"Globalization is taking a beating partly because of our poor understanding of the phenomenon. This well-organized, meticulously researched book is a breath of fresh air in this respect, and is best read cover to cover. Once you have done so, you will reject the hype about globalization as an overpowering force and better recognize the patterns to which it is subject. And that has implications for how globalization should be thought about in a broad range of fields, not just in international economics and international business."

Bernard Yeung, Dean and Stephen Riady Distinguished Professor of Finance and Strategic Management, National University of Singapore (NUS) Business School

"For some time now, there has been an incredible amount of hype about the advent of globalization. As significant as this phenomenon might have been, it has surely been exaggerated by both the popular press and, more worryingly, by academics too. In the last few years, Pankaj Ghemawat has embarked on a much needed crusade to document the actual depth and breadth of this globalization process. The picture that emerges from this academic endeavor is much more nuanced that the one often portrayed in the literature. This magnificent book overviews much of Ghemawat's recent work on this topic and should appeal to a broad range of social scientists interested in globalization."

Pol Antràs, Robert G. Ory Professor of Economics, Harvard University

"At a time of great angst and uncertainty about globalization, it is enormously important to have a fact-based perspective on the phenomenon. That is what *The Laws of Globalization* provides. Solidly grounded in international economics as well as business, this book draws on rigorous research (much of it reported here for the first time), is replete with interesting applications, and is easy to read—all of which should make it appealing to a wide variety of audiences."

Peter Blair Henry, Dean, Richard R. West Professor of Business, and William R. Berkley Professor of Economics & Finance, New York University Leonard N. Stern School of Business

"Pankaj Ghemawat makes readers think again about globalization from new, non-conventional perspectives, always based on data. In this insightful and well-researched book, he describes some key patterns in the globalization process and offers very useful strategic reflections for international companies' senior executives and policy-makers on the implications of the semiglobalized world we live in."

Jordi Canals, Dean Emeritus, IESE Business School

The Laws of Globalization and Business Applications

The Laws of Globalization and Business Applications employs a variety of empirical methodologies to establish two broad regularities that apply to international activity – the law of semiglobalization and the law of distance – and explores some of their implications for business. Part I presents current and historical evidence in support of the law of semiglobalization at the country and the business levels. Part II performs an analogous function regarding the law of distance, showing that the gravity models that international economists have used to analyze merchandise trade between countries also apply to other types of international interactions – and at the industry and firm levels as well. Part III applies these laws to various challenges and opportunities that distance along various dimensions presents to multinational firms. A free online appendix provides additional analysis and documentation to support research applications.

PANKAJ GHEMAWAT is Global Professor of Management and Strategy at New York University's Stern School of Business, where he directs the Center for the Globalization of Education and Management, and the Anselmo Rubiralta Professor of Global Strategy at IESE Business School. He served for more than twenty years on the faculty of Harvard Business School, where in 1991, he became the youngest person ever to be appointed a full professor. Recent honors include the Booz Eminent Scholar Award of the International Management Division of the Academy of Management and the McKinsey Award for the best article published in Harvard Business Review. He served on the AACSB's taskforce on the globalization of management education, and authored the report's recommendations about what to teach students about globalization, and how.

Additional Content Online: A free online appendix is available at www. ghemawat.com/laws. The online appendix expands upon the empirical basis for *The Laws of Globalization and Business Applications* by providing additional analyses, technical notes, and references. It also includes links to tools and maps designed to help readers generate their own analyses and tailor their views of globalization according to their locations and interests.

The Laws of Globalization and Business Applications

Pankaj Ghemawat

CAMBRIDGE
UNIVERSITY PRESS

TETON COUNTY LIBRARY
JACKSON, WYOMING

CAMBRIDGE
UNIVERSITY PRESS

University Printing House, Cambridge CB2 8BS, United Kingdom

One Liberty Plaza, 20th Floor, New York, NY 10006, USA

477 Williamstown Road, Port Melbourne, VIC 3207, Australia

4843/24, 2nd Floor, Ansari Road, Daryaganj, Delhi – 110002, India

79 Anson Road, #06-04/06, Singapore 079906

Cambridge University Press is part of the University of Cambridge.

It furthers the University's mission by disseminating knowledge in the pursuit of education, learning and research at the highest international levels of excellence.

www.cambridge.org
Information on this title: www.cambridge.org/9781107162921
DOI: 10.1017/9781316678503

© Pankaj Ghemawat 2017

This publication is in copyright. Subject to statutory exception and to the provisions of relevant collective licensing agreements, no reproduction of any part may take place without the written permission of Cambridge University Press.

First published 2017

Printed in the United States of America by Sheridan Books, Inc.

A catalogue record for this publication is available from the British Library

Library of Congress Cataloging-in-Publication data
Names: Ghemawat, Pankaj, author.
Title: The laws of globalization and business applications /
by Pankaj Ghemawat.
Description: Cambridge, UK: Cambridge University Press, 2017. |
Includes bibliographical references and index.
Identifiers: LCCN 2016026396 | ISBN 9781107162921 (hardback) |
ISBN 9781316615027 (pbk.)
Subjects: LCSH: Globalization – Economic aspects. | International trade. |
International business enterprises. | International economic relations.
Classification: LCC HF1365.G525 2017 | DDC 337–dc23
LC record available at https://lccn.loc.gov/2016026396

ISBN 978-1-107-16292-1 Hardback
ISBN 978-1-316-61502-7 Paperback

Cambridge University Press has no responsibility for the persistence or accuracy of URLs for external or third-party internet websites referred to in this publication, and does not guarantee that any content on such websites is, or will remain, accurate or appropriate.

To my parents, Mahipal and Shanta Ghemawat,
Who are the two greatest reasons I am an academic.

Contents

Introduction

As final edits were underway on this book, the United Kingdom shocked the world by voting to leave the European Union. The "Brexit" vote was immediately characterized as "the most significant political risk the world has experienced since the Cuban Missile Crisis," more than half-a-century earlier.[1] In addition to reflecting a souring of sentiment about globalization in advanced economies, it fed into an ongoing debate about whether globalization was advancing or in retreat. And in regard to this book, about which I was already scheduled to stage a "showcase panel" the week after the Brexit vote at the annual meeting of the Academy of International Business, it raises the question: did British voters break The Laws of Globalization?"

To answer that question, one must first specify the laws—the broad empirical regularities—adverted to in the title of this book:

- The law of semiglobalization: International interactions, while nonnegligible, are significantly less intense than domestic interactions.
- The law of distance: International interactions are dampened by distance along cultural, administrative, and geographic dimensions and are often affected by economic distance as well.

Both laws clearly hold for the United Kingdom. Starting with the law of semiglobalization, flows across the UK's borders (especially people flows but also trade and capital flows) were large enough to provoke a backlash, yet they still fall far short of what one would expect if borders (in this case even intra-EU borders) had ceased to matter. Thus, the UK's (gross) exports account for about one-third of its GDP, about the same as the world as a whole and far below a zero-border effect benchmark of 96% (100% minus the UK's share of world GDP). And first-generation immigrants comprise only 13% of the UK's population, although Britons think—as reported across three different surveys—that 24–31% of the country's population was born abroad.[2] Even with "Little Englanders" in charge, it is extremely unlikely that the UK's international flows would shrink so much as to become irrelevant.

Turning to the law of distance, the UK's international ties are disproportionately centered on Europe. In 2015, 45% of the UK's exports went to the EU

1

and it drew slightly over one-half its imports from there. Adding in Switzerland brings the Continental share of the UK's merchandise exports to over one-half as well, versus 15% for the U.S. and 6% for China. Given physical proximity, the EU is likely to continue to be the UK's largest export-import partner by far, unless the terms of separation are very acrimonious (like India-Pakistan, to invoke a rather different example of Brexit). And it is not that the UK is particularly narrow in terms of its international engagement: rather, the reverse. In the 2014 edition of the DHL Global Connectedness Index, which I co-developed with Steven A. Altman and the 2016 iteration of which will be released shortly after this book, the UK ranked second out of 140 countries in terms of the breadth of its trade flows and first if one also accounts for breadth of international capital, information and people connections. The UK's ties to countries beyond the EU—the US is its largest destination country for exports—illustrate the non-geographic dimensions of the law of distance. The models estimated in Chapter Five indicate that sharing both a common language as well as colony-colonizer ties (as the UK and US do) boosts trade by 341% and FDI by 656%!

The laws of semiglobalization and distance supply a stable frame of reference in an ambiguous environment. They also have important policy implications. Recognizing how limited globalization is reminds us of the potential gains from further cross-border integration and, especially when the data help deflate exaggerations about globalization levels (what, following Clare Booth Luce, I refer to as globaloney),[3] can help reduce or even reverse fears about globalization. Thus, return to the example of Britons, on average, overestimating immigrant stocks by nearly if not more than 100%. Simply informing survey respondents about the actual amount of immigration reduces the proportion who think there are "too many migrants" in the UK by more than 40%! My 2011 book, *World 3.0: Global Prosperity and How to Achieve It*, looks more broadly at the consequences of globalization in an imperfect world and ways policymakers might manage its unfavorable side effects while exploiting its promise.

Concerning business rather than public policy, firms need to understand how much cross-border activity there is (or could be) in their industries and how its distribution is affected by cultural, administrative, geographic, and economic (CAGE) distance. Note that while Brexit aims to expand the administrative distance between the UK and the EU, firms can still tap into commonalities or proximity along the other dimensions of distance. My 2007 book, *Redefining Global Strategy*, is devoted to elaborating strategies for doing business in a world where borders and distance still matter.

This book assembles empirical support—using a wide range of methodologies and updated data—for the two laws of globalization, which are intended to have the status of scientific laws in the sense of describing important regularities that hold over long periods of time (as distinct from scientific theories that posit a mechanism or explanation of observed phenomena) (McComas 2003). It will be up to the reader to judge whether that appellation is warranted after considering the evidence assembled in this book of the pervasiveness and potency of the two laws (or of the home bias and the distance effects that underlie them).

It is worth noting – especially since one of the (anonymous) reviewers of this manuscript was confused about this point – that the two laws are *not* the same. The law of semiglobalization pertains to the depth of globalization and the law of distance to its breadth – two constructs that are defined in Chapter 1. Conceptually, there is no reason why the first law should imply the second: why, for instance, a limited amount of merchandise crossing a national border should be expected to exhibit distance sensitivity, as opposed to being evenly distributed across foreign countries. And the claim that the second law implies the first one – that all border effects can be reduced to distance effects if the latter are defined broadly enough – is problematic as well. Although it is true that more elaborate measurement of distance tends to reduce the estimated magnitude of national border effects, they usually do not disappear.

The two laws of globalization are generalizations – within the international domain[4] – of the two laws of geography proposed by Waldo Tobler, a leading geographer (Tobler 1970, 1999, 2004):[5]

- The phenomenon external to [a geographic] area of interest affects what goes on in the inside. (Tobler 1999, 87)
- Everything is related to everything else, but near things are more related than distant things. (Tobler 1970, 236)

My first law of globalization adds an upper bound to Tobler's lower bound on outside influences. In addition to positing that international influences are non-negligible, it makes the point that national borders still matter a great deal: that there is substantial home bias. A range of considerations are cited in general support of the first law, but the most play is given to the one that people seem to find the most convincing: data assembled for the *DHL Global Connectedness Index* that measure the depth of globalization implied by a wide range of international trade, capital, information and people flows.[6]

My second law generalizes Tobler's focus on geographic distance to also encompass measures of cultural, administrative/political, and (with some qualifications) economic distance. Unifying empirical support is provided by an exercise that takes the small number of distance-related variables commonly used in international economics to analyze merchandise trade and examines how well they also appear to explain other international interactions. From the perspective of distance as a common core construct, the worst-case outcome would be if none of these distance-related variables mattered in the context of other interactions. And it would be best if they not only mattered but implied some stability, across interactions, in assessments of whether two countries are relatively close or far apart. This latter conclusion is the one that is supported by the empirical evidence.

As a bonus, the two laws are counterintuitive or at least nonobvious to many people even after they have been pointed out. Thus, they directly contradict the assertion by Thomas Friedman, the *New York Times* columnist and perhaps the most prominent geopolitical pundit of our time,[7] that "The World Is Flat," and, the corollary that we have witnessed the creation of "a global, Web-enabled playing field that allows for…collaboration on research and work in real time, without regard to geography, distance or, in the near future, even language" (Friedman 2005, 176). In Friedman's world, neither of the two laws of globalization would apply.

And it isn't just journalists who subscribe to inflated notions of globalization or globaloney. Consider some other pieces of evidence that point in the same direction:

- When Pascal Lamy, the former director general of the World Trade Organization (WTO), invited me to address the national envoys to the WTO as part of an attempt to restart the Doha Round of trade negotiations, an over-whelming majority agreed with the quote provided earlier from Friedman over "semiglobal" and "local" alternatives[8] – even though it raised existential questions about what they were doing in Geneva!
- When I surveyed the readers of the blog that I write for *Harvard Business Review*, 62 percent of them agreed with Friedman, versus 28 percent who opted for the semiglobal alternative and 10 percent for the local alternative – even though the blog post went on to argue that the dominant view constituted globaloney.[9]
- More recently, I surveyed over 3,000 students from 138 countries who partici-pated in my massive open online course (MOOC) on Coursera. Students from every country overestimated levels of globalization—on average supposing international interactions to be almost five times as intense as they actually are.[10]

Although globaloney does seem to persist across countries, education levels, gen-ders, and so on, there *is* general agreement among international economists, at least, that international integration is far from complete. Yet even international economists still find the law of distance – even in its narrow form concerning just merchandise trade – nonobvious, to the point where it has been proposed as a better answer to mathematician Stanislaw Ulam's challenge to Paul Samuelson to "name me one proposition in all of the social sciences which is both true and non-trivial" than the answer that Samuelson (eventually) came up with: comparative advantage.[11] Furthermore, my empirical work fitting (the same) distance-related variables to a broad range of international interactions (described in several chap-ters in Parts II and III of this book) reinforces the utility of thinking about distance as key to analyzing globalization in general, not just merchandise trade.

The regression analyses presented in Chapter 5 – and in other chapters in Parts II and III of this book – fit well with modern social scientists' emphasis on statistical methods based on probabilistic reasoning, even though they should be read as highlighting robust regularities in the data rather than testing hypothe-ses. That said, the empirical methods employed in this book, especially in Part I, range well beyond regressions. Thus, Chapter 1 uses (simple) text mining to identify particularly influential definitions of globalization out of the many that have been proposed, and presents some basic measurements – an approach that is typically ranked at the bottom of most hierarchies of empirical research, for example, de Groot (1969) – to sort through them. Chapter 2 adds in surveys of individuals in order to delve deeper into patterns of globaloney. Chapter 3 takes a historical tack, employing Neustadt and May's (1986) method of similarities and differences to assess what is new, from a business perspective, about the current wave of globalization (relative to the wave that preceded World War I) and what is not. Chapter 4 has a hybrid structure, conditioning the pictures that it paints of globalization at (mostly) large firms on consideration of the constraints that prevent most firms, especially smaller ones, from engaging in any international trade or investment. The pictures themselves might be described by a political scientist as "configurative-idiographic" (Eckstein 1992) and are based on a review of the relevant literature, cases, and a survey of large companies.

The variety of methodological approaches employed is related to my long-term efforts to apply advances from related fields to international business research, in line with Dunning's (1989) plea for more interdisciplinary work of this sort. And it also reflects the primacy of my overarching interest in the phenomenon of globalization itself, over precommitment to a particular methodology for studying it.

Another distinctive feature of this book from an empirical perspective is its reliance, wherever possible, on cross-country evidence rather than evidence drawn from a single country. Thus, the chapters on globalization at the country level draw heavily on data compiled for the *DHL Global Connectedness Index*. And the chapters on globalization at the business level aim for broad coverage as well – at least when compared to the conclusion that roughly two-thirds of empirical articles published in major international business journals between 1992 and 2003 relied on single-country samples (Yang, Wang, and Su 2006).

Substantively, Part I of this book, after sorting through different definitions of globalization, focuses on marshaling evidence in support of the law of semiglobalization at the country and then the business level. Part II performs an analogous function regarding the law of distance. Part III then puts the two laws to work by applying them, chapter by chapter, to contemporary challenges and opportunities that cultural, administrative, geographic, and economic distance present to multinational firms. Additional empirical content is covered in an online appendix available at www.ghemawat.com/laws, along with tools, maps, and other research and teaching materials. The online content enables readers to customize the material by location, industry, etc.—essential to grasping how a semiglobalized world looks very different from different perspectives.

Covering so much ground would not have been possible without the help of a large number of people. I am especially grateful to my coauthors in this regard. Steven Altman, the executive director of the Center for the Globalization of Education and Management at NYU Stern, has worked with me for years now – on *World 3.0* and the *DHL Global Connectedness Index* as well as on this book – and has coauthored five of the chapters that follow in addition to providing invaluable help and commentary on the remainder. Thomas Hout, formerly a senior vice president at the Boston Consulting Group and my coauthor on numerous articles about competition in and out of China, was an ideal partner for thinking about differences in business ownership and governance around the world. Geoffrey Jones, my former colleague at the Harvard Business School and one of the world's leading historians of international business, did more than contribute to the chapter on globalization over time: he helped guide it. And Sebastian Reiche, my colleague at IESE Business School, has helped me learn much more about culture and leadership in an international context than will be evident from our coauthored chapter in this book. None of them should necessarily be assumed, however, to agree with the content of the chapters other than the ones that they coauthored.

I am also grateful to my IESE colleagues Fabrizio Ferraro and Morten Olsen and to Niccolò Pisani of the University of Amsterdam and Herman Vantrappen of Akordeon for ongoing research collaborations that are described briefly in this book. Many other colleagues have also read and commented on earlier versions of some of the material presented herein. And Juan Alcacer at Harvard Business School, Mauro Guillén at Wharton, Donald Lessard at MIT, Lilach Nachum at Baruch College, and Robert Salomon at NYU Stern provided comments on some of the materials prepared specifically for this book. Once again, however, my collaborators and other friends should not be assumed to agree with all of the book's contents.

Given how long this book has been in the making, many members of my research team, past and present, have also made valuable contributions to it, including Phillip Bastian, Joel Bevin, Adrià Borràs Carbonell, Paola Elice, Jordi Ollé Garmendia, Tamara de la Mata López, Yi Mu, Erica Ng, Víctor Pérez García, and Iacopo Tonini. Thousands of my students over the years, for whom some of these chapters were originally written, have been extremely helpful sources of feedback as well. Marta Domenech at IESE has provided continuity in administrative support for a long number of years now, and my former assistant at the Harvard Business School, Sharilyn Steketee, dealt meticulously with the issues involved in getting the manuscript ready for publication. I am also very grateful for generous financial support from the Division of Research at IESE Business School and from the Center for the Globalization of Education and Management at NYU's Stern School of Business.

Finally, it is a particular pleasure to undertake this publishing venture with Cambridge University Press. After receiving the IESE-Fundacion BBVA Economics for Management Prize in 2008 (for my early work on the topic of globalization and strategy), I was invited to write a book for Cambridge. I reluctantly came to the conclusion that I wasn't ready then, but I am delighted that their interest did not lapse.

Notes

1 Eurasia Group president Ian Bremmer tweeted this characterization on June 24, 2016.
2 See the 2014 and 2015 editions of the Ipsos MORI "Perils of Perception" surveys as well as the 2013 edition of the German Marshall Fund of the United States "Transatlantic Trends" survey.
3 See, for instance, Krebs (1987).
4 Some of the same insights apply within countries, at the regional and even local levels. See, for instance, "Competitiveness and Interregional as Well as International Trade: The Case of Catalonia" (Ghemawat, Llano, and Requena 2010) and my book chapter, "From International Business to Intranational Business" (Ghemawat 2015), based on my speech accepting the 2014 Eminent Scholar award from the International Management Division of the Academy of Management.
5 Tobler's articulation of his laws prompted an interesting debate about what laws are and whether the social sciences can aspire to any. See Flyvbjerg (2001, 44–45) and Tobler (2004).
6 See Pankaj Ghemawat and Steven A. Altman, "The DHL Global Connectedness Index 2014" at dhl.com/gci.
7 Philip Tetlock and Dan Gardner, the authors of *Superforecasting*, rate Thomas Friedman as the top "celebrity forecaster" of our time based on a combination of status, relevance of work to world politics, and difficulty of pinning down his/her forecasts and also assert that "there are no hard facts about Friedman's track record, only endless opinions" (2015, 3). It is worth adding that, based on my own calculations, Friedman's book, *The World Is Flat*, has probably sold more copies than all other books ever written about globalization combined!
8 The semiglobal alternative presented was "There is a balance on the spectrum between 'local' and 'global' that represents the 'sweet spot'…[and makes for] 'the race to the middle" (from Rick Wagoner, the former CEO and Chairman of General Motors) and the local alternative was "In real estate, the mantra is 'location, location, location.' For global brand managers, it might be 'localize, localize, localize" (from Orit Gadiesh, the Chairman of the management consulting firm Bain & Company). The workshop itself was held at WTO headquarters in Geneva on November 2, 2010.
9 The semiglobal and local alternatives presented to HBR readers were the same as the ones presented to the national envoys to the WTO. The blog post, dating from May 31, 2011, and titled "Globalization in the World We Live in Now: World 3.0," can be found at http://blogs.hbr.org/cs/2011/05/globalization_in_the_world_we.html.
10 This survey is discussed further in the final substantive section of Chapter Two.
11 See Keith Head and Thierry Mayer's "What Separates Us? Sources of Resistance to Globalization," which notes that "Ulam probably did not mean a logical or mathematical truth since social science is supposed to make *empirically* true claims" (2013, 1201; emphasis in original).

References

de Groot, Adrianus Dingeman. 1969. *Methodology: Foundations of Inference and Research in the Behavioral Sciences*, Psychological Studies, No. 6. The Hague: Mouton.
Dunning, John H. 1989. "The Study of International Business: A Plea for a More Interdisciplinary Approach." *Journal of International Business Studies* 20 (3):411–436. doi: 10.2307/155185.

Eckstein, Harry. 1992. "Configurative-Idiographic Study." In *Regarding Politics: Essays on Political Theory, Stability, and Change*, 136–138. Berkeley: University of California Press. http://publishing.cdlib.org/ucpressebooks/view?docId=ft0k40037v&chunk.id=d0e2728&toc.id=d0e2725&brand=ucpress.

Flyvbjerg, Bent. 2001. *Making Social Science Matter: Why Social Inquiry Fails and How It Can Succeed Again*. Oxford, UK; New York: Cambridge University Press.

Friedman, Thomas L. 2005. *The World Is Flat: A Brief History of the Twenty-First Century*. New York: Farrar Straus and Giroux.

Ghemawat, Pankaj. 2003. "Semiglobalization and International Business Strategy." *Journal of International Business Studies* 34 (2):138–152. doi: 10.1057/PALGRAVE.JIBS.8400013.

———. 2007. *Redefining Global Strategy: Crossing Borders in a World Where Differences Still Matter*. Boston, MA: Harvard Business School Press.

———. 2011. "Globalization in the World We Live in Now: World 3.0." *Harvard Business Review* (May 31, 2011). http://blogs.hbr.org/cs/2011/05/globalization_in_the_world_we.html.

———. 2011. *World 3.0: Global Prosperity and How to Achieve It*. Boston, MA: Harvard Business Review Press.

———. 2015. "From International Business to Intranational Business." In *Emerging Economies and Multinational Enterprises*, edited by Laszlo Tihanyi, Elitsa R. Banalieva, Timothy M. Devinney, and Torben Pedersen, 5–28: Emerald Group Publishing Limited.

Ghemawat, Pankaj, and Steven A. Altman. 2014. "DHL Global Connectedness Index 2014: Analyzing Global Flows and Their Power to Increase Prosperity." Deutsche Post DHL. www.dhl.com/gci.

Ghemawat, Pankaj, Carlos Llano, and Francisco Requena. 2010. "Competitiveness and Interregional as Well as International Trade: The Case of Catalonia." *International Journal of Industrial Organization* 28 (4):415–422. doi: 10.1016/j.ijindorg.2010.03.013.

Head, Keith, and Thierry Mayer. 2013. "What Separates Us? Sources of Resistance to Globalization." *Canadian Journal of Economics/Revue canadienne d'économique* 46 (4):1196–1231. doi: 10.1111/caje.12055.

Krebs, Albin. 1987. "Clare Boothe Luce Dies at 84: Playwright, Politician, Envoy." *New York Times*. www.nytimes.com/learning/general/onthisday/bday/0310.html.

McComas, William F. 2003. "A Textbook Case of the Nature of Science: Laws and Theories in the Science of Biology." *International Journal of Science and Mathematics Education* 1 (2):141–155. doi: 10.1023/B:IJMA.0000016848.93930.9c.

Neustadt, Richard E., and Ernest R. May. 1986. *Thinking in Time: The Uses of History for Decision-Makers*. New York, London: Free Press; Collier Macmillan.

Tetlock, Philip E., and Dan Gardner. 2015. *Superforecasting: The Art and Science of Prediction*. New York: Crown Publishers.

Tobler, Waldo. 1970. "A Computer Movie Simulating Urban Growth in the Detroit Region." *Economic Geography* 46 (Supplement: Proceedings. International Geographical Union. Commission on Quantitative Methods):234–240. doi: 10.2307/143141.

———. 1999. "Linear Pycnophylactic Reallocation–Comment on a Paper by D. Martin." *International Journal of Geographical Information Science* 13 (1):85–90. doi: 10.1080/136588199241472.

———. 2004. "On the First Law of Geography: A Reply." *Annals of the Association of American Geographers* 94 (2):304–310. doi: 10.1111/j.1467-8306.2004.09402009.x.

Yang, Zhilin, Xuehua Wang, and Chenting Su. 2006. "A Review of Research Methodologies in International Business." *International Business Review* 15 (6):601–617.

Part I

The Law of Semiglobalization

1   Defining and Measuring Globalization

Pankaj Ghemawat and Steven A. Altman

This chapter begins by considering the etymology of "globalization" and how the phenomenon has been perceived by the public and in the media. It then reviews how globalization has been defined, with a focus on the academic literature, and with particular emphasis on business and economics. It goes on to consider how globalization might be measured at the country level and argues for a primary focus on the depth (also referred to as intensity) and the breadth (also referred to as extensity) of countries' international interactions. Measuring globalization on this basis – as we do biennially for the *DHL Global Connectedness Index* – suggests that, overall, globalization decreased during the economic crisis of 2008 and has been slow to recover. This distinguishes our index from other leading globalization indexes with which comparisons are feasible.

Origins and Opinions

The word "globalization" is a relatively recent addition to the English lexicon. It first appeared in *Webster's Dictionary* in 1961 (Kilminster 1997, 257), and according to the current edition, its first use came a decade earlier in 1951. Its roots can be traced back to the terms "global" (which took on the meaning of "world scale" in the late nineteenth century) and "globalize" (which appeared in the 1940s) (Merriam-Webster 2015). By contrast, its cousin, "international," is much older, having been introduced by Jeremy Bentham in 1789 (Bentham 1823). Bentham needed the term to describe the legal relations between sovereign nations and people from different nations (Janis 1984, 409).

The ideas that now find their expression in terms of globalization are older than the word itself, of course, just as relationships between sovereign states existed before Jeremy Bentham gave them a name. David Livingstone remarked in 1872 that "the extension and use of railroads, steamships, telegraphs, break down nationalities and bring peoples geographically remote

The authors wish to thank Phillip Bastian for his assistance with writing and research for this chapter.

into close connection commercially and politically. They make the world one, and capital, like water, tends to a common level" (Livingstone and Waller 1874, 215). Jules Verne published *Around the World in 80 Days* in 1873, bringing the idea of circling the world by steamship and railway into the public imagination. Verne's Phileas Fogg speaks of the world having grown smaller as a result of the technology of his day (Verne 1873) – an idea that still resonates with today's digital natives, many of whom are fans of Thomas Friedman's *The World Is Flat* (Friedman 2005). And speaking of the age that ended with World War I, John Maynard Keynes was able to write that "the inhabitant of London could order by telephone, sipping his morning tea in bed, the various products of the whole earth, in such quantity as he might see fit, and reasonably expect their early delivery upon his doorstep" (Keynes 1919, 9).

Discussion of potential harms associated with these trends also predates the term "globalization." The expression "World War" was first used before either of the conflicts we now know by that name. It was first mentioned in 1898 in the *New York Times* and was used alternately with "The Great War" as the appellation for the first such war from its outbreak in 1914 (Harper 2015). Meanwhile, worries about foreign ownership began as early as the late nineteenth century. In the 1880s and 1890s, Americans became angry at the increased foreign ownership of US land, while US foreign direct investment in Europe created resentment there (Jones 1996, 253). In 1901, English journalist W. T. Stead published a book called *The Americanization of the World* and by the 1920s, Japanese writers worried about the Americanization of Japan (Rydell and Kroes 2005, 9). Fears of "Coca-Colonization" date back at least to the 1940s (Jones 1996, 251).

It was only in the past twenty years, however, that "globalization" became the word of choice used to describe these ideas: In the early 1990s, the US Library of Congress catalog listed less than fifty publications per year related to globalization, but from 2002 to 2014, there were more than a thousand every year.[1] Indeed, the fascination with globalization has itself become a global phenomenon, with every major world language having developed a word for it, from 全球化 (quánqiúhuà) in Chinese to *küreselleşme* in Turkish (Scholte 2005).[2]

Public opinion, on balance, is positive toward at least some aspects of globalization – especially in emerging economies – but is changeable and subject to important caveats. The *Pew Spring 2014 Global Attitudes Survey* reports a global median (based on data from forty-four countries) of 81 percent of respondents believing "growing trade and business ties" to be either very good or somewhat good for their countries. However, only 45 percent have a similar view about foreign companies buying domestic ones, and a mere 26 percent see trade as lowering prices (Pew Research Center and Roper Center 2014). Surveys by the *Chicago Council on Global Affairs* indicate that most

Americans "believe that globalization, especially the increasing connections of our economy with others around the world" is mostly good for the United States, and depict a trend of falling public support for globalization from 2004 to 2010, followed by a rising trend through 2014 (Smeltz, Daalder, and Kafura 2014, 37).

Media reports on globalization in the United States, however, have tended toward the negative. Using the AlchemyAPI sentiment analysis engine, we looked at articles matching the search term "globalization" in the *New York Times*, *Washington Post*, and *Wall Street Journal* over the period 2005–2015. All three publications showed a consistent tendency toward negative coverage, although the *Wall Street Journal* has been less negative than the others since 2012. Interestingly, however, using the same parameters with three English-language Chinese publications, *China Daily*, *Shanghai Daily*, and *Xinhua News*, showed a much more positive stance. Similar results were obtained using two other sentiment analysis engines.[3]

These tendencies in public and media sentiment are, of course, just averages that mask a wide dispersion of views about globalization, reflecting, in part, varying conceptions of the phenomenon itself. To attempt to bring greater clarity, we need to start by being explicit about how we choose to define the term, and why. We will then operationalize its measurement at the country level.

Defining Globalization

Journalists, social commentators, and academics have proposed a multitude of definitions of globalization. The term has been used to denote liberalization, Westernization, homogenization, economic growth *and* decline, equality *and* inequality, and so on.

To get a handle on the diversity of definitions, it is useful to start with previously assembled compendia of them. Given our interest in business and the scholarly focus of this book, we turned to two compendia assembled by business school affiliates, Eric Beerkens (2006) and Cynthia Stohl (2005).[4] Restricting each author cited in the compendia to one definition, we narrow the list to forty-two definitions. Some of the heterogeneity across them can be illustrated with the word cloud in Figure 1.1.[5] Unsurprisingly, "world" is the most common word, with "process," "new," "social," "economic," and "national," also standing out. Nevertheless, it is also clear that there were many other associations as well.

Given this diversity, an obvious expedient is to concentrate on definitions that have been particularly influential in terms of academic citations. We initially searched Google Scholar for results matching "globaliz OR globalis AND," followed by the author and year of the definition from Beerkens's and Stohl's work. The most cited reference in the general academic literature is

Figure 1.1 Word cloud showing definitions of globalization.
Source: Authors' analysis of Beerkens (2006) and Stohl (2005).

Arjun Appadurai's 1996 book *Modernity at Large: Cultural Dimensions of Globalization.* Beerkens characterizes Appadurai's definition as "a process of cultural mixing or hybridization across locations and identities" (Beerkens 2006, 1).[6]

However, the phrase that Beerkens uses does not appear in Appadurai's book. In fact, Appadurai in a private communication indicates that "'hybridization' is too weak and general a feature to be a good definition. My own argument in regard to the cultural side of globalization is that 'cultural heterogenization always outpaces cultural homogenization'" (Appadurai "Defining Globalization" 2015).

Appadurai is, obviously, one of the leading commentators on one of the key issues around globalization – whether in fact it does lead to cultural homogenization (1996). Many of his ideas are also relevant to markets for cultural goods. But they don't put business and economics at center stage, which is our intention. So we decided to emphasize that body of literature and the definitions cited by academics therein.[7]

Unfortunately, while Google Scholar is frequently used for this type of work, it covers academic literature very broadly and does not allow searches on particular subjects. In addition, it uses a proprietary algorithm that is subject to some opacity. Google Scholar is designed to prioritize the best matches and find as many matches as possible. Although this may allow a researcher to find scholarly works with relative ease, it is not ideal for more specific searches.[8]

Noting the issues with Google Scholar, we turned to Business Source Complete, which has a more straightforward search algorithm and better-documented features, and also focuses on business and economics literature. In an attempt to be more systematic about finding references to the actual definitions, text-mining techniques were used, starting with the development of a set of keywords from each definition. To determine if the definition itself is cited, a search was conducted to see if these keywords appeared within forty words of each other, which corresponds to approximately two sentences in English, according to an oft-cited linguistics study (Sichel 1974). We limit the search to articles containing the name of the cited author and year together, as well as to those published after 2000 to reduce bias toward older definitions.[9]

The top result using this method is from Held et al.'s 1999 book, *Global Transformations: Politics, Economics, and Culture.* The definition is as follows:

Globalization can be thought of as a process (or set of processes) which embodies a transformation in the spatial organization of social relations and transactions – assessed in terms of their extensity, intensity, velocity and impact – generating transcontinental or interregional flows and networks of activity, interaction, and the exercise of power. (Held et al. 1999, 16)

While Held et al. do *not* say that globalization is an unstoppable force, as some commentators seem to believe, their language, with its talk of transformation, tends to suggest forward momentum for the process. What is more helpful from our perspective, though, is that their definition starts to suggest ways of measuring globalization: the topic of the next section.

Measuring Globalization

When deciding how to measure a phenomenon, a first critical decision concerns the unit of analysis to use. Globalization can take place – and could, in a sense, be measured – at levels ranging from the very macro down to the individual.[10] We begin by looking at globalization at the country level – in terms of interactions between countries[11] – although later in this book, we will also explore globalization at the industry, company, and (more selectively) individual levels.

Held et al.'s definition suggests that globalization has four "spatio-temporal dimensions": extensity, intensity, velocity, and impact (Held et al. 1999, 17). This book emphasizes two of their four dimensions: intensity and extensity. Henceforth, we use the term *depth* for measurements of intensity and *breadth* for measurements of extensity.

Depth measures how much of an economy's activities or flows are international by comparing the size of its international flows (and stocks accumulated from prior year flows) with relevant measures of its domestic activity. This tracks the law of semiglobalization, which states that international interactions are significantly less intense than domestic interactions. Chapter 2 demonstrates that most global flows have a depth of under 30 percent.

Previous research has criticized depth measures, since small countries tend to rank much higher on them than large ones (Squalli and Wilson 2011). This is in part a mathematical artifact, as the analogy of Jew-Gentile marriages illustrates. The intensity of such marriages will inevitably be higher for Jews if there are fewer of them than for Gentiles, but that need not imply that Jews are more open to intermarriage.

Many adjustments have been proposed to address this problem, but more important than the details of the differences among them is the distinction between measuring the *state* of globalization and *openness* to globalization. As Kam Ki Tang and Amy Wagner put it in the specific context of trade, "if the purpose is to measure trade intensity or trade dependency, then the [trade intensity index] will be an appropriate measure. However, if the purpose is to measure trade openness, it has a limitation of being biased against large economies" (2010, 2). Since our aim is to measure the actual level of globalization, we focus on depth (intensity) measures and later regress them on country size and other variables to see if the observed relationships align with a priori expectations.

Breadth, the second integral part of our globalization index, complements depth by looking at how widely the international component of a given type of activity is distributed across countries. In line with the second law of globalization – the law of distance – we expect breadth to be limited by distance effects, with countries interacting more with other countries that are culturally, administratively, geographically, and (often) economically close rather than distant.[12]

To illustrate the importance of incorporating breadth into assessments of global connectedness, consider the southern African country of Botswana. The trade depth of Botswana is high, with merchandise imports and exports together summing to 102 percent of the country's GDP. Yet, Botswana's trade is very limited in its geographic scope: 61 percent of Botswana's exports went to the UK in 2013. Another 13 percent were sent to neighboring South Africa. Only 1 percent were destined for the world's largest importer, the United States (Ghemawat and Altman 2014, 145).

Our conception of breadth deliberately departs from Held et al.'s view of extensity, which emphasizes transcontinental and interregional flows. Our analysis of regionalization indicates that, on average, 53 percent of international trade, capital, information, and people flows take place within rather than between roughly continental regions (Ghemawat and Altman 2014, 92). While Held et al. suggest excluding such intraregional activity, doing so would yield a severely incomplete picture of countries' international linkages. Furthermore, there is a great deal of subjectivity in defining regions and even continents to which measures that discard all intraregional data are particularly sensitive. We return to regionalization in Chapter 10, analyzing it there using several region classifications.[13]

We actually use several types of breadth measures to summarize distributions of interactions, as explained further in Chapter 5. At the country level, our primary breadth measure compares the destinations of a country's international flows to all other countries' shares of the same type of flows in the opposite direction. A country would earn the highest possible breadth score for exports if its exports are distributed across destinations in exact proportion to the rest of the world's imports.[14] Higher breadth scores suggest greater indifference to distance. For world-level analysis, we complement this measure with simpler alternatives such as the average distance traversed by international flows and the proportion that take place within versus between regions.

Velocity, as defined by Held et al., is largely a result of developments in transportation and, especially over the past few decades, communications. One of the problems with measuring communications velocity, however, is the movement to real time: (minimal) time lags in communication seem to be asymptoting toward zero and have been headed in that direction for a long time now. Thus, the transatlantic telegraph cable reduced the time that it took for information to travel between New York and London from more than a week to less than an hour in the 1860s (O'Rourke and Williamson 1999, 219–220; Fouchard 2016, 32–33). International transportation lags for physical goods can still range into weeks and even months, but at least in terms of lower bounds, there isn't evidence of rapid change in the recent period (since 2005) on which our measurement exercise focuses. So given insufficient variation over the time frame we analyze, as well as limitations in data availability across countries, we do not incorporate velocity into our measurement of globalization.

The fourth element highlighted by Held et al., the impact of globalization on social relations and transactions, is crucially important. Indeed, one of us (Ghemawat 2011) wrote a whole book, *World 3.0*, on the social impact of globalization and how its side effects might be managed. But impact is not the primary consideration here; the measurement of globalization is. And mixing up measures of the phenomenon itself with measures of its putative implications seems like a bad basis for actually testing those performance implications.

To what types of international interactions should the depth and breadth measures be applied? Although no one master list stands out, there seems to be general agreement that trade, capital, information, and people flows are all worth considering. Thus, Michael Mussa, an economist, highlights "trade, factor movements [of capital and people], and communication of economically useful knowledge and technology" (2000, 9), while anthropologist Arjun Appadurai cites "ideas and ideologies, people and goods, images and messages, technologies and techniques" (2000, 5) – and has written, most recently, a book about finance (Appadurai *Banking* 2015). In the chapters that follow, a variety of international interactions will be considered, ranging from standard ones such as merchandise trade to nonstandard ones such as patterns of who follows whom on Twitter, but they can all be related to one of the four "pillars" around which we construct the *DHL Global Connectedness Index* (www.dhl.com/gci): trade, capital, information, and people.

The *DHL Global Connectedness Index* measures trade based on imports and exports of merchandise and of services. For depth measures, these are normalized by GDP. Capital is measured using data on foreign direct investment (FDI) and portfolio equity. For each of these, we consider stocks of foreign assets and liabilities as well as flows of capital.[15] The bases of normalization for the capital depth measures vary: GDP for FDI stocks, gross fixed capital formation for FDI flows, and market capitalization for portfolio equity stocks and flows. Information flows are measured by international internet bandwidth (as a proxy for international internet traffic), international phone calls, and trade in printed publications. People movements are measured using data on migrants, international university students, and tourist arrivals. On the information and people pillars, depth is calculated on a per capita basis (based on overall population except in the cases of international internet bandwidth, which is measured per internet user, and international students, which is compared to total tertiary enrollment).

Once all of the depth and breadth metrics have been calculated, panel normalization is performed and the index is aggregated using an importance-based weighting scheme. Given our aforementioned focus on business and economics, the trade and capital pillars are each assigned 35 percent of the total index weight, and the information and people pillars are each assigned 15 percent. Finally, we apply equal weights to depth and breadth. The technical details are described at greater length in each edition of the *DHL Global Connectedness Index*.

At a broader level, it is worth adding that the *DHL Global Connectedness Index* focuses strictly on measuring actual interactions between countries.[16] Symmetric to the argument about excluding performance implications, policy enablers are left out of the globalization index so as to enhance its value in policy analysis.

The index is calculated entirely based on hard data, with no reliance on analysts' opinions or surveys – which is particularly useful given the tendency to globaloney that was mentioned in the introduction and that will be discussed further in Chapter 2. It has come to incorporate more than one million data points covering both depth and breadth across 140 countries that account for 99 percent of the world's GDP and 95 percent of its population. The inclusion of breadth greatly increases the amount of data required: between all possible country pairs rather than only between each country and the rest of the world.

Other Globalization Indexes

For many years, scholars relied primarily on World Bank and International Monetary Fund (IMF) data on trade and capital flows across borders to determine the level of globalization and the extent to which different countries were "globalized." Also on offer since the turn of the century are a number of indexes that attempt more multifaceted analysis – of the flows not only of goods and money, but also of people and information – across borders.

The first globalization index to attract significant attention was produced by the consulting firm A.T. Kearney in collaboration with *Foreign Policy* magazine, and was released in 2001. As that index has not been released since 2007, it will not be addressed further here. There are, however, four other globalization indexes that have been published more than once and continue to be updated: the *KOF Index of Globalization*, the *Ernst & Young (E&Y) Globalization Index* (developed in cooperation with the Economist Intelligence Unit), the *Maastricht Globalization Index (MGI),* and the *McKinsey Global Institute Connectedness Index (McK).*

These other globalization indexes, to the extent they measure actual interactions rather than their enablers, concentrate almost entirely on depth. An analysis of the fifty-six economies included in all of the indexes shows that the correlation coefficient between depth ranks on the *DHL Global Connectedness Index* and ranks on the *KOF*, *E&Y*, and *MGI* indexes is between 0.81 and 0.84 (on *McK*, it is a much lower 0.34 for reasons we will discuss later). By contrast, the correlation coefficient between breadth ranks and ranks on all the other indexes ranges from 0.34 to 0.47. The *Ernst & Young Globalization Index* added one simple breadth measure – the share of main trading partners in total trade – in its 2012 edition, but the other three indexes incorporate none. The exclusion of breadth from other indexes is particularly noteworthy since the (co)authors of the *KOF index* and the *MGI* write that "an important criticism of many indices…is that, strictly speaking, they measure internationalization and regionalization rather than globalization" (Dreher et al. 2010, 179, 181). In other words, they seem to agree with Held et al. on the importance of separating out intraregional and interregional international flows.

The *KOF Index of Globalization*, introduced in 2006 and produced by ETH Zurich, combines a wide range of metrics, going all the way back to 1970. It divides globalization into the spheres of economic, political, and social integration and uses indicators of each of these to build the index. These indicators are weighted based on principal-component analysis to ensure maximum variation, which has conceptual appeal but does result in weights that are hard for us, at least, to reconcile with our priors. For example, international transfers as a percent of GDP receives only a 0.4 percent weight, whereas membership in international organizations receives 7 percent. Even odder, probably, are the allocations of a 5 percent weight to McDonald's restaurants and another 5 percent to Ikea stores, especially when juxtaposed against a 4 percent weight for all of merchandise trade.

In terms of types of measures rather than weights attached to them, the *KOF index* mixes together enablers of globalization (such as tariff rates and capital account restrictions) and actual levels of connectedness (such as trade and capital flows). More than half of its weight is allocated to indicators that we deem to reflect policy and technological enablers of globalization. Furthermore, some of the measures, for example, internet and television penetration, seem more like general indicators of economic development rather than of globalization. While internet and television connectivity can facilitate international information flows, data presented in Chapter 2 indicate that they are primarily used for domestic communication.

The *Ernst & Young Globalization Index*, last updated (as of this writing) in (2012), is somewhat closer to the *DHL Global Connectedness Index*. This index was designed by the Economist Intelligence Unit and is based primarily on their data. The weights of the main pillars are based on a survey of business leaders: 22 percent on trade, 21 percent on capital and finance, 21 percent on technology exchange and ideas, 19 percent on movement of people, and 17 percent on cultural integration. Note that four of these five pillars coincide at least roughly with those of the *DHL Global Connectedness Index*. However, subcomponents of the *Ernst & Young Index* adding up to 27 percent of the total are based on subjective measures – the Economist Intelligence Unit's analyst ratings. In addition, this index covers only sixty countries.

Although Ernst & Young's use of a business leader survey to set its weights has the advantage of focusing on the interests of its audience, it has some problems. First, none of the pillar weights is particularly distant from one-fifth. More importantly, however, the use of a survey can be problematic since even prominent business leaders are prone to believing in globaloney, as we discuss in Chapter 2.

The *Maastricht Globalization Index*, most recently published in 2014, takes a somewhat different approach. While higher values for most of the indexes covered here (including the *DHL Global Connectedness Index*) would generally be seen positively – at least by people who believe increased interconnectedness is a good thing – the *MGI* departs from that by including indicators on military spending and ecological footprints of exports and imports. This index is subdivided into five pillars: political, economic, social and cultural, technological, and environmental, each of which receives an equal weight. While allotting 20 percent of the total weight to the environmental footprint of imports and exports raises questions, the *MGI* generally seems built on defensible indicators, many of which also underpin our index.

Finally, the *McKinsey Global Institute Connectedness Index (McK)* also draws on many of the same indicators as the *DHL Global Connectedness Index* (and its initial release acknowledged having built upon our work) (Manyika et al. 2014, 61). *McK* does look beyond depth, as reflected in the correlations described earlier in this section. However, rather than complementing depth with breadth, *McK* combines "flow intensity [depth] with each country's share of the global total to offer a more accurate perspective on its significance in world flows" (Manyika et al. 2016, 56). Although the "significance" of a country's international activities beyond its own borders is interesting, we view this as only indirectly related to a country's actual level of globalization (shares in global flows themselves being a function of depth and country size). Nonetheless, rather than viewing this as a problem, *McK* argues in their methodological appendix that intensity measures "artificially boost small countries," prompting the inclusion of countries' shares in world flows to "correct" for this (Manyika et al. 2016, 125). In light of our earlier discussion of Squalli and Wilson (2011), upon which *McK* drew in constructing their index, we view this as arbitrary at best.

Changes in Globalization over Time

The discussion in the previous section should have highlighted the range of choices in constructing a globalization index – even if one only chooses to measure depth. To gain a sense of the comparative attractiveness of these indexes relative to each other as well as to the *DHL Global Connectedness Index*, it is useful to consider their recent evolution. Before the onset of the crisis in 2007, when globalization was unequivocally rising and the only question of interest was "by how much," the differences between indexes were less striking. The *DHL Global Connectedness Index 2014*, like other indexes, shows that from 2005 to 2007, globalization increased (see Figure 1.2).

In 2008, however, the financial crisis provided an important checkpoint for globalization indexes. According to the *DHL Global Connectedness Index*, globalization dropped off in 2008, decreased significantly in 2009, and even by 2013, had not fully recovered to 2007 levels. In contrast, the other indexes reported only a slowing or stagnation around the financial crisis – not a dropoff. Figure 1.3 compares trends in the depth of globalization reported by the *DHL Global Connectedness Index* and globalization trends based on the other indexes. The *KOF*, *Ernst & Young*, and *Maastricht* indexes all focus on depth, but did not show any decline as a result of the 2008 global financial crisis: only *KOF* registered as much as a brief pause.[17] (We exclude the *McKinsey* index from this section because that index has not released trend data.[18])

This difference is *not* due to differences in the schemes employed to aggregate data across countries. Global trends reported by the other indexes reflect

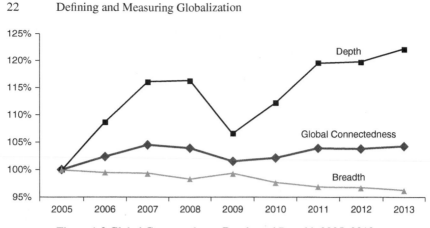

Figure 1.2 Global Connectedness, Depth, and Breadth 2005–2013.
Source: Figure 1.4 of *DHL Global Connectedness Index 2014*, p. 16.

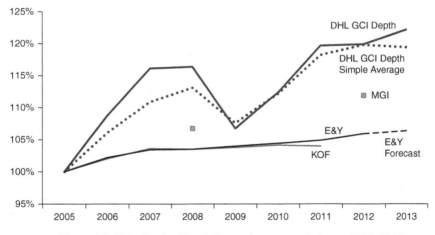

Figure 1.3 Globalization Trend Comparison across Indexes, 2005–2013.
Source: Authors' calculations based on index values referenced.

simple averages across countries' scores. However, given the tremendous variation across countries in terms of size and participation in international interactions, the *DHL Global Connectedness Index* (starting in its 2012 edition) adopts a system that permits the calculation of weighted averages at a global level as well as at intermediate levels of aggregation. To check that the differences between the *DHL Global Connectedness Index* and the other indexes are not driven by this focus on weighted versus simple averages, we recomputed our depth trends using simple averages (the dotted line in Figure 1.3). Even with this alternate averaging method, the *DHL Global Connectedness Index* remains the only index to register a significant drop in the wake of the crisis.

The crisis-era decline in globalization that the *DHL Global Connectedness Index* reports seems to fit better with contemporaneous accounts than the trend depicted by other indexes. The *Economist*'s February 2009 issue proclaimed that "the integration of the world economy is in retreat on almost every front," and highlighted drop-offs in trade, capital, and people flows. The same article also noted a change in popular rhetoric about globalization, stating that "the economic meltdown has popularised a new term: deglobalisation" (Economist 2009). And former US deputy treasury secretary Roger C. Altman addressed increased roles of national governments in regulation and protectionism in his 2009 *Foreign Affairs* article entitled "Globalization in Retreat" (2009, 5). Jean Pisani-Ferry and Indhira Santos spoke of an "end (for now) of a rapid expansion of globalization" in a March 2009 article, pointing to public participation in the private sector, financial fragmentation, and increased tariffs (2009, 8).

Since the end of the crisis, we seem to have entered an age of ambiguity, in which perception of the trajectory of globalization has been uncertain at best and contradictory at worst. Thus, within one month in 2015, the *Washington Post* offered its readers the full range of possibilities. On August 30, 2015, it published a piece by Robert J. Samuelson (Samuelson, 2015) called "Globalization at Warp Speed," but less than a month later, on September 20, 2015, the *Washington Post* Editorial Board (Editorial Board, 2015) wrote a piece entitled "The End of Globalization?"

This ambiguity suggests a particular need for timely measures of globalization. If a globalization index is to be a useful tool for business practitioners and policymakers, new data must be available on a regular basis to inform decision making. The *DHL Global Connectedness Index* is released with an eleven-month lag since the end of the most recent year measured. By contrast, *KOF* is usually published with a twenty-eight-month lag, and the most recent editions of the *McK*, *E&Y*, and *MGI* indexes were published with twenty-seven-, twenty-four-, and sixteen-month lags respectively. In addition, we are actively engaged in efforts to improve on this lag where possible – particularly in measuring depth, which along several pillars can be quite volatile over time.[19]

Conclusion

The term "globalization" rose to prominence in the late 1990s and 2000s, and has taken on a wide variety of meanings. The definition by Held et al. has been particularly influential in the business and economics literature. Building on this definition, we propose depth (or intensity) and breadth (or extensity) as primary measures of globalization. We compare this methodology, embodied in the *DHL Global Connectedness Index*, with other globalization indexes.

Our empirical work on depth and breadth also suggests two adjustments to how globalization is defined. First, the globalization trends captured on the *DHL Global Connectedness Index* show that levels of globalization can both rise and fall. This suggests that definitions should emphasize not only forward movement but also allow for reversals. Second, empirical work on breadth shows that the majority of international interactions take place within rather than between major world regions. Excluding intraregional interactions, as Held et al.'s conception of extensity suggests, would result, in our view, in a severely incomplete view of international interactions.

The notions of depth and breadth we discuss in this chapter underlie the chapters that follow in Parts I and II of this book (even though the precise measures from the *DHL Global Connectedness Index* are often modified as necessary). Depth at the country level, over time, and from a company perspective are the foci of Chapters 2 through 4, which establish the law of semiglobalization, and breadth is the focus of Chapters 5 through 7, which cover the law of distance. Finally, depth and breadth are brought together in joint applications of the two laws in Chapters 8 through 11 in Part III.

Notes

1 Keyword search of Library of Congress Catalog, January 2016.
2 Scholte (2005) claims there is no word in Swahili, but a Google Translate search returns the word "utandawazi," which does appear to link to sites that are about globalization.
3 The sentiment analysis was performed on articles downloaded from *Factiva* using a search for the term "globalization" in each of the six publications on October 30, 2015. AlchemyAPI is a project of IBM Watson and can be found at www.alchemyapi.com. The other two sentiment analysis engines tested were GetSentiment (www.getsentiment.io) and MeaningCloud (www.meaningcloud.com). All three showed a more positive view of globalization in the Chinese English language press; however, only two (AlchemyAPI and GetSentiment) showed that the US newspapers were more negative than positive.
4 Nayef Al-Rodhan and Gérard Stoudmann also produced a compendium of definitions of globalization. For this analysis, we chose to exclude it, as it included many sources from the popular media and was not as closely tied to the business and economics literature. See Al-Rodhan and Stoudmann (2006).
5 This word cloud was generated using an application called Wordle, which measures word usage in a given text. After identifying the specific language, the application assigns each word a numeric weight based on how many times it appears in the text. A word's numeric weight corresponds to a font size, so the more times a word appears, the more space it occupies in the word cloud. Wordle then positions the largest words

across the field and distributes the smaller words among them. In this word cloud, words appearing on a list of the most frequently used words in the English language have been omitted. See Feinberg (2010).

6 Stohl summarizes Appadurai's definition from the same book as: "globalization is characterized by two forces, mass migration and electronic mediation" in Stohl (2005, 232).

7 Culture is a salient piece of the impact of globalization, and certainly a large piece of the body of literature on the subject. A search of the *New York Times* for articles containing "globalization" in Factiva shows a rising proportion appearing in the cultural sections of the paper as compared to the business and finance sections. Across those two categories, the proportion of stories in sections focused on culture (e.g., Arts/Culture, Dining, Travel, Fashion) rose from 42 percent during 2000–2002 to 55 percent during 2013–2015.

8 Searching for definitions of globalization is a difficult problem in text analysis due to the ambiguities around how citations are styled. While we can easily determine if a document cites a particular source, determining whether the document actually cites the definition is more difficult. A verbatim quote is relatively easy to find, but given that definitions could go on for several sentences, it is not clear where to draw boundaries for a verbatim definition. This question is further complicated by the fact that many authors will paraphrase the quote. Paraphrasing may incorporate some unique phrases and words from the original, but not the quote itself. By leveraging proximity based searching techniques, we can get around certain issues of fuzziness. Google Scholar is built around the Google search engine, which is designed for a much different purpose. Google Search is primarily used to find websites, and web designers regularly use tricks to maximize their search engine visibility. As a result, Google is careful not to release clear details of how their search engine works. In addition, it is designed to provide the maximum number of results and rank the best matches first. Thus, putting limitations on the search results might still return results that we would prefer to exclude – just with a lower ranking than the ideal results. While these features of Google Scholar can be useful when searching for articles, they make it less useful in text analysis.

9 The authors wish to acknowledge the helpful assistance of Professor Timothy Hannigan, University of Alberta, in conducting this analysis.

10 For some thoughts in this regard, refer to chapter 15 of Ghemawat (2011).

11 For compactness, the term "countries," as used throughout this book, is meant to refer to what *Asia-Pacific Economic Cooperation (APEC)* calls "economies." Thus, Hong Kong, Macau, and Taiwan are separated from Mainland China. In most cases, British Overseas Territories and Crown Dependencies, Overseas Collectivities and Territories of France, Constituent Countries of Denmark and the Netherlands, and United States Territories are given the same treatment where applicable.

12 As defined in the CAGE Framework, first introduced in Ghemawat (2001).

13 We also discuss in Chapter 10 some of the challenges associated with classifying countries into regions.

14 For a more detailed explanation, refer to Ghemawat and Altman (2014, 78–80).

15 Although data are also available on foreign-held debt, we exclude these from the index on normative grounds.

16 International internet bandwidth is a departure from this focus, employed due to the insufficient availability of country-level international internet traffic data.

17 It should be noted that the *Maastricht* index is reported for only three years: 2000, 2008, and 2012, so the lack of evidence of a decline during the crisis on that index may reflect its timing rather than its methodology.

18 McKinsey does discuss global trends (see, in particular, Exhibit E1 of their 2016 report), but based on a narrower set of indicators rather than their index itself.

19 In order to offer more timely tracking of globalization, we are developing additional measures which we have tentatively named the *Quarterly Updated International Connectedness (QUIC)* index and the *FASTtrade* indicator. Like the *DHL Global Connectedness Index*, these indicators attempt to measure changes in globalization levels, although they are focused on trade and capital depth, as these change more rapidly over time than the other pillars. They are intended to reduce the time lag substantially over annual indexes, as well as to provide more data points.

References

Al-Rodhan, Nayef R. F., and Gérard Stoudmann. 2006. "Definitions of Globalization: A Comprehensive Overview and a Proposed Definition." In *Pillars of Globalization*. Genève: Éditions Slatkine, Geneva Centre for Security Policy.

Altman, Roger C. 2009. "Globalization in Retreat: Further Geopolitical Consequences of the Financial Crisis." *Foreign Affairs* 88 (4):2–7.

Appadurai, Arjun. 1996. *Modernity at Large: Cultural Dimensions of Globalization*, Public Worlds. Minneapolis, MN: University of Minnesota Press.

    2000. "Grassroots Globalization and the Research Imagination." *Public Culture* 12 (1):1–19. doi: 10.1215/08992363-12-1-1.

    2015. *Banking on Words: The Failure of Language in the Age of Derivative Finance*. Chicago; London: The University of Chicago Press.

    2015. "Defining Globalization." E-mail to Pankaj Ghemawat, 10/29/2015 6:05 PM.

Beerkens, Eric. 2006. "Globalisation: Definitions and Perspectives." http://blog.beerkens.info/global.htm.

Bentham, Jeremy. 1823. *An Introduction to the Principles of Morals and Legislation*. 2 ed. London: W. Pickering.

Dreher, Axel, Noel Gaston, Pim Martens, and Lotte Van Boxem. 2010. "Measuring Globalization – Opening the Black Box. A Critical Analysis of Globalization Indices." *Journal of Globalization Studies* 1 (1):166–185.

Economist. 2009. "Globalisation: Turning Their Backs on the World." *Economist* (February 19, 2009). www.economist.com/node/13145370.

Editorial Board. 2015. "The Post's View: The End of Globalization?" *Washington Post*. www.washingtonpost.com/opinions/the-end-of-globalization/2015/09/20/b48b9f60-5e2f-11e5-9757-e49273f05f65_story.html.

Ernst & Young. 2012. "Looking Beyond the Obvious: Globalization and New Opportunities for Growth (2012 Globalization Index)." Accessed October 16, 2015. www.ey.com/gl/en/issues/driving-growth/globalization---looking-beyond-the-obvious---2012-index.

Feinberg, Jonathan. 2010. "Wordle." In *Beautiful Visualization: Looking at Data through the Eyes of Experts*, edited by Julie Steele, and Noah P. N. Iliinsky, 37–58. Sebastopol, CA: O'Reilly.

Fouchard, Gérard. 2016. "Historical Overview of Submarine Communication Systems." In *Undersea Fiber Communication Systems*, edited by José Chesnoy, 21–51. 2nd ed. Amsterdam; Boston: Academic Press.

Friedman, Thomas L. 2005. *The World Is Flat: A Brief History of the Twenty-First Century*. New York: Farrar Straus and Giroux.

Ghemawat, Pankaj. 2001. "Distance Still Matters: The Hard Reality of Global Expansion." *Harvard Business Review* 79 (8):137–147.

2011. *World 3.0: Global Prosperity and How to Achieve It*. Boston, MA: Harvard Business Review Press.

Ghemawat, Pankaj, and Steven A. Altman. 2014. "DHL Global Connectedness Index 2014: Analyzing Global Flows and Their Power to Increase Prosperity." Deutsche Post DHL. www.dhl.com/gci.

Harper, Douglas. 2015. "World War (n.)." In *Online Etymology Dictionary*. www.etymonline.com/index.php?term=world+war&allowed_in_frame=0.

Held, David, Anthony G. McGrew, David Goldblatt, and Jonathan Perraton. 1999. *Global Transformations: Politics, Economics and Culture*. Stanford, CA: Stanford University Press.

Janis, M. W. 1984. "Jeremy Bentham and the Fashioning of 'International Law'." *American Journal of International Law* 78 (2):405–418.

Jones, Geoffrey. 1996. *The Evolution of International Business: An Introduction*. London; New York: Routledge.

Keynes, John Maynard. 1919. *The Economic Consequences of the Peace*. London: Macmillan and Co., Limited.

Kilminster, Richard. 1997. "Globalization as an Emergent Concept." In *The Limits of Globalization: Cases and Arguments*, edited by Alan Scott, 257–283. London; New York: Routledge.

Livingstone, David, and Horace Waller. 1874. *The Last Journals of David Livingstone, in Central Africa, from 1865 to His Death*. 2 vols. London: John Murray.

Manyika, James, Jacques Bughin, Susan Lund, Olivia Nottebohm, David Poulter, Sebastian Jauch, and Sree Ramaswamy. "Global Flows in a Digital Age: How Trade, Finance, People, and Data Connect the World Economy." McKinsey Global Institute, April 2014. www.mckinsey.com/insights/globalization/global_flows_in_a_digital_age.

Manyika, James, Susan Lund, Jacques Bughin, Jonathan Woetzel, Kalin Stamenov, and Dhruv Dhingra. "Digital Globalization: The New Era of Global Flows." McKinsey Global Institute, March 2016. www.mckinsey.com/business-functions/mckinsey-digital/our-insights/digital-globalization-the-new-era-of-global-flows.

Merriam-Webster. 2015. "Globalization." *Merriam-Webster.com*. www.merriam-webster.com/dictionary/globalization.

Mussa, Michael. 2000. "Factors Driving Global Economic Integration." Paper presented at Conference. Global economic integration: Opportunities and challenges, Jackson Hole, WY, August 25, 2000. www.kansascityfed.org/Publicat/sympos/2000/S00muss.pdf.

O'Rourke, Kevin H., and Jeffrey G. Williamson. 1999. *Globalization and History: The Evolution of a Nineteenth-Century Atlantic Economy*. Cambridge, MA: MIT Press.

Pew Research Center, and Roper Center. 2014. "Pew Global Attitudes & Trends Question Database." www.pewglobal.org/question-search/?qid=1011&cntids=&stdids=; Excel download available at: https://ropercenter.cornell.edu/cfide/pewglobal/export.cfm?qstnTextID=1011&cntIDs=&stdIDs=.

Pisani-Ferry, Jean, and Indhira Santos. 2009. "Reshaping." *Finance & Development* (March):8–12.

Rydell, Robert W., and Rob Kroes. 2005. *Buffalo Bill in Bologna: The Americanization of the World, 1869–1922*. Chicago: University of Chicago Press.

Samuelson, Robert J. 2015. "Globalization at Warp Speed." *Washington Post* (August 30, 2015). www.washingtonpost.com/opinions/globalization-at-warp-speed/2015/08/30/152d3f0c-4d9d-11e5-84df-923b3ef1a64b_story.html.

Scholte, Jan Aart. 2005. *Globalization: A Critical Introduction*. 2nd ed. New York: Palgrave Macmillan.

Sichel, H. S. 1974. "On a Distribution Representing Sentence-Length in Written Prose." *Journal of the Royal Statistical Society. Series A (General)* 137 (1):25–34. doi: 10.2307/2345142.

Smeltz, Dina, Ivo H. Daalder, and Craig Kafura. 2014. "Foreign Policy in the Age of Retrenchment: Results of the 2014 Chicago Council Survey of American Public Opinion and U.S. Foreign Policy." Chicago, IL: The Chicago Council on Global Affairs. www.thechicagocouncil.org/publication/foreign-policy-age-retrenchment-0.

Squalli, Jay, and Kenneth Wilson. 2011. "A New Measure of Trade Openness." *World Economy* 34 (10):1745–1770. doi: 10.1111/j.1467-9701.2011.01404.x.

Stohl, Cynthia. 2005. "Globalization Theory." In *Engaging Organizational Communication Theory & Research: Multiple Perspectives*, edited by Steve May, and Dennis K. Mumby, 223–261. Thousand Oaks, CA: Sage Publications.

Tang, Kam Ki, and Amy Wagner. 2010. "Measuring Globalization Using Weighted Network Indexes." 31st General Conference of The International Association for Research in Income and Wealth, St. Gallen, Switzerland, August 22–28, 2010. www.iariw.org/papers/2010/4cTang.pdf.

Verne, Jules. 1873. *Around the World in Eighty Days*. Translated by George M. Towle. Boston, MA: James R. Osgood and Company.

2   The Depth of Globalization

This chapter presents empirical evidence for the law of semiglobalization: "International interactions, while non-negligible, are significantly less intense than domestic interactions." The bulk of the evidence presented here is organized around the four categories of international interactions introduced in Chapter 1: Trade, Capital, Information, and People. Although I discuss the four categories one by one, it is important to remember that there are complementarities among them, as well as some substitution effects. Thus, people flows have been found to stimulate both trade[1] and information flows (Perkins and Neumayer 2013); information flows are positively associated with capital flows (Portes and Rey 2005); some foreign direct investment substitutes for trade, and so on.

In each section, most of the evidence presented takes the form of quantity measures, specifically depth ratios. Depth ratios – as described in Chapter 1 – look at the international proportion of activities that could take place either within or across national borders. A standard example is the ratio of exports to GDP as an indicator of trade intensity. Where possible, I also present price measures, because economic theory implies that rising levels of cross-border integration should decrease price dispersion across countries. Thus, this chapter treats markets as the primary locus of cross-border integration and focuses on economic evidence on the extent to which they are integrated. It supplies market-level context for Chapters 3 and 4, which place greater emphasis on globalization at the firm level, and its focus on recent evidence also complements the longer-run historical perspective on globalization provided in Chapter 3. This chapter concludes with some data on how much people overestimate depth levels, and why it matters.

Throughout this chapter, wherever possible, depth data are presented based on worldwide averages captured over extended periods (annual data in most cases). However, it is important to recognize up front that there is substantial – and systematic – variation around those averages. At the country level, depth measures are positively associated with countries' per capita GDPs and negatively related to country size and remoteness (Ghemawat and Altman 2014, 25).

At the individual level, globetrotting celebrities and senior business executives are often outliers on depth metrics pertaining to international travel and relationships. Furthermore, some forms of connectedness are subject to temporal variation in the form of spikes during particular kinds of events, for example, more highly correlated stock price movements during major selloffs and greater international news coverage during terrorist attacks and natural disasters.

Trade Flows

Trade flows are the most obvious quantity measure of product market integration. World exports of goods and services rose from 1 percent of world GDP in 1820 to 31 percent in 2014, but the deepening of trade intensity has not been monotonic. The proportion of world output traded across borders reached its first peak of roughly 8 percent immediately before the Great Depression and then plummeted amid a wave of protectionism. After World War II, this metric soared from 6 percent in 1950 up through its previous peak and continued growing with few interruptions until reaching the unprecedented level of 32 percent in 2008. While the subsequent financial crisis and macroeconomic downturn led to a drop-off in 2009 to 27 percent, the ratio of exports to GDP was back near its all-time high by 2011.[2] Since 2011, services trade intensity has started to increase again while merchandise trade intensity has faltered (see Figure 2.1).

Although the large expansion of international trade over the past half-century provides evidence of rising product market integration, for trade economists the question of why there isn't even more trade draws more interest than the record levels it has reached. To see the room for increase, consider a hypothetical benchmark in which national borders do not affect buying patterns at all. In such a situation, buyers in a particular nation would be as prone to obtain goods and services from foreign producers as domestic ones, and the share of imports in total domestic consumption would equal 1 minus the nation's share of world GDP (Helpman 1987; Frankel 2001; Eaton and Kortum 2002). For example, since the US economy accounted for about 22 percent of world GDP in 2014, the US import/GDP ratio would, at this benchmark, equal 1 minus the US share of world GDP, or 0.78, as would, under the first-order assumption of balanced trade, the US export/GDP ratio. However, the actual ratios are less than one-quarter of these hypothetical ratios! On a global basis, this hypothetical benchmark implies world imports equal to 92 percent of world GDP in 2011, up from 77 percent in 1960 due to the rise of emerging economies and the creation of new borders; for example, the break-up of the former Soviet Union (Head and Mayer 2013).

The line with slope −1 in Figure 2.2 traces out this hypothetical benchmark of perfect product market integration at the country level as national shares of world GDP vary, with the world's twenty largest economies by GDP in US dollars (at market exchange rates) plotted on the chart. Note that most of

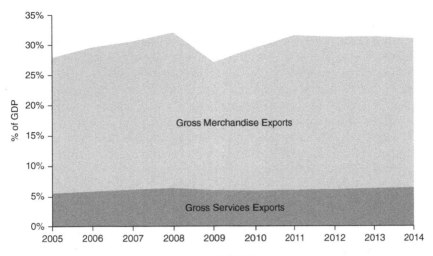

Figure 2.1 Trade Depth Ratios, 2005–2014.
Sources: Merchandise and Commercial Services Trade (BPM 6) data from the World Trade Organization (WTO) Statistics database, GDP data from IMF WEO (April 2015).

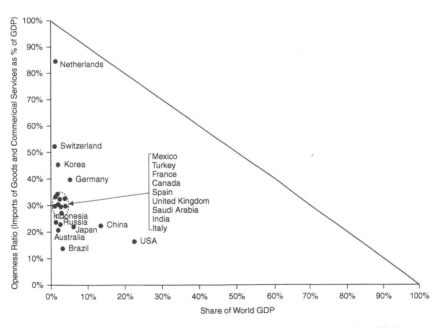

Figure 2.2 Actual versus Perfect Product Market Integration, 20 Largest Economies, 2014.
Note: Countries listed in brace appear in descending order by openness ratio.
Sources: Calculated from WTO Statistics Database and IMF World Economic Outlook Database (October 2015).

the nations cluster close to the origin and all fall well below the hypothetical benchmark – including the Netherlands, the highest example on the chart, which ranks as the world's most globally connected economy on the 2014 *DHL Global Connectedness Index*.[3] The main exceptions to this rule are trading hubs such as Hong Kong and Singapore, which report imports of nearly double their GDP, but re-export a large proportion of them.

Examples such as Hong Kong and Singapore also illustrate how traditional (gross) depth ratios overstate the extent of trade integration, because products that cross national borders multiple times are counted each time. With the rise of multi-country supply chains, the effect of this double- and triple-counting becomes significant for many countries, not only trading hubs. In 2010, an estimated 28 percent of the value of gross exports of goods and services was foreign value added (value from a country other than where the exports are registered). This implies that exports really account for closer to 20 percent of global value added rather than more than 30 percent (UNCTAD 2013, 123). Adjusting for multicountry supply chain effects also brings into clearer focus the deeper trade in goods as compared to services. Exports account for about 40 percent of value added in goods-producing sectors (agriculture and industry) but only 15 percent in the service sector.[4]

Figure 2.3 compares export depth across industries in 2014, and here the issue of double and triple counting arises again as the available data do not permit calculations on a value-added basis.[5] At the top of the figure is microwave ovens, 72 percent of which were exported in 2014. The concentration of 75 percent of microwave oven manufacturing in China suggests that economies of scale combine with labor cost arbitrage to boost this figure. At the other extreme, the industry with the lowest depth among those analyzed was electricity, of which only 3 percent is traded across national borders. Here, national regulations and infrastructure as well as transmission losses over long distances come into play. Recall that gross exports of all types of goods and services accounted for 31 percent of world GDP in 2014, providing a benchmark against which industries may be characterized as more or less deeply integrated across borders than the world economy as a whole.[6]

The three types of energy in Figure 2.3 exemplify how trade intensities can vary widely even among industries within a single sector. Crude petroleum, the price of which is used to predict global macroeconomic trends, is unsurprisingly higher than the average across all goods and services, with 37 percent of production exported in 2013. Coal falls below the average with a depth score of 19 percent, and, as already mentioned, only 3 percent of electricity is traded across national borders. Analysis at the level of the energy sector as a whole would miss these large differences.

Industries with high export intensity tend to export products with high value-to-weight ratios, as illustrated in Figure 2.4.[7] This is unsurprising since high

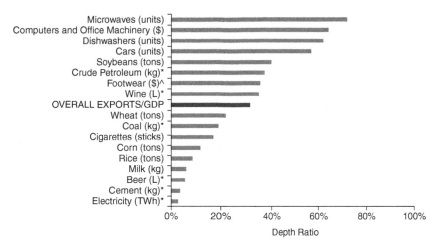

Figure 2.3 Industry Depth Comparisons, 2014 or Most Recent.
Note: * 2013; ^ Retail value used in denominator (rather than production value).
Sources: Microwaves: Production and Exports data from Euromonitor Passport; Computers and Office Machinery: Production and Exports data from Euromonitor Passport; Dishwashers: Production and Exports data from Euromonitor Passport; Cars: Consumption data from OICA (New registrations of passenger cars), Imports data from UN Comtrade (HS96 8703), adjustment to account for trade in used cars based on Henry Kamau, "Trade in Second-Hand Vehicles" presentation to the UNEP PCFV, July 7, 2016; Soybeans: Production and Exports data from Grain Market Report (International Grains Council); Crude Petroleum: Production data from UN Energy Statistics Database, Exports data from UN Comtrade (SITC4 3330); Footwear: Consumption data from Euromonitor Passport, Imports data from UN Comtrade (SITC4 851); Wine: Consumption data from Euromonitor Passport, Imports data from UN Comtrade (HS as reported 2204) with gaps filled in using data from Euromonitor Passport; Wheat: Production and Exports data from Grain Market Report (International Grains Council); Coal: Production data from UN Energy Statistics Database, Exports data from UN Comtrade (HS02 2701); Cigarettes: Production and Exports data from Euromonitor Passport; Corn: Production and Exports data from Grain Market Report (International Grains Council); Rice: Production and Exports data from Grain Market Report (International Grains Council); Milk: Consumption data from Euromonitor Passport, Imports data from UN Comtrade (HS as reported 0401); Beer: Consumption data from Euromonitor Passport, Imports data from UN Comtrade (HS02 2203); Cement: Production data from USGS 2013 Minerals Yearbook, Exports data from UN Comtrade (HS as reported 2523); Electricity: Production and Exports data from International Energy Agency Statistics, 2015.

value-to-weight ratios help mitigate the costs associated with international trade. Note that Figure 2.4 reflects the value-to-weight ratios of traded goods

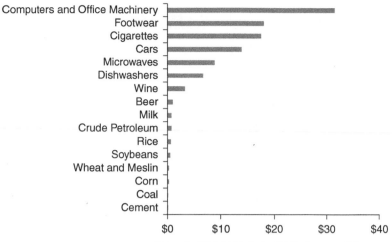

Figure 2.4 Value-to-Weight Comparison (Value of Exported Goods in USD/kg), 2014.
Source: UN Comtrade. Computers and Office Machinery: HS as reported 8471, 8472, 8443; Footwear: SITC4 851; Cigarettes: HS as reported 240220; Cars: HS96 8703; Microwaves: HS as reported 851650; Dishwashers: HS96 842211; Wine: HS as reported 2204; Beer: HS02 2203; Milk: HS as reported 0401; Crude Petroleum: SITC4 3330; Rice: HS as reported 1006; Soybeans: HS as reported 1201; Wheat and Meslin: HS as reported 1001; Corn: HS as reported 1005; Coal: HS02 2701; Cement: HS as reported 2523.

within each of the industries analyzed; the value-to-weight ratios of nontraded goods in the same industries may differ from those shown. Industries with higher trade intensity also tend to have higher R&D intensity since international sales (via either trade or local production abroad) help firms spread fixed R&D costs over greater sales volumes.

Viewed in terms of prices rather than quantities, the ultimate in market integration is achieved when two (or more) markets are yoked together by the so-called Law of One Price (LOP), that is, prices equalize across them. Implicit in LOP is a (strong) zero-arbitrage-profits principle. Note that the degree of price integration of product markets can be high even when the quantity flows across them are limited, for example, for commodities whose local prices are pegged to world benchmark prices, particularly ones with high value-to-weight ratios. Except for (nearly) perfect commodities, however, lack of data on local currency prices of identical products across countries generally hampers tests of price integration. Studies that *have* been conducted to test LOP generally conclude that cross-country price dispersions tend to be large and to die down at a slow pace, and there is little evidence of recent movement toward smaller dispersions or speedier dampening (for a survey of the literature, see Rogoff 1996). Thus, the evidence is murky, but it is not possible to conclude that price measures indicate increasing (or decreasing) integration or globalization of product markets.

Capital Flows

Trade is not the only way in which the cross-border integration of product markets is accomplished: foreign direct investment (FDI), which involves product-specific investment across borders, is an obvious alternative. My own preferred normalization is to look at how large total FDI flows are in relation to global gross fixed capital formation, because this permits a (rough) answer to the question of how much of real investment around the world consists of investments being made by companies outside their home countries. While FDI, like trade, soared to unprecedented levels after World War II, its growth has been even more volatile. The ratio of FDI outflows to gross fixed capital formation reached 14 percent in 2000 amid a wave of cross-border mergers but then declined to only 8 percent in 2001 and 6 percent in 2003. By 2007, it had recovered to a peak value of 16 percent, but it collapsed again amid the global financial crisis and after a modest recovery stagnated at 7 percent between 2012 and 2014.[8]

There has also been substantial study of the international mobility of capital more broadly defined, although as in the case of trade, the professional curiosity of economists has focused on smaller-than-expected flows (or stocks). Probably the most famous "anomaly" of this sort is the one Martin Feldstein and Charles Horioka (1980) uncovered by calculating a 90 percent correlation between domestic savings and domestic investment across a panel of countries, much higher than benchmark models that assume perfect capital mobility would lead us to expect. Another anomaly that points in the same direction is based on analysis suggesting that investors hold much smaller proportions of their wealth in foreign securities than they would if they were diversifying well internationally (only one-third the level expected without "home bias" among investors from advanced economies and one-tenth among investors from emerging economies in 2008) (Coeurdacier and Rey 2013). US and Brazilian investors, for example, hold 77 percent and 99 percent of their portfolios in domestic equities even though the United States and Brazil account for only 33 percent and 2 percent of world market capitalization, respectively (Coeurdacier and Rey 2013). The depth of international equity investment, however, has been on a rising trend: international portfolio equity stocks rose from 27 percent of world stock market capitalization in 2005 to 36 percent in 2014.[9]

Data on other aspects of capital market integration are spottier, but Figure 2.5 does summarize several additional depth metrics. These metrics all fall in

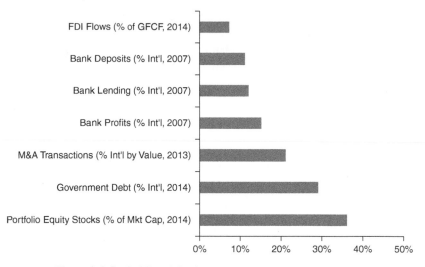

Figure 2.5 Capital Depth Ratios.
Sources: Outward FDI flows (% of GFCF): World Investment Report 2015 (UNCTAD); Bank Deposits (% Int'l, 2007), Bank Lending (% Int'l, 2007), Bank profits (% Int'l, 2007): Claessens and Van Horen (2012); M&A Transactions, excluding Spin-offs (% Int'l, 2013): Thomson Research; Government Debt (% Int'l, 2014): Euromonitor Passport; Portfolio Equity Stock (% of Market Capitalization of listed companies, 2014): Equity Investment Inward Stock from IMF's Balance of Payments and International Investment Position Statistics; Market Capitalization of listed companies from Euromonitor Passport.

between the levels already cited for FDI and portfolio equity. Roughly, 29 percent of government debt was foreign owned in 2014.[10] On the basis of available (partial) data on M&A transactions, 21 percent of the value and 23 percent of the number of transactions that took place in 2013 were combinations between firms located in different countries.[11] Banking was less international, with foreign banks taking 11 percent of deposits, making 12 percent of loans, and generating 15 percent of bank profits in 2007 (Claessens and Horen 2012) – figures that have probably since declined.

All the discussions of capital so far have been partial in the sense of focusing on subsets of capital flows.[12] Figure 2.6 tracks total gross capital flows (loans, portfolio debt and equity, and FDI)[13] across national borders as a percentage of GDP from 1980 to 2012, and highlights the dramatic run-up in international capital flows, debt as well as equity, that took place before the global financial crisis and their subsequent collapse in 2008. As shown in Figure 2.7, the precrisis expansion of international capital flows was driven primarily by loans and portfolio investment (debt and equity) inflows into advanced economies. From 2003 to 2007, 86 percent of the growth of total capital flows came from inflows

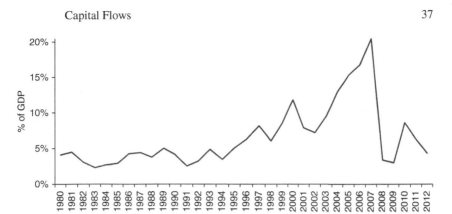

Figure 2.6 Gross Capital Inflows as Percentage of GDP, 1980–2012.
Sources: Gross capital inflow data 1980–2011 drawn from World Bank (2013); capital flows in 2012 estimated based on growth rate of capital flows shown in "Capital: Just in Case." (2013); GDP data from IMF World Economic Outlook database (October 2013).

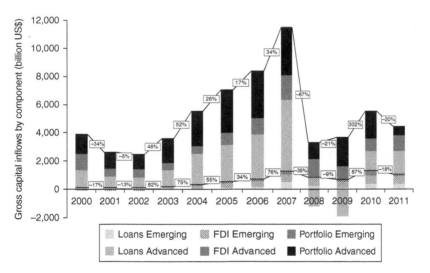

Figure 2.7 Gross Capital Inflows by Component, 2000–2011.
Note: Advanced and emerging economies are as classified in that source, rather than corresponding to the IMF classification scheme used elsewhere in this book.
Source: Gross capital flow data drawn from World Bank, "Capital for the Future," (2013).

into advanced economies, and FDI never contributed more than 20 percent of the inflows into advanced economies over that period.[14]

Much of this run-up, extending even farther back, to 1980, seems to have reflected European rather than global financial market integration. From 1980 to 2007, 56 percent of the global growth in capital flows and, since 2007, 72 percent of the decline, took place in Western Europe (Lund et al. 2013). The introduction of the Euro ushered in a wave of progress toward the European Union's (EU) longstanding goal of creating a single European capital market. Intra-EU foreign bank exposures rose 215 percent from 2000 to 2008. In late 2007, 40 percent of interbank claims of Euro area banks were on banks in other EU member countries, as were 25 percent of their equity holdings. Bond markets were even more integrated with bonds from other EU countries making up 54 percent of the EU bond portfolios of Euro area banks. Integration did not, however, extend to retail lending. At the end of 2007, 85 percent of intra-EU loans by Euro area banks were still domestic, 12 percent were to other Euro area countries, and 3 percent were to non-Euro area EU countries (IMF 2013).

After the onset of the crisis, however, much of the prior increase in Europe's financial integration was reversed. Interbank claims on other Euro area financial institutions fell by 42 percent after September 2008, and lending to other non-Euro area EU members by 23 percent. Cross-border loans to private sector entities dropped 40 percent. Euro area banks reduced their overall exposure to other Euro area countries' bonds by 55 percent and to non-Euro area EU members' bonds by 50 percent, contributing to rising home bias in EU banks' sovereign debt portfolios (Acharya and Steffen 2013) and to fears of a sovereign debt doom loop. In Spain and Italy, domestic sovereign debt came to account for more than three quarters of national banks' sovereign debt portfolios (Uhlig 2013). Cross-border equity exposure also fell 8 percent and 23 percent vis-à-vis other Euro area countries and non-Euro area EU members respectively (IMF 2013).

Price-based measures of capital market integration – with price integration reinterpreted in terms of the equalization of rates of return on common or comparable securities across national boundaries – supply additional evidence about the continued segmentation of capital markets. A comparison of one-year interest rates on sterling-denominated assets sold in London and in New York provides one example (Obstfeld and Taylor 1997). Figure 2.8 tracks the standard deviation of differences in returns in the two cities as an inverse measure of capital market integration over more than one hundred years. The data indicate significant cross-border integration of capital markets prior to 1914, the breakdown of that integration in the interwar period, and its recovery in the postwar period (consistent with historical patterns that I discuss in Chapter 3).

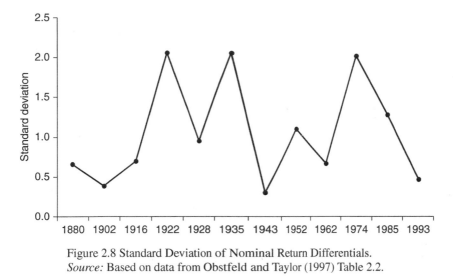

Figure 2.8 Standard Deviation of Nominal Return Differentials.
Source: Based on data from Obstfeld and Taylor (1997) Table 2.2.

Qualitatively similar conclusions are suggested by comparing real rather than nominal returns, although that increases the standard deviation of the dispersion of returns, presumably reflecting the effects of currency risk, both nominal and real (Obstfeld and Taylor 1997; for further discussion of currency risk, see Frankel 1992, 197). A somewhat different form of price-based evidence, that pertaining to spillovers of asset price movements between markets does suggest a trend toward greater integration of equity and foreign exchange markets (IMF April 2016).[15]

Information Flows

Since it can be congealed in products, embedded in capital equipment, or transferred between countries within multinational firms, the cross-border flows already discussed can carry knowledge flows – frequently treated as the most meaningful information flows – across national borders as well. This section focuses on cross-border flows of information in pure, disembodied, "knowledge-based" form. This focus offers a relatively simple benchmark: since disembodied knowledge has a "nonrival" character – that is, its use in one market, whether defined in geographic or product-related terms, does not preclude its application to others – perfect cross-border integration in this context should imply that information or knowledge, once developed anywhere in the world, is available everywhere else as well. But intrinsic intangibility does mean that information flows are harder to measure than, say, merchandise trade. And one must proceed channel by channel since there is no overarching measure of cross-border information flows. With those caveats, it seems that there have been substantial increases in the intensity of cross-border information flows over time and, a bit more definitely, that cross-border integration in this regard nevertheless remains very incomplete. Consider internationalization channel by channel.

During 2013, people around the world, on average, spoke on international telephone calls for about 150 minutes, up from 88 minutes in 2005.[16] This means that the average person still transmits and receives a very limited amount of information via international telephone calls: just about 2.5 hours of conversation content per year! These figures exclude calls that neither originate nor terminate via traditional telephone lines, but even adding in a rough estimate for computer-to-computer calls, international calling minutes still account for less than 5 percent of total international and domestic minutes (see Figure 2.9). The international share of telephone calls, thus, remains limited even though the per-minute cost of international calls fell 95 percent from 1980 to 2010 (Head and Mayer 2013).

The internet has been celebrated for making distance (and borders) irrelevant, but internet use also remains primarily domestic. While international internet bandwidth per internet user has soared from 6,200 bits per second in 2005 to 52,600 in 2013 (8.5 times its 2005 level), it only measures the potential for international connectivity rather than actual international communications. There are some technical issues involved with measuring the proportion of internet traffic that crosses international borders. Nonetheless, one estimate indicates it has remained steady at roughly 17–18 percent since 2006.[17] And for E-commerce, which blends information and trade flows, the international proportion of revenues was estimated at 16 percent in 2013 (PayPal 2013).[18]

Information flows on social media are also primarily domestic. A published estimate indicates that only 16 percent of Facebook friends are located across national borders, and newer unpublished research points toward an even lower share (Ugander et al. 2011). On Twitter, an estimated 25 percent of followers are located in different countries from the people they follow. But only 14 percent of followers are located in a foreign country that doesn't share the same dominant language (Takhteyev, Gruzd, and Wellman 2012). Twitter is probably more "globalized" than Facebook because of the tendency to follow news rather than friends.

Research I conducted in collaboration with TCS Innovation Labs finds that active followers on Twitter (defined as followers who re-tweet) are more likely to be domestic than passive followers. This research reaffirms the importance of a common language, but also shows that language is far from the only cultural commonality that promotes communication. Thus, string matching suggests that about one-third of foreign followers of Indian Twitter users have

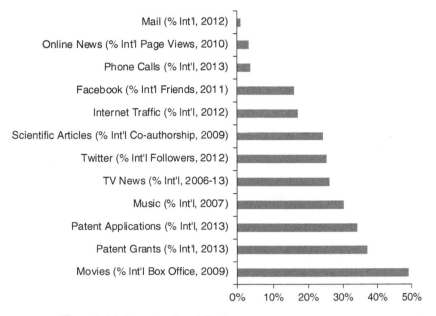

Figure 2.9 Information Depth Ratios.

Sources: Mail (% Int'l, 2012): Universal Postal Union (UPU); Online News (% Int'l Page Views, 2010): Unpublished analysis of Google Ad Planner data conducted by Ethan Zuckerman; Phone Calls (% Int'l, 2013): International Telecommunication Union and Telegeography; Facebook (% Int'l Friends, 2011): Ugander (2011); Internet Traffic (% Int'l, 2012): rough estimate based on data from Cisco Visual Networking Index and Telegeography; Scientific Articles (% Int'l Co-authorship, 2009): Scellato, Franzoni, and Stephan (2015); Twitter (% Int'l Followers, 2012): Takhteyev, Gruzd, and Wellman (2012); TV News (% Int'l, 2006–13): (Media Tenor 2006; Porath and Mujica 2011; Aalberg et al. 2013); Music (% Int'l, 2007): Ferreira and Waldfogel (2013); Patent Applications and Grants (% Int'l, 2013): Euromonitor Passport; Movies (% Int'l Box Office Revenue, 2009): estimate based on data from Box Office Mojo, Reliance Entertainment, Screen Digest, Screenline, Entgroup (Enbase), Press Reports.

Hindu names – far out of line with the infrequency of such names (probably 1–2 percent of the total) outside India – suggesting important ethnic/religious bridges across borders.

Analyses of other forms of communication over the internet reinforce the conclusion that people primarily use it to communicate domestically rather than across international borders. A study of instant messages on MSN Messenger shows that users who communicate with each other are sixteen times as likely to be in the same country (and twenty-seven times as likely to speak the same language) compared to users who do not communicate (Leskovec and Horvitz 2008). E-mail exchanges on Yahoo Mail are also significantly more intense among users who are geographically proximate and share cultural ties (State et al. March 2013).

With respect to general awareness of developments in other countries, it is useful to consider the (mainly national) media's coverage of foreign stories. Data aggregated across three cross-country studies suggest that the average foreign share of TV news coverage is about 26 percent (Media Tenor 2006; Porath and Mujica 2011; Aalberg et al. 2013). Furthermore, roughly one-third to one-half of foreign news coverage focuses on the home country's foreign affairs, indicating that the purely foreign share of TV news is probably in the mid-to-high teens (Porath and Mujica 2011; Pew Research Center various editions). People also seldom view foreign news websites. Page views on news websites from foreign countries constitute 1 percent of total page views of news websites in Germany, 2 percent in France, 5 percent in the UK, and are in single digits in all countries for which data are available – as low as 0.1 percent in China.[19]

Several studies also report a persistent decline in the intensity of international news coverage over time (see, for instance, Papathanassopoulos 2002; Reinemann et al. 2012; Aalberg et al. 2013). On the front pages of major US newspapers, the share of foreign stories declined from 27 percent in 1987 to 11 percent in 2010 (Weaver and Willnat 2012). In the major British press, the foreign share of coverage shrank by about 40 percent between 1979 and 2009 (Moore 2010). There is also evidence that foreign news stories tend to present the countries covered in a negative light. According to one study, one-third of foreign stories analyzed "painted a negative picture of the protagonists" as compared to only one-fifth presenting positive news (Schatz and Kolmer 2010, 140). Furthermore, cross-country historical data show a trend toward more negative news coverage from 1979 to 2010 (Leetaru 2011).

Another avenue for international transmission of information is via the translation of books and local printing of translated editions. However, relatively few titles are actually translated into foreign languages. In the United States and the UK, just 3 percent of the books published are translated from foreign languages, and only 1 percent of fiction. The share of translated books is higher in non-English-speaking countries, for example, 14 percent in France and 8 percent in Germany. Overall, translations from English dominate, with a two-thirds share of all translated books in Europe ("Stories from Elsewhere" 2012).

Cultural products such as music and movies provide other potential avenues for international information flows. Fernando Ferreira and Joel Waldfogel (2013) analyze music consumption and report that 30 percent was international in 2007, down from 50 percent in the 1980s. Depth ratios for movies, however, are higher. In 2009, foreign films accounted for an estimated 49 percent of global box office revenues, largely reflecting the popularity of Hollywood movies in many countries.[20] Although an updated depth ratio for box office revenues is not available, China's rising share of world box office revenues since 2009 has almost certainly driven it down.

Data on international collaboration in research also point to continued localization of knowledge, even in the face of rising informational connectivity. In 2009, 24 percent of published scientific articles in the fields of biology, chemistry, earth science, and materials science, were internationally coauthored (by coauthors based in different countries) (Scellato, Franzoni, and Stephan 2015). However, international coauthorship had increased substantially over the previous two decades, up from only 10 percent in 1990 and 23 percent in 2005 (Leydesdorff and Wagner 2008, 319). Across a broader range of fields, an estimated 25–35 percent of published articles have international coauthors (Ghemawat and Pisani 2014).

International patenting data provide another research-based perspective on the globalization of information flows. In 2013, 34 percent of patent applications came from nonresidents of the countries where the patents were sought and 37 percent of patent grants were awarded to nonresidents.[21] The proportion of "domestic" patents with at least one foreign coinventor is much lower, only 7 percent between 2009 and 2011 (OECD 2013). A study of patent citations in five large industrialized countries also finds that patents whose inventors reside in the same country are typically 30–80 percent more likely to cite each other than inventors from other countries, and that, on average, these citations come one year sooner (Jaffe and Trajtenberg 1999).

In business, direct evidence on the size of knowledge transfer costs within firms, while fragmentary, also fits with the law of semiglobalization. One influential early study of technology transfers in the chemicals, petroleum refining, and machinery sectors concluded that transfer costs account for an average of 19 percent of total project costs – and range from 2 percent to 59 percent (Teece 1977). Yet another outcome-based perspective that points in the same direction is supplied by the observation that location matters for international competitiveness in large part because of locally dense information flows, as exemplified most vividly by internationally successful clusters.[22] While it would be an exaggeration to say that location is destiny, such perspectives do serve as a reminder that the availability of information transmission capacity is necessary for information to travel, but it is usually not sufficient.

People Flows

The intensity of international people flows has risen more modestly over time than the intensity of trade, capital, and information flows. Starting with migration, the proportion of the world's population living outside of the country

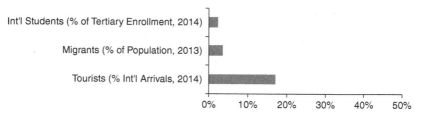

Figure 2.10 People Depth Ratios.
Sources: International Students (% of Tertiary Enrollment, 2014): Foreign Students as % of All Higher Education Students in Euromonitor Passport; Migrants (% of Population, 2013): United Nations, Department of Economic and Social Affairs (2013). Trends in International Migrant Stock: Migrants by Destination and Origin (United Nations database, POP/DB/MIG/Stock/Rev.2013), and World Development Indicators (WDI); Tourists (% Int'l Arrivals, 2014): UNWTO (2015).

where they were born is roughly the same today as it was in 1910, about 3 percent[23] (see Figure 2.10). While the physical and informational costs associated with migration have declined over time, policy restrictions – visa and work permit requirements – have been put in place to restrict its growth. Visas were generally not required to travel between countries before 1913, and the United States did not begin requiring immigrants to obtain visas until 1924 (Foner 2000, as cited in UNDP 2009; Ng and Whalley 2008). There are, however, indications of a recent increase. The United Nations data indicate that first generation migrants rose from 3.1 percent of world population in 2005 to 3.4 percent in 2013 (United Nations 2013).

Migration patterns reflect the persistence of economic gains as a motivation for international people flows. Among migrants from developing countries, 80 percent move to countries with higher scores on the UN's *Human Development Index* (UNDP 2009, 23). Only 49 percent of migrants from emerging economies, however, move to advanced economies, indicating very substantial migration from relatively less to relatively more developed emerging economies.[24] Emigration rates are the highest out of middle-income countries, as poverty itself constrains mobility from the poorest countries (UNDP 2009, 24). The countries with the highest share of immigrants in their populations are countries that employ large contingents of migrant workers, most notably Persian Gulf countries such as Qatar, where foreigners make up more than 70 percent of the population.

To turn from quantity to price-based measures, the obvious indicator to consider with respect to migration is cross-border convergence of wages as a measure of the integration of labor markets. Data on the evolution of average GDP per worker adjusted for Purchasing Power Parity (PPP) – a rough proxy

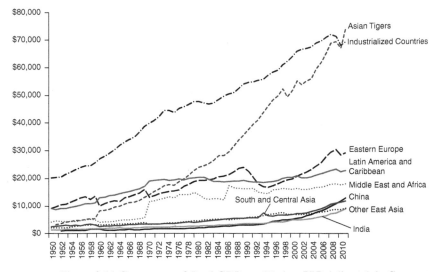

Figure 2.11 Convergence? Real GDP per Worker, PPP Adjusted, in Constant 2005 International Dollars (Chain Series), 1950–2010.
Source: Compiled from Penn World Table, version 7.1. (November 2012).

for average wages – across countries indicate that while incomes in industrialized countries have tended to converge, a few Asian "tigers" have been the only countries able to break away from the rest of the developing world and catch up with the industrialized world (see Figure 2.11).[25] More sophisticated tests confirm this conclusion and indicate that the failure of most developing countries to catch up can be reconciled only with a weaker notion of convergence – conditional convergence (Barro and Sala-i-Martin 1995). Conditional convergence allows for differences in the steady state incomes toward which different economies are trending based on differences along dimensions such as investment, education, and population growth. Human capital turns out, in attempts to fit conditional convergence models to the data, to have a particularly marked effect on the predicted extent of convergence.

In addition to migration, a long-term people flow, there are also more focused indicators of cross-border movements of people. International student mobility represents a medium-term people flow. In 2014, 2.2 percent of the world's university students were enrolled in degree programs outside of their home countries, up only slightly from 2.1 percent in 2005.[26] International tourism, a short-term people flow, is more intense and growing more rapidly. In 2014, roughly 16–18 percent of tourist trips were international, and there were more than 1 billion international tourist arrivals for the first time ever, up from only 674 million in 2000 (UNWTO 2015). Nonetheless, adding up all kinds of

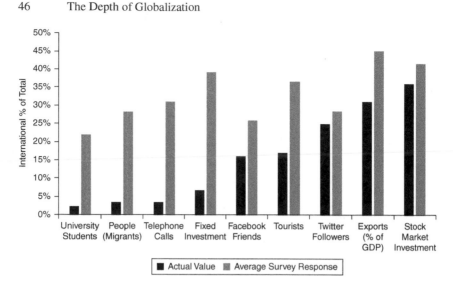

Figure 2.12 US Perceptions of Globalization versus Hard Data.
Source: Surveys conducted for author via the SurveyMonkey platform. Actual values based on sources cited for each variable as referenced in this chapter.

people flows, Khanna (2010) roughly estimates that 90 percent of the world's population never leave the countries where they were born. Even if that figure were "merely" 80 percent, it would still be very striking.

Globaloney and Its Correlates

This chapter has focused, so far, on providing a data-driven characterization of globalization depth to support the law of semiglobalization. But as a reminder of the broader message behind both this chapter and the previous one – the importance of measurement – it is useful to circle back to the divergence between actual globalization depths and the more elevated perceptions of them that tend to be prevalent. I already cited some evidence along these lines in the introduction and attached the label of globaloney to the phenomenon. Given its incidence, globaloney is worth describing and discussing in a bit more detail.

To do so, I will rely on surveys I have run that link individuals' calibrations of the depth of globalization to some of their personal attributes – and to their assessments of globalization's implications. One recent survey asked a sample of US adults – differentiated by age, gender, levels of education, income, and other characteristics – to guess the depth of globalization of each of the nine indicators listed in Figure 2.12. The gray bars indicate that respondents persisted with guessing in the 20–40 percent range (although they went as high as 45 percent for exports as a percentage of GDP), and the black bars (showing actual depth ratios) indicate that guesses in the 0–20 percent range would have served better in two-thirds of the categories. Taking a simple average across ratios of the survey responses to the actual values for the nine categories to create a "globaloney index," the respondents guessed globalization levels to be 4.5 times as large as their actual values!

Globaloney of this sort seems to be a global problem rather than just localized to the United States. A survey of more than 3,000 students from 138 countries at the beginning of my massive open online course (MOOC) on the Coursera platform revealed that each country for which a meaningful average could be calculated exhibited overestimation – with an average globaloney index of 4.8!

These large multiples serve as a reminder of the limits to the supposed wisdom of crowds: assessments of globalization depth seem to be subject to systematic biases. I have speculated elsewhere (e.g., in my book *World 3.0*) about various factors, including psychological biases and social influences, that might be at work. The surveys provide some additional grist for such discussion. Younger people have higher globaloney indexes than older people – 5.0 for those aged 18–29 versus 4.6 for those above 60[27] – which is suggestive of social influences of various sorts. Moreover, students from emerging economies have somewhat higher globaloney indexes than those from advanced economies – 4.9 versus 4.6[28] – which may reflect enthusiasm for globalization as an escape from economic backwardness (and is also consistent with the sentiment analysis in the previous chapter suggesting more positivity around globalization in emerging economies). Globaloney does tend to diminish with higher education: high school graduates average a globaloney index of 5.5 versus 4.5 for master's graduates.[29] But disappointingly, especially from the perspective of a business school professor, undergraduate or master's degrees in business administration or finance are *not* associated with lower levels of globaloney than commensurate educational qualifications in other fields. In fact, globaloney indexes tend to be slightly, if insignificantly, higher for business administration/finance graduates!

Although such variation deserves additional documentation and analysis, what seems even more striking is how little the contingencies described end up mattering in the aggregate. The differences between the better-calibrated subgroups and the worse-calibrated ones have to do with globaloney indexes in the range of 4–5 for the former and 5–6 for the latter – both very far from the ideal level of 1. Once again, globaloney appears to be a general bias.

The survey data also provide some indications of why the general bias is worth resisting – for reasons that go beyond the basic advisability of confronting intuitions with measurements. The surveys suggest, first of all, that people who have more exaggerated perceptions of the depth of globalization also worry more about its harmful social consequences for income inequality, global warming, and the like. Exaggerated assessments of the depth of globalization could lead, via overwrought concerns about globalization's harms, to dysfunctional antiglobalization policies, as I warned in *World 3.0*. And in terms of business rather than public policy, globaloney correlates with agreement with dubious propositions about global strategy that essentially ignore the discontinuities that arise at national borders, that is, the law of semiglobalization (the dubious propositions themselves are elaborated at length in chapter 1 of my 2007 book, *Redefining Global Strategy*).

Conclusion

This chapter has provided evidence for the law of semiglobalization based on data on the depth of globalization of international trade, capital, information, and people flows (and stocks). Many measures of the international integration of markets have increased dramatically in recent decades. Yet the depth of cross-border integration of such markets remains quite limited, or *semiglobalized*. And the fact that nearly all of the depth metrics I present fall below 30 percent makes it hard to envision a scenario in which the world would reach a state of (nearly) complete globalization within any reasonable business planning horizon. Conversely, some observers see in the recent declines in trade and FDI flows signs of deglobalization. But although even slight drop-offs could have major consequences, given the parametrization, the extreme case in which cross-border integration can be ignored seems unlikely to be reached. Thus, *semiglobalization* is not only an appropriate description of the world today, but also one likely to prove robust for the foreseeable future because of the broad domain of possibilities covered.

The conclusion that the world is *semiglobalized* may or may not strike the average reader as very definite, but it is worth pointing out that it does have very definite, and favorable, implications for the added value of thinking explicitly about globalization and business. With either totally segmented or totally integrated country markets, one would effectively be back to the single-country base case that is implicit in much thinking about business, and wouldn't really need any new globalization-related thinking. Semiglobalization is *the* state of the world in which it can pay to work with a more complex model than the single-country one.

In terms of implications for future research, there is clearly room to improve on the depth measures presented in this chapter – and to analyze the determinants of variations in depth. But additional argument about the law of semiglobalization itself seems unlikely to me to be as productive a source of new insights as many of the research opportunities identified in later chapters.

In contrast, there is much more that needs to be done to alleviate globaloney in general. I would guess that in the part of the educational space with which I am most familiar, MBA programs at leading business schools, probably more than one-half of the students, overall, graduate thinking that the world is flat.

And given that companies account for the overwhelming majority of international trade and FDI flows, more accurate perceptions of the levels of globalization on the part of those who run them might add to social welfare as well as private profits. Chapters 3 and 4 unpack some of the challenges and opportunities semiglobalization presents to firms and their managers.

Notes

1 Doubling the number of immigrants from a particular country is associated with 9 percent higher imports from that country according to Hatzigeorgiou (2010). See also Lin (2011).

2 For additional perspective as well as a full list of sources employed here, refer to Figure 3.2 in Chapter 3

3 The *DHL Global Connectedness Index* 2011, 2012, and 2014 as well as the Depth Index of Globalization 2013, elaborated by Pankaj Ghemawat and Steven A. Altman, provide additional global measures of the extent of globalization and also provide equivalent country-level measures for 140 countries.

4 Calculation based on comparison of trade in value added from World Investment Report (UNCTAD 2013, 123, 137) with sectoral composition of GDP data from World Bank World Development Indicators database.

5 For all industries except those without such data available (computers and office machinery, footwear), depth scores are calculated based on quantity rather than value to avoid analytical problems associated with price mark-ups at various stages of distribution. Additionally, other factors that create general fuzziness around these calculations include: the issue discussed in the text of products being counted each time they cross borders in a multi-country supply chains, difficulties with matching product category definitions across data sources for numerators and denominators, inventory stock changes, inventory shrinkage, sales that take place outside of formal retail channels, as well as more basic data availability and quality constraints.

6 Note that the 31 percent benchmark used here reflects exports as a percentage of GDP without the adjustment to remove double-counting discussed earlier in this section. Because industry level analysis permits some distinction between finished goods and intermediate goods, the problem of double-counting is not as severe here as in global and country level analysis, though it still cannot be removed entirely. Thus, a more precise placement of this benchmark would probably fall somewhere between 20 percent and 30 percent.

7 The correlation coefficient between the values on Figures 2.3 and 2.4 is 0.56.

8 Based on data from UNCTAD (2015).

9 Based on portfolio equity data from the IMF's Balance of Payments and International Investment Position Statistics (2016), and Market Capitalization from Euromonitor Passport. The data employed here cover sixty-four countries.

10 Based on data from Euromonitor Passport covering ninety-seven countries.

11 Based on available data from Thomson Research (value was only available for 40 percent of transactions). Spinoffs were excluded from this analysis.

12 Foreign direct investment currently accounts for roughly one-half of total foreign investment, but its share was significantly smaller at the start of the twentieth century. (See Bloomfield 1968, 3–4; cited in Bordo, Eichengreen, and Irwin 1999, 35).

13 The categorization of flows here reflects that shown in the data source employed, World Bank (2013). The loans category consists primarily of lending by bank and nonbank financial institutions; however, this category also includes all "other" capital flows that are classified neither as FDI nor as portfolio investment.

14 Calculation based on data from World Bank (2013). In this section, advanced economies are those economies designated as advanced and emerging economies are those designated as developing in the same report, rather than the IMF classifications employed elsewhere in this book.

15 See, however, the analysis of portfolio equity in Chapter 5 for evidence of the continued distance-sensitivity of stock market investment.

16 Estimate based on data reported in Telegeography International Traffic Database.

17 This estimate is generated by dividing the Average International Internet Traffic reported by Telegeography by Cisco's estimate of the Total Internet IP Traffic as reported in various editions of Cisco's Visual Networking Index forecasts (Cisco VNI 2015). Note that the classification of traffic on private IP networks is ambiguous in this analysis and could potentially push the international share up to 22 percent.

18 Based on data from the United States, the UK, Germany, Brazil, China, and Australia.

19 Data on page views of foreign news websites are from an unpublished analysis of Google Ad Planner data conducted by Ethan Zuckerman.

20 Estimate based on data from Box Office Mojo, Reliance Entertainment, Screen Digest, Screenline, Entgroup (Enbase), Press Reports.

21 Based on data from Euromonitor Passport covering ninety-one countries.

22 The other (overlapping) reasons for the localization of international competitiveness identified by Porter (1990) are sophisticated local demand and the local availability of specialized inputs and complements as well as basic factors of production.

23 "A report by the ILO counted 33 million foreign nationals in 1910, equivalent to 2.5 percent of the population covered by the study (which was 76 percent of the world population at the time)" (UNDP 2009, n. 53, 125).

24 Calculation based on United Nations (2013) with countries classified as advanced or emerging based on the country classifications in the October 2013 edition of the IMF World Economic Outlook database.

25 Based on simple averages across all countries with data reported in each year (sample generally grows over time as data on a larger number of countries becomes available). Series "rgdpwok" with "version 2" of China data. Region classification for this figure is unique and does not follow the *DHL Global Connectedness Index* regions used in Chapter 10. Asian Tigers: Hong Kong, Singapore, South Korea, Taiwan; Industrialized Countries: Australia, Austria, Belgium, Canada, Denmark, France, Germany, Great Britain, Greece, Ireland, Italy, Japan, Netherlands, New Zealand, Norway, Portugal, Spain, Sweden, Switzerland, United States; Other South and Central Asia: Afghanistan, Armenia, Azerbaijan, Bangladesh, Bhutan, British Indian Ocean Territory, Georgia, Kazakhstan, Kyrgyzstan, Maldives, Nepal, Pakistan, Sri Lanka, Tajikistan, Turkey, Turkmenistan, Uzbekistan; Other East Asia: Cambodia, Indonesia, Laos, Malaysia, Mongolia, Philippines, Thailand, Timor-Leste, Vietnam; Eastern Europe: Albania, Armenia, Belarus, Bosnia and Herzegovina, Bulgaria, Croatia, Cyprus, Czech Republic, Estonia, Finland, Hungary, Latvia, Lithuania, Macedonia, Moldova, Montenegro, Poland, Romania, Russia, Serbia, Slovakia, Slovenia, Turkey, Ukraine; Latin America

and Caribbean: Argentina, Bahamas, Barbados, Belize, Brazil, Bolivia, Chile, Colombia, Costa Rica, Cuba, Dominican Republic, Ecuador, El Salvador, Grenada, Guatemala, Guyana, Haiti, Honduras, Jamaica, Mexico, Nicaragua, Panama, Paraguay, Peru, Puerto Rico, St. Kitts and Nevis, St. Lucia, St. Vincent and the Grenadines, Suriname, Trinidad and Tobago, Uruguay, Venezuela; Middle East and Africa: Algeria, Angola, Bahrain, Benin, Botswana, Brunei, Burkina Faso, Burundi, Cameroon, Cabo Verde, Central African Republic, Chad, Congo, Cote d'Ivoire, Djibouti, Egypt, Eritrea, Ethiopia, Gabon, Gambia, Ghana, Guinea-Bissau, Iraq, Israel, Jordan, Kenya, Kuwait, Lebanon, Lesotho, Liberia, Libya, Madagascar, Malawi, Mali, Mauritius, Morocco, Mozambique, Namibia, Niger, Nigeria, Oman, Qatar, Rwanda, Saudi Arabia, Senegal, Sierra Leone, Somalia, South Africa, Sudan, Swaziland, Syria, Tanzania, Togo, Tunisia, Uganda, United Arab Emirates, Yemen, Zambia, Zimbabwe.

26 Calculation based on student mobility data from Euromonitor Passport covering 114 countries.

27 Based on data aggregated from across both of the two surveys described earlier in this section (the broad sample of US adults via SurveyMonkey and the international sample of students in my Coursera MOOC).

28 Based on Coursera student sample only.

29 Based on broad sample of US adults (via SurveyMonkey) only.

References

Aalberg, Toril, Stylianos Papathanassopoulos, Stuart Soroka, James Curran, Kaori Hayashi, Shanto Iyengar, Paul K. Jones, Gianpietro Mazzoleni, Hernando Rojas, David Rowe, and Rodney Tiffen. 2013. "International TV News, Foreign Affairs Interest and Public Knowledge." *Journalism Studies* 14 (3):387–406. doi: 10.1080/1461670x.2013.765636.

Acharya, Viral V., and Sascha Steffen. 2013. "The 'Greatest' Carry Trade Ever? Understanding Eurozone Bank Risks." National Bureau of Economic Research Working Paper Series 19039, May 2013. www.nber.org/papers/w19039.

Barro, Robert J., and Xavier Sala-i-Martin. 1995. *Economic Growth*, McGraw-Hill Advanced Series in Economics. New York: McGraw-Hill.

Bloomfield, Arthur I. 1968. "Patterns of Fluctuation in International Finance before 1914." Princeton Studies in International Finance, International Finance Section, Department of Economics, Princeton University. www.princeton.edu/~ies/IES_Studies/S21.pdf.

Bordo, Michael D., Barry Eichengreen, and Douglas A. Irwin. 1999. "Is Globalization Today Really Different Than Globalization a Hundred Years Ago?" National Bureau of Economic Research Working Paper Series 7195, June 1999. www.nber.org.ezp-prod1.hul.harvard.edu/papers/w7195.pdf.

Cisco VNI. 2015. "Cisco Visual Networking Index: Forecast and Methodology, 2014–2019 White Paper." www.cisco.com/c/en/us/solutions/collateral/service-provider/ip-ngn-ip-next-generation-network/white_paper_c11-481360.pdf.

Claessens, Stijn, and Neeltje van Horen. 2012. "Foreign Banks: Trends, Impact and Financial Stability." International Monetary Fund Working Paper 12/10, January 1, 2012. www.imf.org/external/pubs/ft/wp/2012/wp1210.pdf.

Coeurdacier, Nicolas, and Hélène Rey. 2013. "Home Bias in Open Economy Financial Macroeconomics." *Journal of Economic Literature* 51 (1):63–115. doi: 10.1257/jel.51.1.63.

Eaton, Jonathan, and Samuel Kortum. 2002. "Technology, Geography, and Trade." *Econometrica* 70 (5):1741–1779.

Economist. 2012. "Stories from Elsewhere: Books in Translation." *Economist (Online)*. The Economist Newspaper NA, Inc. Available at ProQuest: http://search.proquest.com./docview/1023122745.

——— 2013. "Capital: Just in Case." *Economist*. www.economist.com/news/special-report/21587383-capital-controls-are-back-part-many-countries-financial-armoury-just-case.

Euromonitor International. "Passport Database." Accessed 2015 & 2016. www.euromonitor.com/passport.

Feldstein, Martin, and Charles Horioka. 1980. "Domestic Saving and International Capital Flows." *Economic Journal* 90 (358):314–329.

Ferreira, Fernando, and Joel Waldfogel. 2013. "Pop Internationalism: Has Half a Century of World Music Trade Displaced Local Culture?" *The Economic Journal* 123 (569):634–664. doi: 10.1111/ecoj.12003.

Foner, Nancy. 2000. *From Ellis Island to JFK: New York's Two Great Waves of Immigration.* New Haven, New York: Yale University Press; Russell Sage Foundation.

Frankel, Jeffrey A. 1992. "Measuring International Capital Mobility: A Review." *American Economic Review* 82 (2):197–202.

——— 2001. "Assessing the Efficiency Gain from Further Liberalization." In *Efficiency, Equity, and Legitimacy: The Multilateral Trading System at the Millennium*, edited by Roger B. Porter, Pierre Sauvé, Arvind Subramanian, and Americo Beviglia Zampetti, 81–105. Washington, DC: Brookings Institution Press.

Ghemawat, Pankaj, and Steven A. Altman. 2011. "DHL Global Connectedness Index 2011." Deutsche Post DHL. www.dhl.com/en/about_us/logistics_insights/studies_research/global_connectedness_index/global_connectedness_index_2011/gci_results.html.

——— 2012. "DHL Global Connectedness Index 2012." Deutsche Post DHL. www.dhl.com/en/about_us/logistics_insights/studies_research/global_connectedness_index/global_connectedness_index_2012/gci_results.html.

——— 2013. "Depth Index of Globalization 2013." IESE Business School. www.ghemawat.com/dig/.

——— 2014. "DHL Global Connectedness Index 2014: Analyzing Global Flows and Their Power to Increase Prosperity." Deutsche Post DHL. www.dhl.com/gci.

Ghemawat, Pankaj, and Niccolò Pisani. 2014. "Extent, Pattern, and Quality Effects of Globalization in Scientific Research: The Case of International Management." work in progress.

Hatzigeorgiou, Andreas. 2010. "Migration as Trade Facilitation: Assessing the Links between International Trade and Migration." *The B.E. Journal of Economic Analysis & Policy* 10 (1). doi: 10.2202/1935-1682.2100.

Head, Keith, and Thierry Mayer. 2013. "What Separates Us? Sources of Resistance to Globalization." *Canadian Journal of Economics/Revue canadienne d'économique* 46 (4):1196–1231. doi: 10.1111/caje.12055.

Helpman, Elhanan. 1987. "Imperfect Competition and International Trade: Evidence from Fourteen Industrial Countries." *Journal of the Japanese and international economies* 1 (1):62–81.

Heston, Alan, Robert Summers, and Bettina Aten. November 2012. "Penn World Table Version 7.1." Center for International Comparisons of Production, Income and Prices at the University of Pennsylvania. www.rug.nl/research/ggdc/data/pwt/pwt-7.1.

International Monetary Fund (IMF). March 2013. "European Union: Publication of Financial Sector Assessment Program Documentation – Technical Note on Financial Integration and Fragmentation in the European Union." IMF Country Report 13/71. International Monetary Fund. www.imf.org/external/pubs/ft/scr/2013/cr1371.pdf.

October 2013. "World Economic Outlook (WEO) Database." www.imf.org/external/pubs/ft/weo/2013/02/weodata/index.aspx.

April 2015. "World Economic Outlook (WEO) Database." www.imf.org/external/pubs/ft/weo/2015/01/weodata/index.aspx.

2016. "Balance of Payments and International Investment Position Statistics." Last Modified January 26, 2016. http://data.imf.org/?sk=7A51304B-6426-40C0-83DD-CA473CA1FD52.

April 2016. "Global Financial Stability Report." World Economic and Financial Surveys. International Monetary fund. www.imf.org/External/Pubs/FT/GFSR/2016/01/pdf/text_v2.pdf.

Jaffe, Adam B., and Manuel Trajtenberg. 1999. "International Knowledge Flows: Evidence from Patent Citations." *Economics of Innovation & New Technology* 8 (1–2):105–136.

Khanna, Parag. 2010. "Remapping the World (in List of 10 Ideas for the Next 10 Years)." *Time*, March 22, 2010, 42–43.

Leetaru, Kalev. 2011. "Culturomics 2.0: Forecasting Large-Scale Human Behavior Using Global News Media Tone in Time and Space." *First Monday* (August 2011). http://journals.uic.edu/ojs/index.php/fm/article/view/3663.

Leskovec, Jure, and Eric Horvitz. 2008. "Planetary-Scale Views on a Large Instant-Messaging Network." Proceedings of the 17th international conference on World Wide Web, Beijing, China. http://dl.acm.org/citation.cfm?id=1367620.

Leydesdorff, Loet, and Caroline S. Wagner. 2008. "International Collaboration in Science and the Formation of a Core Group." *Journal of Informetrics* 2 (4):317–325. doi: 10.1016/j.joi.2008.07.003.

Lin, Faqin. 2011. "The Pro-Trade Impacts of Immigrants: A Meta-Analysis of Network Effects." *Journal of Chinese Economic and Foreign Trade Studies* 4 (1):17–27. doi: 10.1108/17544401111106789.

Lund, Susan, Toos Daruvala, Richard Dobbs, Philipp Härle, Ju-Hon Kwek, and Ricardo Falcón. March 2013. "Financial Globalization: Retreat or Reset?". McKinsey Global Institute. www.mckinsey.com/insights/global_capital_markets/financial_globalization.

Media Tenor. 2006. "Different Perspective: Locations, Protagonists and Topic Structures in International TV News." *Media Tenor* (April):62–65.

Moore, Martin. 2010. "Shrinking World: The Decline of International Reporting in the British Press." *Media Standards Trust* (November). http://mediastandardstrust.org/wp-content/uploads/downloads/2010/11/Shrinking-World-FINAL-VERSION.pdf.

Ng, Eric C. Y., and John Whalley. 2008. "Visas and Work Permits: Possible Global Negotiating Initiatives." *Review of International Organizations* 3 (3):259–285. doi: 10.1007/s11558-008-9033-6.

Obstfeld, Maurice, and Alan M. Taylor. "The Great Depression as a Watershed: International Capital Mobility over the Long Run." National Bureau of Economic Research Working Paper Series 5960, March 1997. www.nber.org/papers/w5960.

OECD. 2013. "OECD Science, Technology and Industry Scoreboard 2013: Innovation for Growth." www.oecd-ilibrary.org/science-and-technology/oecd-science-technology-and-industry-scoreboard-2013_sti_scoreboard-2013-en.

Papathanassopoulos, Stylianos. 2002. *European Television in the Digital Age: Issues, Dynamics and Realities.* Cambridge: Polity Press in association with Blackwell Publishers.

PayPal. 2013. "Executive Summary." Modern Spice Routes: The Cultural Impact and Economic Opportunity of Cross-Border Shopping. https://www.paypalobjects. com/webstatic/mktg/pdf/PayPal_ModernSpiceRoutes_Report.pdf.

Perkins, Richard, and Eric Neumayer. 2013. "The Ties That Bind: The Role of Migrants in the Uneven Geography of International Telephone Traffic." *Global Networks* 13 (1):79–100. doi: 10.1111/j.1471-0374.2012.00366.x.

Pew Research Center. various editions. "The State of the News Media." www.journalism .org/category/publications/state-of-the-media/.

Porath, William, and Constanza Mujica. 2011. "Las Noticias Extranjeras En La Televisión Pública Y Privada De Chile Comparada Con La De Catorce Países." *Comunicación y Sociedad* 24 (2):333–370.

Porter, Michael E. 1990. *The Competitive Advantage of Nations.* New York: Free Press.

Portes, Richard, and Hélène Rey. 2005. "The Determinants of Cross-Border Equity Flows." *Journal of International Economics* 65 (2):269–296. doi: 10.1016/ j.jinteco.2004.05.002.

Reinemann, Carsten, James Stanyer, Sebastian Scherr, and Guido Legnante. 2012. "Hard and Soft News: A Review of Concepts, Operationalizations and Key Findings." *Journalism* 13 (2):221–239. http://jou.sagepub.com/cgi/content/abstract/13/2/221.

Rogoff, Kenneth. 1996. "The Purchasing Power Parity Puzzle." *Journal of Economic Literature* 34 (2):647–668.

Scellato, Giuseppe, Chiara Franzoni, and Paula Stephan. 2015. "Migrant Scientists and International Networks." *Research Policy* 44 (1): 108–120.

Schatz, Roland, and Christian Kolmer. 2010. "News Coverage of Foreign Place Brands: Implications for Communication Strategies." In *International Place Branding Yearbook 2010: Place Branding in the New Age of Innovation*, edited by Frank M. Go, and Robert Govers, 134–146. Basingstoke: Palgrave Macmillan.

State, Bogdan, Patrick Park, Ingmar Weber, Yelena Mejova, and Michael Macy. March 2013. "The Mesh of Civilizations and International Email Flows." *arXiv:1303.0045 [cs.SI].* http://arxiv.org/abs/1303.0045.

Takhteyev, Yuri, Anatoliy Gruzd, and Barry Wellman. 2012. "Geography of Twitter Networks." *Social Networks* 34 (1):73–81. doi: 10.1016/j.socnet.2011.05.006.

Teece, David J. 1977. "Technology Transfer by Multinational Firms: The Resource Cost of Transferring Technological Know-How." *Economic Journal* 87 (346):242–261.

TeleGeography. 2015. "Telegeography Report & Database." www.telegeography.com/ research-services/telegeography-report-database/.

Ugander, Johan, Brian Karrer, Lars Backstrom, and Cameron Marlow. "The Anatomy of the Facebook Social Graph." arXiv:1111.4503 [cs.SI], November 11, 2011. http://arxiv.org/abs/1111.4503.

Uhlig, Harald. "Sovereign Default Risk and Banks in a Monetary Union." National Bureau of Economic Research Working Paper Series 19343, August 2013. www.nber.org/papers/w19343.

UNCTAD. 2013. "World Investment Report 2013: Global Value Chains: Investment and Trade for Development." United Nations. http://unctad.org/en/PublicationsLibrary/wir2013_en.pdf.

    2015. "World Investment Report 2015: Reforming International Investment Governance." United Nations. http://unctad.org/en/PublicationsLibrary/wir2015_en.pdf.

UNESCO. "UNESCO Institute for Statistics." www.uis.unesco.org/.

United Nations (UN). "The International Migration Report 2013." Population Division of the Department of Economic and Social Affairs of the United Nations Secretariat, December 2013. http://esa.un.org/unmigration/documents/worldmigration/2013/Full_Document_final.pdf.

United Nations Development Programme (UNDP). 2009. "Human Development Report 2009: Overcoming Barriers: Human Mobility and Development." http://hdr.undp.org/sites/default/files/reports/269/hdr_2009_en_complete.pdf.

United Nations World Tourism Organization (UNWTO). 2015. "UNWTO Tourism Highlights, 2015 Edition." http://mkt.unwto.org/publication/unwto-tourism-highlights-2015-edition.

Weaver, David H., and Lars Willnat. 2012. *The Global Journalist in the 21st Century*, Routledge Communication Series. New York, NY: Routledge.

World Bank. 2013. "Capital for the Future: Saving and Investment in an Interdependent World." World Bank. http://go.worldbank.org/T3OEGQAH20.

World Trade Organization (WTO). "WTO Statistics Database." http://stat.wto.org/Home/WSDBHome.aspx?Language=E.

3   Globalization in Historical Perspective

Pankaj Ghemawat and Geoffrey G. Jones

Chapter 2 provided recent evidence for the law of semiglobalization, showing that the integration of markets across national borders remains far from complete (see Figure 3.1).[1] This chapter places the current depth of globalization in historical context. It also begins a transition – which will be completed in the next chapter – from focusing on markets as the locus of integration to examining the firms that operate within and across those markets. In Chapter 4, recent data will be presented on the globalization of business at the level of individual functions (finance, marketing, etc.) within firms.

The emphasis on firms in this chapter and the next reflects how the law of semiglobalization describes *the* state of the world that attaches importance to firms' cross-border activities. Perfect cross-border integration of markets for products or inputs would limit the value of the bridges firms can build across borders. In addition, perfectly separated national markets would dispense with the need for cross-border activities. It is between those extremes of complete separation and integration that the scope, complexity, and profit impact of firms' cross-border activities are maximized. This chapter examines the role firms have played over time in promoting international trade and investment. It takes a chronological perspective organized around a first wave of globalization that stopped after World War I and a second wave that started after World War II and has continued at least up to the 2008 global financial crisis (see Figure 3.2).

The First Wave

In 1500 CE, the world's export-to-GDP ratio was estimated to have been only about 0.1 percent, and international trade mostly occurred within geographic regions: the costs and hazards of interregional transportation by land, for example, along the Silk Road between Europe and China, were extremely high. But improvements in seafaring technology in the fifteenth and subsequent centuries by West Europeans eased trade with India and China, each of which had an economy significantly larger than all of Europe's at the time. Particularly critical was the discovery of a sea-route to the East, around the Cape of Good

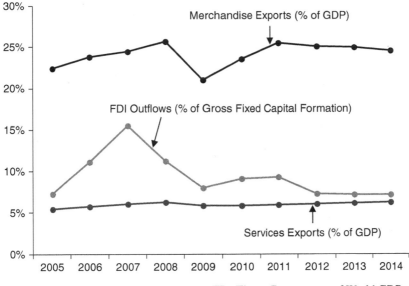

Figure 3.1 Exports and Outward FDI Flows (Percentages of World GDP and GFCF, 2005–2014).
Sources: World Trade Organization (WTO), International Monetary Fund (IMF) (April 2015), UNCTAD (2015).

Hope, by the Portuguese navigator, Vasco da Gama, in 1497. The sea-route sparked a surge in the trade of luxuries between Europe and Asia, starting with trade in spices that could be sold for more than a hundred times as much in Europe as in their Asian countries of origin. Nonetheless, very high costs and risks limited the returns from trade: about half of the ships that set sail from Portugal for the East in the sixteenth and early seventeenth centuries never returned.

A major development in the seventeenth century was the chartering of the first *joint stock trading companies* in Europe to trade with particular countries, most notably the English and Dutch East India Companies. These companies focused on pooling risks across investors as well as *arbitraging* differences in costs and willingness to pay between Asia and Europe (since they also purchased goods in Europe for sale in Asia). In so doing, they undertook hundreds of thousands of transactions every year (Carlos and Nicholas 1988, 401). Although not remotely comparable to the volumes of such flows in a large modern multinational, these requirements were sufficient to create the need for several hundred administrative personnel at the headquarters of the English East India Company and to force the replacement of owner-managers with salaried managers organized into hierarchies that included committees to

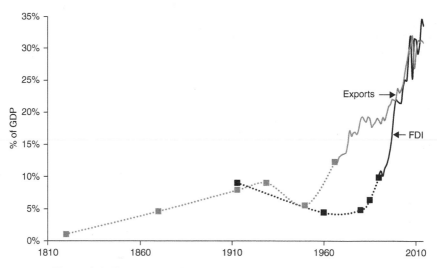

Figure 3.2 Exports and Outward FDI Stock (Percentage of World GDP, 1820–2014).

Sources: Exports 1820: Angus Maddison, Monitoring the World Economy 1820–1992, OECD 1995; Exports 1870–1950: Angus Maddison, The World Economy Volume 1: A Millennial Perspective and Volume 2: Historical Statistics. Development Centre Studies. OECD Publishing, 2006; Exports 1966–2014: World Bank World Development Indicators, World Trade Organization Statistics Database, and IMF World Economic Outlook; FDI 1913–1985: World Investment Report 1994; FDI 1990–2014: World Investment Report 2015.

control accounts, buying, private trade, presidencies, shipping, and treasure. The company began to experiment with contracts and incentives to motivate and control these managers. Eventually, it introduced a system of merit-based appointments that provided a model for the British and Indian civil service and – early in the nineteenth century – set up what may have been the world's first corporate university, the East India College, to train officers. Thus, it actually set up many of the systems for modern management that are commonly supposed to have been pioneered by companies much later in the nineteenth century. But by then, the English East India Company itself had gone out of business, after a long political as well as commercial decline because of liberal sentiments in Britain, jealousy of its commercial rights, and apprehensions about its security apparatus and empire overseas. The Indian Mutiny/War of Independence of 1857 brought the Company's possessions in India under the direct control of the British Crown.

That did not mark the end of all the original trading companies: Hudson's Bay Company, incorporated by English royal charter in 1670, still operates as a retailer in Canada and the United States. And others entered the fray. British-owned trading houses such as Jardine Matheson participated in the forced opening of the China market, originally trading Indian opium for Chinese tea. German traders such as Metallgesellshaft secured control of the global nonferrous metal trade (Becker 1998). When Japan reopened to the world with the Meiji Restoration in 1868, several dozen trading companies modeled on Jardine Matheson and other British merchant houses were set up to ease the effects of more than 200 years of isolation. By 1914, trading companies handled 51 percent of Japanese exports and 64 percent of imports, and Mitsui Bussan alone – part of the Mitsui diversified holding company – accounted for 20 percent of Japan's exports and imports. In the 1990s, six general trading companies, led by Mitsubishi and Mitsui, continued to handle roughly 40 percent of Japan's exports and 70 percent of its imports (Dicken 2011, 417).

To look beyond trading companies, overall trade grew particularly explosively starting in the early nineteenth century – a few decades after modern economic growth began with the industrial revolution. The world's export-to-GDP ratio increased from 1 percent in 1820 to 5 percent by 1870 and 8 percent by 1913,[2] even though GDP itself was starting to grow much faster than population in parts of the world. Much of this increase was due to the expansion of trade beyond luxuries to agricultural and mineral commodities. World markets emerged for foodgrains after the mid-nineteenth century, aided by the shift from sail to steam and other improvements in transportation. Meat followed foodgrains, although perishability meant that the trade was organized around large vertically integrated firms that coordinated flows from slaughter to sale. Significant trade emerged in minerals as well, usually on the back of FDI. These and other commodities dominated international trade in the first wave of globalization, although trade in manufactures, particularly textiles, grew to be significant as well.

Telecommunications technology was important in enabling the increasing integration of many commodity markets during the first wave of globalization. In the 1850s, Siemens and Halske pioneered the development of telegraph and cable equipment, and established workshops in St. Petersburg (Russia) and London to install and maintain products manufactured in Berlin. Siemens Global cable systems were built and operated by giant utility firms, especially the British-owned Globe Telegraph and Trust Company (Jones and von Siemens 2012). These developments, and particularly the deployment of the first transatlantic cables, forced significant price convergence of commodities for which a few reference prices served to summarize conditions in geographically separate product markets – and for widely traded financial instruments. Thus, price differentials between the London and New York markets for US Treasury bonds fell by 69 percent when the first transatlantic cable was introduced in 1866 (Kavesh, Garbade, and Silber 1978; O'Rourke and Williamson 1999, 220).

Britain, the first country to experience the effects of the industrial revolution, was also well positioned geographically vis-à-vis global economic shifts. Europe and the United States' combined share of world GDP increased from about one-quarter – less than China's – in 1820 to about half by the end of the century (Maddison 2006), and Britain was situated right between those two growing regions. It became the pacesetter at industrial transformation *and* specialization: a major shift from agriculture to industry and rapid urbanization turned the country into a big importer of grains and a big exporter of manufactures. But British manufactured exports focused on traditional sectors such as textiles rather than new, higher-tech ones such as chemicals and electrical machinery. And after 1870, it steadily lost ground to Continental Europe, particularly Germany. Great Britain's share of world merchandise exports fell from 24 percent in 1870 to 19 percent in 1913. Britain *was* responsible, however, for a growing global share of high value-added financial services, including insurance. By one estimate, the three largest exporters, the UK, the United States, and Germany, collectively accounted for two-thirds of world exports (Bairoch and Kozul-Wright March 1996).

Britain continued to dominate international capital flows to a much greater extent than international trade through to the end of the first wave of globalization. Some of this took the form of bank intermediation: British banks started setting up large branch networks across the British Empire in the 1830s. The 1840s, for example, saw British interests floating a bank called the Oriental Bank Corporation in Bombay that quickly moved its head office to London and then constructed a branch network all over South Asia, South Africa, and Australia. It entered Japan in the 1860s, and floated the Japanese government's first foreign loans in the early 1870s before collapsing in 1884. Subsequently, British overseas banks such as HSBC focused on a particular region (Jones 1993, 20–23, 7). In addition to bank intermediation, large amounts of securities, typically debt obligations based on measurable revenue-generation potential (of governments, railways, etc.) were also invested across borders, in the form of *foreign portfolio investment*. Then there was the emergence, especially in the closing decades of the nineteenth century and early in the twentieth, of large volumes of *foreign direct investment* (FDI). Through the late nineteenth and early twentieth centuries, Britain was the dominant home country for FDI: its share of the worldwide stock of FDI was between 40 and 45 percent in 1913.

More than one-half and perhaps as much as 80 percent of British FDI was accounted for by what Mira Wilkins calls *free-standing enterprises* (Wilkins 1998, 11). In addition to obtaining its source capital from the UK, a typical firm of this sort would be organized as a standalone entity in London, under British law, and would typically operate in just one country. It might own a discrete foreign asset such as an Argentine railway, a US mine, or an Iranian oilfield that was managed locally by a British expatriate. Thus, freestanding enterprises were "born global." They served, in effect, as project financing syndicates with delegated project management that transferred capital to foreign countries while taking advantage of cross-country differences in institutional infrastructure, particularly contract enforcement, to reduce transaction costs. Although termed free-standing, many were clustered through various linkages, especially around trading companies, which established new ventures and then did initial public offerings in London or other markets – not unlike modern-day business groups (Jones 2000).

In terms of sectors, data on listed companies suggest that before World War I, about 85 percent of British FDI was concentrated in (and spread relatively evenly across) resource-based sectors, railways, and other utilities and services (Corley 1994, 80). The geographic scope of British FDI was broad, and British firms accounted for the bulk of investment in the British Empire outside Canada (where the United States led). The colonial context was even more evident in FDI from France, the third largest source overall, in developing countries: this was, after all, the high point of the age of the empire. Most French (and German) manufacturing investments, however, were located in Europe (Wilkins 1991).

FDI from the United States presents an interesting contrast. The United States had, of course, historically been a technological follower. Thus, its textile yarn industry got off the ground when Samuel Slater, known as the "Father of the American Industrial Revolution" in the United States and "Slater the Traitor" in Britain, carried from the latter to the former not only Richard Arkwright's spinning technology but also the highly disciplined, profitable factory system he had developed. But, ultimately, it was the United States rather than Britain that overtook China as the largest single economy in the world based on GDP measured at purchasing power parity (PPP), in 1890 (Maddison 2010). As of 1914, US FDI continued to be dominated by the resource-based sector – mining, agriculture, and petroleum accounted for 54 percent of total investment – but manufacturing accounted for another 18 percent. Geographically, 72 percent of US investment was concentrated in the Americas, led by Canada and Mexico, but investments to seek out new markets for manufactures – as opposed to resource-seeking investments aimed at arbitraging differences in costs and availability – focused on Canada, Europe, and Russia. Large-scale enterprises with significant administrative hierarchies spearheaded such manufacturing FDI, unlike the freestanding firms that accounted for the bulk of British FDI – although this also meant that domestic operations typically dominated international activities in terms of size and methodology.

Unlike traditional *vertical multinationals* in agriculture and mining, which used outputs from some countries as inputs into their operations elsewhere (i.e., exploited differences across countries), manufacturing multinationals

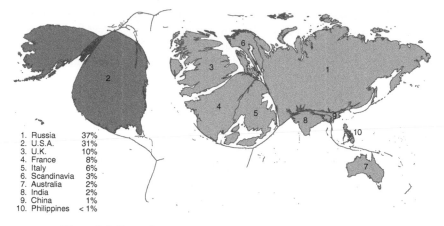

1. Russia	37%	
2. U.S.A.	31%	
3. U.K.	10%	
4. France	8%	
5. Italy	6%	
6. Scandinavia	3%	
7. Australia	2%	
8. India	2%	
9. China	1%	
10. Philippines	< 1%	

Figure 3.3 Singer Sales Distribution, 1910.
Note: Based on unit sales, not revenues.
Source: Adapted from Geoffrey Jones and David Kiron, "Globalizing Consumer Durables: Singer Sewing Machines before 1914," HBS Case 9-804-00.

were *horizontal multinationals* that replicated parts of their business models across the countries in which they operated to turn out broadly the same range of products (i.e., exploited similarities). Singer, the US-based manufacturer of sewing machines, was an unusually successful early example (Jones and Kiron 2008). Its key challenges concerned not manufacturing but the marketing, distribution, and retailing of a consumer durable with a cost comparable to US per capita income at the time. Singer's innovations in response to this challenge – which included the development of hire purchase and then the invention of direct selling by door-to-door salesmen – were both a way to collect money and expand the market where retail infrastructure was weak. Many of these innovations originated outside the United States and were then transferred back home. Investment in foreign manufacturing was complemented by a network of branch offices that ultimately came to be overseen by three regional offices, in New York, London, and Hamburg. By the early 1900s, Singer held 90 percent of its market despite *not* being the technological leader, and was the seventh largest firm in the world by sales (Gordon 2008, 671). Its sales profile was also unusually dispersed, even by the standards of today's multinationals: Russia, not the United States, was its largest single market (see Figure 3.3).

The Great Reversal

The first wave of globalization stalled and, based on measures of market integration, went into reverse after World War I. The most obvious reason had to do with disruptions of the international political (and economic) order. Singer, for example, lost its entire Russian business as a result of the revolution in 1917. And France lost two-thirds of its entire foreign investment. The Communist Revolution was the first case of large-scale expropriation of FDI. Also striking, however, were the sequestrations of German-owned affiliates by US, British, and other Allied governments during World War I, which not only reduced the stock of German FDI to virtually zero, but also signaled the end of the era when foreign companies could operate in most countries on more or less the same terms as domestic ones. Receptivity to foreign firms did not recover after the end of World War I. Although the United States shifted from being the world's largest debtor nation to being a net creditor over the course of the war, growing nationalism resulted in major restrictions on foreign ownership in shipping, telecommunications, resources, and other industries.

While trade flows did recover during the 1920s, the Wall Street crash of 1929 and its global spread finally ended the first wave of globalization. Tariffs and exchange controls proliferated. Immigration plummeted as governments introduced quotas and work visas. And capital market integration went into reverse as the gold standard collapsed and the international monetary system disintegrated into regional currency areas. However, in other respects, globalization might be considered as "constrained" rather than reversed (Jones 2010, 125–134; Miller 2012, 10; Jones 2013, 5, 33–43). Thus, the global consumer market that had emerged during the late nineteenth century persisted. The Nazi regime in Germany after 1933 pursued highly autarkic trade policies alongside its anti-Semitic and xenophobic behavior, but the German public remained avid consumers of Hollywood movies and American cosmetic brands.

Nevertheless, new subworlds based on alternative currency areas did appear after the collapse of the gold standard in the early 1930s. The Sterling Area, the Franc Area, and the Dollar Area shaped flows of capital and of trade during the 1930s, and were significant influences on international business and trade for several decades thereafter. Thus, on the eve of World War II, the British Empire accounted for 75 percent of all non-oil British foreign investment (Wilkins 1991, 163–167).[3] Distinct spheres of influence were also evident in the proliferation of international cartels, which governed 40 percent of world trade by the end of the 1930s (Fear 2008, 279). While the US government was officially suspicious of international cartels, major US firms, whether in oil or manufactured goods (GE dominated the world electric lamp cartel, which sold 85 percent of lamps in the world) were extremely important actors in them. Such cartels persisted as major forces in Europe and Japan for decades and continue to be significant in some key commodities (e.g., oil) and some other sectors critical to globalization (e.g., international shipping and air transport).

Less obviously, the shift in output from agriculture to manufacturing and the decades it took most firms – unlike Singer – to figure out how to sell differentiated manufactures rather than commodities overseas played a role as well. Some have even argued that this shift was more important than the upheavals of the interwar era. Thus, in the United States, trade plummeted from 24 percent of GDP in 1920 to just 11 percent by the end of the decade – a level that would not be exceeded over the next thirty years – before the Smoot-Hawley Tariff Act of 1930 led directly to the Great Depression (Greenwald and Kahn 2009, 19). The infrastructure developed to trade commodities had to be improved to handle differentiated products that lacked well-defined reference prices, could not be shipped in bulk, and often required substantial local adaptation, marketing, and aftersales support. To this day, trade in differentiated manufactures remains more sensitive to proximity and common language/colonial ties than trade in commodities (Rauch 1999).

After the horrors and disruption of World War II, much of the world shut itself off from globalization. Communism closed Russia, and then Eastern Europe, China, and elsewhere to global capitalism. These regimes instead attempted their own noncapitalist globalization: postwar Communist rulers encouraged their countries to specialize in particular sectors and trade with one another. Until political relations between Communist China and the Soviet Union deteriorated in the late 1950s, this Communist subworld covered a significant fraction of the world. The state-led model also attracted developing countries whose independence often intertwined with a backlash against Western capitalism. Thus, India engaged in large-scale state planning in order to promote industrial catch-up *à la* the Soviet Union – with which it also developed close trading and technological relationships.

The Second Wave

Globalization eventually did resume its onward march in the decades after World War II, with trade surging starting in the 1960s and FDI in the 1980s (see Figure 3.2). Drivers included changes in governmental policy, the expansion of globalization beyond commodities as companies figured out how to sell differentiated manufactures, and, to some extent, services, across borders, the increasing intensity of investments in intangible assets such as technology and marketing expertise subject to some cross-border economies of scale, and advances in information technology in particular. What resulted, in addition to more globalization, were both a broader range of strategies than pure arbitrage and more elaborate attempts at coordination within and across organizational boundaries. Moreover, in the past few decades, emerging markets reemerged as an engine of world growth, and companies from them as new players on the global scene.

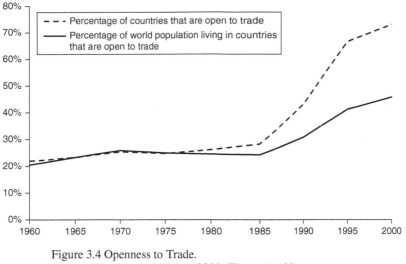

Figure 3.4 Openness to Trade.
Source: Wacziarg and Welch (2008, Figure 1, 188).

The Role of Government

The General Agreement on Tariffs and Trade (GATT), eventually replaced by the World Trade Organization, served as a platform for global negotiations that greatly reduced artificial barriers to trade. Regionally, the European Common Market and other integration initiatives provided impetus for more trade. So did broader moves by countries to open up. Thus, a classification of countries as closed or open based on trade barriers, as well as on whether they were "socialist," black market premia for hard currency, and state monopolization of major exports, suggested significant increases in openness to trade since the 1960s, especially in the last two decades of the twentieth century (see Figure 3.4). The countries that remained open throughout this period (e.g., the United States and quite a number in Western Europe) also experienced large declines in tariffs and other contrived trade barriers, to levels generally well below those prevailing in the early twentieth century. In addition, even countries classified as remaining closed (e.g., China, India, and Russia) did integrate more with the global economy.

The visible hand of government and the challenges of globalizing differentiated manufactures continued to affect the development of multinationals in the decades that followed World War II. The vertical integration of natural resource companies, a key feature of the first global economy, came under pressure as host governments objected to having their resources owned by foreigners – although large oil, minerals, and fruit companies and other vertical multinationals retained some of their importance through their downstream control of distribution, access to markets, and (limited) contractual protections. And a new generation of trading companies emerged, such as Philipp Brothers and later Glencore, that purchased commodities from suppliers in developing countries that were now state-owned and sold them worldwide (Jones and Storli 2012).

During the second wave of globalization, governments continued to matter a great deal – and arguably even more so now than at the crest of the first wave of globalization. The rapid expansion of the state sector was a factor. In one sample of industrialized countries, for example, the share of governmental expenditures in total GDP increased from about 10 percent in 1870 to 46 percent in 1996 (Tanzi and Schuknecht 2000, Table I.1, p. 6). The breakup of empires in the course of the twentieth century also contributed, as the number of independent countries increased from an all-time low of about sixty at the beginning of the twentieth century to nearly 200 by 2000 (Alesina, Spolaore, and Wacziarg 2000). Others pointed to the shifting distribution of power across countries rather than their number as a problem. In 2013, Pascal Lamy, then head of the World Trade Organization, invoked multipolarity as one of the key reasons for the failure to conclude the Doha round of trade talks despite more than a decade of negotiation:

Power is shifting from West to East and shifting quickly. Countries like India, China, Brazil, and Indonesia would, quite rightly, like a great share in the management of world affairs. But those who have held power for many decades are ready to accept this only if the emerging countries also take a larger share of the burden. (Basu 2013)

In contrast, during the first wave of globalization, governments rarely intervened in international economic affairs. Trade was the sole exception: governments such as those in Germany and the United States relied on tariffs as the largest source of governmental revenue, and after 1870 the United States led the world in raising tariffs in order to also facilitate import substitution in manufacturing. But there were almost no restrictions on foreign investments in the United States or elsewhere – they were not even monitored. Nor were there many restrictions on labor mobility, although by the late nineteenth century the United States had begun to restrict Asian immigration, and almost entirely prohibited it after World War I.

World War I and the Great Depression were turning points. Governments were everywhere in the lives of multinationals after 1914 – expropriating, regulating, providing incentives, and so on – and this has remained the case. As a result, administrative arbitrage – arbitraging between governments and their rules and regulations – achieved some prominence alongside more traditional economic arbitrage. Examples include global shipping and flags of convenience, location of financial activities in loosely regulated offshore financial centers, of dirty manufacturing in countries with weak environmental restrictions, and the broad use of foreign affiliates to reduce tax burden – a focus of mounting public outrage and tough talk from many governments that is discussed further in Chapter 4. But such international administrative arbitrage notwithstanding, it remained easy to assign nationalities, as in clear roots in one country, to almost all firms, even the most internationalized – arguably easier than at the peak of the first wave of globalization (Jones "Nationality" 2005). Even the very few long-running exceptions to this rule seemed to have come under pressure recently: thus, the traditional two-headed Anglo-Dutch structures at Unilever and Shell had finally been consolidated.

Sectoral Shifts

Horizontal multinationals in manufacturing continued to struggle with the challenges of globalizing differentiated manufactures. But through to the 1960s there was little rationalized production in such companies; subsidiaries tended to operate on a standalone basis, intrafirm trade was very low, and when it did take place, tended to be one way, from home to abroad. This was partly a legacy of the welter of exchange controls and tariffs of the interwar years. But it also reflected continued lags in building up the kinds of intangible assets that pioneers such as Singer had started to amass a century earlier. Intangible assets such as technological knowhow and marketing expertise tended to exhibit increasing returns to scale and (partial) fungibility across locations, but it was often difficult to contract out their services. Therefore, they spurred the international expansion of horizontal multinationals despite large differences across national markets. To this day, R&D intensity and advertising intensity are robust predictors of the incidence of horizontal MNEs in manufacturing, presumably because such expenditures serve as proxies for the underlying importance of intangible assets.[4]

What did change – particularly about advanced economies – in the period after World War II was the shift of economic activity and particularly employment toward services. Thus, between 1953 and 2005, service sector employment in the United States, Western Europe, and Japan rose from 52 percent of total employment to 84 percent.[5] In tandem, service firms swelled the ranks of globalizers. During the 1950s, consultants, ad agencies, hotels, and film distributors went global, spreading management practices and lifestyles. The globalization of these firms' footprints did, however, present some performance challenges. Among the top fifty law firms, for example, a negative relationship persisted in 2010 between the percentage of overseas partners in a firm and its profit per equity partner (Beaton 2011, 19).

The biggest changes in services were due to banks. The creation of the Euromarkets in the late 1950s by British overseas banks such as the Bank of London and South America revolutionized the world financial system (Schenk

1998). Over the next two decades, the growing pool of offshore capital increasingly impinged on the ability of governments to regulate financial systems. The new unregulated financial markets were and remained clustered in places such as London, and offshore centers such as the Cayman Islands, where they were disconnected from "real world" activity such as foreign trade. Financial market liberalization – including the removal of controls on international capital flows – accelerated in the 1970s, and has been cited as a contributor to a resurgence of banking crises in that decade after several decades of near-invisibility in major economies. From the mid-1980s through the end of the 1990s, countries accounting for a quarter of the world's GDP were routinely in crisis in any given year (Reinhart and Rogoff 2013). Nonetheless, trade in the services sector continued to remain limited, illustrated by the fact that services account for roughly 70 percent of global GDP but only about 20 percent of global trade.[6] New analysis of trade in value added, however, indicates that accounting for services content embodied in manufacturing exports, for example, in the form of labor services, perhaps doubles the "services" share of world exports. Even on this basis, however, trade in services is still only about one-third as intense as trade in merchandise.[7] And by 2012, roughly two-thirds of global FDI was in the service sector, up from half in 1990 (UNCTAD 2014).

Some services such as haircuts were, of course, intrinsically untradeable. Trade and particularly FDI in others, although feasible, required a sophisticated system of rules and regulation that not all World Trade Organization members were equipped to operate – nor politically willing to do so, as evidenced by the breakdown of the Doha round of trade talks. Policy restrictions continued to be particularly pronounced in transportation and professional services. Some analysts nonetheless concluded that services globalization represented a great opportunity, although not a simple one: that a given percentage cut in service barriers would produce greater gains than those from a comparable cut in merchandise trade barriers (Decreux and Fontagné 2011). Others asserted an analogy with the decades it took firms to figure out how to sell differentiated manufactures rather than commodities overseas:

We are currently in a period like that from 1920 to 1950, in which changes in the composition of economic activity – then the trend toward differentiated manufacturing; now the move toward locally produced and consumed services – outweigh the impact of improving transportation and communications on globalization. It is likely to be a period in which economic globalization declines in importance. (Greenwald and Kahn 2009, 19)

Intangible Asset/Information Intensity

As the relative importance of commodities declined and the emphasis on selling differentiated manufactures and, to a lesser extent, services across

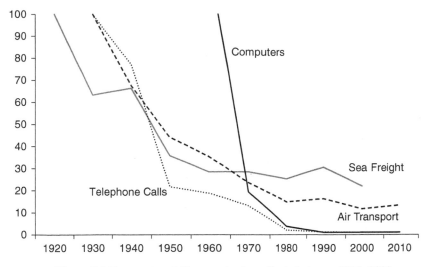

Figure 3.5 Transport and Communications Costs Indexes, 1920–2009.
Sources: Adapted from UNDP (1999), p. 30, with Air Transport (average revenue per passenger kilometer) updated to 2009 based on ICAO, "Regional Differences in International Airline Operating Economics: 2008 and 2009."

borders went up during the postwar period, the intensity of investments in intangible assets shot up. Thus, in the United States, which led on this metric, gross business investment in intangibles increased from slightly over 4 percent of nonfarm business output at the end of World War II to nearly 14 percent by 2007 – with about one-half of the total being accounted for by investments in R&D and brand equity – while the rate of investment in tangible assets hovered between 10 percent and 12 percent (Corrado and Hulten 2010). In addition, investment in information technology (IT) in the form of both hardware and software came to account for a significant proportion of total investment.

IT was the big technological story of the second wave of globalization, especially in the past few decades. Which is not to say that transportation technology didn't experience significant improvements as well (see Figure 3.5). The development of shipping containers facilitated "unitization" or the shipping of less-than-full shiploads (note the continuing response to the challenges of differentiated manufactures vs. commodities), slashed handling costs and times, and permitted more efficient multimode shipments in which maritime transport interfaced with rail or road. However, the advent of OPEC (state-sponsored cartels continued to be entirely legitimate in many commodities – if ineffective in most) and recurrent peaks in the price of oil slowed progress. And the jet plane not only improved air transport costs and times, especially on the North Atlantic route that still dominated interregional interactions in the early decades of the second wave, but also opened up new markets (e.g., for perishables) and permitted the development of quick-response global supply chains. As a result, air transportation is estimated to account for about 40 percent of world trade by value. But again, fuel prices have flattened the cost trajectory recently, and environmental concerns loom ever larger.

The IT revolution itself – the development of transistors and microprocessors, massive increases in processing power, the internet revolution, and the prospect of a new digital wave around social media, mobility, analytics, big data, and the cloud – is a familiar story that will not be repeated here. What is worth emphasizing here is that the significant improvements in the speed and richness with which information could be exchanged between places had profound implications for how global organizations connected themselves up internally as well as externally to suppliers, buyers, and others.

Strategy and Organization

In addition to the *arbitrage* strategies aimed at exploiting differences that vertical multinationals had traditionally pursued, the second wave of globalization saw more and more horizontal multinationals also wrestling with the tension between *adaptation* to adjust to differences and *aggregation* to overcome differences. They sought to remain locally relevant while exploiting at least some similarities across countries to tap economies of scale or scope.[8] But this was often hard to get right, as illustrated by Ford's attempts over nearly a century to develop a "world car." The runaway success of Ford's fully standardized "any color so long as it's black" Model T in the early 1900s inspired the company to build a giant plant modeled on its River Rouge complex in the United States in the UK, even though the market there was much smaller. Utilization problems were compounded by insufficient adaptation to local demand (e.g., use of powerful US engines while local preferences were shifting to smaller cars with lower operating costs) and rising trade barriers that stymied planned exports to France and Germany. GM historically achieved stronger results in Europe by allowing its subsidiaries there to pursue strategies more tailored to local markets. Ford nonetheless continued to pursue its vision of a "world car" despite setbacks such as the 1981 Ford Escort, which was planned as a "totally common vehicle" across the United States and Europe but was launched with only a single common part across the regions – with even that part changed six months later. Later attempts did achieve more parts commonality, however, and in the 2010s, Ford was again pursuing its world car ambitions – but so far, the original Model T is the only exception to the rule regarding the unworkability of complete standardization in autos.[9]

Overall, improvements in IT, rising levels of globalization, and deepening intangible asset-intensity prompted many multinationals to expand their attempts at cross-border coordination well beyond the traditional emphasis on resource allocation across and monitoring of national operations by headquarters. Multinationals typically started out by tying foreign ventures to the parent with loose organizational links because of their riskiness as well as the prohibitive costs of establishing an elaborate organization to administer them.[10] As foreign operations matured, they typically established an international division to coordinate such functions as transfer pricing, finance, and the distribution of exports among production units. As foreign operations became even more important, however, the mismatch between domestic and international structures prompted a search for alternatives ranging from global product divisions and geographic divisions to matrix structures involving more elaborate coordination across products or geographies, which became more popular over the 1990s and 2000s.[11]

Increasing integration within multinational firms also involved transforming their subsidiaries in foreign countries – to the point where free-standing subsidiaries had been deemed an endangered species (Birkinshaw 2001, 381). However, once again, rhetoric seems to have outrun reality: thus, a study of the foreign affiliates of US multinationals finds that intrafirm trade is concentrated among a small number of large affiliates within large multinational corporations; the median affiliate ships nothing to the rest of the corporation (Ramondo, Rappoport, and Ruhl 2015). Cross-border geographical and functional integration proved very difficult to achieve, especially for companies where borders had previously been sharply drawn. Thus, the regional integration of the European Union prompted Unilever's top management to promote pan-European integration at Unilever as well, starting in the 1950s; but in the early twenty-first century, the company was still struggling to integrate the production and marketing facilities of its European firms (Jones and Miskell 2005).

In addition to attempts to achieve greater coordination internally, leading multinationals also paid more attention in the 1990s and 2000s to strategic alliances involving significant interorganizational coordination. This change is typically attributed to the development of the internet, the diffusion of models for outsourcing, and the push in many lines of business to provide integrated solutions from participants across the entire value chain. Thus, according to rough estimates based on a range of data sources, alliances' share of revenues for the top 1,000 US public corporations increased from about 1 percent in 1980 to between 6 and 7 percent by 1990, 15 percent by 1995, and 20 percent by 1998.[12]

Value chains in the consumer electronics industry exemplified the new reliance on webs of external partners. Taiwan's Foxconn assembled an estimated 40 percent of the world's consumer electronics in 2011 for clients such as

Apple, Dell, Amazon, Samsung, and Sony. Apple and other Foxconn clients, however, came under fire for working conditions at Foxconn's plants, including a spate of suicides, illustrating some of the difficulties associated with managing such extended supply networks (Duhigg and Barboza 2012).

Emerging Markets

Foxconn also exemplified an even larger change in the world economy: the changing role of emerging countries, particularly China and India, which will be discussed further in Chapters 5 and 11. China and India had accounted for nearly one-half of world GDP between them in 1820 (at PPP). By the end of the first wave of globalization, that figure had fallen to about 15 percent as their income levels stagnated. China and India became suppliers of primary commodities – cotton, tea, and so on – so they continued to be important to the global economy, but they captured little value from it. They truly became peripheral only with the second wave of globalization, when Communist China and state-planned India opted out of the global economy. By 1980, their share of world GDP had dropped to only 5 percent.[13] By contrast, the GDP of the United States had grown to 22 percent of the world total, while the countries that now make up the EU-28 accounted for 30 percent. China and India have since turned around, rising to 20 percent by 2010 (slightly larger than either the United States or the EU). China also became the world's largest merchandise exporter, accounting for 10 percent of the world total that year, versus 8 percent each for the United States and Germany. China's share of world GDP surpassed that of the United States in 2014 and is forecast to reach 25 percent by 2040 (slightly more than the United States and EU combined). Figure 3.6 summarizes these GDP shifts and Figure 3.7 tracks emerging economies' share of global totals for a broader range of variables from 1980 to 2014.

Overall, the data in Figures 3.6 and 3.7 suggest a severing of the link between market size and income that had lasted most of the twentieth century. The largest markets for most products had long been developed countries but now, emerging markets in general and China in particular often led. And for some products and services (consumer durables, telecommunications, construction inputs), the shift was occurring at a very high velocity. Thus, in autos – a particularly large, asset-intensive industry that one might think of as slow-moving – emerging markets' share of new vehicle registrations increased from 33 percent in 2005 to 56 percent in 2014![14]

In response to this shift, multinationals from advanced economies (again) expanded their horizons to encompass such markets. Once again, large-scale resource-seeking investments – although the resource being sought was often labor rather than some mineral or other commodity – appeared to precede large-scale market-seeking investments. Penetrating emerging markets posed

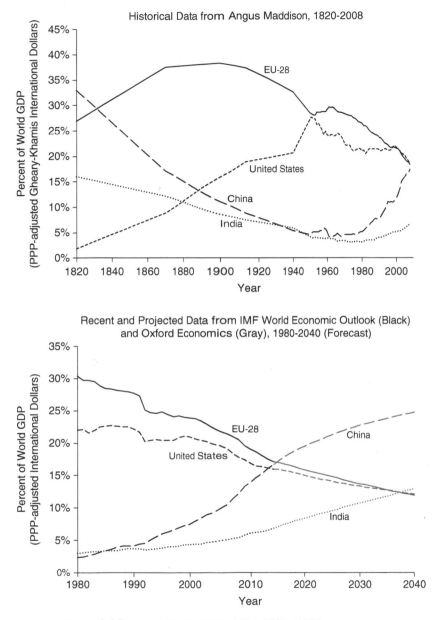

Figure 3.6 Shares of World GDP (PPP), 1820–2040F.
Sources: Maddison (Historical Statistics); IMF World Economic Outlook Database (October 2015); 2017–2030: Oxford Economics Projections (2016).

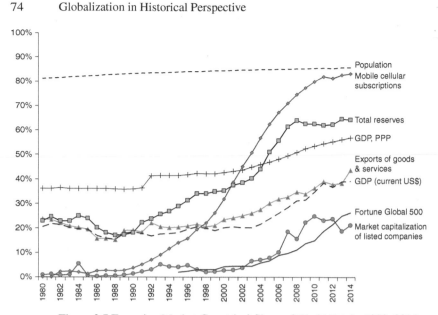

Figure 3.7 Emerging Market Countries' Share of World Totals, 1980–2014.
Notes: Emerging market countries are those classified as emerging market and developing economies by the International Monetary Fund (IMF). Exports of goods and services, market capitalization of listed companies, and total reserves are in current US $; GDP PPP is in current international dollars. Market capitalization of listed companies' data exclude Ecuador and South Africa.
Sources: World Bank World Development Indicators 2015, April 2015, IMF World Economic Outlook Database, October 2015; Fortune Global 500 lists, Fortune magazine.

particular challenges. Price points were generally much lower. Companies from advanced countries also had to deal with greater distances than, say, faced by a US multinational expanding into Europe along dimensions such as cultural values, the quality of institutions, infrastructure, and human resources. And they often also had to contend with low-cost, fast-moving local companies.

Emerging Competitors

Large companies were actually one of the dimensions along which emerging economies' share of the world total lagged, as indicated in Figure 3.7. Nevertheless, even here, their influence was increasing rapidly: in 2014, 132 of the firms in the Fortune Global 500 hailed from emerging countries, versus only 10 in 1995. A new set of competitors was emerging in the global arena. Some Latin American, Asian, and other firms had grown substantially behind protective tariffs during the 1950s–1980s, reaching decent scale and developing their own capabilities, even if they were rarely internationally competitive. With the removal of many of these restrictions, the most competitive of them were intent on expanding abroad. And they were joined as credible multinational challengers by Chinese private companies – although size-based rankings were still dominated by state-owned companies, which accounted for more than three-quarters of the 90+ Chinese companies on the Fortune Global 500 and more than one-half of the companies from other emerging economies – vs. 4 percent of the companies from advanced economies.

Such multinational challengers had, with a particular focus on China and India, been characterized as lower cost, better adapted to their home market, and often nimbler than established multinationals but lacking the latter's marketing expertise, technological knowhow, and management systems. Industry-level patterns provided some support for this characterization: established multinationals tended to do better in China and India in industries with higher differentiation potential – that is, with high R&D and advertising intensity – and local companies in industries with lower differentiation potential (Ghemawat and Hout 2008, 2016).[15] Further support came from the macro observation that investment rates in intangible assets tended to be much lower in emerging economies. China was a partial exception, with an intangible investment rate in 2010 of 10 percent of nonfarm business output (vs. less than 3 percent in India), focused on software, R&D, and design (Hao August 2012). But this level was low relative to Chinese rates of investment in tangible assets and appeared not to be yielding commensurate increases in output, perhaps because it seemed to be driven top-down by Chinese policymakers (Hao September, 2012).

Although going head-to-head with incumbent multinationals in advanced countries as well as in one's own was one option for companies from emerging economies, it wasn't the only one. Shifts in world demand presumably combined with low levels of intangible assets and continued restrictions on foreign competitors in many sectors to make focusing on the home market a more attractive option for a company from an emerging economy than a company from an advanced one. Burgeoning commercial links among emerging economies represented another possible focus: trade between emerging markets, for example, had recently been by far the fastest growing component of world trade.[16] Focusing by region or subregion was another, probably even more common option: for example, many Latin American companies that internationalized became regionally focused "MultiLatinas." Other bases for expanding – for example, by following diaspora or colonial-era linkages – further multiplied the possibilities.

From a historical perspective, the multinational challengers from emerging economies were not entirely without precedent. Some business enterprises from emerging economies extended their operations across national borders during the first wave of globalization as well. Thus, the Patiño tin company from Bolivia acquired mines overseas, smelters in Britain and the United States, and shipping and transport interests, but was nationalized in 1952. Many of the other earlier multinational challengers also succumbed to interventionist governments and regulations between the interwar years and the 1980s. Recent developments regarding the rise of emerging markets and emerging competitors are examined further in Chapter 11.

Conclusion

What does this comparison between the two waves of globalization suggest about the future evolution of the second one? In terms of just absolute levels, Figure 3.2 reminds us that current trade and FDI intensities are three to four times as high as the peak intensities reached during the first wave. Short-to-medium-run people flows across borders have probably grown significantly more rapidly, and cross-border information flows have exploded. So this peak is in a rather different place, involving much more cross-border integration along most respects – except in terms of the ties of empire – than the previous one.

In terms of momentum, there has certainly been a weakening in recent years in the growth of globalization but, again from Figure 3.2, this hasn't yet lasted as long as did the weakening that went before the great reversal. And more importantly, policymakers do not seem to have been tempted to follow up on the global financial crisis with sweeping protectionism, unlike in 1929–1930 in the United States. So another possible difference between the two peaks is that there may have been some learning from the (first) great reversal – although, as of this writing, the looming threat of isolationism in advanced economies suggests at least some uncertainty about whether or not this pattern will continue.

Whether the second wave might end in a great reversal is presumably sensitive to what policymakers, in governments and the private sector, decide to do. Looking the drivers of globalization during the second wave and thinking back to the first wave, it seems hard to imagine the technological changes that have increased levels of globalization being unwound. What look more reversible – despite the possible learning from the (first) great reversal cited – are policy changes that, broadly speaking, have mostly been prointegrationist in the period since World War II, that is, have tried to encourage more trade and FDI.

The sectoral shifts between the time of the first wave and the second wave suggest that in terms of governmental policies that are likely to move the needle in a positive direction, services still represent an area of substantial opportunity. And since international interactions in services often require FDI, market access and a host of other issues need to be sorted out and acted upon, which is more complex than simply reducing barriers to trade in merchandise.

The increased intensity of intangible assets and information flows/technology in the economy at large and in multinational firms in particular and, relatedly, the complex forms of cross-border coordination that many multinationals are now attempting hint at global management challenges, solved and unsolved. We look at these in more detail, function by function, in Chapter 4.

Finally, the increasing share of the world economy accounted for by emerging economies and the rising number of large competitors from these economies, particularly China, are the other changes that stand out from comparison of the first and second waves of globalization. At least as a baseline, it seems reasonable, given demographics and some other considerations, to assume that growth rates in emerging economies will be at least slightly higher than in advanced economies, that is, that the big shift toward emerging economies will continue, if perhaps at a slower pace than in recent years. These trends and their implications are discussed in some depth in Chapter 11.

Notes

1 For additional coverage of trade and capital depth trends, refer to chapter 3 of Ghemawat and Altman (2014).
2 1820 value from Maddison (1995), specifically Chapter 2 tables (available at: www .ggdc.net/MADDISON/Monitoring_the_world/1995_Monitoring_the_World/ TextTables/tables_chapter2.pdf). 1913 value from Maddison (2006, Table F-5, p. 362).
3 Based on data from Conan (1960) and exclusive of oil-related foreign investments.
4 See Caves for a more precise statement of the necessary conditions for horizontal MNEs and an overview of the empirical evidence on their incidence (2007, 1–13, 29–45, and 105–108).
5 Calculation based on Angus Maddison dataset contained in Groningen Growth and Development Centre (GGDC) 10-sector database, www.rug.nl/research/ggdc/data/ 10-sector-database. These data include government as well as commercial services.
6 Based on 2010 data reported in the World Bank's World Development Indicators.
7 Based on UNCTAD (2013, 137) and World Bank World Development Indicators. See also Escaith (2013). For additional details, refer to the Trade Flows section in Chapter 2.
8 The "AAA" strategies of adaptation, aggregation, and arbitrage are discussed briefly in chapters 4 and 6 and in much more detail in chapters 4–7 of Ghemawat (2007).
9 The material in this paragraph is drawn from Sturgeon and Florida (2000), Scheele (2004), Jones *Multinationals* (2005, 175).
10 The discussion in this paragraph follows the richly detailed review of the literature in Caves (2007, chapter 3).
11 Stopford and Wells (1972) describe the tension among these organizational forms. Data presented in Chapter 4 indicate rising incidence of matrix organizations

between the late 1990s and late 2000s, and declining use of functional structures over the same period.

12 Data through 1995 based on Freidheim (1998), and since then, on Warren Company (2002); these sources themselves rely on a range of others that they cite in more detail.

13 The historical estimates, compiled by Angus Maddison, use the Gheary-Khamis method of valuing PPP. By contrast, the more recent data compiled by the IMF use a version of the Gini-Eltetö-Köves-Szulc (GEKS) method. Since we are constrained by the availability of data using different price valuations, we present them separately in the two panels of Figure 3.6. The Gheary-Khamis method produces higher percentages for developing economies, including China and India. The figures reported in the text for 1980 to 2040 are based on the IMF data and thus, the GEKS method. For more information on different methods of measuring purchasing power, see Deaton and Heston (2008).

14 Based on data from Euromonitor Passport.

15 Details in prepublication version of 2008 article, available from the authors.

16 See Figure 11.5 in chapter 11.

References

Alesina, Alberto, Enrico Spolaore, and Romain Wacziarg. 2000. "Economic Integration and Political Disintegration." *American Economic Review* 90 (5):1276–1296. doi: 10.1257/aer.90.5.1276.

Bairoch, Paul, and Richard Kozul-Wright. March 1996. "Globalization Myths: Some Historical Reflections on Integration, Industrialization and Growth in the World Economy." United Nations Conference on Trade and Development, Kings College, Cambridge. http://unctad.org/en/docs/dp_113.en.pdf.

Basu, Nayanima. 2013. "If Countries Don't Want to Negotiate and Agree, a WTO Head Can't Do Much." *Business Standard*, January 28, 2013, 4.

Beaton, George. 2011. "Mega Trends in Professional Services." Gro Pro Conference, April 19, 2011.

Becker, Susan. 1998. "The German Metal Traders before 1914." In *The Multinational Traders*, edited by Geoffrey Jones, 66–85. London New York: Routledge.

Birkinshaw, Julian. 2001. "Strategy and Management in MNE Subsidiaries." In *The Oxford Handbook of International Business*, edited by Alan M. Rugman, and Thomas L. Brewer, 380–401. New York: Oxford University Press. www.oxfordscholarship.com/view/10.1093/0199241821.001.0001/acprof-9780199241828-chapter-14.

Carlos, Ann M., and Stephen Nicholas. 1988. "'Giants of an Earlier Capitalism': The Chartered Trading Companies as Modern Multinationals." *Business History Review* 62 (3):398–419. doi: 10.2307/3115542.

Caves, Richard E. 2007. *Multinational Enterprise and Economic Analysis*. 3rd ed. Cambridge; New York: Cambridge University Press.

Conan, A. R. 1960. *Capital Imports into Sterling Countries*. London; New York: Macmillan; St. Martin's Press.

Corley, T.A.B. 1994. "Britain's Overseas Investments in 1914 Revisited." In *The Making of Global Enterprise*, edited by Geoffrey Jones. London; Portland, OR: F. Cass.

Corrado, Carol A., and Charles R. Hulten. 2010. "How Do You Measure a 'Technological Revolution'?" *The American Economic Review* 100 (2):99–104. doi: 10.2307/27804971.

Deaton, Angus, and Alan Heston. 2008. "Understanding PPPs and PPP-Based National Accounts." No. w14499. National Bureau of Economic Research.

Decreux, Yvan, and Lionel Fontagné. 2011. "Economic Impact of Potential Outcome of the DDA." CEPII Working Papers 2011–2023, October 20, 2011. http://ssrn.com/abstract=2004831.

Dicken, Peter. 2011. *Global Shift: Mapping the Changing Contours of the World Economy*. 6th ed. Thousand Oaks, CA: Sage.

Duhigg, Charles, and David Barboza. 2012. "In China, Human Costs Are Built into an iPad." *New York Times*, January 25, 2012, Business Day | The iEconomy. www.nytimes.com/2012/01/26/business/ieconomy-apples-ipad-and-the-human-costs-for-workers-in-china.html.

Escaith, Hubert. 2013. "Trade in Tasks and Global Value Chains: Stylized Facts and Implications." WTO Trade Data Day, January 16, 2013.

Fear, Jeffrey. 2008. "Cartels." In *The Oxford Handbook of Business History*, edited by Geoffrey Jones, and Jonathan Zeitlin. Oxford England; New York: Oxford University Press. www.oxfordhandbooks.com/view/10.1093/oxfordhb/9780199263684.001.0001/oxfordhb-9780199263684-e-012.

Freidheim, Cyrus. 1998. *The Trillion-Dollar Enterprise: How the Alliance Revolution Will Transform Global Business*. Reading, MA: Perseus Books.

Ghemawat, Pankaj. 2007. *Redefining Global Strategy: Crossing Borders in a World Where Differences Still Matter*. Boston, MA: Harvard Business School Press.

Ghemawat, Pankaj, and Steven A. Altman. 2014. "DHL Global Connectedness Index 2014: Analyzing Global Flows and Their Power to Increase Prosperity." Deutsche Post DHL. www.dhl.com/gci.

Ghemawat, Pankaj, and Thomas Hout. 2008. "Tomorrow's Global Giants? Not the Usual Suspects." *Harvard Business Review* 86 (11):80–88.

2016. "Can China's Companies Conquer the World? The Overlooked Importance of Corporate Power." *Foreign Affairs* 95 (2): 86–98.

Gordon, Andrew. 2008. "Selling the American Way: The Singer Sales System in Japan, 1900–1938." *Business History Review* 82 (4):671–699.

Greenwald, Bruce C., and Judd Kahn. 2009. *Globalization. The Irrational Fear That Someone in China Will Take Your Job*. Hoboken, NJ: John Wiley & Sons.

Hao, Xiaohui (Janet). August 2012. "Intangible Investment in China Has Grown Rapidly – but Is It Efficient?" *China Center for Economics and Business: Chart of the Week* (China-COTW-8-24-12). The Conference Board. www.conference-board.org/publications/publicationdetail.cfm?publicationid=2317.

September, 2012. "China – Increasing Intangible Investment Not Yielding Commensurate Increases in Output." *China Center for Economics and Business: Chart of the Week* (China-COTW-9-17-12). The Conference Board. www.conference-board.org/publications/publicationdetail.cfm?publicationid=2319.

International Monetary Fund (IMF). "Direction of Trade Statistics (DOTS)." Last Modified August 25, 2015. http://data.imf.org/DOT.

October 2015. "World Economic Outlook (WEO) Database." www.imf.org/external/pubs/ft/weo/2015/02/weodata/index.aspx.

Jones, Geoffrey. 1993. *British Multinational Banking, 1830–1990*. Oxford England; New York: Clarendon Press; Oxford University Press.

2000. *Merchants to Multinationals: British Trading Companies in the Nineteenth and Twentieth Centuries*. Oxford UK; New York: Oxford University Press.

2005. *Multinationals and Global Capitalism: From the Nineteenth to the Twenty-First Century*. Oxford; New York: Oxford University Press.

2005. "Nationality and Multinationals in Historical Perspective." Harvard Business School working paper 06-052.

2010. *Beauty Imagined: A History of the Global Beauty Industry*. Oxford: Oxford University Press.

2013. *Entrepreneurship and Multinationals: Global Business and the Making of the Modern World*. Northampton, MA: Edward Elgar Pub.

Jones, Geoffrey, and David Kiron. "Globalizing Consumer Durables: Singer Sewing Machine before 1914." HBS Case No. 9-804-001, Harvard Business School Publishing, Boston. https://hbr.org/product/Globalizing-Consumer-Dura/an/804001-PDF-ENG.

Jones, Geoffrey, and Peter Miskell. 2005. "European Integration and Corporate Restructuring: The Strategy of Unilever, C.1957–C.1990." *The Economic History Review* 58 (1):113–39. doi: 10.1111/j.1468-0289.2005.00300.x.

Jones, Geoffrey, and Espen Storli. 2012. "Marc Rich and Global Commodity Trading." HBS Case No. 9-813-020, Harvard Business School Publishing, Boston. https://hbr.org/product/marc-rich-and-global-commodity-trading/813020-PDF-ENG.

Jones, Geoffrey, and Bjoern von Siemens. 2012. "Werner von Siemens and the Electric Telegraph." HBS Case No. 9-811-004, Harvard Business School Publishing, Boston.

Kavesh, Robert A., Kenneth D. Garbade, and William L. Silber. 1978. "Technology, Communication and the Performance of Financial Markets: 1840–1975." *Journal of Finance* 33 (3):819–32. doi: 10.1111/j.1540–6261.1978.tb02023.x.

Maddison, Angus. 1995. *Monitoring the World Economy, 1820–1992*, Development Centre Studies. Paris; Washington, DC: Development Centre of the Organisation for Economic Co-operation and Development; OECD Publications and Information Center distributor.

2006. "The World Economy: Volume 1: A Millennial Perspective." *Development Centre Studies*. OECD Publishing. http://dx.doi.org/10.1787/9789264022621-en.

2010. "Historical Statistics of the World Economy: 1–2008 AD." www.ggdc.net/maddison/Historical_Statistics/vertical-file_02-2010.xls.

Miller, Michael B. 2012. *Europe and the Maritime World: A Twentieth-Century History*. Cambridge: Cambridge University Press.

O'Rourke, Kevin H., and Jeffrey G. Williamson. 1999. *Globalization and History: The Evolution of a Nineteenth-Century Atlantic Economy*. Cambridge, MA: MIT Press.

Ramondo, Natalia, Veronica Rappoport, and Kim J. Ruhl. 2015 "Intrafirm Trade and Vertical Fragmentation in U.S. Multinational Corporations." National Bureau of Economic Research Working Paper Series No. 21472, August 2015. www.nber.org/papers/w21472.

Rauch, James E. 1999. "Networks Versus Markets in International Trade." *Journal of International Economics* 48 (1):7–35. doi: 10.1016/S0022-1996(98)00009-9.

Reinhart, Carmen M., and Kenneth S. Rogoff. 2013. "Banking Crises: An Equal Opportunity Menace." *Journal of Banking & Finance* 37 (11):4557–73. doi: 10.1016/j.jbankfin.2013.03.005.

Scheele, Nick. 2004. "It's a Small World after All…or Is It?: The State of Globalization in the Worldwide Automotive Industry." In *The Global Market: Developing a Strategy to Manage across Borders*, edited by John A. Quelch, and Rohit Deshpande, Chapter 7. San Francisco: Jossey-Bass.

Schenk, Catherine R. 1998. "The Origins of the Eurodollar Market in London: 1955–1963." *Explorations in Economic History* 35 (2):221–38. doi: 10.1006/exeh.1998.0693.

Stopford, John M., and Louis T. Wells. 1972. *Managing the Multinational Enterprise: Organization of the Firm and Ownership of the Subsidiaries*, The Harvard Multinational Enterprise Series. New York: Basic Books.

Sturgeon, Timothy J., and Richard Florida. 2000. "Globalization and Jobs in the Automotive Industry." MIT Industrial Performance Center Working Paper 00-012, November 2000. http://ipc.mit.edu/sites/default/files/documents/00-012.pdf.

Tanzi, Vito, and Ludger Schuknecht. 2000. *Public Spending in the 20th Century: A Global Perspective*. Cambridge, UK; New York: Cambridge University Press.

UNCTAD. 2012. "World Investment Report 2012: Towards a New Generation of Investment Policies." United Nations. http://unctad.org/en/PublicationsLibrary/wir2012_embargoed_en.pdf.

— 2013. "World Investment Report 2013: Global Value Chains: Investment and Trade for Development." United Nations. http://unctad.org/en/PublicationsLibrary/wir2013_en.pdf.

— 2015. "World Investment Report 2015: Reforming International Investment Governance." United Nations. http://unctad.org/en/PublicationsLibrary/wir2015_en.pdf.

United Nations (UN). "United Nations Commodity Trade Statistics Database." http://comtrade.un.org/db/.

United Nations Development Programme (UNDP). 1999. "Human Development Report 1999: Globalization with a Human Face." http://hdr.undp.org/sites/default/files/reports/260/hdr_1999_en_nostats.pdf.

Wacziarg, Romain, and Karen Horn Welch. 2008. "Trade Liberalization and Growth: New Evidence." *The World Bank Economic Review* 22 (2): 187–231.

Warren Company. 2002. "Strategic Alliance Best Practice User Guide." www.warrenco.com/2._User_Guide_-ASAP_Intro_-_v2.pdf.

Wilkins, Mira. 1991. *The Growth of Multinationals*, The International Library of Critical Writings in Business History. Aldershot, Hants, England; Brookfield, VT, USA: E. Elgar.

— 1998. "The Free-Standing Company Revisited." In *The Free-Standing Company in the World Economy, 1830–1996*, edited by M. Wilkins and H. G. Schröter. Oxford University Press.

4   The Globalization of Business

Firms doing business beyond the borders of their home countries generate many types of international interactions – most obviously trade and capital flows but also some people and information flows.[1] The incomplete international integration of markets opens up the opportunity for firms to create economic value by themselves bridging the borders and distance that separate markets. This framing highlights how understanding the globalization of firms – both externally as market participants and internally in terms of the functions they perform – is essential to understanding the phenomenon of globalization itself.

This chapter looks at the state of globalization of business firms. It parallels Chapter 2, which also focused on the current state of globalization, but at the level of markets rather than firms. And it complements the historical discussion in Chapter 3 in terms of its temporal focus and by affording an opportunity to probe the more complex forms of cross-border coordination that some multinationals are now attempting. In order to be as concrete as possible, this chapter drills down to the globalization of specific functional areas within firms: marketing, operations, R&D, finance, accounting, organization, and leadership. In addition to reviews of the literature and some of my own company case studies and surveys, it is informed by a recent project cosponsored by NYU Stern's Center for the Globalization of Education and Management, which I head, and the Center for Global Enterprise (a think tank set up by Samuel Palmisano, the former Chairman and CEO of IBM) that commissioned thought leaders across six functional areas to take an up-to-date look at globalization from a business perspective.[2]

The methodology used to assemble this large, diverse literature into relatively concise functional characterizations bears comment as well. The tremendous heterogeneity among firms around the world – in terms of size and, relatedly, participation in globalization – implies that the broad global averages used in Chapter 2 to characterize how deeply globalized markets are would work less well at the firm level. Limited availability of data about firms, especially small firms, as compared to countries also limits the feasibility of parallel treatment. So this chapter relies on a rather different empirical tradition, of configurative-idiographic empiricism from political science.[3] Data on more limited samples of firms, typically very large firms, are combined with qualitative insights as a basis for painting pictures of the functional challenges and practices associated with globalization. And these functional pictures are preceded by an introductory section that puts them into context by looking at how key measures of firm globalization vary with firm size.

The evidence suggests that the law of semiglobalization applies at the level of firms as well as markets. The overwhelming majority of firms do not operate across national borders, indicating that international interactions are indeed less intense than domestic ones from their perspective. And second, even the few (typically large) firms that do operate across national borders seem to be subject to border effects internally – despite rhetoric about multinationals as globally integrated pools of capital, people, knowledge, and so on.

Firm Globalization and Firm Size

The two most obvious ways of measuring firms' cross-border activities – although there are others that will be looked at as well – pertain to two types of international activity of particular interest to business people: exports (and sometimes imports) and FDI. Looking at firm-level data, there is a striking (if obvious) difference from the country level: unlike countries, many firms, especially smaller ones, report no exports (or imports). And the fraction that has engaged in FDI is much lower still – and even more tilted toward even larger firms.

Given participation constraints, with many firms engaging in neither of these modes of globalization, reliance on population averages would be tricky. A two-stage approach of looking at participation constraints first (in this section) and then (in the sections that follow) at how firms that participate in globalization do so fits with conditional probability as well as common sense.

To start with trade, according to a fact sheet from the US Department of Commerce, based on 2010 data:

Less than one percent of America's 30 million companies export[4] – a percentage that is significantly lower than all other developed countries. And of U.S. companies that do export, 58 percent export to only one country … Small and medium-sized companies account for 98 percent of U.S. exporters, but represent less than one-third of the known export value of U.S. goods exports. (United States Department of Commerce 2011)

This (less than) one-third share can be compared with calculations by the US Small Business Administration that small and medium enterprises (SMEs) with fewer than 500 employees account for between 40 and 50 percent of private sector payroll, employment, and output, and 64 percent of net new private-sector jobs (Office of Advocacy 2012). The US Census data underlying these

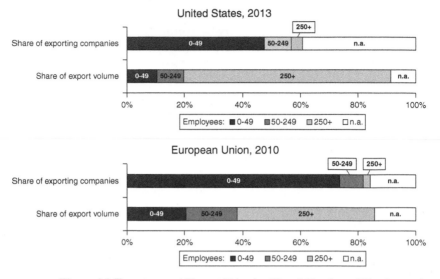

Figure 4.1 Exporters and Export Value by Firms' Number of Employees in the United States and European Union.
Source: Eurostat, International Trade by Enterprise Characteristics (2010) and US Census Bureau.

characterizations also indicate that importers are even sparser and similarly concentrated in value terms (United States Census Bureau 2013).[5]

EU data exhibit the same broad patterns, but with export participation rates in the range of several percentage points rather than 1 percent, and with smaller firms playing a somewhat larger role in exports than in the United States, as shown in Figure 4.1 (Eurostat 2012). This reflects, among other things, the smaller sizes of individual EU members compared to the United States and the relatively easy accessibility of other EU members.

Globalization through multinationalization – FDI to buy or build affiliates in foreign countries – is even rarer and even more the domain of large firms. To start with the United States, the Commerce Department officially tallies about 3,800 multinationals (defined as firms with FDI in at least one country) in 2012, which represents slightly more than 0.01 percent of the thirty million firms baseline cited earlier.[6] National borders clearly massively constrain investment patterns: more so, for instance, than industry boundaries. Thus, there are many more establishments in the United States that operate in five-plus product markets, and, obviously, the horizontal diversification level of multiplant enterprises is even higher. By implication, many more US firms have diversified horizontally across industries than have internationally, which makes internationalization constraints more rather than less interesting, as discussed further in Chapter 7.

As in the case of exports, US firms lag in terms of the proportion that participate in FDI. Thus, Denmark, less than one-fiftieth the size of the United States, reports significantly more multinationals – more than any other country in fact (UNCTAD 2009)! Consistent with the market-level analysis in Chapter 2 indicating that smaller and wealthier countries are more deeply internationalized, such countries also tend to be home to more multinationals. If multinational headquarters intensity is measured as the ratio of the number of multinationals from a country to its GDP, a 1 percent increase in GDP (economy size) is associated with a 0.4 percent decrease in multinational headquarters intensity, while a 1 percent increase in GDP per capita (level of economic development) is associated with a 0.8 percent increase in multinational headquarters intensity.[7]

Overall, in 2014, there were between 80,000 and 100,000 multinational firms around the world,[8] or less than 0.1 percent of estimates of the total number of businesses around the world.[9] The number of multinationals had roughly doubled since 1990, in line with the expansion of the world economy.[10] Multinationals had been estimated to drive 80 percent of world trade as well as 75 percent of private sector R&D and 40 percent of productivity growth (Dobbs et al. 2015). Although around two-thirds (or more) of the world's multinationals were based in advanced economies, multinationals from emerging economies were increasingly in evidence, as described further in Chapter 11.

The world's multinational firms had approximately 890,000 foreign affiliates in 2014 (UNCTAD 2015, 146), which generated an estimated 10.2 percent of all value added around the world (i.e., produced 10.2 percent of world GDP), up from roughly 5 percent in the 1980s but down slightly from a peak of 11.0 percent in 2007, as shown in Figure 4.2. Foreign affiliates of multinationals also generated 33 percent of world exports of goods and services in 2014, and 3 percent of employees around the world worked for them (i.e., worked outside of the country where their employer was headquartered) (World Bank WDI 2013; UNCTAD 2015, 18; International Labour Organization (ILO)).[11] Total sales of foreign affiliates of multinationals were 54 percent larger than the world's *total* exports of goods and services, indicating that foreign affiliates comprise a significantly larger part of international business activity than exports (UNCTAD 2013, 18; World Bank WDI 2013). Refer to Figure 4.3 for country-by-country comparisons of foreign affiliates' share of value added and employment across a sample of OECD members.

Turning to the size distribution of multinationals, roughly one-third of US multinationals and two-thirds of UK multinationals in the 1980s and 1990s were small and medium enterprises (SMEs); however, across both countries,

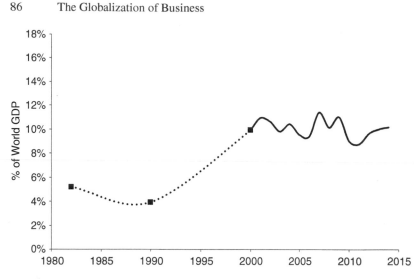

Figure 4.2 Value Added of Foreign Affiliates as Percentage of World GDP.
Notes: The 2011–2015 editions of the World Investment Report provide data
on the variable "Value-added (product) of foreign affiliates"; the 2001–2010
editions provide data on the variable "Gross product of foreign affiliates." For
each year, the value used is the one reported in the most recent edition. The
2006 value refers to the 2005–2007 "precrisis" average.
Source: UNCTAD World Investment Report, Various Editions.

SMEs held less than 3 percent of foreign assets (UNCTAD and Fujita 1993;
Buckley 1997). So FDI is much more skewed in value terms toward larger
firms than exports (refer back to Figure 4.1 for data on exports).

The limited globalization of SMEs reflects constraints such as lack of familiarity
with foreign markets and fixed costs associated with exploring and developing
them. The function-by-function material that follows illustrates some of the
practical challenges that underpin some of these fixed costs. Still, many SMEs do
express great enthusiasm for globalization and some – particularly those serving
a "deep niche" across countries via strong technical capabilities and selling to
other firms rather than to end consumers – have achieved significant international
success (Kohn 1997). And digital optimists have claimed that digitization might
increase the number of companies that export as much as sixfold (DMCC 2016).

The idea of deep technical depth also hints at an additional correlation – not
involving direct causality – between size and globalization: firms that are more
productive, broadly defined, are more likely to grow large as well as to engage
in international activity. In fact, a series of intraindustry models predicts that
only the more productive firms will engage in international activity and of
those, only the most productive will engage in FDI, with the remainder settling
for exports and the least productive firms staying at home (Helpman, Melitz,

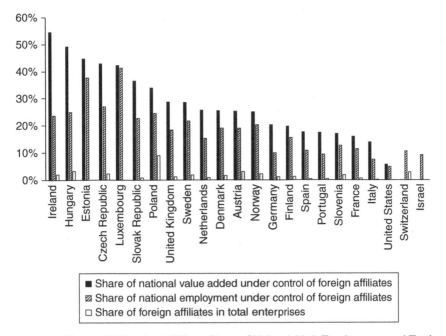

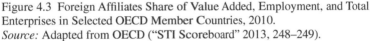

Figure 4.3 Foreign Affiliates Share of Value Added, Employment, and Total Enterprises in Selected OECD Member Countries, 2010.
Source: Adapted from OECD ("STI Scoreboard" 2013, 248–249).

and Yeaple 2004). And even ones that stay at home may face shutdown threats as a result of increases in globalization (Sutton 2012): competition can internationalize even if a firm itself doesn't.

While large firms are more international than SMEs, even the world's largest firms by revenue generate the majority of their sales in their home countries. In 2013, the average firm in the 2014 Fortune Global 500 (among those reporting such data) earned 54 percent of its revenue in its home country and 65 percent of its revenue within its home "broad triad" region. Only 11 percent of these firms generated at least 20 percent of their sales – whether through trade or FDI – in each of the three "broad triad" regions.[12] While these results do indicate a higher proportion of "global" firms than were found in Rugman and Verbeke (2004) and in updates to that study – as discussed in Chapter 10 – they still affirm the limited globalization of the world's largest firms by revenue. And even among firms with highly globalized sales, home bias – the shadow of border effects – may be manifest along other dimensions. Thus, BMW has a dispersed sales footprint across regions,[13] but, as illustrated in Figure 4.4, it still concentrates its production and workforce at home in Germany.

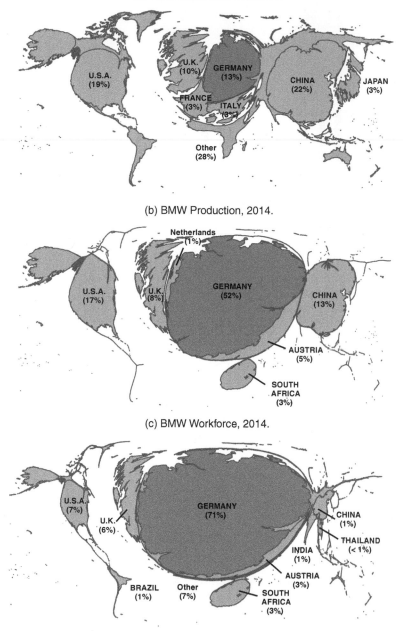

(a) BMW Sales (Volume), 2014.

U.K. (10%)
GERMANY (13%)
U.S.A. (19%)
CHINA (22%)
JAPAN (3%)
FRANCE (3%)
ITALY (3%)
Other (28%)

(b) BMW Production, 2014.

Netherlands (1%)
GERMANY (52%)
U.S.A. (17%)
U.K. (8%)
CHINA (13%)
AUSTRIA (5%)
SOUTH AFRICA (3%)

(c) BMW Workforce, 2014.

U.S.A. (7%)
GERMANY (71%)
U.K. (6%)
CHINA (1%)
THAILAND (< 1%)
INDIA (1%)
AUSTRIA (3%)
BRAZIL (1%)
Other (7%)
SOUTH AFRICA (3%)

Figure 4.4 Rooted Maps of BMW Sales, Production, and Workforce, 2014. *Sources:* Based on sales data from BMW 2014 Annual Report, production data from OICA, and workforce data from BMW Sustainable Value Report 2014.

To summarize this section, the relative sparsity of trading firms and, especially, multinationals suggests that international interactions with buyers and suppliers are less intense than domestic interactions from the perspective of the overwhelming majority of firms. And the discussion of how firms that take part in international trade and FDI tend to be dominated – in value terms – by very large firms sets the stage for the sections that follow that look at multinationals, mostly very large ones, to ascertain to what extent doing business across national borders presents different functional challenges and elicits different responses than a single-country context might.

Marketing

Marketing is the function that brings firms into contact with local customers, distribution channels, media environments, and so on, often forcing substantial adaptation to respond to cross-country differences. There is a great deal of evidence that even experienced exporters often underadapt to foreign markets (Dow 2006). What is more controversial is how much large global companies – which typically engage in FDI as well as exports, cluster in marketing-intensive sectors, and leverage intangible assets such as brands (Caves 1971) – need to adapt their marketing strategies.

The 1980s saw a surge of interest in Theodore Levitt's assertion that customers everywhere want the same thing, permitting ever-increasing levels of standardization (Levitt 1983). This is a view that most marketing academics have abandoned in the face of evidence accumulated over subsequent decades.[14] So have many marketing professionals. Thus, Sir Martin Sorrell, CEO of WPP, the world's largest marketing services company, estimated in 2013 that "no more than 15 percent of the business we do at WPP is truly global – if by global you mean that we use the same marketing methods throughout the world" (quoted in Ghemawat, Altman, and Strauss, 7). Consider some illustrations related to the "4Ps" of marketing (and refer to Table 4.1 for one pair of marketing experts' comparison of levels of internationalization across elements of the marketing mix):

> **Products.** Survey research indicates that cultural distance strongly affects product acceptance in foreign markets, leading to extensive product adaptation requirements (Powers and Loyka 2010). According to a recent literature review, firms tend to standardize product design, quality, and features more than other parts of the marketing mix, but often suffer performance penalties as a result (Steenkamp 2015). Significant competitive advantages of the sort the Apple iPad or Coke Classic possess can mitigate the need for local product variation but usually fail to eliminate it: the iPad's

Table 4.1 *Planning Grid for Marketing Decisions*

Marketing Mix Elements	Global ● ◕ ◑ ◔ ○ Local
Product Design	●
Brand Name	●
Product Positioning	●
Packaging	◑
Advertising Theme	◕
Pricing	◕
Advertising Copy	○
Distribution	◕
Sales Promotion	○
Customer Service	◔

Source: Quelch and Jocz (2012, 185).

software interface and Coke Classic's sweetness vary around the world. Variation is even more evident when one looks at Coke's overall product portfolio. In Japan – its second most profitable market (Hill, Jones, and Schilling 2014, 267) – cola is only a small part of total sales: Coke offers more than 200 products there, many of them unique to the country (Ghemawat 2007, chapter 1).

Price. A few multinationals target the same relative positioning everywhere, but actual price levels tend to vary across markets, and decisions about them to be decentralized (Bradley 2005, chapter 1). Thus, despite being an iconic offering from a multinational known for its appetite for standardization, McDonalds' Big Mac is priced very differently around the world – so much so that it is used (lightheartedly) by *The Economist* as a basis for estimating

effective currency under- or overvaluation ("The Big Mac Index").[15]
The pressures – and room – to vary prices have been reduced by
increased integration within some regions (e.g., Europe) but have
been greatly increased by the attention many multinationals are
paying to emerging markets – which differ more from developed
markets than the latter do from each other, as elaborated in Chapter
11 (and so create greater pressures to vary all 4Ps).

Promotion. Whether to use the same global brand around the world
is still controversial. Some experts recommend doing so – except
in case of obvious contraindications such as harmful local connota-
tions or local unpronounceability – on the grounds that branding
is the biggest source of leverage afforded by global as opposed to
local marketing (Steenkamp 2015). Leverage from global branding is limited, however, by the limited globalization of most
brands themselves and evidence that effective promotions are often
location-specific. Thus, data on 10,000 top brands in 31 countries
compiled by market research firm Millward Brown indicate that
only 16 percent of the brands studied are, roughly, among the top
15 by sales in their categories in more than one country, and only
3 percent in more than seven countries (Hollis 2008, 50).[16] The
same study also finds that the top performing advertisements in one
country seldom perform as well in others and sometimes perform
much worse, and concludes that "while using the same ad cam-
paign across borders may offer cost efficiencies, the savings real-
ized may not outweigh the benefit offered by local engagement"
(Hollis 2009, 2). The placement of advertisements in media channels is even more localized than the advertising content itself, with
one senior executive estimating that 99 percent of media spending
is executed locally because of the importance of local knowledge
in ensuring advertisements reach their target audiences.[17] In light of
these limitations, many global marketers now place more emphasis
on standardizing taglines and images to achieve global consistency
and scalability for a firm's best creative ideas while leaving room
for adaptation. For example, advertisements might feature voice-
over rather than actors speaking to facilitate more efficient script
adaptation and language translation.

Place. While examples already cited such as iPads and Big Macs pertain to consumer products subject to pull strategies, differences in
distribution structures loom (even) larger in business-to-business
marketing. Even when distribution structures are the same, channels typically have to be set up country by country – and according to one study, most of the relationships established at the time

of market entry, especially into emerging markets, eventually fail (Arnold 2000). In developed markets, channels are supposed to be relatively short, efficient, and involve a few large distributors versus the opposite in emerging markets (Steenkamp 2015). Distribution decisions tend, like pricing, to be very decentralized (Bradley 2005, chapter 1).

Business-to-business marketing to large, multinational accounts *does* increasingly involve global or regional account management in which inter- actions with multinational customers are coordinated and partially standard- ized (Bink and Yip 2007). Also, many multinationals discourage national subsidiaries from reinventing the wheel and encourage them, instead, to adopt and adapt marketing programs that have succeeded elsewhere – part of the ongoing quest to achieve some degree of aggregation or cross-border economies of scale. But overall, the global marketing discussion has shifted from competing the same way everywhere to careful consideration of which countries to compete in and how much to coordinate across them, with some asserting that marketing is, overall, the least centralized of major functional areas (Bradley 2005).

Operations

On the supply side rather than the demand side, firms that operate across national borders disaggregate their value adding activities across multiple countries to try to perform them in the most advantageous locations. Such multicountry supply chains may involve arm's length trade, foreign direct investment, or, in between those extremes, a variety of contractual modes. And these diverse modes of coordination have been facilitated by the deployment of information technology (IT) that enables the extensive use of e-tenders, elec- tronic data interchange, and other digital coordination mechanisms and makes the offshoring of some services and manufacturing activities possible. Thomas Friedman's *The World Is Flat* (2005) can be read as an IT-inspired paean to the increasing interest in the 2000s in the globalization of supply chains as opposed to the globalization of markets.

Data help put some of these possibilities in perspective. In terms of moti- vations for globalization, establishing foreign production facilities to produce closer to foreign markets seems to dominate production overseas (typically at lower cost) for export back to home, at least for US multinationals. In 2009, 61 percent of sales of foreign affiliates of US multinationals were to customers in the country where the affiliate was located, 30 percent were to customers in other foreign countries, and only 9 percent were to customers in the United States (Barefoot and Mataloni 2011). In terms of the mode of international coordination, aggregate estimates indicate that in 2010, of the nearly 80 percent of trade that took place within global value chains orchestrated by multinational firms, 42 percent was within multinational firms themselves, 16 percent within their networks of contract manufacturing partners, licensees, franchisees, and so on, and 42 percent was through multinationals trading on an arms-length basis with other multinationals or with domestic firms (UNCTAD 2013). A survey of (large) companies in advanced economies supplies a similar characterization, finding that about one-third of their manufacturing capacity is in their home countries, one-third under the control of their foreign affiliates, and one-third managed by external partners (Geissbauer and D'heur 2010, 9). Of course, for some companies such as Cisco, the percentage of production outsourced – mostly to low-cost offshore locations – exceeds 90 percent (Harrington and O'Connor 2009). But so far, estimates that a quarter of all US jobs might eventually be offshoreable turn out to be an order of magnitude higher than rough estimates of actual levels of offshoring (Otterman 2004; Blinder 2009).

Of course, even high levels of offshoring do not necessarily imply standardization. As firms move their production into new countries, they often find it advantageous to vary their production methods to reflect differences in cost structures. In countries with lower labor costs, for example, using more labor-intensive methods can reduce cost and increase flexibility. Production methods also vary across locations due to differences in environmental regulations, availability of natural resource and other inputs, proximity to suppliers and its implications for inventory management, and so on. Such variation must, of course, be weighed against its implications for cross-country economies of scale. Even if varying a production process might maximize local efficiency, higher engineering costs, missed opportunities for bulk purchasing of inputs, lost interchangeability of components, and greater operational complexity could overshadow that advantage.

In fact, since 2010, analysts had begun to suggest that the shift of manufacturing operations to emerging economies in pursuit of labor cost savings – particularly Western multinationals moving production to Asia – had run its course and that firms might even begin to shorten their production chains, bringing operations back home or to countries closer to home. This perspective reflected multiple concerns about far-flung supply networks, such as rising labor costs in China (which had become the default destination for much labor-intensive assembly), worries about transporting goods over long distances due to energy prices and concerns about climate change, supply chain vulnerabilities exposed by the 2011 earthquake and tsunami in Japan, protectionist rumblings during the economic crisis, and so on. Technology also played a role in such prognostications. Fracking had boosted US competitiveness, particularly in energy-intensive sectors, and automation and 3D printing might lead to more localized manufacturing, although large improvements in the costs of the new technologies were generally thought to be required for this to happen.

Given uncertainty about these trends, it is also useful to look at data on recent developments. The Boston Consulting Group (BCG) estimated in 2014 that China already had higher average manufacturing costs than Mexico and that its cost advantage vis-à-vis the United States had narrowed significantly (Sirkin, Zinser, and Rose 2014). And a BCG survey in 2013 indicated that a majority of executives of large US manufacturing companies were planning or actively considering shifting back production from China (BCG 2013). However, aggregate data on the ratio of US manufacturing imports to US domestic manufacturing value added did not – at least through 2013 – provide evidence of large-scale reshoring back to the United States.[18]

Beyond simple debates about shifting more production offshore or back closer to home, practitioners have begun to rediscover academic experts' advocacy of tiered supply chains that mix local and offshored production to achieve not just efficiencies but agility and adaptability as well – of particular importance under conditions of product proliferation and shortening product life cycles (Lee 2004). Another important theme involves shifting from focusing on physical flows of products to also looking at virtual flows of information, or so-called hybrid supply chains, in recognition of increasing information and intangible asset-intensity. And when one superimposes these developments on the multiple dimensions of choice mentioned at the beginning of this section – and on the shift by firms beyond focusing on arbitrage (e.g., mining minerals and exporting them without additional processing) to embracing strategies that involve more adaptation to local differences and aggregation in the pursuit of international economies of scale, the picture that emerges is a variegated one that requires sophisticated decision making by multinationals rather than either finding one best place to produce for the world or building single-country supply chains. Thus, according to McKinsey, "building the supply chain of the future ... means ditching today's monolithic model in favor of splintered supply chains that dismantle complexity, and using manufacturing networks to hedge uncertainty" (Malik, Niemeyer, and Ruwadi 2011, 62).

Research and Development

R&D is like marketing in being key to the creation of intangible assets that help propel firms across borders and resembles operations in terms of presenting trade-offs between concentration of activities in a few locations to achieve scale economies versus dispersion to tap into distinct local capabilities. R&D decisions are also swayed, however, by the concentration of most R&D in a small number of countries – 31 percent in the United States in 2013, 22 percent

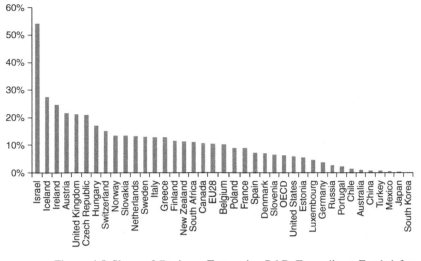

Figure 4.5 Share of Business Enterprise R&D Expenditure Funded from Abroad, 2013.
Source: Adapted from OECD Main Science and Technology Indicators (2015, 81).

in Europe, 18 percent in China, and 10 percent in Japan (Grueber and Studt 2013) – as well as the issues related to intellectual property rights that are discussed later in this section.

Despite stagnation in overall R&D intensity, recent years have seen an increasing emphasis by firms on performing R&D abroad and a broadening of its scope beyond the traditional focus on adapting technologies developed at home to foreign markets. A simple average across seventeen OECD countries indicates a significant increase in the share of business R&D financed from abroad, from 4.3 percent in 1985 to 10.4 percent in 2005 – and similar changes in the share of locally invented patents assigned to foreign firms (Thomson 2013) – but only a very limited further increase in R&D financed from abroad, up to 10.6 percent, by 2011.[19] (Refer to Figure 4.5 for a comparison of the share of business R&D expenditures funded from abroad across a set of OECD countries.)

Very large and R&D-intensive firms do tend to exceed these averages, and by an apparently widening margin. For instance, a survey of 209 R&D-intensive multinationals indicated that in 2001, 33 percent of spending for West European companies, 32 percent for North American ones, and 11 percent for Japanese ones occurred outside their home countries/regions, implying an average of 22 percent (Edler, Meyer-Krahmer, and Reger 2002).[20] For such companies, internationalization levels seem to have increased significantly since then.

According to a survey by Booz & Company, 184 R&D-intensive multinationals spent 55 percent of their R&D budgets outside of their home countries in 2007 (Jaruzelski and Dehoff 2008). A follow-up by PwC Strategy& of 207 such companies indicates a further increase by 2014, to 60 percent (Jaruzelski, Schwartz, and Staack 2015).

The internationalization of R&D activities opens up room for divergence between its origin (where the company commissioning it is from) and its destination (where R&D is actually conducted). The same PwC Strategy& study of 207 R&D-intensive companies indicates that North American and European firms remain the largest corporate R&D spenders, accounting for 45 percent and 30 percent of total expenditures, respectively, compared to 25 percent for the Asian firms in the sample; however, Asia has surpassed them as a destination, accounting for 35 percent of total expenditures, versus 33 percent for North America and 28 percent for Europe (which was the number one destination in 2007).

Asia's rise mainly reflects large-scale growth in R&D spending by foreign firms, especially in China and India, whereas Europe's decline is driven by decreasing spending there by European *and* non-European firms combined with strong European R&D spending in other parts of the world (Jaruzelski et al. 2015). As a result, Asia is the only region in which, based on PwC Strategy&'s sample, corporate R&D originating outside the region has come to exceed 50 percent of the total (Jaruzelski et al. 2015). And Asia is also the key driver of the increasing share of R&D being conducted in emerging economies, although it is worth noting differences in the types of R&D activities undertaken there. Thus, Chinese R&D is much more heavily weighted toward product and service development and away from basic and applied research than is the case for United States and Europe (Grueber and Studt 2013).

The rapid growth of R&D expenditures in China – estimated at 18 percent annually in real terms between 2001 and 2011 (National Science Board 2014) – has led one source to project that China will (on a PPP basis) overtake the United States as the world's largest R&D spender by 2019 (OECD 2014). In fact, in terms of the number of patent applications, China already surpassed the United States in 2011, but it still lags the United States in terms of total *patent* grants, particularly grants overseas, presumably due to quality shortcomings, and the same broad pattern applies to other emerging economies: their share of patent grants is significantly lower than their share of patent applications (Alcacer, Beukel, and Cassiman 2015). That said, there are some significant differences even among emerging economies: in India, most applicants were foreign firms, unlike in China, and a significantly greater proportion of Indian innovations were applied overseas.

The shifts toward Asia and toward emerging economies both appear to reflect the effects of proximity to large markets. According to a 2015 PwC Strategy& survey of 369 senior R&D executives and innovation leaders, the most important advantages of moving R&D functions to China comprised proximity to high-growth markets (71 percent), to key manufacturing sites (59 percent), and to key suppliers (54 percent), followed by lower development costs (53 percent), and other cost-related reasons (Jaruzelski et al. 2015).

Nonetheless, firms' R&D expenditures continue to be biased toward their home countries. Thus, one study focused on patent application data for 156 large, R&D-intensive firms between 1995 and 2002 and found that firms in the UK and United States conducted three to four times as much R&D at home as they would if they located R&D "freely in accordance with countries' attractiveness," versus more than twenty times as much for Japanese firms and with the larger continental European countries covered falling somewhere in between (Belderbos, Leten, and Suzuki 2013, 771).[21] Increased globalization of R&D has somewhat reduced these multiples, but calculations based on updated data from the same source for the sample of the world's top 2000 R&D investors during the period 2010–2012 indicate the continuation of high levels of home (regional) bias, with roughly 80 percent of patent applications being generated by inventors residing in the same region as where the companies being considered are headquartered (European Union 2015, 80).[22]

Belderbos et al. (2013) also conclude that home bias is higher when home countries offer relatively strong protection in terms of intellectual property rights. Alcacer et al. elaborate on some problems firms face in enforcing their intellectual property (IP) rights:

IP protection remains fragmented and it is very costly to develop a comprehensive IP footprint worldwide. Furthermore, larger numbers of applications are causing backlogs and delays in numerous Patent and Trademarks Offices; as a consequence, weaker patents and industrial designs are granted. Litigation over the validity and violation of IP rights has also become expensive, and its outcome uncertain. Suits and counter-suits among different players in the value chain across countries are more common due to weaker patents, a hyper-fragmented IP space, and the costs of patenting globally. (Alcacer et al. 2015, 2)

Alcacer et al. also point to a range of approaches, beyond formal IP tools such as patenting, that firms use to try to capture value from their IP: market-mechanisms such as versioning/lead times, complexity (making an innovation more difficult to copy), secrecy, and sales/licensing, as well as public initiatives such as policy advocacy and participation in standard setting organizations and patent pools. And they note that firms often use these multiple mechanisms in combination.

Finance

Firms from different home countries adopt different mixes of equity and debt financing. Equity finance is especially important in economies such as the United States and the UK, whereas banks play a greater role in others such as Japan and Germany. These differences, as well as the institutional factors that underpin them, are described further in Chapter 9. Financing practices in emerging economies also tend to differ from those in advanced economies due to the former's generally weaker regulations, transparency, accountability, and internal governance practices (Hrnjic, Reeb, and Yeung 2015).

To turn to the extent to which firms tap *foreign* sources of capital and look first at equity, listings by foreign companies accounted for just 6 percent of total stock market listings in mid-2015 as well as 6 percent of the actual value of shares traded through electronic order books through the first half of that year (WFE 2015). And even for companies listed on exchanges in more than one country, the home country or region continues to dominate equity financing. Thus, although Deutsche Bank is listed in Frankfurt and New York, at the end of 2014, 57 percent of its shares were held by shareholders in Germany (up sharply over the previous two years), 21 percent in other EU countries, and only 13 percent in the United States (Deutsche Bank 2014, 39). However, there *is* a significant difference between firms from advanced versus emerging economies, with one study indicating that between 1991 and 2009, the former raised only 9 percent of their equity abroad on a yearly basis as compared to 32 percent for the latter (Ceballos, Didier, and Schmukler 2010).[23]

Debt financing is more globalized, overall, than equity financing. Over the same period from 1991 to 2009, firms raised about one-third of their debt capital internationally. Again, there was substantial variation based on countries' levels of economic development. Firms from advanced economies raised 32 percent of their debt capital abroad, as compared to 42 percent by firms from emerging economies (Ceballos et al. 2010).

The efforts by firms from emerging economies, in particular, to raise capital abroad as well as the importance of financial centers suggest significant efforts to arbitrage cross-border differences. But they fall far short of implying fully integrated internal capital markets within firms given the reliance – across debt and equity – on domestic sources for 61 percent of financing (Ceballos et al. 2010). And while larger firms are significantly more internationalized in this respect – 10 percent of the firms that tap foreign capital markets collect about two-thirds of the funds raised internationally (Gozzi, Levine, and Schmukler 2010) – the example of Deutsche Bank suggests that it would be a mistake to treat individual multinationals as integrated pools of capital. So does the fact that US firms are holding trillions of dollars offshore to mitigate high domestic tax rates – behavior that is discussed further in the next section. The practical implications, as summarized by one researcher are:

In managing their internal markets to create a competitive advantage, finance executives must delicately balance the financial opportunities they offer with the strategic opportunities and challenges presented by operating in multiple institutional environments, each of which has its own legal regime and political risks…A global finance function must do three things well: Establish the appropriate geographic locus of decision making… at a geographic level where other strategic decisions are made … create a professional finance staff that rotates globally … [and] codify priorities and practices that can be adapted to local conditions. (Desai 2008, 110)

Accounting

Accounting also varies greatly across countries, mainly, like finance, because of institutional differences. Briefly, governance in Anglo-Saxon countries, which is based on common law and focused on shareholders, emphasizes public disclosure because dispersed owners tend to lack direct access to management. In Continental Europe, in contrast, governance is based on civil law and focused on stakeholders – who have direct access to management – and so does not rely as much on public disclosure. Asian governance typically fuses civil law with some type of group structure and therefore more closely resembles Continental governance. As a result, share prices are more responsive to public earnings reports in Anglo-Saxon countries than in Continental Europe or East Asia, where reserves tend to be used to smooth out payouts to major stakeholders over time (Ball, Kothari, and Robin 2000).

The trend toward adoption of International Financial Reporting Standards (IFRS) is expected to force more similarity on these accounting traditions. More than 120 jurisdictions, including all members of the European Union, have either entirely adopted or incorporated aspects of IFRS into their financial reporting. However, the United States and China are still to adopt IFRS. US Generally Accepted Accounting Principles (GAAP) are converging with IFRS standards, but only about 500 publicly traded firms in the United States currently apply the latter (Danjou 2015). Similarly, China, instead of abandoning its accounting standards, has been eliminating those that lead to accounting treatments incompatible with IFRS – and, in regard to related party transactions between state owned enterprises (which still dominate Chinese business), has secured modifications to IFRS to conform to Chinese standards, which are much less stringent (Hinks 2012; Selling 2013, 155). Other key jurisdictions that neither oblige nor restrict the use of IFRS are Japan, India, Switzerland, Bermuda, and Cayman Islands. Overall, 52 percent of the Fortune Global 500 use IFRS as of 2014, followed by US GAAP with 29 percent of the total (Danjou 2015).

IFRS, while influenced by the Anglo-Saxon tradition, is rooted more in principles and less in prescriptive rules than US (and Chinese) GAAP. Extra discretion presumably widens the scope of operation of the general inference that accounting quality is determined by the incentives that firms have to provide high-quality financial statements as well as by the accounting standards themselves – a pattern that is evident when one looks, for instance, at the quality of the financial statements put out by Chinese privately owned companies versus state-owned companies, or by Chinese companies that seek to raise money on equity markets versus ones that don't (Lee, Walker, and Zeng 2014).

Such considerations lead one review to conclude that even "complete" adoption of IFRS *won't* produce uniform financial reporting: "most market and political forces will remain local for the foreseeable future so...there inevitably will be substantial differences among countries in implementation of IFRS, which now risk being concealed by a veneer of uniformity" (Ball 2006, 5). This suggests perpetuation of the current situation, in which accounting mostly occurs on a country-by-country basis – even when global clients rely on global accounting firms (who, ironically, are barred from being auditors in China) – and financial statements aren't strictly comparable across countries.

Tax accounting merits separate comment because it is quite distinct from financial accounting: in the United States, tax law is formally separate from the GAAP used to prepare public financial statements. While firms everywhere engage in tax planning, multinationals face an expanded array of options, associated with differences in corporate income tax rates around the world. And despite the steady decline in corporate income tax rates in OECD countries, for example, from an average level close to 50 percent in the early 1980s to a band centered on 20–30 percent in the 2010s, multinationals are judged to be increasing profit-shifting from high tax to low tax jurisdictions (OECD 2011; Economist 2013). Note that rising intangibility facilitates profit-shifting because it allows, for instance, tax planning that vests ownership of intangible assets in low-tax countries to which subsidiaries in countries where the final sales take place pay royalties.

Taxing multinationals has attracted additional attention in the wake of the global financial crisis thanks to the heightened fiscal pressures faced by governments coupled with aggressive tax-avoidance by high-profile multinationals: shifting profits out of particular high-tax jurisdictions (e.g., by Starbucks, Google, and Amazon out of the UK), holding huge amounts of cash overseas in order to avoid high corporate income tax rates, and even shifting corporate headquarters (e.g., tax-inversion through acquisition) to lower-tax jurisdictions. The latter two approaches were particularly favored by US firms facing the highest corporate income tax rates in the OECD – 39 percent.[24]

Several multilateral initiatives aim to deal with the issues raised by such cases, as well as to restrict the activities of offshore financial centers. Thus, the OECD launched an "Action Plan on Base Erosion and Profit Shifting" in 2013, at the request of the G20 finance ministers (OECD 2013). Fifteen specific action items were identified, and plans were announced to create a "multilateral instrument" to speed the process of updating bilateral tax treaties. Nonetheless, the centrality of taxation authority to countries' sovereign power and uneven support – the United States, home to many leading online firms, was apparently less supportive than many European countries – loomed as issues with this process as of 2015. Although this and other initiatives might somewhat tighten restrictions on firm behavior, they fall far short of targeting complete elimination of opportunities for tax arbitrage.

Organization

The organizational challenge most closely associated with multinationalization has been described as "designing systems that retain sufficient unity and coherence to operate as a common enterprise and, at the same time, to allow sufficient latitude and flexibility to adapt to greatly varying circumstances" across locations (Richard Scott, quoted in Westney and Zaheer 2009, 341). Multinationals address this challenge both in the design of their organizational structures as well as via the use of various mechanisms that facilitate coordination across separate organizational units. A variety of trends such as the growth of emerging economies, improvements in telecommunications and information technology, rising emphasis on innovation outside of firms' home countries, and greater collaboration with external partners all point toward firms attempting more complex and information-intensive organizational coordination than was the case when the focus was primarily on headquarters allocating resources among national subsidiaries and tracking their financial performance.

In the design of multinationals' organizational structures, the adoption of regional/area structures has long been a typical approach for firms with broad geographic footprints. Regional structures take advantage of the greater similarity among countries within as compared to between regions, as described in Chapter 10. Many multinationals, however, such as those with diverse product portfolios and broad geographic footprints, find the need to group organizational units based on multiple dimensions (e.g., by product group and by region). Thus, a survey indicates a shift among large multinationals toward matrix structures that attempt to coordinate along more than one dimension, as shown in Table 4.2.

A variant on the matrix is the front-back organization, studied by Galbraith (1993), in which a relatively decentralized front-end feeds off a back-end "platform" that is relatively centralized and coordinated. This can be thought of as an unbalanced matrix that puts products above geographies and is supposed to imply lower levels of management costs, lateral communications, and

Table 4.2 *Organization of Large Multinationals (Percent of Respondents)*

	2007	Late 1990s
Functional organization	24	42
Area organization	21	25
Product organization	16	18
Matrix organization	37	14
Other	1	1

Source: Pankaj Ghemawat and David J. Collis, Globalization Survey, 2007.

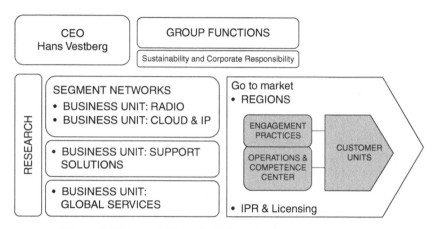

Figure 4.6 Ericsson's Front-Back Organization.
Source: Adapted from Ericsson (2015).

duality than the global matrix – but higher than the multidivisional organization (Kobashi and Konomi 2015). Ericsson's representation of itself, as illustrated in Figure 4.6, supplies an example.

The figure indicates that research is integrated at Ericsson but doesn't register that information technology is as well, as in the use of a single integrated IT network, perhaps because that is considered too obvious to mention. Also not evident in the figure is the global standardization of certain processes directly under group functions: sourcing, capital allocation, and core human resource policies. And then there is standardization from a production and marketing standpoint around global product platforms. So in Ericsson's case, most of the functional areas covered in this chapter embody significant, deliberate centralization. The big exception is the decentralized market-facing front-end, particularly the "Customer Units."

Ericsson supplies just one illustration of where the line between a centralized platform and a decentralized front-end might be drawn. In the 1990s, industries such as autos and home appliances put a great deal of effort into pushing that line forward by reducing the number of product platforms they relied on, that is, placed more emphasis on integrating product design and manufacturing. And more recently, there has been much interest in going all the way to market with IT platforms that enable rapid, asset-light globalization. Thus, LinkedIn (founded in 2002) ostensibly operates in 200 countries, Airbnb (2008) in 190, and Uber (2009) in 68.[25] The few conventional multinationals with such broad footprints have taken decades if not a century or longer to put them into place.

Of course, some of these would-be global platforms do face challenges from local competitors, especially in large markets and in categories in which network economies are largely national rather than global and where there are large cultural or administrative differences of the sort introduced and elaborated in the next few chapters. The extent to which "global" platforms manage, through the depths of their commitment to particular markets, to withstand local challengers remains to be seen Ghemawat (2016).

Even the relatively simple front-back structure and, *a fortiori*, the more complicated matrix structure are often difficult to implement and sometimes result in confusion and conflict as people and units struggle to juggle multiple bosses. The additional managerial overhead associated with multiple reporting dimensions can also add to costs. Furthermore, organizational redesigns themselves are expensive and disruptive. These and other limitations prompt multinationals to focus on strengthening their coordination capacity in ways that do not require the restructuring of formal reporting relationships. The cross-unit linking and networking mechanisms that organizations employ for this purpose are various, and vary over time, but some examples can be specified (note that mechanisms focused on the mix and capabilities of a firm's leadership team are reserved for the next section):

- Creating standing committees, centers of excellence, global virtual teams, task forces, and so on, that span geographic areas or other organizational units
- Developing a strong corporate culture to bridge national cultural differences
- Enforcing a company-wide common language policy to ease communication
- Rotating managers between countries (not just exporting them from headquarters)
- Holding key meetings outside of the home country
- Reserving spots at a "corporate university" for talent from outside the home country.

Information technology can also help improve connectivity among far-flung organizational units. However, online interactions tend to mirror offline relationships, which are most intense among people who are located close to each other. Thus, gaining the full benefits of information technology often requires using it in conjunction with some of the organizational linking mechanisms summarized here and the mobility initiatives described in the next section.

All this ferment, while encouraging, is also a reminder that neither practitioners nor researchers have yet figured out the optimal way to organize complex global companies – and that even the best such companies continue to face significant organizational challenges. Thus an analysis of public companies by McKinsey suggests that even high-performing global organizations lag "local champions" in areas such as establishing a shared vision, engaging employees around the world, maintaining professional standards, encouraging innovation of all kinds, and building relationships with governments, communities, and other businesses (Dewhurst, Harris, and Heywood 2011).

Leadership

Levels of internationalization of most firms' workforces are typically limited: as mentioned previously, only 3 percent of all employees are based outside their employer's home country, although this proportion does rise as high as 57 percent among the world's 100 largest (nonfinancial) firms ranked by foreign assets (UNCTAD 2014). But from the standpoint of strategy setting and organizational coordination, the globalization of a firm's leadership is more salient than the simple proportion of its workforce located abroad. Therefore, this section will focus on the globalization of firms' senior leadership – an individual-level measure of firm globalization – before turning to expatriation and other forms of workforce mobility, developing international competencies, and broader human resource policy.

The limited globalization of firms' leadership teams – both with respect to national origins and capabilities – appears to have emerged as a binding constraint on how well firms deal with their international opportunities. Thus, in terms of direct performance effects, a 2013 study reports that national diversity on the top management team "is among the few diversity attributes that help increase firm performance" and "the effects of international experience and functional diversity diminish over time, whereas the impact of nationality diversity becomes stronger" (Nielsen and Nielsen 2013, 378, 380). National diversity at the top can also have a positive signaling effect on a firm's ability to recruit and retain foreign talent. A much more extended treatment of the literature on this topic can be found in Ghemawat and Vantrappen (2015), who also present descriptive statistics based on hand-collected data about the extent to which the CEOs and the top management teams of the world's largest firms, the Fortune Global 500, are natives of the countries where those firms are headquartered. The data indicates a very large degrees of home bias overall: among the 2013 Fortune Global 500, 87 percent of firms were led by a native CEO and 85 percent of top management team members (direct reports to CEOs) were

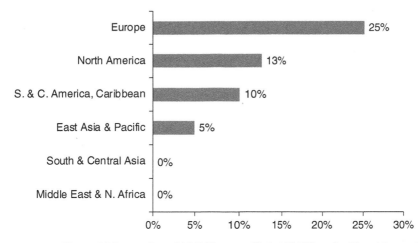

Figure 4.7 Proportion of 2013 Fortune Global 500 Firms Led by a Non-native CEO, by Region.
Source: Data compiled from firm websites by Pankaj Ghemawat and Herman Vantrappen. For additional details, refer to Ghemawat and Vantrappen (2015).

natives (and with the rest of the home region accounting for a disproportionate share of the non-natives).[26] The dearth of foreign talent at the top is even more severe when focusing on the subset of the Fortune Global 500 based in emerging economies: only 2 percent of those "emerging giants" were led by a non-native CEO, and the average top management team among those firms had only 3 percent non-native members. At the opposite end of the spectrum, the countries with the most multinationality at the top were small countries mainly in Europe: 71 percent of the Swiss firms on the Fortune Global 500 were led by a non-native CEO. Figures 4.7 and 4.8 provide region-wise comparisons of the prevalence of non-native CEOs and top management team members in the Fortune Global 500.

The proportion of non-native CEOs leading Fortune Global 500 companies has remained basically stable since 2008, decreasing from 14 percent to 13 percent, despite significant CEO turnover. But there appears to be an acculturation effect – once a company gets used to having a non-native CEO, it is much more likely to accept non-natives in the future. And firms led by a non-native CEO tend to have far more diverse top management teams, with 45 percent non-native members as compared to only 11 percent among firms led by native CEOs. A closer examination of the data on non-native CEOs also indicates a high positive correlation between the probability of a large multinational nominating a non-native CEO and its overall level of internationalization, as measured based on the foreign share of firms' sales, assets, and

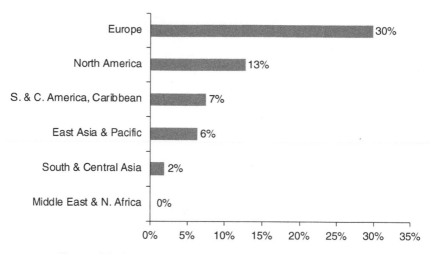

Figure 4.8 Average Non-native Proportion of Top Management Team Members in 2013 Fortune Global 500 Firms, by Region.
Source: Data compiled from firm websites by Pankaj Ghemawat and Herman Vantrappen. For additional details, refer to Ghemawat and Vantrappen (2015).

employees.[27] Firms from more deeply globalized countries on the *DHL Global Connectedness Index* are also more likely to be led by non-native CEOs.[28]

Expatriation is another avenue for companies to transfer knowledge and relationships across borders. However, there are indications that companies are reducing their reliance on expatriates to save money (expatriates typically cost 2–3 times as much as locals) and to improve localization. According to one study, the proportion of expatriates in senior management roles in multinationals in China, India, Brazil, Russia, and the Middle East declined from 56 percent to 12 percent between the 1990s and the 2000s (Holstein 2008). Overall, data on a small sample of large companies suggest that the proportion of expatriates in large global companies is usually less than 1 percent of total employment – often only around 0.1 percent (Ghemawat and Vantrappen 2013).

There is also evidence that for US and European multinationals, expatriates still take longer, on average, to ascend the corporate ladder than managers who continue to work within their home countries, indicating a need for greater focus on integrating mobility programs with career paths and talent management strategies (Hamori and Koyuncu 2011). The pattern that even at leading international business schools, top multinationals still tend to recruit graduates only to work in their home countries – if they recruit non-natives at all – suggests that limited integration of mobility into career paths extends all the way back to firms' recruitment policies.

Firms do, however, appear to be embracing a wider range of mobility initiatives that extend beyond the traditional model of sending senior-level employees abroad on "expatriate packages." A 2010 survey projects both the number of employees on international assignments as well as the number of countries where the average firm sends its assignees to increase 50 percent by 2020 (PwC 2012). Some large companies distinguish among traditional expatriates, inpatriates, short-term assignees, international business travelers, and self-initiated assignees, and develop different career models for them. One cautionary note: while short-term international assignments can indeed be useful, research indicating that it takes at least three months to become immersed in a new location and appreciate how business works there suggests a need for some caution about what can be accomplished over very short time frames (Gail Naughton, as quoted in Bisoux 2007). In addition, cross-border virtual teams and other cross-unit linking arrangements discussed in the previous section can complement a firm's mobility initiatives.

Finally, experience alone is not sufficient for the development of global leadership capabilities.[29] So educational programs – particularly those that sensitize executives to cross-country differences and their business implications – are also essential and complementary to experiential learning. Nonetheless, cultural diversity training programs must be carefully designed to avoid potential pitfalls. A recent study shows that students who took a cultural psychology class increased their levels of cultural awareness but were also more prone to stereotyping than a control group.[30] Chapter 8 provides further discussion of national cultural differences and the implications for companies.

Conclusion

Relatively few firms – typically, larger ones – engage in international trade and even fewer, larger firms are the ones that tend to make foreign direct investments, that is, officially become "multinationals." And the international reach of most firms that are multinational is generally quite limited: for example, the modal number of foreign countries in which a US multinational operates is one, and the median number three. It is only among very large multinationals that one sees attempts to achieve significant levels of cross-border coordination. And even for these firms, footprints still tend to be centered on home countries or regions, as are workforces, and especially their senior leaders. This rootedness is one affirmation that the law of semiglobalization applies to companies as well as countries.

So is the observation that despite efforts at many companies to increase levels of cross-border coordination, their marketing, operations, accounting, and so on vary significantly across the countries where they operate. Multinationals seldom market in exactly the same way across countries, nor are operational tasks performed at one best place – or a few – around the world. While firms' R&D and financing may spread out across national borders, there is no free-flowing global pool of knowledge or capital that companies can take advantage of without accounting for cross-country differences and local idiosyncrasies. Multinational firms do generate consolidated global accounting results, but their subsidiaries still have to comply with the national accounting rules of the countries where they are located. Organizationally, multinationals are more complex than purely domestic firms and face substantial challenges in staffing up with people – especially leadership team members – who are equipped to understand the various contexts in which a firm operates and to create value across them.

Looking across all these functional areas, some strategic themes also stand out and can be summarized in terms of the adaptation, aggregation, and arbitrage (AAA) strategies briefly introduced in Chapter 3. Looking function by function suggests needs for cross-country variation that forces some adaptation on even the most "global" of companies in lieu of the pursuit of pure aggregation strategies designed to maximize cross-border economies of scale or scope. Present economic and political trends seem to be raising the salience of adaptation relative to aggregation, as proposed in Ghemawat (2011, 304) and emphasized by GE Chairman Jeff Immelt in a widely cited speech at NYU Stern's 2016 MBA Commencement (Immelt 2016).[31] And arbitrage strategies, while they continue to be practiced, seem the object of much less excitement than when I first began writing about them in the mid-2000s (Ghemawat 2003). Further discussion of these AAA strategies will be deferred until Chapter 6, after the second law of globalization has been introduced and elaborated.

This chapter concludes Part I, in which we have seen how the law of semi-globalization applies to markets and to firms. Home bias applies at both levels, and has persisted over time: international interactions and cross-border coordination continue to be much more limited than the levels we would expect to see if national borders didn't matter. In Part II, we shift focus to the cross-border interactions that do take place, border effects notwithstanding, and examine how they are shaped by the law of distance.

Notes

1 For a review of the role of multinationals in shaping international economic integration, refer to Acs and McCann (2011).

2 The six functional areas (and the thought leaders involved) were global versus local marketing (Jan-Benedict Steenkamp); creating, managing, and protecting intellectual property (Juan Alcacer, Karin Beukel, and Bruno Cassiman); building government trust (David Beier and Edward Freeman); corporate culture and leadership (Sebastian Reiche), economic and financial management (Emir Hrnjic, David Reeb, and

Bernard Yeung); and global supply chains (Guilio Buciuni and Gary Pisano). All of the papers written for this project are available at the Center for Global Enterprise website (http://thecge.net).

3 For more information about configurative-idiographic studies, see Eckstein (1992).

4 This percentage would be closer to 5 percent if one focused on exporters as a percentage of all multiperson enterprises.

5 Analysis based on known trade value (the portion of US total trade that can be matched to specific companies). In 2013, there were 304,223 exporting companies and 184,208 importing companies, among which 83,199 companies both imported and exported.

6 Computations are based on Bureau of Economic Analysis data and were kindly carried out at the author's request by Jim Fetzer in fall 2014.

7 In a linear regression based on UNCTAD data on number of multinationals headquartered in different countries (UNCTAD 2009), both GDP and GDP per Capita were significant at the 0.01 level and those two variables alone explained nearly one-third of the variation in MNE headquarters intensity across the available sample of 121 countries.

8 UNCTAD (WIR 2015, 146) lists 100,000 multinational firms whereas Dobbs et al. (2015) reports 84,000 (defined as parent firms and excluding multinational corporations headquartered in low tax jurisdictions such as Ireland, Luxembourg, the Netherlands, and Hong Kong, and in Caribbean countries).

9 Dun & Bradstreet identifies 122 million active companies worldwide, out of the total 251.3 million companies available in their database, as of December 2015. This implies at least 100 million firms in the world. See Dun & Bradstreet (2015).

10 Dobbs et al. (2015) estimate that the number of multinationals reached 2.3 times its 1990 level in 2013. Global economic output in real terms was 2.3 times as large in 2013 as in 1990 at PPP and 1.8 times at market exchange rates, according to data from the IMF World Economic Outlook database (April 2015).

11 The global estimates of multinational activity presented in this paragraph are necessarily rough, and estimates from other sources do vary somewhat. The FDI Contribution Index published in UNCTAD's (2012) World Investment Report indicates that the contribution of foreign affiliates of multinationals to value added in 2009 was 12.7 percent in developed countries, 12.2 percent in developing economies, and 21.7 percent in transition economies. Across those same three categories, respectively, foreign affiliates' contributions to employment were 7.5 percent, 7.9 percent, and 3.0 percent, to wages and salaries 14.6 percent, 15.4 percent, and 11.2 percent, to R&D expenditures 24.2 percent, 24.1 percent, and 15.4 percent, and to capital expenditures 10.5 percent, 11.6 percent, and 25.7 percent.

12 Calculation based on data compiled from annual reports of the 2014 Fortune Global 500; 301 and 320 firms reported data on regional and international sales, respectively. The analysis discussed here and the definition of a "global" firm utilized are based on Rugman and Verbeke (2004).

13 Based on the criteria used in Rugman and Verbeke (2004), BMW is classified as "bi-regional" rather than "global" because its North American sales value falls short of the 20 percent threshold; however, based on sales volume (rather than value) mapped in Figure 4.4, BMW does appear to meet the criteria for "global" status.

14 For a generally unfavorable retrospective on Levitt's views, see Quelch and Deshpande (2004).

15 In its January 7, 2016 issue, *The Economist* described the Big Mac index as follows: "The Big Mac index is a lighthearted guide to whether currencies are at their 'correct' level. It is based on the theory of purchasing-power parity (PPP), the notion that global exchange rates should eventually adjust to make the price of identical baskets of tradable goods the same in each country. Our basket contains just one thing, a Big Mac hamburger."

16 Percentages cited in Hollis (2008) reflect the cutoff for inclusion in the BrandZ study that normally includes the top sixteen brands by category, roughly 70 percent of sales.

17 Interview by Pankaj Ghemawat of Adam Smith, futures director at WPP's media buying umbrella firm, GroupM, in 2012. For more, refer to Ghemawat et al. (2013).

18 World Bank's World Development Indicators data show that US manufacturing imports as a percent of US manufacturing value added rose from 79 percent in 2010 to 84 percent in 2011 and 86 percent in 2012–2013.

19 Note that the 1985 and 2005 data are from Thomson (2013), and the 2011 data from OECD ("STI Scoreboard" 2013).

20 The sample was skewed toward Japanese companies, which accounted for nearly half the responses to the survey on which these estimates are based.

21 For smaller European countries, the home bias multiples exceed the Japanese level, nearly reaching 100 times in the case of Finland.

22 Switzerland is, thanks to its global pharmaceutical companies (as well as not being part of the EU), the outlier, with only 25 percent of inventors located within the country. The proportions are higher for Japan (91 percent), the United States (78 percent), and the EU (74 percent).

23 The sample used in this analysis includes capital raising issues by firms in 153 countries: 291,842 debt issues, 100,919 equity issues, and 147,980 syndicated loans issues. Emerging economies in this context are those classified as all non-high-income economies (for consistency with material elsewhere in this book, rather than the classification employed in the original source).

24 Based on 2015 combined (central and subcentral government) corporate income tax rate data reported in Table II.2 of the OECD Tax Database. Accessed May 2016 at https://stats.oecd.org/Index.aspx?DataSetCode=TABLE_II1.

25 Data as reported on company websites as of March 2016.

26 In these calculations, no adjustments were made for corporate inversions or other changes of domicile that can increase the share of non-natives without actually changing a firm's leadership or operations. Thus, Accenture is treated as having a 100 percent non-native top management team after having shifted its place of incorporation to Ireland.

27 This is based on UNCTAD's Transnationality Index (TNI), which is calculated as the average of the following three ratios: foreign assets to total assets, foreign sales to total sales, and foreign employment to total employment. For a complete analysis, refer to Ghemawat and Vantrappen (2013).

28 National diversity on large firms' boards of directors also tends to be limited, as detailed in Ghemawat and Vantrappen (2015).

29 Online survey conducted by Harvard Business Review in 2007.

30 Buchtel (2014), cited in Reiche (2015). For a general critique of cross-cultural training research and practice, see Reiche, Lee, and Quintanilla (2014).

31 Immelt announced that GE would pivot to localization in response to rising anti-globalization and antibusiness sentiment as well as governmental dysfunction.

References

Acs, Zoltan J., and Philip McCann. 2011. "Globalization: Countries, Cities and Multinationals." *Regional Studies* 45 (1):17–32.

Alcacer, Juan, Karin Beukel, and Bruno Cassiman. 2015. "Capturing Value from IP in a Global Environment." Draft prepared for Workshop on Business Models for Speed and Scale, New York, April 2015.

Arnold, David. 2000. "Seven Rules of International Distribution." *Harvard Business Review* 78 (6):131–137.

Ball, Ray. 2006. "International Financial Reporting Standards (IFRS): Pros and Cons for Investors." *Accounting and Business Research* 36, Supplement 1 (Special Issue: International Accounting Policy Forum):5–27. doi: 10.1080/00014788.2006.9730040.

Ball, Ray, S. P. Kothari, and Ashok Robin. 2000. "The Effect of International Institutional Factors on Properties of Accounting Earnings." *Journal of Accounting and Economics*, February, 1–51.

Barefoot, Kevin B., and Raymond J. Mataloni, Jr. 2011. "Operations of U.S. Multinational Companies in the United States and Abroad: Preliminary Results from the 2009 Benchmark Survey." *Survey of Current Business* November:29–48. Bureau of Economic Analysis. www.bea.gov/scb/pdf/2011/11%20November/1111_mnc.pdf.

Belderbos, Rene, Bart Leten, and Shinya Suzuki. 2013. "How Global Is R&D? Firm-Level Determinants of Home-Country Bias in R&D." *Journal of International Business Studies* 44:765–786. doi: 10.1057/jibs.2013.33.

"The Big Mac Index: Global Exchange Rates, to Go." *The Economist*, Last Modified July 16, 2015. www.economist.com/content/big-mac-index.

Bink, Audrey J. M., and George S. Yip. 2007. "Managing Global Accounts." *Harvard Business Review* 85 (9):102–111.

Bisoux, Tricia. 2007. "Global Immersion." *BizEd* 6 (4):44–49. www.e-digitaleditions.com/i/58060-julyaugust2007/45.

Blinder, Alan S. 2009. "How Many US Jobs Might Be Offshorable?" *World Economics* 10 (2):41–78.

BMW. 2014. "Annual Report 2014." www.bmwgroup.com/bmwgroup_prod/e/0_0_www_bmwgroup_com/investor_relations/finanzberichte/bmw-group-geschaeftsbericht-2014.shtml.

——— 2014. "Sustainable Value Report 2014." www.bmwgroup.com/bmwgroup_prod/com/en/_common/_pdf/BMW_Group_SVR2014_EN.pdf.

Boston Consulting Group, The. "Majority of Large Manufacturers Are Now Planning or Considering 'Reshoring' from China to the U.S." Press Release, September 24, 2013. www.bcg.ch/media/PressReleaseDetails.aspx?id=tcm:85-144944.

Bradley, Frank. 2005. *International Marketing Strategy*. 5th ed. New York: Financial Times/Prentice Hall.

Buchtel, Emma E. 2014. "Cultural Sensitivity or Cultural Stereotyping? Positive and Negative Effects of a Cultural Psychology Class." *International Journal of Intercultural Relations* 39:40–52. doi: 10.1016/j.ijintrel.2013.09.003.

Buckley, Peter J. 1997. "International Technology Transfer by Small and Medium Sized Enterprises." *Small Business Economics* 9 (1):67–78. doi: 10.1023/A:1007912100301.

Caves, Richard E. 1971. "International Corporations: The Industrial Economics of Foreign Investment." *Economica* 38 (149):1–27. doi: 10.2307/2551748.

Ceballos, Francisco, Tatiana Didier, and Sergio L. Schmukler. "How Much Do Developing Economies Rely on Private Capital Markets?", July 2010. Working paper available at http://siteresources.worldbank.org/DEC/Resources/CDSUseofPrivateCapitalMarketsJul222010.pdf.

Danjou, Philippe. 2015. "L'extension Du Domaine… Des IFRS (the Extension of the Scope of IFRS)." *Finance & Gestion* (Mars/March):39–40. Available in French at: www.ifrs.org/Features/Documents/Philippe-Danjou-Extension-du-domaine-des-IFRS-February-2014.pdf; English version at: www.ifrs.org/Features/Documents/Philippe-Danjou-article-Extension-of-scope-of-IFRS-February-2014.pdf.

Desai, Mihir A. 2008. "The Finance Function in a Global Corporation." *Harvard Business Review* 86 (7/8):108–112.

Deutsche Bank. 2014. "Leveraging Strengths, Rising to the Challenges, Earning Trust: Annual Review 2014." https://annualreport.deutsche-bank.com/2014/ar/servicepages/downloads/files/dbfy2014_annual_review.pdf.

Dewhurst, Martin, Jonathan Harris, and Suzanne Heywood. 2011. "Understanding Your 'Globalization Penalty'." *McKinsey Quarterly* 2011 (3):12–15.

Dobbs, Richard, Tim Koller, Sree Ramaswamy, Jonathan Woetzel, James Manyika, Rohit Krishnan, and Nicoló Andreula. 2015. "Playing to Win: The New Global Competition for Corporate Profits." September. McKinsey Global Institute. www.mckinsey.com/insights/corporate_finance/the_new_global_competition_for_corporate_profits.

Dow, Douglas. 2006. "Adaptation and Performance in Foreign Markets: Evidence of Systematic Under-Adaptation." *Journal of International Business Studies* 37 (2):212–226. doi: 10.1057/palgrave.jibs.8400189.

Dubai Multi Commodities Centre (DMCC). 2016. "The Future of Trade." http://future-oftrade.ae/the-impact-of-digital.

Dun & Bradstreet. 2015. "Dun & Bradstreet's Data Quality." Accessed December 2015. www.dnb.com/company/our-data/data-quality-of-data-as-a-service.html.

Eckstein, Harry. 1992. "Configurative-Idiographic Study." In *Regarding Politics: Essays on Political Theory, Stability, and Change*, 136–138. Berkeley: University of California Press. Available at: http://publishing.cdlib.org/ucpressebooks/view?docId=ft0k40037v&chunk.id=d0e2728&toc.id=d0e2725&brand=ucpress.

Economist. 2013. "The Price Isn't Right." Economist. www.economist.com/news/special-report/21571557-corporate-profit-shifting-has-become-big-business-price-isnt-right.

Edler, Jakob, Frieder Meyer-Krahmer, and Guido Reger. 2002. "Changes in the Strategic Management of Technology: Results of a Global Benchmarking Study." *R&D Management* 32 (2):149–164. doi: 10.1111/1467–9310.00247.

Ericsson. 2015. "Company Facts." Accessed December 2015. www.ericsson.com/thecompany/company_facts.

European Union. 2015. "2015 EU Industrial R&D Investment Scoreboard." http://iri.jrc.ec.europa.eu/scoreboard15.html.

Eurostat. 2012. "International Trade by Enterprise Characteristics." Last Modified September 2012. Accessed 2010. http://ec.europa.eu/eurostat/statistics-explained/index.php/International_trade_by_enterprise_characteristics.

Friedman, Thomas L. 2005. *The World Is Flat: A Brief History of the Twenty-First Century*. New York: Farrar Straus and Giroux.

Galbraith, Jay R. 1993. "The Value Adding Corporation: Matching Structure with Strategy." In *Organizing for the Future: The New Logic for Managing Complex Organizations*, edited by Jay R. Galbraith, and Edward E. Lawler, 15–42. San Francisco: Jossey-Bass.

Geissbauer, Reinhard, and Michael D'heur. 2010. "2010–2012 Global Supply Chain Trends: Are Our Supply Chains Able to Support the Recovery?" June 2010. PRTM Management Consultants. www.consultancy.nl/media/PRTM%20Supply%20Chain%20Trends%202010-2012-1019.pdf.

Ghemawat, Pankaj. 2003. "The Forgotten Strategy." *Harvard Business Review* 81 (11):76–84.

2007. *Redefining Global Strategy: Crossing Borders in a World Where Differences Still Matter*. Boston, MA: Harvard Business School Press.

2011. *World 3.0: Global Prosperity and How to Achieve It*. Boston, MA: Harvard Business Review Press.

2016. "What Uber's China Deal Says About the Limits of Platforms," Harvard Business Review, August 10. https://hbr.org/2016/08/what-ubers-china-deal-says-about-the-limits-of-platforms.

Ghemawat, Pankaj, Steven A. Altman, and Robert Strauss. "WPP and the Globalization of Marketing Services." IESE Business School Case Study SM-1600-E, June 2013. www.ieseinsight.com/fichaMaterial.aspx?pk=104567&idi=2&origen=3&idioma=2.

Ghemawat, Pankaj, and Herman Vantrappen. 2013. "World's Biggest Companies: Still Xenophobic, after All These Years." *Fortune*, June 24, 2013. http://fortune.com/2013/06/24/worlds-biggest-companies-still-xenophobic-after-all-these-years/.

2015. "How Global Is Your C-Suite?" *MIT Sloan Management Review* 56 (4):73–82.

Gozzi, Juan Carlos, Ross Levine, and Sergio L. Schmukler. 2010. "Patterns of International Capital Raisings." *Journal of International Economics* 80 (1):45–57.

Grueber, Martin, and Tim Studt. "2014 Global R&D Funding Forecast." *R&D Magazine*, Battelle Memorial Institute, December 2013. www.battelle.org/docs/tpp/2014_global_rd_funding_forecast.pdf.

Hamori, Monika, and Burak Koyuncu. 2011. "Career Advancement in Large Organizations in Europe and the United States: Do International Assignments Add Value?" *International Journal of Human Resource Management* 22 (4):843–862. doi: 10.1080/09585192.2011.555128.

Harrington, Kevin, and John O'Connor. 2009. "How Cisco Succeeds at Global Risk Management." *Supply Chain Management Review*, July–August, 10–17.

Helpman, Elhanan, Marc J. Melitz, and Stephen R. Yeaple. 2004. "Export Versus FDI with Heterogeneous Firms." *American Economic Review* 94 (1):300–316. doi: 10.1257/000282804322970814.

Hill, Charles W. L., Gareth R. Jones, and Melissa A. Schilling. 2014. *Strategic Management: An Integrated Approach*. 11th ed. Stamford, CT: Cengage Learning.

Hinks, Gavin. 2012. "IFRS: Where Next for Global Convergence?" *Financial Management* (March):32–34. Chartered Institute of Management Accountants (CIMA). www.fm-magazine.com/assets/pdf/FM_April%202012.pdf.

Hollis, Nigel. 2008. *The Global Brand: How to Create and Develop Lasting Brand Value in the World Market*. New York: Palgrave Macmillan.

"Culture Clash: Globalization Does Not Imply Homogenization." Millward Brown's POV, May 2009. www.millwardbrown.com/docs/default-source/insight-documents/points-of-view/MillwardBrown_POV_CultureClash.pdf.

Holstein, William J. 2008. "The Decline of the Expat Executive." *strategy+business*. (Originally published by Booz & Company). www.strategy-business.com/article/li00086?pg=all.

Hrnjic, Emir, David M. Reeb, and Bernard Yeung. "Styles of Financial Management." Draft prepared for Workshop on Business Models for Speed and Scale, Center for Globalization of Education and Management (CGEM); Center for Global Enterprise (CGE), New York, March 2015.

Immelt, Jeffrey R. 2016. "The World I See: Jeff Immelt's Advice to Win in Time of Anger about Globalization." New York University Stern School of Business. May 20, 2016. MBA Commencement Address. www.gereports.com/the-world-i-see-immelts-advice-to-win-in-the-time-of-globalization/.

International Labour Organization (ILO). "Statistics and Databases." www.ilo.org/global/lang--en/index.htm.

International Monetary Fund (IMF). April 2015. "World Economic Outlook (WEO) Database." www.imf.org/external/pubs/ft/weo/2015/01/weodata/index.aspx.

Jaruzelski, Barry, and Kevin Dehoff. 2008. "Beyond Borders: The Global Innovation 1000." *strategy+business* Winter (53). (Originally published by Booz & Company). www.strategy-business.com/article/08405.

Jaruzelski, Barry, Kevin Schwartz, and Volker Staack. 2015. "The 2015 Global Innovation 1000: Innovation's New World Order (Study Report)." *Strategy&*. PwC. www.strategyand.pwc.com/reports/2015-global-innovation-1000-media-report.

Kobashi, Tsutomu, and Natalie Konomi. 2015. "Idiosyncrasies of the Front-Back Organization" *Bulletin of Aichi Institute of Technology* 50:200–203. http://repository.aitech.ac.jp/dspace/bitstream/11133/2882/1/%E7%B4%80%E8%A6%8150%E5%8F%B7%28p200-p203%29.pdf.

Kohn, Tomás O. 1997. "Small Firms as International Players." *Small Business Economics* 9 (1):45–51. doi: 10.1023/A:1007999614414.

Lee, Edward, Martin Walker, and Cheng Zeng. 2014. "Do Chinese Government Subsidies Affect Firm Value?" *Accounting, Organizations and Society* 39 (3):149–169. doi: http://dx.doi.org/10.1016/j.aos.2014.02.002.

Lee, Hau L. 2004. "The Triple-A Supply Chain." *Harvard Business Review* 82 (10):102–112.

Levitt, Theodore. 1983. "The Globalization of Markets." *Harvard Business Review* 61 (3):92–102.

Malik, Yogesh, Alex Niemeyer, and Brian Ruwadi. 2011. "Building the Supply Chain of the Future." *McKinsey Quarterly* 2011 (Winter):62–71. www.mckinsey.com/insights/operations/building_the_supply_chain_of_the_future.

Nielsen, Bo Bernhard, and Sabina Nielsen. 2013. "Top Management Team Nationality Diversity and Firm Performance: A Multilevel Study." *Strategic Management Journal* 34 (3):373–382. doi: 10.1002/smj.2021.

OECD. 2011. "Tax Trends in OECD Countries." OECD 50th Anniversary: Challenges in Designing Competitive Tax Systems, Paris, France, June 30, 2011. www.oecd.org/ctp/48193734.pdf.

2013. "*Action Plan on Base Erosion and Profit Shifting*." Paris: OECD Publishing. http://dx.doi.org/10.1787/9789264202719-en.

"OECD Science, Technology and Industry Scoreboard 2013: Innovation for Growth." STI Scoreboard, OECD Publishing. www.oecd-ilibrary.org/science-and-technology/oecd-science-technology-and-industry-scoreboard-2013_sti_scoreboard-2013-en.

2014 "China Headed to Overtake EU, US in Science & Technology Spending, OECD Says." OECD Media office. www.oecd.org/newsroom/china-headed-to-overtake-eu-us-in-science-technology-spending.htm.

2015. "Table 62. R&D Expenditure of Foreign Affiliates as a Percentage of R&D Expenditures of Enterprises." *Main Science and Technology Indicators* 1:81. OECD Publishing.

Office of Advocacy. 2012. "Frequently Asked Questions About Small Business." Small Business Adminsitration. www.sba.gov/sites/default/files/FAQ_Sept_2012.pdf.

OICA. International Organization of Motor Vehicle Manufacturers. www.oica.net/.

Otterman, Sharon. "Trade: Outsourcing Jobs." Council on Foreign Relations, February 4, 2004. www.cfr.org/pakistan/trade-outsourcing-jobs/p7749.

Powers, Thomas L., and Jeffrey J. Loyka. 2010. "Adaptation of Marketing Mix Elements in International Markets." *Journal of Global Marketing* 23 (1):65–79. doi: 10.1080/08911760903442176.

PwC. 2012. "Talent Mobility 2020: The Next Generation of International Assignments." PricewaterhouseCoopers. www.pwc.com/gx/en/issues/talent/future-of-work/global-mobility-map.html.

Quelch, John A., and Rohit Deshpande. 2004. *The Global Market: Developing a Strategy to Manage across Borders*, The Jossey-Bass Business & Management Series. San Francisco: Jossey-Bass.

Quelch, John A., and Katherine E. Jocz. 2012. *All Business Is Local: Why Place Matters More Than Ever in a Global, Virtual World*. New York: Portfolio/Penguin.

Reiche, B. Sebastian. "The Role of Global Leadership for Cross-Border Expansion: Project on Business Models for Speed and Scale." Draft prepared for Workshop on Business Models for Speed and Scale, Center for Globalization of Education and Management (CGEM); Center for Global Enterprise (CGE), New York, March 2015.

Reiche, B. Sebastian, Yih-teen Lee, and Javier Quintanilla. 2014. "Cross-Cultural Training and Support Practices of International Assignees." In *The Routledge Companion to International Human Resource Management*, edited by David G. Collings, Geoffrey T. Wood, and Paula M. Caligiuri, 308–323. London: Routledge.

Rugman, Alan M., and Alain Verbeke. 2004. "A Perspective on Regional and Global Strategies of Multinational Enterprises." *Journal of International Business Studies* 35 (1):3–18.

Selling, Thomas. 2013. "Bumps in the Road to IFRS Adoption: Is a U-Turn Possible?" *Accounting Horizons*, March, 155–167.

Sirkin, Harold L., Michael Zinser, and Justin Rose. 2014. "The Shifting Economics of Global Manufacturing: How Cost Competitiveness Is Changing Worldwide" *BCG Perspectives*. www.bcgperspectives.com/content/articles/lean_manufacturing_globalization_shifting_economics_global_manufacturing/.

Steenkamp, Jan-Benedict E. M. "Global Brands in a Semiglobalized World: Securing the Good and Avoiding the Bad." Draft prepared for Workshop on Business Models for Speed and Scale, Center for Globalization of Education and Management (CGEM); Center for Global Enterprise (CGE), New York, April 2015.

Sutton, John. 2012. *Competing in Capabilities: The Globalization Process*, Clarendon Lectures in Economics. Oxford: Oxford University Press.

Thomson, Russell. 2013. "National Scientific Capacity and R&D Offshoring." *Research Policy* 42 (2):517–528. doi: 10.1016/j.respol.2012.07.003.

UNCTAD. 2009. "World Investment Report 2009: Transnational Corporations, Agricultural Production and Development." United Nations. http://unctad.org/en/docs/wir2009_en.pdf.

2012. "World Investment Report 2012: Towards a New Generation of Investment Policies." United Nations. http://unctad.org/en/PublicationsLibrary/wir2012_embargoed_en.pdf.

2013. "World Investment Report 2013: Global Value Chains: Investment and Trade for Development." United Nations. http://unctad.org/en/PublicationsLibrary/wir2013_en.pdf.

2014. "World Investment Report 2014: Investing in the SDGs: An Action Plan." United Nations. http://unctad.org/en/PublicationsLibrary/wir2014_en.pdf.

2015. "World Investment Report 2015: Reforming International Investment Governance." United Nations. http://unctad.org/en/PublicationsLibrary/wir2015_en.pdf.

UNCTAD, and Masataka Fujita. 1993. *Small and Medium-Sized Transnational Corporations: Role, Impact, and Policy Implications.* New York: United Nations: Programme on Transnational Corporations.

United States Census Bureau. 2013. "Profile of U.S. Importing and Exporting Companies." United States Department of Commerce. www.census.gov/foreign-trade/Press-Release/edb/2013/index.html.

United States Department of Commerce. 2011. "Exporting Is Good for Your Bottom Line." International Trade Administration. http://trade.gov/cs/factsheet.asp.

Westney, D. Eleanor, and Srilata Zaheer. 2009. "The Multinational Enterprise as an Organization." In *The Oxford Handbook of International Business*, edited by Alan M. Rugman, 341–366. 2nd ed. Oxford; New York: Oxford University Press.

World Bank. 2013. "World Development Indicators: GDP (Current US$)." World Bank national accounts data, and OECD National Accounts data files. http://data.worldbank.org/indicator/NY.GDP.MKTP.CD?order=wbapi_data_value_2013+wbapi_data_value+wbapi_data_value-last&sort=desc.

World Federation of Exchanges (WFE). 2015. "World Federation of Exchanges: Connecting Exchanges and Stakeholders." Last modified June 2015. www.world-exchanges.org/.

Part II

The Law of Distance

5 The Breadth of Globalization and Distance

This chapter provides empirical evidence at the country level for the law of distance: "International interactions are dampened by distance along cultural, administrative, and geographic dimensions and are often affected by economic distance as well." It parallels Chapter 2, which supplied country-level evidence for the law of semiglobalization. Chapter 2 focused on national borders and the intensity of interactions across them, and concluded that the depth of globalization remains limited: that most interactions that could occur either within or across borders are domestic. This chapter focuses on the interactions that *do* occur across national borders and analyzes the breadth of their distribution across partner countries. Chapter 6 provides a complementary look at the distribution of cross-border interactions at the industry and firm levels.

The first section of this chapter supplies evidence of the limited breadth of globalization. It focuses on comparing the average physical distances[1] over which international interactions take place to (hypothetical) frictionless benchmarks and confirms that the actual distances traversed are much shorter than would be expected in a world where the law of distance did not hold. These comparisons are complemented with a series of cartograms based on countries' international interactions that help illustrate how the law of distance applies across space. And although much of the emphasis in this section is on geographic distance, it provides some evidence of limited breadth across other dimensions of distance as well.

The second section introduces Ghemawat (2001)'s CAGE Distance Framework, which will be used throughout Part II to identify dimensions of distance that shape international interactions and, thus, help explain the limited breadth of globalization. The dimensions of distance highlighted by the framework are the same ones flagged in the law of distance: cultural, administrative, geographic, and economic. The CAGE Distance Framework will also provide the structure around which Part III's discussion of business applications is organized.

The third section of this chapter draws on and extends the large literature on gravity modeling in international economics to calibrate the effects of distance along each of the CAGE dimensions. In order to generate estimates that are comparable across different types of international interactions, it fits a standard gravity model to eleven types of trade, capital, information, and people flows. The results provide strong empirical support that the law of distance applies across them.

The fourth section focuses on the persistence of distance effects over time. This section begins with a brief discussion of what trade economists have found in their gravity-based analysis of distance effects over the past half-century. It then turns to trends since the mid-2000s, which point toward international interactions taking place across greater distances but their breadth continuing to lag the levels implied by frictionless benchmarks.

The fifth section illustrates the policy relevance of gravity modeling by using it to analyze the shifting patterns of international influence among the European Union, the United States, and China in terms of changing trade patterns.[2] Current merchandise trade patterns are compared to those predicted by a gravity model, and then the model is employed to project trade patterns in 2040. The emphasis here on public policy fits with the country-level focus of this chapter; implications of the law of distance for business policy are discussed in Chapter 6, drawing on that chapter's industry- and firm-level analysis.

The Limited Breadth of Globalization

The breadth of globalization, as discussed in Chapter 1, is related to what David Held et al. call globalization's *extensity*, as opposed to its depth (*intensity*) (1999, 1–86). There are obviously many different ways of summarizing a distribution of interactions into a single measure of breadth, and some are better suited than others to particular levels of analysis. When measuring breadth at the country level, measures that calibrate breadth against a common yardstick regardless of countries' geographic locations have special appeal.

For country-level comparisons, the *DHL Global Connectedness Index* measures breadth based on the similarity of a country's distribution of international flows across partner countries to the rest of the world's distribution of those flows in the opposite direction. The example of inbound tourism in the Bahamas illustrates the intuition behind this measure. More than 80 percent of tourists visiting the Bahamas come from only one country, the United States, which is the source of less than 10 percent of all outbound tourists worldwide. While the Bahamas ranks second in the world on tourist arrivals per capita (a depth metric), the disparity between the origins of its inbound tourists and the rest of the world's outbound tourists ranks the breadth of the Bahamas' inbound tourism among the world's lowest.

Overall, the breadth of globalization, measured thus, seems to be positively related to country size. In particular, bigger countries tend to have export portfolios that are more diversified across country markets and industries – a regularity apparently not previously noted in the literature, which Ghemawat and Olsen (2016) document and rationalize theoretically.[3] Breadth is also positively related to GDP per capita (Ghemawat and Altman 2014).

Herfindahl-type concentration measures are another indicator that can be utilized to evaluate the breadth of international interactions at the country level. Babones and Farabee-Siers (2012) present such an analysis of merchandise trade, and the 2014 edition of the *DHL Global Connectedness Index* provides concentration metrics across nine types of trade, capital, information, and people flows and stocks as an alternative to its primary breadth measure. This measure, like the previous one, indicates that larger countries tend to have broader distributions of international activity across partners.

For breadth analysis at the world level, which is the focus of this section, worries about bias due to variations in how far individual countries are from others do not arise and so simpler measures can be employed. Therefore, the primary metric I use here will be the average distance traversed by international interactions. This metric is both intuitive and readily comparable to frictionless benchmarks. Regionalization measures (tracking the proportion of a given type of activity that takes place within the boundaries of a multicountry region) provide another simple way of thinking about breadth, but consideration of them is deferred until Chapter 10.

The average distance between any two randomly selected countries around the globe is about 8,500 km, providing a very rough (unweighted) benchmark of the average distance that international interactions might extend in a frictionless world. For the analysis of merchandise trade, Head and Mayer (2013) provide a more sophisticated benchmark that follows the same logic as the frictionless benchmark utilized in Chapter 2: each country consumes imports from every other country in proportion to partners' shares of world GDP. On the basis of 2013 GDP data, that benchmark implies that merchandise trade flows, on average, would be expected to traverse 8,236 km.[4] In 2013, the actual average distance traversed by merchandise trade was 4,798 km, only 58 percent as far as implied by Head and Mayer's frictionless benchmark (see Figure 5.1).

Figure 5.2 presents the average distances across which a variety of types of goods were exported in 2014. Only one of the products traveled an average of more than 8,500 km. Soybeans were shipped the longest distance (12,530 km), partly due to the unique patterns of production and consumption of that commodity: the three largest directional flows (all destined for China – from Brazil, the United States, and Argentina) add up to more than half of the world total. Long-distance trade in bulk commodities such as soybeans is also eased by the absence of requirements to learn about and cater to subtle variations in product preferences across markets. Microwave ovens were traded over the second longest distances (7,975 km) – over three quarters of them were exported by China alone. Electricity (875 km) and milk (1,543 km) were traded over the

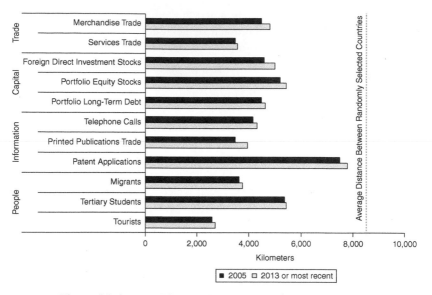

Figure 5.1 Average Distance Traversed by International Interactions, 2005 versus 2013.
Source: Adapted from *DHL Global Connectedness Index* 2014, Figure 1.3.

shortest distances, presumably because of problems associated with transmission and spoilage respectively.

Foreign Direct Investment (FDI) and Portfolio Equity measured as stocks were held at greater average distances than traversed by merchandise trade: 5,003 km and 5,433 km respectively. However, even portfolio equity stocks are invested across far shorter distances than frictionless benchmarks imply. Substituting stock market capitalization for GDP in Head and Mayer's benchmark for trade, an analogous frictionless benchmark for portfolio equity stocks is 8,936 km.[5] Although portfolio equity transactions are "weightless" in the sense that no physical transportation is required, prior studies have confirmed that distance dampens stock market investment even within countries (Coval and Moskowitz 1999; Grinblatt and Keloharju 2001; Portes and Rey 2005).

For information and people flows, substituting population for GDP in the trade benchmark implies a frictionless benchmark of 7,635 km.[6] All of the flows studied fall far short of the benchmark except patents (average distance 7,790 km), though it is worth keeping in mind that international patenting activity is highly concentrated in a few locations spread across North America, West Europe, and East Asia.[7] International students cover the second longest distance among these categories (5,422 km) owing to the concentration of the world's top universities in a small number of advanced economies,

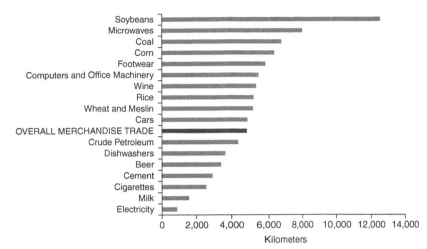

Figure 5.2 Average Distance Traversed by a Sample of Traded Goods, 2014 or Most Recent.

Source: Based on exports data from UN Comtrade unless otherwise noted. Soybeans: HS as reported 1201; Microwaves: HS as reported 851650; Coal: HS02 2701; Corn: HS as reported 1005; Footwear: SITC4 851; Computers and Office Machinery: HS as reported 8471, 8472, 8443; Wine: HS as reported 2204; Rice: HS as reported 1006; Wheat and Meslin: HS as reported 1001; Cars: HS96 8703; Crude Petroleum: SITC4 3330; Dishwashers: HS96 842211; Beer: HS02 2203; Cement: HS as reported 2523; Cigarettes: HS as reported 240220; Milk: HS as reported 0401; Electricity: IEA (2016).

which results, in particular, in large flows from Asia to the United States and Europe.[8] At the opposite extreme, tourism – based on international tourist arrivals (excluding daytrips) – takes place over the shortest average distance, only 2,719 km.

This discussion has focused, so far, on physical distance, but it is important to emphasize that the law of distance applies more broadly. Consider the example of linguistic distance as a type of cultural distance: 22 percent of trade and 34 percent of migration take place between countries that share a common language, as compared to frictionless benchmarks (analogous to those used previously) of 11 percent for trade and 13 percent for migration. A similar pattern shows up using finer-grained measures of linguistic distance that take into account how some (different) languages are more closely related than others.[9] And to cite an example related to administrative distance, 47 percent of trade and 50 percent of migration take place between countries that have free trade agreements, as compared to frictionless benchmarks of 17 percent and 16 percent.[10]

Maps (cartograms) that preserve countries' relative locations but resize them in proportion to a focal country's international interactions can help make intuitions about the law of distance more vivid. Here, maps are presented based on selected country-level trade, capital, information, and people flows. Since each map can reflect only one type of interaction from the perspective of a single focal country, these constitute a narrow set of examples. Several hundred (multicolored) maps of this type can be found at www.ghemawat.com/maps. And the econometric evidence presented later in this chapter will show that many of the patterns apparent from these maps apply more generally.

Consider Figure 5.3, which maps Germany's merchandise exports (top) and outward foreign direct investment stocks (bottom). Germany was the world's third largest merchandise exporter in 2013, and derived 39 percent of its GDP from merchandise exports, significantly more than the largest exporter (China, with 23 percent) or the second largest (the United States, with 9 percent). While Germany is famed as a "global" export powerhouse, a full 70 percent of its merchandise exports went to other countries within Europe. France was Germany's top export destination, even though France was only the world's fifth largest economy. Other countries that share borders with Germany also appear much larger than they do on normal maps (where countries are scaled by geographic size). Nonetheless, two of Germany's top six export destinations are relatively distant countries: the United States (#4) and China (#6). These examples of the world's two largest economies illustrate the need to control for the size of export destinations when analyzing the effects of distance on export volumes, which is the purpose of the map's shading scheme.

As the shading on the map indicates, all of the countries where Germany's exports make up more than 15 percent of the destination country's imports are located within Europe.[11] And even within Europe, distance exerts a significant influence. Thus, all of the countries where Germany's exports account for more than 25 percent of imports are adjacent to Germany, with the sole exception of Hungary, which is only slightly more removed. In addition, in the bottom panel of Figure 5.3, Germany's outward FDI stock is almost as focused on nearby countries as its exports, despite the fact that Germany's outward FDI stock more closely mirrors the rest of the world's inward FDI stock than that of any other country, that is, has the highest breadth score.[12] Roughly two-thirds of Germany's outbound foreign direct investment was in European countries in 2011.

Figures 5.4 and 5.5 provide examples of other types of international interactions. Figure 5.4 maps Singapore's outbound international telephone calls. Singapore ranks third worldwide on the number of minutes per capita its residents spend calling people in other countries, but over 60 percent of those calls are to just three countries: India (35 percent), Malaysia (19 percent), and

(a) Merchandise Exports, 2013.

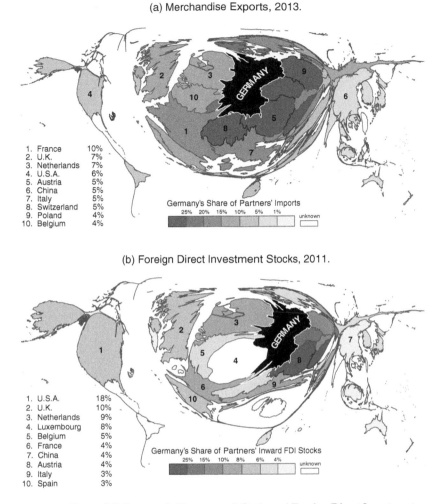

1. France   10%
2. U.K.   7%
3. Netherlands   7%
4. U.S.A.   6%
5. Austria   5%
6. China   5%
7. Italy   5%
8. Switzerland   5%
9. Poland   4%
10. Belgium   4%

Germany's Share of Partners' Imports
25% 20% 15% 10% 5% 1%   unknown

(b) Foreign Direct Investment Stocks, 2011.

1. U.S.A.   18%
2. U.K.   10%
3. Netherlands   9%
4. Luxembourg   8%
5. Belgium   5%
6. France   4%
7. China   4%
8. Austria   4%
9. Italy   3%
10. Spain   3%

Germany's Share of Partners' Inward FDI Stocks
25% 15% 10% 8% 6% 4%   unknown

Figure 5.3 Germany's Exports and Outbound Foreign Direct Investment.
Sources: Based on exports from IMF Direction of Trade Statistics (DOTS)
and FDI from OECD.

China (9 percent). Figure 5.5 maps the origins of the foreign-born population
in the United Arab Emirates, the country with the highest proportion of its
population born abroad (84 percent in 2013).[13] There is a high concentration of
migrants from nearby countries: 38 percent came from India, 15 percent from
Bangladesh, 13 percent from Pakistan, and 10 percent from Egypt.

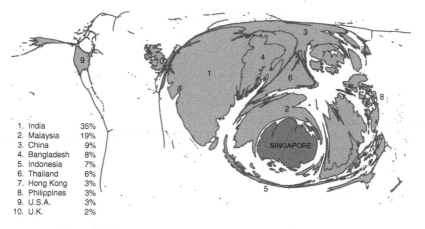

1. India	35%
2. Malaysia	19%
3. China	9%
4. Bangladesh	8%
5. Indonesia	7%
6. Thailand	6%
7. Hong Kong	3%
8. Philippines	3%
9. U.S.A.	3%
10. U.K.	2%

Figure 5.4 Singapore's Outbound International Phone Calls, 2012.
Source: Based on data from Telegeography's International Traffic Database.

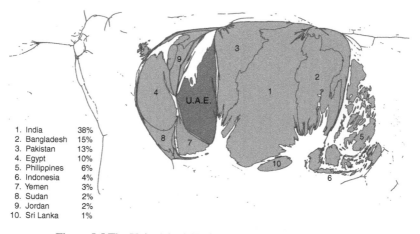

1. India	38%
2. Bangladesh	15%
3. Pakistan	13%
4. Egypt	10%
5. Philippines	6%
6. Indonesia	4%
7. Yemen	3%
8. Sudan	2%
9. Jordan	2%
10. Sri Lanka	1%

Figure 5.5 The United Arab Emirates' Foreign Born Population, 2013.
Source: Based on data from UN Migrant Stock 2013.

None of these maps look much like standard world maps. They are highly distorted – and the distortions conform to clear patterns rather than appearing random. The next section introduces the CAGE Distance Framework, which identifies an intuitive set of distance dimensions that help explain the patterns on these maps. The following section will then provide econometric support for these inferences by using them to estimate gravity models of global trade, capital, information, and people flows.

The CAGE Distance Framework at the Country Level

Ghemawat (2001)'s CAGE Distance Framework identifies four dimensions of distance that shape – and in most cases dampen – international interactions: cultural, administrative, geographic, and economic. The names given to the dimensions were intended to be intuitive, although there has occasionally been some confusion about the meaning of the administrative leg of the framework. Rather than administrative, this dimension could have been called institutional or political, but that would have made for a less interesting acronym. Additionally, there are some drivers of international interactions that are not easily classified. Colonial ties, for example, tend to imply both cultural and administrative similarities, that is, can be thought of as bridges across both types of differences. The CAGE Framework is meant to draw the attention of researchers and policymakers to multiple salient dimensions of distance rather than to provide a mutually exclusive classification scheme.

The effects of all four CAGE dimensions are apparent in the maps in Figures 5.3 through 5.5. The geographic concentration of international interactions is obvious across all of the maps and has already been discussed in the previous section. Cultural factors also feature prominently across several of the maps. The intensity of Germany's exports to Austria and Switzerland is boosted by linguistic as well as other cultural ties; the concentration of Singapore's international phone calls in China, Malaysia, and India fits with Singapore's ethnic composition and related family and business linkages; and seven of the top ten source countries of the United Arab Emirates' immigrants share Islam with the UAE as the dominant religion (although the largest source, India, does not). Regional administrative integration also seems likely to contribute to the concentration of Germany's exports and FDI within the European Union (EU); similarly, ASEAN ties presumably give Singaporeans an additional reason to call neighboring countries, and historical colonial ties probably contribute to the volume of calls to the UK. The effects of economic distance are most apparent on the map of the UAE's foreign – born population: migrant laborers come to the UAE from populous countries with much lower wage levels.[14]

Table 5.1 elaborates a set of country characteristics within each of the CAGE dimensions that tend to shape international interactions. These lists are not meant to be exhaustive, but rather to illustrate common examples of each dimension of distance. The most distinctive feature of the CAGE Framework is that it highlights the bilateral attributes of country pairs (or multilateral attributes of groups of countries) as well as the unilateral attributes of individual countries. Most of the frameworks that have been proposed for thinking about differences across countries (or locations) focus on just unilateral attributes, that is, they assume that countries can be assessed

Table 5.1 *The CAGE Framework at the Country Level*

	Cultural Distance	Administrative Distance	Geographic Distance	Economic Distance
Country Pairs (Bilateral)	• Different languages • Different ethnicities; lack of connective ethnic or social networks • Different religions • Lack of trust • Different values, norms, and dispositions	• Lack of colonial ties • Lack of shared regional trading bloc • Lack of common currency • Political hostility	• Physical distance • Lack of land border • Differences in time zones • Differences in climates / disease environments	• Rich/poor differences • Other differences in cost or quality of natural resources, financial resources, human resources, infrastructure, information or knowledge
Countries (Unilateral / Multilateral)	• Insularity • Traditionalism	• Nonmarket/ closed economy (home bias vs. foreign bias) • Lack of membership in international organizations • Weak institutions, corruption	• Landlockedness • Lack of internal navigability • Geographic size • Geographic remoteness • Weak transportation or communication links	• Economic size • Low per capita income

Source: Reproduced from Table 2-1 of Pankaj Ghemawat, *Redefining Global Strategy*, Harvard Business School Press 2007 (page 41).

one by one against a common yardstick. Note that this characterization applies not only to cardinal indices such as the *World Economic Forum's Global Competitiveness Index* or *Transparency International's Corruption Perceptions Index* but also to ordinal ranking schemes such as Michael Porter's "diamond" framework for diagnosing the (relative) international competitiveness of different countries as home bases in specific industries. But such indexicality is restrictive since it is incapable of capturing bilateral differences of the sort necessary to envision countries as existing in (and even occupying) space in relation to each other (i.e., as nodes in a network) instead of arraying them along a common yardstick.[15]

Having drawn that distinction, it is useful to add that unilateral influences *can* conceptually be bedded down with bilateral influences. A formal link is supplied by a unilateral measure of isolation (or integration), which captures country-specific attributes that generally decrease (or increase) a country's involvement in cross-border economic activities and that can be treated as a common component of that country's distances along various dimensions from other countries. For example, isolated countries characterized by unique, ingrown cultures, closed administrative policies, physical remoteness, or extremely high or low incomes can be thought of as being relatively distant from everywhere else. The gravity modeling that follows in the next section will focus on bilateral influences, employing country fixed effects to capture unilateral country characteristics.

Although the focus here has been on introducing the CAGE Distance Framework at the country level, it is important to note that this framework is also widely used in industry- and firm-level analysis. Chapter 6 will discuss how the sensitivity of interactions to particular dimensions of CAGE distance varies across industries, and will also examine applications of the framework at the firm level, and the final section of this chapter will discuss a country-level public policy application.

Gravity Models and the Calibration of Distance Effects

Gravity models calibrate the effects of distance on international interactions, providing insight into factors that limit the breadth of globalization and shape the patterns observed in the maps discussed in the preceding sections. These models are so named because of the resemblance to Newton's law of universal gravitation in physics, which posits that the gravitational force between two bodies is directly proportional to the product of their masses and inversely proportional to the square of the distance between them. Similarly, gravity models in economics relate trade (and other interactions) between countries to the sizes of their economies and the physical distance between them as well as to other factors expected to inhibit or promote interactions.

To understand the basic intuition behind gravity models, consider, once again, Germany's merchandise exports. Figure 5.6 plots the intensity of Germany's exports (normalized by partner countries' GDPs) against their distances from Germany in kilometers (with both transformed into natural logarithms).[16] In this example, physical distance "explains" 59 percent of the variation in export intensity across destination countries. The slope of the regression line (−1.1) quantifies how the intensity of Germany's exports varies with distance in the form of an elasticity. If distance from Germany increases by 1 percent, one should expect the intensity of Germany's exports to decline by 1.1 percent. Gravity models typically extend the same logic to interactions between all countries (rather than to or from only one country) and are often augmented to incorporate multiple types of distance rather than just physical distance as explanatory variables.

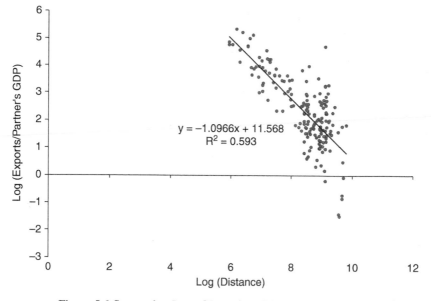

Figure 5.6 Scatterplot: Log of Intensity of Germany's Merchandise Exports versus Log of Distance from Germany.
Source: Based on data from IMF Direction of Trade Statistics, IMF World Economic Outlook Database, and CEPII.

The forerunners of today's gravity models can be found in nineteenth-century models of intranational people flows, for example, Desart's (1846) study of passenger traffic on Belgium's railway network and Ravenstein's (1889) analysis of migration within the UK (Odlyzko 2014). Beckerman (1956) produced an early example of a study showing a significant negative correlation between physical distance and trade flows. The traditional econometric specification for the analysis of trade flows was introduced by Jan Tinbergen (1962).

Since that time, gravity models have come to be recognized for their success at producing "some of the clearest and most robust findings in economics" (Leamer and Levinsohn 1995, 1384). However, "prior to 1979, the absence of rigorous theoretical microeconomic foundations for the gravity equation in international trade inhibited its use for policy work and left the equation on the periphery of mainstream international trade research" (Bergstrand and Egger 2011, 543). Since then, several papers have laid the theoretical foundations for gravity models of international trade, among them Anderson (1979), Bergstrand (1985, 1989), Krugman (1980), Anderson and van Wincoop (2003), Helpman, Melitz, and Rubinstein (2008), Chaney (2008), and Olivero and Yotov (2012).

International economists have estimated literally thousands of gravity models of merchandise trade, and published hundreds of papers reporting their results. Keith Head and Thierry Mayer's chapter in the *Handbook of International Economics* (2014) provides a summary of the results of 2,508 gravity models, drawn from 159 papers. Across all of the models, the median elasticity of trade with respect to physical distance is roughly −1.[17] This indicates that the rough summary conclusion from the German example is a good first-order approximation of the global effect of physical distance on merchandise trade: from any given country, all else equal (including GDP), if one trading partner is half as far away as another, one should expect trade with the closer country to be twice as large as trade with the one farther away.[18]

To illustrate the magnitude of the distance effects implied by this calibration, consider the intensity of Germany's exports to the Netherlands, Spain, and Azerbaijan.[19] The distance from Germany to the Netherlands (based on a population-weighted average of distances between major cities in the two countries) is one-fourth as large as the distance from Germany to Spain. Therefore, the rough assumption that halving distance doubles exports intensity implies that for a distance one-fourth as far, exports intensity should quadruple (double twice: 2 x 2 = 4). Indeed, in 2013, the intensity of Germany's exports to Spain was one-fourth the intensity of Germany's exports to the Netherlands. The distance from Germany to Azerbaijan is 8.5 times the distance from Germany to the Netherlands (and double the distance from Germany to Spain), implying that the effect should be doubled again (2 x 2 x 2 = 8). And indeed Germany's exports to the Netherlands were eight times more intense than Germany's exports to Azerbaijan.

The overwhelming majority of research using gravity models focuses on trade flows, particularly merchandise trade.[20] There are, however, examples of gravity-based analyses of other types of interactions as well. Thus, Kimura and Lee (2006) estimate gravity models of services trade among OECD countries and conclude that the gravity model fits trade in services even better than it does merchandise trade. Several studies analyze FDI using gravity models (e.g., Carr, Markusen, and Maskus 2001; Markusen and Maskus 2002; Blonigen, Davies, and Head 2003; Egger 2008), typically finding distance to strongly inhibit FDI even though some (horizontal) FDI might, as a substitute for trade, be expected to be positively associated with distance. Portes and Rey (2005) analyze the effects of distance on portfolio equity investments and find a negative relationship that they associate with informational frictions. There are fewer gravity models of information flows, but Rietveld and Janssen (1990) and Wong (2008) conclude that international telephone traffic displays some of the same patterns as international trade. And studies of international migration (e.g., Lewer and Van den Berg 2008; Mayda 2010; Grogger and Hanson 2011; Ortega and Peri 2013) all find a strong negative effect for physical distance.[21]

Prior studies that analyze international interactions using gravity models typically focus on only one or two types of interactions, customizing their models to the specific domain(s) studied. In order to provide consistent and comparable rather than piecemeal evidence for the law of distance across multiple types of international interactions, Ghemawat and de la Mata (2015) estimate the same standard gravity model for eleven types of trade, capital, information, and people flows using the following equation:

$$\log(F_{odt}) = \beta_0 + \beta_1 \text{Language}_{od} + \beta_2 \text{Colony}_{od} + \beta_3 \text{Agreement}_{odt} + \beta_4 \log(\text{Physical distance})_{od} + \beta_5 \text{Contiguity}_{od} + \beta_6 \log(\text{Income disparities})_{odt} + \beta_7 \log(\text{Size})_{odt} + \varphi_o + \varphi_d + \varphi_t + u_{odt}$$

$\log(F_{odt})$ refers to the natural log of the flow from country o to country d in year t. Language_{od}, Colony_{od}, Agreement_{odt}, and Contiguity_{od} are binary variables that take the value 1 (rather than 0) if, respectively, the two countries share a common language, if one colonized the other at some point in history, if they are linked by a trade agreement (any trade agreement for analysis of trade flows, regional trade blocs for other kinds of flows), or if they are geographically contiguous or adjacent. $\log(\text{Physical distance})_{od}$ is the natural log of the population-weighted average distance between major cities in the two countries; $\log(\text{Income disparities})_{odt}$ is the natural log of the ratio (higher over lower) of the two countries' per capita incomes; and $\log(\text{Size})_{odt}$ is the natural log of the product of the two countries' GDPs (for analyzing trade and capital flows) or populations (for analyzing information and people flows). Finally, φ_o and φ_d are country-fixed effects; φ_t represents year-fixed effects; and u_{odt} the error term.[22] Errors are clustered by country pair to avoid potential heteroscedasticity problems and to relax the assumption of independence across observations for the same country pair over the period studied. The data are based primarily on the dyadic dataset covering the period from 2005 to 2011 assembled for the *DHL Global Connectedness Index 2012* (Ghemawat and Altman 2012) (for additional details, refer to the online appendix at www.ghemawat. com/laws). In order to reduce problems associated with data availability and quality, coverage is restricted to the sample of ninety-seven countries used by Baier and Bergstrand (2007), which account for 92 percent of the world's GDP and 88 percent of its population.[23]

The explanatory variables in the gravity model obviously correspond to the dimensions of distance identified in the previous section's discussion of the CAGE Distance Framework. Common language is an indicator of cultural similarity. Colony-colonizer ties and trade agreements reflect administrative links. Physical distance and contiguity correspond to the geographic dimension of the framework. And income disparities provide an indicator of economic distance.

Table 5.2 summarizes the results of Ghemawat and de la Mata's baseline specification, estimated using ordinary least squares (OLS). The coefficients for merchandise exports are generally consistent with the median coefficients estimated for the structural gravity equations that Head and Mayer (2014) report. Physical distance is statistically significant at the 0.01 level across every one of the flows analyzed, and the coefficients (which may be interpreted as elasticities), with the exception of international patenting activity, range from –0.9 to –1.9.

Recall that the example of Germany's merchandise exports corresponds to a physical distance effect of –1.1. This model indicates that physical distance has even stronger negative effects for merchandise exports across a large sample of countries (–1.5) as well as for most of the other types of activity analyzed. The distance effect for international patenting activity is much smaller (–0.3), presumably because patenting activity is highly concentrated in a handful of wealthy countries, leading to a large share of the total variability in this flow being captured by the fixed effects and the size variable. Also, note that these estimates of the effects of physical distance reflect the inclusion in the model of a second geographic variable, common border. Prior research on merchandise trade indicates that gravity models that do not include this variable typically find even more strongly negative distance effects (Disdier and Head 2008). Here, common border achieves significance six times out of eleven, with its strongest effects on migrants and tourists.

The nongeographic explanatory variables also tend to be significant with the expected signs. Starting with the cultural dimension of the CAGE Distance Framework, the coefficient for common official language is positive and significant almost across the board – except in the case of portfolio long-term debt – and generally larger for people and informational interactions. Under the administrative dimension, colony-colonizer performs about as well as common language but trade agreements/regional blocs perform much more poorly, often failing to have the predicted sign, let alone achieving significance. This analysis, however, treats all regional blocs equally rather than taking into account how some (most notably the EU) involve far deeper and broader integration than others (e.g., Mercosur). Finally, the ratio of countries' per capita incomes, the economic distance variable, is significant in ten of eleven cases: the only interaction on which it does *not* have a significant effect is merchandise trade – which may be part of the reason why it has not been employed as frequently as the other independent variables in that context. Differences in per capita income generally depress international interactions, except in the cases of service exports, migrants, and phone calls, which are positively related to such differences. For merchandise trade, the insignificant coefficient reflects the fact that trade flows for some products are motivated by (labor cost) arbitrage whereas others are dampened by differences in demand patterns that are correlated with levels of economic development.[24] Industry-level analysis in Chapter 6 will show that this variable is indeed significant with a negative sign for some products and with a positive sign for others.

Table 5.2 *General Gravity Model, OLS Estimation*

	(1)	(2)	(3)	(4)	(5)
	Trade		Capital		
Dependent Variable	Merchandise exports	Services exports	FDI outward stocks	Portfolio equity assets stocks	Portfolio long-term debt stocks
Independent Variables					
Common official language	0.765*** (0.0619)	0.380*** (0.100)	0.755*** (0.143)	0.556*** (0.145)	0.0856 (0.120)
Colonial linkage	0.717*** (0.136)	0.695*** (0.160)	1.266*** (0.195)	0.512** (0.233)	0.176 (0.182)
Trade agreement	0.314*** (0.0607)	0.135 (0.0965)			
Regional bloc			0.101 (0.171)	0.207 (0.143)	0.740*** (0.130)
Physical distance (logged)	−1.510*** (0.0373)	−0.974*** (0.0559)	−1.210*** (0.0756)	−1.011*** (0.0714)	−0.925*** (0.0574)
Common border	0.532*** (0.158)	0.131 (0.170)	−0.0140 (0.225)	0.388* (0.218)	−0.0604 (0.178)
Ratio of per capita income (max / min, logged)	−0.0177 (0.0157)	0.430*** (0.0422)	−0.377*** (0.0794)	−0.401*** (0.0603)	−0.559*** (0.0484)
Product of GDPs (logged)	0.571*** (0.0388)	0.576*** (0.0652)	0.226** (0.0933)	0.498*** (0.113)	0.243*** (0.0858)
Constant	15.34*** (0.582)	15.49*** (1.127)	14.35*** (1.237)	6.570*** (1.592)	7.584*** (1.140)
Observations	63,384	10,726	13,514	16,206	16,967
Adjusted R-squared	0.777	0.881	0.751	0.766	0.762

Notes: Robust standard errors in parentheses, clustered by country pair.
Source: Ghemawat and de la Mata (2015).
*** $p<0.01$, ** $p<0.05$, * $p<0.1$.

Dependent Variable	(6)	(7)	(8)	(9)	(10)	(11)
		Information			People	
	Outgoing phone calls	Printed publications exports	Patent applications	Emigrant stocks	Tertiary students inbound[a]	Tourist arrivals
Independent Variables						
Common official language	0.990***	1.854***	0.638***	1.162***	1.176***	0.954***
	(0.0848)	(0.0838)	(0.0710)	(0.0754)	(0.0832)	(0.0911)
Colonial linkage	0.713***	1.420***	0.750***	1.183***	1.428***	0.445*
	(0.122)	(0.162)	(0.107)	(0.155)	(0.160)	(0.241)
Regional bloc	−0.0553	0.135	−0.367***	−0.793***	0.164*	0.561***
	(0.0953)	(0.115)	(0.0983)	(0.111)	(0.0994)	(0.175)
Physical distance (logged)	−1.132***	−1.917***	−0.274***	−1.401***	−1.149***	−1.545***
	(0.0504)	(0.0474)	(0.0426)	(0.0378)	(0.0451)	(0.0584)
Common border	0.421***	0.236	0.467***	1.239***	0.241	0.759***
	(0.105)	(0.162)	(0.116)	(0.163)	(0.152)	(0.226)
Ratio of per capita income (max / min, logged)	0.183***	−0.266***	−0.0607**	0.110***	−0.114***	−0.0800**
	(0.0244)	(0.0214)	(0.0249)	(0.0222)	(0.0280)	(0.0316)
Product of populations (logged)	0.932***	0.463	2.593***	−0.311***	0.215	1.747***
	(0.181)	(0.388)	(0.386)	(0.0622)	(0.313)	(0.325)
Constant	15.11***	12.64***	23.91***	14.12***	17.11***	31.92***
	(1.516)	(2.372)	(4.064)	(0.731)	(2.570)	(2.714)
Observations	13,752	36,894	11,004	38,352	18,837	10,752
Adjusted R-squared	0.893	0.701	0.820	0.802	0.715	0.879

[a] Tertiary Students has been analyzed based on data up to 2010.

Table 5.3 *Percentage of Variance Explained by Distance Variables*

	R-squared of gravity models with			% of the remaining variance explained by physical distance [C2-C1]/ [1-C1]	% of the remaining variance explained by all distance variables [C3-C1]/ [1-C1]
	C1: Size variables (GDP, pop'n) and fixed effects	C2: Physical distance, size variables and fixed effects	C3: Standard set of variables and fixed effects		
Merchandise exports	0.679	0.771	0.777	29%	31%
Services exports	0.827	0.869	0.881	24%	31%
FDI outward stocks	0.661	0.732	0.751	21%	27%
Portfolio equity assets stocks	0.705	0.758	0.766	18%	21%
Portfolio long-term debt stocks	0.672	0.747	0.762	23%	27%
Tertiary students inbound	0.539	0.672	0.715	29%	38%
Emigrant stocks	0.630	0.767	0.802	37%	46%
Tourist arrivals	0.735	0.865	0.879	49%	54%
Outgoing phone calls	0.793	0.867	0.893	36%	48%
Printed publications exports	0.478	0.664	0.701	36%	43%
Patent applications	0.787	0.800	0.820	6%	15%

Even though Ghemawat and de la Mata (2015) use (almost) exactly the same explanatory variables across all of the interactions, the goodness of fit of the models ranges from 70 percent to nearly 90 percent (with merchandise exports, to which the explanatory variables were "tuned," situated at the median). Of course, some of this explanatory power is unrelated to distance. Consider how goodness of fit changes across three variants on the basic gravity model, as reported in Table 5.3. The first column is based on regressions that include just the fixed effects and the sizes of the country pairs yet manages to explain a large share of the variance, ranging from nearly one-half to more than four-fifths. The second column adds in physical distance to fixed effects and sizes and helps explain about one-quarter of the remaining variance on average, although the precise shares range from 6 percent to 49 percent, as reported in the second-last column. The third column adds in the remaining distance variables and further boosts overall explanatory power, although by lesser amounts. In the case of merchandise trade, in particular, the share of remaining variance explained goes up from only 29 percent to 31 percent, although larger improvements are achieved for the other flows.

These results might seem to suggest that at least in the case of trade in goods, augmenting physical distance with the other distance variables adds very little. But it is important to remember that some of the other distance variables are significantly correlated with physical distance. Therefore, attributing all the additional variance accounted for by the specification in the second column relative to the first one to physical distance likely overstates its real contribution. A safer conclusion is that augmenting physical distance with other distance variables seems to make even more sense for other international interactions than it does for merchandise trade – where such augmentation has long been common.

Ghemawat and de la Mata (2015) also report a second set of regressions using the Poisson Pseudo-Maximum Likelihood (PPML) estimation in order to address econometric concerns about the basic OLS model, most notably robustness to zero values (these results are also provided in the online appendix at www.ghemawat.com/laws). Zero values arise when a subset of the country pairs in the model do not have any interactions of a given type reported in a particular year. Zero values account for 30 percent or more of all of the flows studied – up to a high of 77 percent for patents – except for merchandise trade, where their share is 12 percent and phone calls, where Telegeography's subsample of countries, which reports no zero values, was utilized. The PPML model, calculated following the method specified by Santos Silva and Tenreyro (2006), finds distance effects that continue to be broadly significant but a bit weaker than under OLS. Looking in the aggregate at the six distance-related variables across the eleven types of international interactions, these are significant more than two-thirds of the time (71 percent) at least at the 0.1 level under PPML, versus four-fifths of the time under OLS.

A final point from Ghemawat and de la Mata (2015) follows from the construction of composite distance metrics using the methodology developed for the CAGE Comparator online distance analysis tool (see www. ghemawat.com/cage).[25] These composite distances are calibrated for each type of interaction based on all of the distance-related gravity coefficients, converted into effect multipliers and scaled to be comparable to kilometers of physical distance. Correlations across the composite distances for different flow types tend to be quite high. For example, composite distance for merchandise trade has correlations above 0.9 with composite distance for five of the ten other interactions studied, as shown in Figure 5.7. Composite distance, especially for flows with weight, also tends to be strongly correlated with physical distance. These results point to the conclusion that countries that are relatively distant from each other with respect to a particular type of interaction also tend to be far when other types of interactions are concerned, lending support to the view that the law of distance is a fundamental attribute of globalization rather than a narrower regularity that applies only to merchandise trade.

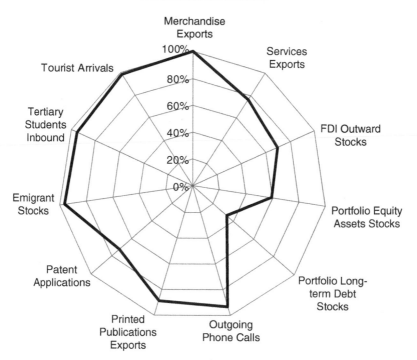

Figure 5.7 Correlation between Distance Implied by Coefficients for Merchandise Exports and Distances Implied by Coefficients for Other Flows Based on OLS Estimates.
Source: Ghemawat, Pankaj, and Tamara de la Mata. "Globalization and Gravity." unpublished working paper, IESE Business School, 2015, Figure 1A.

The Persistence of Distance Effects over Time

Many of the most visible costs associated with operating across physical distance have plummeted over the past century. According to one study, sea freight rates dropped 70 percent between 1920 and 1960 (UNDP 1999, 30). Per-ton-kilometer air freight rates fell 92 percent from 1955 to 2004 (Hummels 2007). The cost of international telephone calls fell more than 10 percent every year between 1999 and 2003, 20 percent in 2001 alone (TeleGeography 2013). With the advent of internet-based phone services, international telecommunications costs have approached zero. In addition, the availability of free online translation services might be presumed to have made linguistic differences less cumbersome, and the speed of many types of international data flows has also increased. These developments might reasonably lead one to suppose that the inhibiting effect of distance on international interactions could be diminishing, and that the law of distance might soon cease to apply.

Contrary to such intuitions, trade researchers using gravity models tend to find that physical distance effects have not declined, and some even report increases over time, leading to what has been termed the "distance puzzle" (Buch, Kleinert, and Toubal 2004) or the "missing globalization puzzle" (Coe, Subramanian, and Tamirisa 2007). Figure 5.8 presents the results of a meta-analysis summarized in Head and Mayer (2013). Depending on the sample and method employed, there may or may not be a trend toward rising distance effects, but there is no appreciable trend toward declining physical distance effects over this time frame.

Work to resolve this "puzzle" continues in the trade literature, with several recently published studies offering econometric specifications that do pick up declining distance effects. See, for example, Coe et al. (2007), Yotov (2012), Lin (2013), and Larch et al. (2014). Carrère et al. (2013) corroborate such results in the case of advanced economies, arguing that the distance puzzle applies only to developing countries. Although this debate continues, given the magnitude of distance effects and their consistency across multiple types of interactions, a scenario in which the law of distance would soon cease to hold seems unlikely. And even if research in this area eventually points to distance effects that are diminishing over time, that would lead to a conclusion that parallels the one in Part I regarding the depth of globalization. There have been large increases in the intensity of many trade, capital, and information flows, but borders continue to matter to a sufficient extent that the law of semiglobalization still holds.

It is worth adding that gravity-based research on the distance puzzle focuses on multidecade time frames, and has not yet examined trends since the mid-2000s, which suggest that international interactions are stretching out over greater distances. The weighted average distance traversed by each of the flows reported in Figure 5.1 has increased since 2005. The average distance covered by merchandise trade rose from 4,479 km in 2005 to 4,798 km in 2013. And FDI stocks stretched out from an average of 4,589 km in 2005 to 5,003 km in 2012 (Ghemawat and Altman 2014).

A large part of the recent rise in the distances spanned by international interactions seems to be a result of the growing proportion of these interactions involving emerging economies, which tend to interact over greater distances than advanced economies, in part due to their geographic locations (as discussed further in Chapter 11). The GDP-weighted average distance between country pairs composed of two emerging economies is 8,672 km, as compared to 6,842 km between two advanced economies and 8,552 km between one

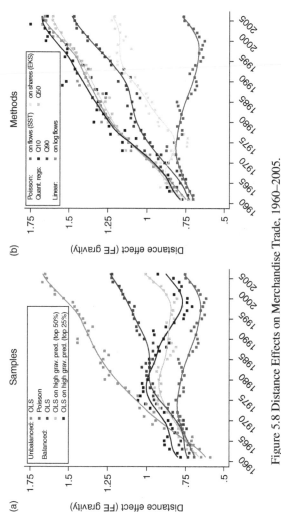

Figure 5.8 Distance Effects on Merchandise Trade, 1960–2005.
Head, Keith, and Thierry Mayer. 2013. "What Separates Us? Sources of Resistance to Globalization." *Canadian Journal of Economics/Revue canadienne d'économique* 46 (4) Figure 5, pg 1210.

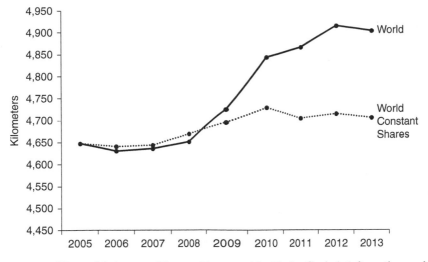

Figure 5.9 Average Distance Traversed by Trade, Capital, Information, and People Flows Covered on the *DHL Global Connectedness Index*, 2005–2013. *Source:* Adapted from Figure 4.4 of the *DHL Global Connectedness Index 2014.*

emerging economy and one advanced economy. Emerging economies average 63 percent higher remoteness scores than advanced economies, based on the remoteness measure in Wei (1996). Policy likely exacerbates geography here in that emerging economies have not, in general, built up the same level of intraregional policy integration as advanced economies. Emerging economies also tend to have large physical infrastructure deficiencies, and in some cases, legacies remain of transport links built to ship resources to former colonial powers rather than to efficiently link countries with their neighbors.

Figure 5.9 juxtaposes the actual increase in (weighted) average distance traversed by the international interactions covered in the *DHL Global Connectedness Index* against an adjusted version of the same analysis in which the distances over which individual countries interact change over time but their weights (as shares of total world interactions) are held constant to remove the composition effects associated with the rise of emerging economies (and the relative decline, in particular, of Europe). This adjustment eliminates most but not all of the increase, indicating that the trend toward international interactions taking place over greater distances is the result primarily – but not entirely – of composition effects. This topic will be examined in greater length in Chapter 10 because, at least with respect to merchandise trade, the upturn in the emerging economies' share of world GDP coincides with the reversal of an earlier decades-long trend of increasing trade regionalization.

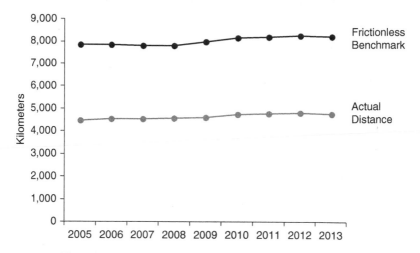

Figure 5.10 Actual Distance Traversed by Merchandise Trade versus Frictionless Benchmark, 2005–2013.
Source: Calculation based on data from IMF Direction of Trade Statistics and IMF World Economic Outlook databases.

Do recent increases in the average distance traversed by international interactions imply a narrowing of the gap between the actual breadth of globalization and frictionless benchmarks? Figure 5.10 compares the evolution of the actual distance traversed by merchandise trade and the evolution of its GDP-based frictionless benchmark over the period from 2005 to 2013. The actual distance rose 319 km, but the benchmark rose even more: 396 km. In percentage terms, however, the actual distance increased (slightly) from 57 percent of the benchmark in 2005 to 58 percent in 2013.

Looking more generally across trade, capital, information, and people flows, the world-level weighted averages of the *DHL Global Connectedness Index* breadth measures indicate that the breadth of globalization has generally fallen further behind frictionless benchmarks over this period (see Figure 5.11).[26] Furthermore, finer-grained analysis of those breadth measures indicates declining breadth in advanced economies and rising breadth in emerging economies. Although the international interactions of both sets of economies are taking place over greater distances than they did in 2005, those of advanced economies have not stretched far enough or fast enough to keep up with the "big shift" of activity to emerging economies described and analyzed in Chapter 11. Returning again to the example of Germany's merchandise exports, the average distance traversed by those exports did increase from 2,703 km in 2005 to 2,821 km in 2013. However, for Germany to have maintained its 2005 share

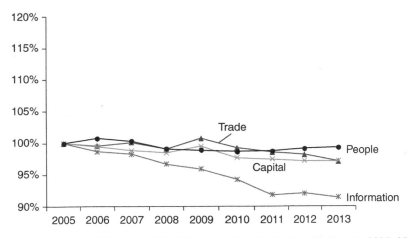

Figure 5.11 *DHL Global Connectedness Index* Breadth Trends, 2005–2013.
Source: Figure 4.5 of *DHL Global Connectedness Index* 2014, p. 63.

of imports in all of its export markets, a rough analysis indicates it would have had to export more than an average distance of 3,037 km in 2013.

Although much of the emphasis in this section has been on merchandise trade, the sense in some quarters that distance effects are diminishing is often related to assertions that the internet makes distance irrelevant. Contrary to such notions, analysis of user activity on Twitter and the crowdfunding site Kiva.org demonstrate that the law of distance also holds in cyberspace. A gravity model of follower relationships on Twitter showed that such relationships are dampened significantly by physical distance and economic distance and rise significantly with cultural and administrative similarity.[27] And Burtch, Ghose, and Wattal (2014) analyzed transactions on Kiva.org and found that lenders prefer culturally similar and geographically proximate borrowers.

To summarize, evidence of various types points to the long-run persistence of the law of distance. Distance effects obtained from gravity models, under typical specifications of those models, have tended not to decline over time. And while recent data point toward interactions stretching out over greater distances since 2005, frictionless benchmarks have shifted out even farther over the same time frame.

An Application: Mapping the World

Data on the breadth of global interactions permit one to answer fundamental questions about globalization, and assuming some stability to the estimated distance coefficients – in line with the previous section – permit some predictions about the future as well. For an application that concerns one of the key geopolitical issues of our time, consider the rise of China. Some assert that the United States will continue to be *the* superpower, and others believe that it will be China.[28] What can usefully be added to this debate on the basis of the kinds of data and analysis stressed in this chapter?

As a basic starting point, consider some of the unilateral comparisons that typically surface in discussions of China's rise. China has already surpassed the United States in terms of GDP at purchasing power parity and is widely expected to do so in terms of GDP at market exchange rates as well in the 2020s. It has also become the world's largest exporter, and has overtaken the United States as the largest single market in many product and service categories. Yet China also remains quite far behind in other areas, such as GDP per capita and output per worker. Given the complexity of the issues and the specific focus here on geopolitical influence, unilateral comparisons provide at best only a partial view. Bilateral indicators that focus specifically on China's position relative to the United States in international networks are, arguably, even more relevant.

The obvious place to start is to analyze China's and others' places in the global trade network since that is one of the key dimensions of economic power. In addition to being the world's largest exporter, China is also the second largest importer, and leads in total trade.[29] In ongoing research with IESE colleagues Fabrizio Ferraro and Jordi Torrents, we find that China has, in terms of trade, surpassed the United States based on one measure of network centrality (betweenness) and is gaining on the United States – but still behind – on another (PageRank, à la Google). Figure 5.12 summarizes the changing positions in the international trade network based on these measures, with the world's third largest trading nation, Germany, also included for purposes of comparison.

A simpler and in some senses even more striking indicator of China's rise in the global trade network is provided by the observation that China has a larger merchandise trading relationship than the United States with 126 of 180 countries for which data were available. This represents 72 percent of the world's GDP (outside the United States and China), up from 54 countries and 41 percent of GDP in 2005. But this is, of course, a very bipolar perspective. A tripolar perspective that also accounts for the European Union suggests that China's rise in merchandise trade has been linked more to leadership positions wrested away from the European Union than the United States – but that the European Union nonetheless remains the world's leading trading power if it is treated as a unified entity.

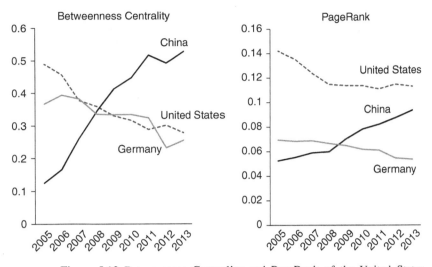

Figure 5.12 Betweenness Centrality and PageRank of the United States, China, and Germany in the Merchandise Trade Network.
Source: Based on author's research with Fabrizio Ferraro and Jordi Torrents from IESE Business School.

The maps in Figure 5.13 depict the evolution of merchandise exports from the United States, European Union, and China. All other countries are shaded according to which of those three provide the greatest share of its imports. The first two panels show the actual trade patterns in 2005 and 2013 respectively. Europe's position stands out, especially in 2005, although that is partly because the EU's twenty-eight countries are larger in terms of combined GDP than the United States or China. In 2005, Europe enjoyed a higher level of exports to 101 of the 150 countries for which data were available (countries accounting for 46 percent of the total GDP of those 150 countries).[30] By 2013, this advantage had eroded to leads in seventy-three countries (35 percent of the GDP of the other countries in the sample). In the same time period, the United States moved from being ahead in thirty-one countries (19 percent of other countries' GDP) to only twenty-seven (15 percent of other countries' GDP), whereas China had a large net gain, from eighteen (27 percent of other countries' GDP) in 2005 to fifty in 2013 (50 percent of other countries' GDP). Thus, although the EU still has more countries in its sphere, China is ahead in countries that represent a greater percentage of world GDP.

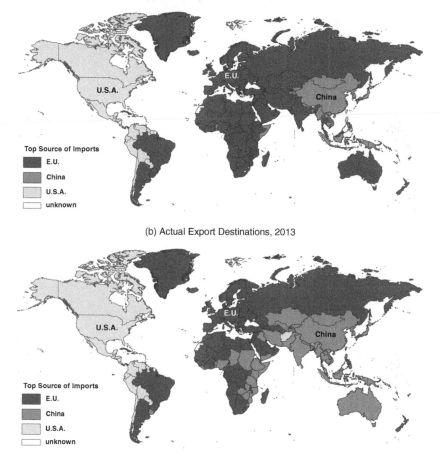

(a) Actual Export Destinations, 2005

Top Source of Imports
- E.U.
- China
- U.S.A.
- unknown

(b) Actual Export Destinations, 2013

Top Source of Imports
- E.U.
- China
- U.S.A.
- unknown

Figure 5.13 Applying Gravity Models to Predict World Merchandise Export Patterns.
Source: Author's Analysis

So far, I have focused on characterizing current positions and their recent evolution in regard to merchandise trade – which did require breadth data but otherwise involved nothing more than data summarization. The obvious next step is to try to use some of the estimates of the coefficients from the merchandise trade gravity model along with growth rate predictions (from other sources) to predict patterns of leadership, starting with the present, where actual patterns supply a reality check. Using the gravity model to predict which of these three exporters would be expected to lead in every other country in 2013 yields the

(c) Gravity Model Predicted Export Destinations, 2013

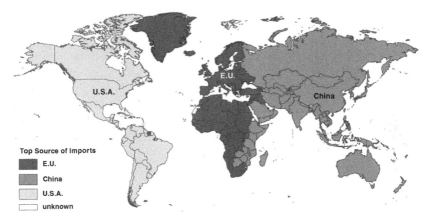

(d) Gravity Model Predicted Export Destinations, 2040

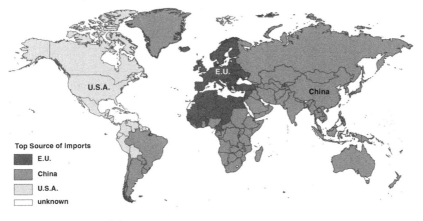

Figure 5.13 (*cont.*)

map in the third panel.[31] The model correctly predicts which of the three economies will be ahead in 115 out of the 150 cases, representing 75 percent of other
countries' GDP. This is encouraging, especially considering that it does not
incorporate any information at all about the products traded (gravity models of
trade at the industry level will be discussed in Chapter 6). Comparing the second
and third panels in Figure 5.13 shows that Europe maintains its lead in more
countries than would be predicted on the basis of cross-country estimates: based
on the coefficients estimated from gravity modeling, the EU should be ahead in
fifty-seven countries, whereas China is predicted to be ahead in fifty-nine.

Looking at the difference between actual trade and gravity-based predictions can show where opportunities lie or where the model is missing key barriers to trade. For example, the four countries with the largest percent difference between model-estimated import percentage and actual import percentage from the United States are Syria, Liberia, Cuba, and Belarus. All four are under some form of sanctions by the United States. Cuba, in particular, is predicted to import 51 percent of its goods from the United States, but the actual percentage is 3 percent. This points to the fact that (apart from trade agreements) the model does not include data on interstate amity/hostility, which is certainly a key determinant of who trades with whom. Unfortunately, no comprehensive, convincing dyadic dataset on these relationships could be found.[32]

If we look once again at the maps, we can find that the clearest difference between the predicted US sphere and actual US sphere is in South America. Brazil and Argentina, the two largest economies in South America, import more from the European Union, but the model predicts that they should fall into the US sphere. And at the other end of the world, Afghanistan is predicted to import 52 percent of its goods from China, but the actual percentage is only 4.3 percent. Although Afghanistan and China share a short common border and China is the largest economy in the region, Afghanistan imported more from the United States in 2013 than from China, presumably due to the US military presence there, and has a much closer trading partnership with its other neighbors, particularly Pakistan. Nevertheless, the gravity model does suggest that there may be a larger role for China to play as an exporter to Afghanistan.

To turn to the future, China is expected to continue growing at a faster rate than the United States. The last panel of Figure 5.13 shows the predictions of the gravity model for 2040 using Oxford Economics' long-term projections for growth in GDP and GDP per capita.[33] Oxford Economics' baseline projections have China and many other emerging markets growing relatively rapidly and, among advanced economies, the United States growing faster than the EU. Using these growth forecasts and the distance coefficients from the gravity model, the EU is predicted to lead in only thirty-three markets (representing 11 percent of other countries' GDP), whereas China increases to eighty-seven (and 75 percent of other countries' GDP), including many in the Americas and most of Africa, and the United States leads in only thirty countries, representing 13 percent of other countries' GDP. In addition, the baseline growth forecasts for China would have to be cut well below the lowest estimates contemplated, for instance, by McKinsey's recent global scenarios for that to have a material impact on leadership patterns (Enriquez, Smit, and Ablett 2015). So in terms of trade, China's rise seems, based on the analysis, more rather than less likely to continue.

Finally, the analysis so far focused on merchandise trade, whereas, as emphasized throughout this book, there are also many other types of international interactions. China generally looks less central in those other respects. Thus, in foreign direct investment, China is catching up with the United States on flows, but only because it is a major destination (the second-ranked one): as a source, it ranks behind Japan as well as the United States. In terms of FDI stocks, the United States had almost nine times as much outward FDI and five times as much inward FDI stock as China in 2014.[34] The network centrality measures confirm the lower relative influence of China in the FDI network, with China's FDI flows ranking eighth on betweenness centrality and fourth on PageRank in 2012.

Several points are clear from this analysis. By every important measure, China is growing in its economic influence. It has made huge strides over the past decade in GDP, trade, and FDI, as well as other measures, although the possibility that it will continue to grow at the rate that it did through 2010 is now widely deemed unlikely. The United States continues to be the single-country leader in every metric except trade, but the twenty-eight-country bloc of the European Union, taken together, has enormous economic influence. Assuming typical growth forecasts, Europe (and to a lesser extent the United States) is projected to cede some of its share in trade and FDI networks, while China is projected to grow its share substantially.

Nonetheless, the CAGE Framework does suggest that the United States and EU have some advantages that will continue well into the future. On the cultural dimension, for example, while Chinese is, by some measures at least, the most spoken language in the world, 96 percent of the Chinese-speaking population resides in mainland China. By contrast, the member states of the EU share common languages with countries on every continent, and English, the primary language of the United States, is the language of international business and diplomacy. In terms of linguistic commonality, the United States shares a common language with 19 percent of rest of the world's GDP, versus 1 percent for China and a weighted average of 7 percent for EU members (Ghemawat and Altman 2014). Under the administrative dimension, trade agreements are the most malleable area of the gravity model's framework, and it does seem that there is a movement over time toward more free trade agreements. The EU has completed trade agreements with fifty-eight countries, compared to only twenty each for the United States and China, which is a great success for a multinational bloc. However, this could mean that much of the "low hanging fruit" is already gone. All three powers are involved in large-scale multilateral negotiations as of this writing.

On the geographic dimension, physical distance is essentially fixed (with a possible caveat about global warming changing polar trade routes), but China will benefit from the changing center of economic gravity. As the "big shift" proceeds, China will become closer to the world's center of GDP. At present, measured on a 0–10 scale, with 10 being the most remote, China scores 5.7, compared to 6.9 for the United States, and an EU average of 2.3. China is, therefore, already closer to world markets than the United States, but the average EU member is much closer.

On the economic dimension of the CAGE Framework, while China's rising GDP per capita may not itself directly expand its trade volume, it does imply a movement toward trade in more differentiated products. Such a change away from purely arbitrage-based exports might confer greater power over the markets to which China exports.

To summarize, China has gained considerable leverage in terms of trade since 2005, and it is a growing force in FDI, though primarily as a destination. One could still argue that China will be the global hegemon in the long if not medium term, with the most obvious rationale being based on domestic (unilateral) factors: China's size in terms of its large population combined with its rising per capita income. In an international rather than domestic context, the typical conjecture is that China's current or soon-to-be-achieved leadership in trade will translate into (or can be leveraged into) leading positions in foreign direct investment and the other dimensions of globalization over time. But the latter argument seems doubtful because even if China does manage to assert dominance in trade and, ultimately, FDI, its marginal positions in terms of most cross-border flows of information and people are not all likely to turn into leading positions as an automatic consequence of such changes.[35]

Conclusion

In 1944, George Orwell lamented how writers of his era continued repeating phrases such as "the abolition of distance," which were fashionable before 1914. Orwell's lament notwithstanding, some of the most popular books on globalization in recent decades followed the same theme, with titles such as *The Death of Distance* (Cairncross 2001) and *The World Is Flat* (Friedman 2005). The empirical evidence presented in this chapter, however, paints a starkly different picture, one where the law of distance is both persistent over time and applies broadly across different types of interactions.

These patterns also suggest that distance effects capture a variety of factors that often dampen international interactions. While transportation costs often come to mind as the most obvious reason why trade might be sensitive to distance, the relevance of distance to both "weighty" and "weightless" interactions suggests that even for trade, transportation costs only partially explain such dampening. One estimate based on studies in international economics indicates that only 4–28 percent of distance-driven trade costs are attributable to transportation costs (Head and Mayer 2013). And according to a literature review in the *Oxford Handbook of International Business,* "the consensus is that the bulk of trading costs are due to trade-reducing factors such as differences in legal systems, administrative practices, market structures, networks, languages, and monetary regimes" (Fratianni 2009, 84).

To conclude, this chapter has covered the law of distance at the country level, and it has also addressed some types of interactions for which a large proportion of country-level activity is directed by firms. An estimated 80 percent of trade takes place within the global value chains of multinational firms (UNCTAD 2013), and foreign direct investment is by definition the province of multinational firms. Firms also actively promote international information and people flows. Chapter 6 turns to industry- and firm-level evidence for and implications of the law of distance.

Notes

1 The term "physical distance" is used here for what is colloquially referred to simply as "distance" (typically measured in kilometers or miles). This term is used rather than "geographic distance" because "geographic distance" is conceived here as a multifaceted construct incorporating physical distance as well as the presence or absence of a common border, climate differences, and so on.

2 For another policy application, refer to Pankaj Ghemawat, "Beyond Brexit: An Initial Analysis and Questions for the AIB Community," *AIB Insights,* Vol. 16, No. 3, 2016.

3 Larger countries are likely to be competitive in more industries, simply because they span more territory, have more diverse cultures, and have larger populations from which to draw exceptional entrepreneurs and firms. Since the distribution of firm size is generally fat-tailed, a few highly productive large firms end up having large effects on aggregate variables at the economy-wide level (Gabaix and Ibragimov 2011; di Giovanni, Levchenko, and Zhang 2014). The exports of smaller countries with relatively few such firms therefore tend to be concentrated in fewer industries, whereas larger countries tend to have export portfolios that are more diversified across industries. In addition, since smaller countries that rely heavily on a few industries will trade less with one another, larger countries are also more likely to have a more diversified export portfolio across countries.

4 Calculation based on data from the IMF World Economic Outlook database, (April 2015).

5 Based on stock market capitalization data from Euromonitor Passport (Euromonitor International). Since outbound investment can flow from countries with relatively smaller to relatively larger stock markets, a more conservative benchmark for portfolio equity might lie in between the GDP based benchmark used for trade and this market capitalization based benchmark. Regardless, the basic point remains that actual investment patterns are far less globalized than the frictionless benchmark.

6 Calculation based on data from the IMF World Economic Outlook database (April 2015).

7 The top five patenting countries (Japan, the United States, Germany, the Republic of Korea, and France) are responsible for 66% of international patent applications; the top five patent offices (the United States, the European Patent Office, China, Japan, and the Republic of Korea) receive 71% of international patent applications.

8 Throughout this chapter, unless otherwise noted, actual distances traversed by international interactions were calculated based on flow data from the "DHL Global Connectedness Index 2014" (see Appendix B of that report for a full list of data sources employed); population weighted distance data ("distw") is from Mayer and Zignago (2011).

9 Using a dataset from Dow and Karunaratna (2006) (L1 in https://sites.google.com/site/ddowresearch/home/scales/languages) that assigns a value from 1 to 5 based on relationships between countries' most spoken languages (where countries with the same primary language, such as Mexico and Uruguay, receive a 1 and countries with primary languages from completely unrelated language families, such as Singapore and South Korea, receive a 5), we find that the average value for merchandise trade is 3.7, compared with a benchmark of 4.1 if language were not a factor. The average value for international migration is 3.2, whereas the benchmark for this is also 4.1.

10 Based on data on free trade agreements reported by the World Trade Organization (WTO).

11 This observation does exclude small countries that in a given year obtain an unsually high proportion of their imports from Germany. In 2013, 35 percent of Bermuda's imports and 16 percent of St. Kitts and Nevis's imports were from Germany. However, due to the small size of these countries, these very high percentages are most likely due to a small number of large shipments rather than being indicative of a general pattern. In fact, there was no year between 2005 and 2012 when more than 15 percent of St. Kitts and Nevis's imports were from Germany, and only one – 2010 – when Bermuda's imports from Germany exceeded 15 percent of their total.

12 Germany ranked first worldwide on outward FDI stock breadth in the "DHL Global Connectedness Index 2014."

13 Non-citizens/temporary migrants are included in this calculation. In this case, most are temporary migrants without a path to citizenship. For details on how migrants are defined in the data sources employed here, refer to United Nations, Population Division/DESA (2013).

14 Note that in the case of wage levels, it is differences rather than similarities that boost interactions.

15 For a more extended discussion of indexicality in a broader social science context, see Abbott (2001).

16 This figure is similar to one in Head and Mayer (2013), which the authors of that paper trace back to a graphic in Isard and Peck (1954).

17 The elasticity across all models in the sample is −0.89 and across the subset of "structural gravity" models is −1.1. For this analysis, all models including country fixed effects or ratio-type methods are considered structural gravity models.

18 The formula to calculate how many times more intensively a country is expected to export to a nearer country as compared to a farther country for any elasticity

and combination of distances is: (Distance from focal country to nearer country ^ Elasticity) / (Distance from focal country to farther country ^ Elasticity). The elasticities appear in the exponents here because both distance and exports were transformed in natural logs in the gravity model regression.

19 Intensity here refers to focal country exports divided by destination country GDP. Thus, for example, the intensity of Germany's exports to the Netherlands is calculated as the value of Germany's exports to the Netherlands divided by the Netherlands' GDP.

20 One indication is provided by Head and Mayer's (2014) chapter on gravity equations in the *Handbook of International Economics:* the subsection on "Gravity models beyond trade in goods" occupies about one page out of a total of 64.

21 A more extensive literature review can be found in Ghemawat and de la Mata (2015).

22 We have also tested models with time-varying fixed effects, and found that this adjustment leads to only minor changes to the results, as reported in the online appendix at www.ghemawat.com/laws.

23 The online gravity modeling feature at www.ghemawat.com/gravity offers the flexibility to extend this analysis to cover additional years, countries, and variables.

24 Note that a similar analysis incorporating data for 224 countries and territories shows a negative and significant sign (as expected). However, this may just reflect the increased likelihood of a statistically significant result with a larger sample. The size of the coefficient for this model under the larger sample remains smaller than for other flows.

25 Composite (or compounded) distance and its research applications will be discussed further in Chapter 7.

26 Breadth is calculated in that study by comparing the distribution of each country's interactions of a given type (e.g., merchandise exports) with the rest of the world's distribution of the same type in the opposite direction (e.g., merchandise imports). A country with exports distributed proportionally to the rest of the world's imports would receive a perfect breadth score (normalized to 1), and the larger the difference between the two distributions the lower the score (normalized to 0). The world aggregate scores shown in Figure 5.11 were constructed by first taking weighted averages across countries by flow type (based on countries' shares of world total flows) and then weighted averages across flows (based on the *DHL Global Connectedness Index* pillar and component weights).

27 This gravity model analysis was performed using a dataset compiled under my direction by TCS Innovation Labs. The CAGE distance variables used here were the same as those in the Ghemawat and de la Mata gravity models reported earlier in this chapter.

28 See, for example, Jacques (2009) and Friedman (2009).

29 Adjusting for foreign content in countries' exports, however, does change these rankings. According to the OECD Trade in Value Added database (October 2015 edition), China remained behind the United States (but ahead of Germany) in terms of domestic value added content of gross exports as of 2011, the most recent year covered. In that year, 32 percent of the value of China's gross exports came from foreign sources, as compared to only 15 percent for the United States (and 26 percent for Germany).

30 Note that thirty countries are excluded: 28 by virtue of being in the EU, and the United States and China.

31 The prediction was performed by plugging the appropriate country data into the regression equation. Fixed effects for exporting and importing country were included. The year fixed effects were not, but this has no impact on the results given the framing of this analysis and how the regression equation is specified.

32 Endogeneity concerns arise as well.

33 Oxford Economics projections for this analysis were current as of April 2015.

34 Author's calculations based on data from UNCTAD.

35 For a company level analysis of China's rise, refer to Ghemawat and Hout (2016).

References

Abbott, Andrew Delano. 2001. *Chaos of Disciplines*. Chicago: University of Chicago Press.

Anderson, James E. 1979. "A Theoretical Foundation for the Gravity Equation." *American Economic Review* 69 (1):106–116.

Anderson, James E., and Eric van Wincoop. 2003. "Gravity with Gravitas: A Solution to the Border Puzzle." *American Economic Review* 93 (1):170–192.

Babones, Salvatore J., and Robin M. Farabee-Siers. 2012. "Indices of Trade Partner Concentration for 183 Countries, 1980–2008." *Journal of World-Systems Research* 18 (2):266–277. American Sociological Association. www.jwsr.org/wp-content/uploads/2012/08/Vol18n2_Babones.pdf.

Baier, Scott L., and Jeffrey H. Bergstrand. 2007. "Do free trade agreements actually increase members' international trade?" *Journal of International Economics* 71(1): 72–95.

Beckerman, W. 1956. "Distance and the Pattern of Intra-European Trade." *Review of Economics and Statistics* 38 (1):31–40. doi: 10.2307/1925556.

Bergstrand, Jeffrey H. 1985. "The Gravity Equation in International Trade: Some Microeconomic Foundations and Empirical Evidence." *Review of Economics and Statistics* 67 (3):474–481.

Bergstrand, Jeffrey H. 1989. "The Generalized Gravity Equation, Monopolistic Competition, and the Factor-Proportions Theory in International Trade." *Review of Economics and Statistics* 71 (1):143–153.

Bergstrand, Jeffrey H., and Peter Egger. 2011. "Gravity Equations and Economic Frictions in the World Economy." In *Palgrave Handbook of International Trade*, edited by Daniel M. Bernhofen, Rod Falvey, David Greenaway, and Udo Kreickemeier, 532–570. Houndmills, Basingstoke; New York: Palgrave Macmillan.

Blonigen, Bruce A., Ronald B. Davies, and Keith Head. 2003. "Estimating the Knowledge-Capital Model of the Multinational Enterprise: Comment." *American Economic Review* 93 (3):980–994.

Buch, Claudia M., Jörn Kleinert, and Farid Toubal. 2004. "The Distance Puzzle: On the Interpretation of the Distance Coefficient in Gravity Equations." *Economics Letters* 83 (3):293–298. doi: 10.1016/j.econlet.2003.10.022.

Burtch, Gordon, Anindya Ghose, and Sunil Wattal. 2014. "Cultural Differences and Geography as Determinants of Online Prosocial Lending." *MIS Quarterly* 38 (3):773–794.

Cairncross, Frances. 2001. *The Death of Distance: How the Communications Revolution Is Changing Our Lives*. Boston: Harvard Business School Press.

Carr, David L., James R. Markusen, and Keith E. Maskus. 2001. "Estimating the Knowledge-Capital Model of the Multinational Enterprise." *American Economic Review* 91 (3):693–708.

Carrère, Céline, Jaime de Melo, and John Wilson. 2013. "The Distance Puzzle and Low-Income Countries: An Update." *Journal of Economic Surveys* 27 (4):717–742. doi: 10.1111/j.1467-6419.2011.00715.x.

Chaney, Thomas. 2008. "Distorted Gravity: The Intensive and Extensive Margins of International Trade." *American Economic Review* 98 (4):1707–1721. doi: 10.1257/aer.98.4.1707.

Coe, David T., Arvind Subramanian, and Natalia T. Tamirisa. 2007. "The Missing Globalization Puzzle: Evidence of the Declining Importance of Distance." *IMF Staff Papers* 54 (1):34–58. www.imf.org/external/pubs/ft/staffp/2007/01/pdf/coe.pdf.

Coval, Joshua D., and Tobias J. Moskowitz. 1999. "Home Bias at Home: Local Equity Preference in Domestic Portfolios." *Journal of Finance* 54 (6):2045–2073. doi: 10.1111/0022-1082.00181.

Desart, Henri-Guillaume. 1846. *Chemin De Fer Direct De Bruxelles Vers Gand, Par Alost, En Communication Avec Les Stations Diverses De La Capitale: Mémoire À L'appui Du Projet Et. À L'égard Des Mouvements.* Bruxelles: E. Devroye.

di Giovanni, Julian, Andrei A. Levchenko, and Jing Zhang. 2014. "The Global Welfare Impact of China: Trade Integration and Technological Change." *American Economic Journal: Macroeconomics* 6 (3):153–183. doi: 10.1257/mac.6.3.153.

Disdier, Anne-Célia, and Keith Head. 2008. "The Puzzling Persistence of the Distance Effect on Bilateral Trade." *Review of Economics and Statistics* 90 (1):37–48.

Dow, Douglas, and Amal Karunaratna. 2006. "Developing a Multidimensional Instrument to Measure Psychic Distance Stimuli." *Journal of International Business Studies* 37 (5):578–602. doi: 10.2307/4540370.

Egger, Peter. 2008. "On the Role of Distance for Outward FDI." *Annals of Regional Science* 42 (2):375–389. doi: 10.1007/s00168-007-0166-y.

Enriquez, Luis, Sven Smit, and Jonathan Ablett. 2015. "*Shifting Tides: Global Economic Scenarios for 2015–25.*" Insights & Publications. McKinsey & Company. www.mckinsey.com/insights/strategy/shifting_tides_global_economic_scenarios_for_2015_25.

Euromonitor International. "Passport Database." Accessed 2015 & 2016. www.euromonitor.com/passport.

Fratianni, Michele. 2009. "The Gravity Model in International Trade." In *The Oxford Handbook of International Business*, edited by Alan M. Rugman, 72–89. 2nd ed. Oxford; New York: Oxford University Press.

Friedman, George. 2009. *The Next 100 Years: A Forecast for the 21st Century.* New York: Doubleday.

Friedman, Thomas L. 2005. *The World Is Flat: A Brief History of the Twenty-First Century.* New York: Farrar Straus and Giroux.

Gabaix, Xavier, and Rustam Ibragimov. 2011. "Rank – 1 / 2: A Simple Way to Improve the OLS Estimation of Tail Exponents." *Journal of Business & Economic Statistics* 29 (1):24–39. doi: 10.1198/jbes.2009.06157.

Ghemawat, Pankaj. "CAGE Distance Analysis." Last Modified 2011. www.ghemawat.com/cage/.

        2001. "Distance Still Matters: The Hard Reality of Global Expansion." *Harvard Business Review* 79 (8):137–147.

Ghemawat, Pankaj, and Steven A. Altman. 2012. "DHL Global Connectedness Index 2012." Deutsche Post DHL. www.dhl.com/en/about_us/logistics_insights/studies_research/global_connectedness_index/global_connectedness_index_2012/gci_results.html.

2014. "DHL Global Connectedness Index 2014: Analyzing Global Flows and Their Power to Increase Prosperity." Deutsche Post DHL. www.dhl.com/gci.

Ghemawat, Pankaj, and Tamara de la Mata. "Globalization and Gravity." Unpublished working paper, IESE Business School, 2015.

Ghemawat, Pankaj, and Thomas Hout. 2016. "Can China's Companies Conquer the World?" *Foreign Affairs* 95 (2):86–98.

Ghemawat, Pankaj, and Morten Olsen. 2016. "Country Size and Export Breadth." Unpublished Working Paper, IESE Business School.

Grinblatt, Mark, and Matti Keloharju. 2001. "How Distance, Language, and Culture Influence Stockholdings and Trades." *Journal of Finance* 56 (3):1053–1073. doi: 10.1111/0022-1082.00355.

Grogger, Jeffrey, and Gordon H. Hanson. 2011. "Income Maximization and the Selection and Sorting of International Migrants." *Journal of Development Economics* 95 (1):42–57. doi: 10.1016/j.jdeveco.2010.06.003.

Head, Keith, and Thierry Mayer. 2013. "What Separates Us? Sources of Resistance to Globalization." *Canadian Journal of Economics/Revue canadienne d'économique* 46 (4):1196–1231. doi: 10.1111/caje.12055.

2014. "Gravity Equations: Workhorse, Toolkit, and Cookbook." In *Handbook of International Economics*, edited by Gita Gopinath, Elhanan Helpman, and Kenneth S. Rogoff, 131–195. Oxford: North-Holland.

Held, David, Anthony G. McGrew, David Goldblatt, and Jonathan Perraton. 1999. *Global Transformations: Politics, Economics and Culture*. Stanford, CA: Stanford University Press.

Helpman, Elhanan, Marc Melitz, and Yona Rubinstein. 2008. "Estimating Trade Flows: Trading Partners and Trading Volumes." *Quarterly Journal of Economics* 123 (2):441–487.

Hummels, David. 2007. "Transportation Costs and International Trade in the Second Era of Globalization." *Journal of Economic Perspectives* 21 (3):131–154.

IEA. 2016. "OECD – Electricity Exports by Destination (Database)." Accessed February 26, 2016. http://dx.doi.org/10.1787/data-00458-en.

International Monetary Fund (IMF). April 2015. "World Economic Outlook (WEO) Database." www.imf.org/external/pubs/ft/weo/2015/01/weodata/index.aspx.

Isard, Walter, and Merton J. Peck. 1954. "Location Theory and International and Interregional Trade Theory." *Quarterly Journal of Economics* 68 (1):97–114.

Jacques, Martin. 2009. *When China Rules the World: The End of the Western World and the Birth of a New Global Order*. New York: Penguin Press.

Kimura, Fukunari, and Hyun-Hoon Lee. 2006. "The Gravity Equation in International Trade in Services." *Review of World Economics* 142 (1):92–121. doi: 10.1007/s10290-006-0058-8.

Krugman, Paul. 1980. "Scale Economies, Product Differentiation, and the Pattern of Trade." *American Economic Review* 70 (5):950–959.

Larch, Mario, Pehr-Johan Norbäck, Steffen Sirries, and Dieter M. Urban. "Heterogenous Firms, Globalization and the Distance Puzzle." IFN Working Paper 957, August 19, 2014. http://ssrn.com/abstract=2483004.

Leamer, Edward E., and James Levinsohn. 1995. "International Trade Theory: The Evidence." In *Handbook of International Economics*, edited by Gene M. Grossman, and Kenneth Rogoff, 1339–1394. Amsterdam: Elsevier Science.

Lewer, Joshua J., and Hendrik Van den Berg. 2008. "A Gravity Model of Immigration." *Economics Letters* 99 (1):164–167. doi: 10.1016/j.econlet.2007.06.019.

Lin, Faqin. 2013. "Are Distance Effects Really a Puzzle?" *Economic Modelling* 31:684–689. doi: 10.1016/j.econmod.2013.01.011.

Markusen, James R., and Keith E. Maskus. 2002. "Discriminating among Alternative Theories of the Multinational Enterprise." *Review of International Economics* 10 (4):694–707.

Mayda, Anna Maria. 2010. "International Migration: A Panel Data Analysis of the Determinants of Bilateral Flows." *Journal of Population Economics* 23 (4):1249–1274. doi: 10.1007/s00148-009-0251-x.

Mayer, Thierry, and Soledad Zignago. 2011. "Geodist Dataset." CEPII, Last Modified December 12, 2011. www.cepii.fr/CEPII/fr/bdd_modele/download.asp?id=6.

Odlyzko, Andrew. "The Forgotten Discovery of Gravity Models and the Inefficiency of Early Railway Networks." University of Minnesota, September 1, 2014. Available at SSRN: http://ssrn.com/abstract=2490241 or http://dx.doi.org/10.2139/ssrn.2490241.

Olivero, María Pía, and Yoto V. Yotov. 2012. "Dynamic Gravity: Endogenous Country Size and Asset Accumulation." *Canadian Journal of Economics* 45 (1):64–92. doi: 10.1111/j.1540-5982.2011.01687.x.

Ortega, Francesc, and Giovanni Peri. 2013. "The Effect of Income and Immigration Policies on International Migration." *Migration Studies* 1 (1):47–74. doi: 10.1093/migration/mns004.

Orwell, George. 2000. *As I Please, 1943–1945*. Edited by Sonia Orwell, and Ian Angus. 3 vols. Vol. 3, The Collected Essays, Journalism, and Letters of George Orwell. New York: Harcourt. Original edition, *Tribune*, May 12, 1944. Reprint, Harcourt, Brace, and World, Inc. 1968.

Population Division/DESA. 2013. "Trends in International Migrant Stock: The 2013 Revision – Migrants by Destination and Origin (CD ROM Documentation)." United Nations. www.un.org/en/development/desa/population/migration/data/estimates/docs/OriginMIgrantStocks_Documentation.pdf.

Portes, Richard, and Hélène Rey. 2005. "The Determinants of Cross-Border Equity Flows." *Journal of International Economics* 65 (2):269–296. doi: 10.1016/j.jinteco.2004.05.002.

Ravenstein, E. G. 1889. "The Laws of Migration." *Journal of the Royal Statistical Society* 52 (2):241–305. doi: 10.2307/2979333.

Rietveld, Piet, and Leon Janssen. 1990. "Telephone Calls and Communication Barriers." *Annals of Regional Science* 24 (4):307–318.

Santos Silva, J. M. C., and Silvana Tenreyro. 2006. "The Log of Gravity." *Review of Economics and Statistics* 88 (4):641–658.

TeleGeography. 2013. "Telegeography Report." https://www.telegeography.com/.

Tinbergen, Jan. 1962. *Shaping the World Economy: Suggestions for an International Economic Policy*. New York: Twentieth Century Fund.

UNCTAD. 2013. "Global Value Chains and Development: Investment and Value Added Trade in the Global Economy." http://unctad.org/en/PublicationsLibrary/diae2013d1_en.pdf.

United Nations Development Programme (UNDP). 1999. "Human Development Report 1999: Globalization with a Human Face." http://hdr.undp.org/sites/default/files/reports/260/hdr_1999_en_nostats.pdf.

Wei, Shang-Jin. "Intra-National Versus International Trade: How Stubborn Are Nations in Global Integration?" National Bureau of Economic Research Working Paper Series 5531, April 1996. http://papers.nber.org/papers/w5531.pdf.

Wong, Wei-Kang. 2008. "Comparing the Fit of the Gravity Model for Different Cross-Border Flows." *Economics Letters* 99 (3):474–477. doi: 10.1016/j.econlet.2007.09.018.

Yotov, Yoto V. 2012. "A Simple Solution to the Distance Puzzle in International Trade." *Economics Letters* 117 (3):794–798. doi: 10.1016/j.econlet.2012.08.032.

6   Distance at the Industry and Company Levels

Pankaj Ghemawat and Steven A. Altman

This chapter provides empirical evidence for the law of distance at the industry and firm levels, complementing the country-level evidence presented in Chapter 5. It also parallels Chapter 4, which provided firm-level evidence for the law of semiglobalization. The more limited availability of data on the breadth of international business activity compared to its depth precludes function-by-function treatment of the sort provided in Chapter 4. We focus, instead, on extending the gravity modeling from the previous chapter to the industry and firm levels before turning to implications for business practice.

We begin by analyzing how the distance sensitivity of merchandise trade and announced greenfield foreign direct investment (FDI) vary across industries. This involves estimating gravity models that incorporate the same CAGE distance effects as the trade and FDI models estimated in Chapter 5. The sensitivity of trade and investment to specific types of distance turns out to depend in predictable ways on the characteristics of the product or service involved.

We then shift from the industry level to the firm level, where most prior empirical work has been based on single-country samples. After a brief discussion of such single-country evidence, we turn to newer multicountry evidence and present a gravity-based analysis of the foreign subsidiary locations of the Fortune Global 500. This analysis confirms that the footprints of the world's largest firms conform to the law of distance. Shifting the analysis to the firm level also allows us to analyze firm characteristics that seem to be associated with firms operating across greater CAGE distance.

The remaining sections of this chapter focus on implications for business practice. The third section discusses qualitative and quantitative applications of the CAGE Distance Framework in business analysis. The fourth section discusses complementary tools and frameworks that are designed to be used with the CAGE Distance Framework. The final substantive section addresses ways in which firms can boost their capacity to deal with distance.

The authors would like to thank Xiaoqian Li and Phillip Bastian for their assistance with the industry level trade and FDI models, respectively.

Table 6.1 *The CAGE Framework at the Industry Level*

Cultural Distance	Administrative Distance	Geographic Distance	Economic Distance
Cultural differences matter the most when: • Products have high linguistic content (TV programs) • Products matter to cultural or national identity (foods) • Product features vary in terms of size (cars) or standards (electrical equipment) • Products carry country-specific quality associations (wines)	Government involvement is high in industries that are: • Producers of staple goods (electricity) • Producers of other "entitlements" (drugs) • Large employers (farming) • Large suppliers to government (mass transportation) • National champions (aerospace) • Vital to national security (telecommunications) • Exploiters of natural resources (oil, mining) • Subject to high sunk costs (infrastructure)	Geography plays a more important role when: • Products have a low value-to-weight or bulk ratio (cement) • Products are fragile or perishable (glass, fruit) • Local supervision and operational requirements are high (services)	Economic differences make the biggest impact when: • Nature of demand varies with income (cars) • Economies of standardization or scale are limited (cement) • Labor and other factor cost differences are salient (garments) • Distribution or business systems are different (insurance) • Companies need to be responsive (home appliances)

Source: Table 2–3 of Ghemawat (2007), p. 50.

The Law of Distance at the Industry Level

Variations in the sensitivity of different industries to specific dimensions of the CAGE Distance Framework were discussed briefly in Ghemawat (2001) and elaborated in some detail in Ghemawat (2007). Table 6.1 characterizes the kinds of industries that are expected to be especially sensitive to each dimension of CAGE distance. This early work on the CAGE Framework at the industry level was informed first qualitatively by case studies and then confirmed quantitatively by the estimation of seventy industry-specific gravity models of merchandise trade (Ghemawat and Mallick 2003). Here, we provide an updated and expanded gravity model analysis at the industry level of merchandise trade and then add a similar analysis of announced greenfield FDI.

The principal econometric challenge with shifting from gravity modeling of aggregate trade and FDI to modeling at the industry level is that the proportion of "zero values" (country pairs with no interactions) increases and ordinary least squares (OLS) regression results become increasingly biased. In the standard OLS specification, the dependent variable (as well as the continuous

Table 6.2 *OLS and PPML Coefficients for Merchandise Trade in All Products*

	(1)	(2)
Dependent variable	Merchandise trade (all products)	
Model	OLS	PPML
Independent variables		
Common official language	0.861***	0.133*
	(0.0598)	(0.069)
Colonial linkage	0.548***	0.0510
	(0.1279)	(0.092)
Trade agreement	0.369***	0.397***
	(0.0518)	(0.0583)
Physical distance (logged)	−1.370***	−0.718***
	(0.0361)	(0.0344)
Common border	0.554***	0.376***
	−0.162	−0.0682
Ratio of per capita income	0.0580***	0.0410
(max/min, logged)	(0.0151)	(0.0270)
Product of GDPs	0.609***	0.520***
(logged)	(0.0376)	(0.0379)
Constant	16.254***	16.822***
	(0.532)	(0.513)
Observations	66,706	76,545
Adjusted R-squared (OLS)/R-squared (PPML)	0.794	0.911
% of zero values	0	12.85

Robust standard errors in parentheses, clustered by country pair. *** $p<0.01$, ** $p<0.05$, * $p<0.1$.

explanatory variables) is logged, forcing exclusion of observations with zero values, even though the absence of a flow is informative. In addition, OLS does not correct for heteroscedasticity, which is a common problem in analyzing country-to-country flows. For these reasons, most of the regressions in this chapter are based on the Poisson Pseudo-Maximum Likelihood (PPML) estimator instead of OLS (Santos Silva and Tenreyro 2006). PPML retains many of the useful features of OLS,[1] but has the advantage of not discarding zero values (Shepherd 2013, 52). However, it should be noted that this – as well as differences in the data samples employed – does mean that the results reported in this chapter are not directly comparable to those in Chapter 5.[2]

Table 6.2 compares OLS and PPML estimates of gravity models for total merchandise trade (as baselines for the industry-level analysis that follows). The PPML coefficients tend to be smaller, as discussed in Chapter 5. The coefficient for colonial linkages becomes insignificant, while the coefficient for common official language is significant only at the 0.1 level, rather than the

0.01 level achieved in the OLS model. In addition, the R-squared[3] of the PPML models tends to be higher than the adjusted R-squared of the OLS models. Because PPML allows the addition of zero values, the number of observations is higher: 13 percent of the PPML observations are zero when we look at all merchandise trade. As we disaggregate to the level of individual industries, the proportion of zeros in the models will grow significantly.

Merchandise Trade by Industry

Using the UN's Comtrade database, which provides dyadic data on merchandise trade at the detailed product level, we are able to examine trade patterns by industry (United Nations 2015).[4] The histograms[5] in Figure 6.1 show the distribution of coefficients across all ninety-seven two-digit HS codes. With the notable exception of physical distance, these distributions peak near the regression coefficients for total merchandise trade (the vertical lines superimposed on the histograms).

The coefficients for the (logged) ratio of GDP per capita are of particular interest, since arbitrage may be more common in this regard than on other dimensions of distance. Recall that the coefficient for this variable was insignificant in Chapter 5. Consistent with that overall pattern, the PPML coefficient for the ratio of GDP per capita is near zero, and fails to achieve statistical significance. However, there are forty-four product categories for which the coefficient is significant and positive, indicating economic arbitrage, and twenty product categories for which it is significant and negative, indicating that economic distance dampens trade.

Although we cannot discuss the coefficients obtained for all of the industries individually, many of the extreme coefficients do conform to intuitions. The product category for which a common language is associated with the largest boost to trade is printed books, newspapers, pictures, and other products of the printing industry. The category for which trade expands the most with a common border and shrinks the most with physical distance is live animals, which are obviously difficult and costly to transport over long distances. Aircraft, spacecraft, and parts thereof are the least sensitive to physical distance, partly because they are themselves vehicles for long-distance transportation. Economic distance (based on the ratio of countries' per capita GDPs) inhibits trade the most for pharmaceutical products (perhaps due to affordability) and boosts trade the most for natural or cultured pearls and precious or semiprecious stones (due to arbitrage). Table 6.3 reports the highest, lowest, and smallest (absolute value) coefficients for each of the distance variables.

The goodness of fit for these models also varies across industries, as summarized in Figure 6.2 and Table 6.4. Recall that, due to the inclusion of fixed

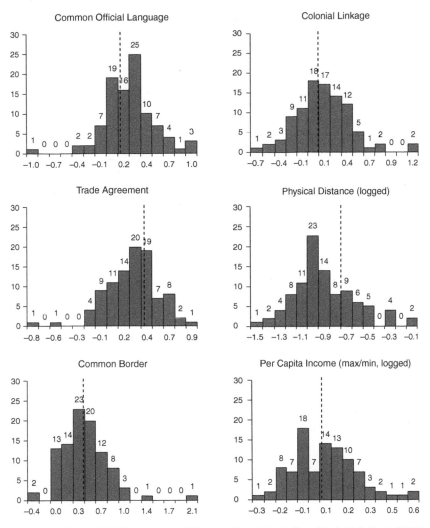

Figure 6.1 Histograms of Distance Variables in Two-Digit H.S. Code PPML Gravity Models of Merchandise Trade (Vertical Line Indicates Model Coefficient for All Products).
Source: Authors' analysis.

effects, R-squared values tend to be high in these types of models. Twenty-six of the two-digit product categories have an R-squared above 0.9 and only nine have an R-squared of less than 0.6. The majority of the estimations that work best involve finished products, whereas several of the worst performing models involve intermediate goods.

Table 6.3 *Highest, Lowest, and Smallest (Absolute Value) Coefficients for Each of the Distance Variables for Two-Digit HS Codes in PPML Gravity Models of Merchandise Trade*

	H.S. Code with Highest Coefficient		Coefficient	S.E.
Common official language	49	Printed books, newspapers, pictures and other products of the printing industry	1.094***	(.132)
Colonial linkage	99	Commodities not specified according to kind	1.250***	(.351)
Trade agreement	79	Zinc and articles thereof	0.975***	(.147)
Common border	01	Live animals	2.188***	(.195)
Physical distance (logged)	88	Aircraft, spacecraft, and parts thereof	0.001	(.137)
Ratio of per capita income (max/min, logged)	71	Natural or cultured pearls, precious or semi-precious stones	0.644***	(.091)

	H.S. Code with Lowest Coefficient		Coefficient	S.E.
Common official language	67	Prepared feathers and down and articles made of feathers or of down	−1.054***	(.351)
Colonial linkage	87	Vehicles other than railway or tramway rolling stock	−0.730***	(.208)
Trade agreement	01	Live animals	−0.858**	(.436)
Common border	80	Tin and articles thereof	−0.497*	(.261)
Physical distance (logged)	01	Live animals	−1.554***	(.190)
Ratio of per capita income (max/min, logged)	30	Pharmaceutical products	−0.375***	(.060)

	H.S. Code with Smallest Coefficient (Absolute Value)		Coefficient	S.E.
Common official language	95	Toys, games and sports requisites; parts and accessories thereof	0.005	(.279)
Colonial linkage	08	Edible fruit and nuts; peel of citrus fruit or melons	0.001	(.196)
Trade agreement	81	Other base metals; cermets; articles thereof	−0.005	(.122)
Common border	50	Silk	0.006	(.305)
Physical distance (logged)	88	Aircraft, spacecraft, and parts thereof	0.001	(.137)
Ratio of per capita income (max/min, logged)	99	Commodities not specified according to kind	−0.001	(.136)

Robust standard errors in parentheses, clustered by country pair.

*** $p < 0.01$, ** $p < 0.05$, * $p < 0.1$.

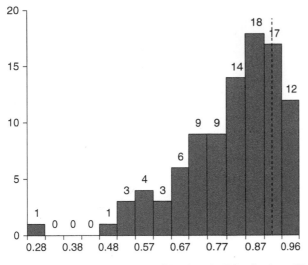

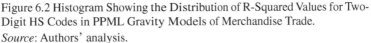

Figure 6.2 Histogram Showing the Distribution of R-Squared Values for Two-Digit HS Codes in PPML Gravity Models of Merchandise Trade.
Source: Authors' analysis.

Greenfield Foreign Direct Investment by Industry

Gravity models of announced greenfield FDI by industry provide further support for the law of distance and, again, reveal systematic variation in distance sensitivity across industries. For this purpose, we rely on the fDi Markets database, developed by the *Financial Times*. This is the most comprehensive database of announced greenfield FDI, providing detailed data on FDI activities by multinationals around the world, although it does suffer from the limitations of being based on FDI announcements, whereas the FDI statistics used in Chapter 5 were based on measures of actual FDI from national account data. Since there are relatively few announced projects for most industries in any given year, the fDi Markets data were aggregated over the period from 2005 to 2014, reducing the total number of observations. Even after cumulating the data across years, two-thirds of the values are zeros, so we again focus on PPML rather than OLS estimation. Table 6.5 shows the differences across the OLS and PPML results for FDI outward stocks (as analyzed in Chapter 5) and announced greenfield FDI from fDi Markets.

Although there are some differences in the two sets of results, the similarities are encouraging. The PPML coefficients are significant at the 0.01 level

Table 6.4 *2-Digit HS Codes with Best and Worst Model Fit in PPML Gravity Models of Merchandise Trade*

Highest R-squared		R-squared	Lowest R-squared		R-squared
46	Manufactures of straw, of esparto or of other plaiting materials	0.987	89	Ships, boats and floating structures	0.259
63	Other made up textile articles; sets; worn clothing and worn textile articles	0.985	99	Commodities not specified according to kind	0.495
			17	Sugars and sugar confectionery	0.519
66	Umbrellas, sun umbrellas, walking sticks, seat sticks, whips, riding-crops	0.985	53	Other vegetable textile fibers; paper yarn and woven fabric of paper yarn	0.520
65	Headgear and parts thereof	0.982			
67	Prepared feathers and down and articles made of feathers or of down	0.981	23	Residues and waste from the food industries	0.538
			24	Tobacco and manufactured tobacco substitutes	0.550
45	Cork and articles of cork	0.971	10	Cereals	0.572
64	Footwear, gaiters and the like; parts of such articles	0.964	75	Nickel and articles thereof	0.575
94	Furniture; bedding, mattresses, cushions and similar stuffed furnishing	0.955	14	Vegetable plaiting materials; vegetable products nes	0.589
95	Toys, games and sports requisites; parts and accessories thereof	0.954	25	Salt; sulfur; earths and stone; plastering materials, lime and cement	0.623
83	Miscellaneous articles of base metal	0.948			

for common official language, colonial linkage, weighted physical distance, and ratio of GDP per capita, but insignificant for regional bloc and common border. The signs are also consistent with expectations (except for the one on common border, which was insignificant). And the physical distance coefficients are remarkably similar. Clearly, the law of distance holds for this dataset as well.

The advantage of using the fDi Markets data is that we are also able to examine the coefficients at the industry level. Note, however, that this

Table 6.5 *OLS and PPML Coefficients for FDI across all Industries*

Dependent variable	(1) FDI outward stocks	(2) Announced Greenfield FDI (fDi Markets)	(3) FDI outward stocks	(4) Announced Greenfield FDI (fDi Markets)
Model	OLS		PPML	
Independent variables				
Common official	0.755***	0.404***	0.390***	0.450***
language	(0.143)	(0.105)	(0.137)	(0.108)
Colonial linkage	1.266***	0.841***	0.380***	0.460***
	(0.195)	(0.160)	(0.140)	(0.111)
Regional bloc	0.101	0.327**	0.0270	0.0744
	(0.171)	(0.149)	(0.0237)	(0.152)
Physical distance (logged)	−1.210***	−0.845***	−0.589***	−0.591***
	(0.0756)	(0.0605)	(0.0951)	(0.0649)
Common border	−0.014	0.188	0.306	−0.104
	(0.225)	(0.152)	(0.191)	(0.121)
Ratio of per capita income	−0.377***	−0.346***	−0.419***	−0.199***
(max/min, logged)	(0.0794)	(0.0359)	(0.0984)	(0.0437)
Product of GDPs	0.226**	0.057	0.382***	0.393***
(logged)	(0.0933)	(0.113)	(0.143)	(0.0757)
Constant	14.350***	10.382***	14.940***	9.988***
	(1.237)	(1.294)	(0.977)	(0.792)
Observations	13,514	2,822	22,328	8,321
Adjusted R-squared (OLS)/ R-squared (PPML)	0.751	0.577	0.767	0.829

Robust standard errors in parentheses, clustered by country pair.

*** $p<0.01$, ** $p<0.05$, * $p<0.1$.

Source: Ghemawat and de la Mata (2015) and authors' calculations.

analysis does not exactly parallel the merchandise exports analysis, in that the categories are aggregated up to only thirty-nine "sectors," versus ninety-seven two-digit product categories in the merchandise trade data. Also, the announced greenfield FDI data include service industries as well as merchandise. Figure 6.3 shows histograms of the estimated coefficients.

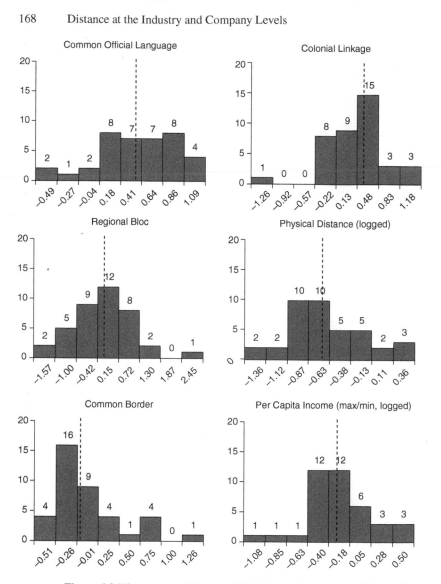

Figure 6.3 Histograms of Distance Variables in Sector-Level PPML Gravity Models of Announced Greenfield FDI (Vertical Line Indicates Model Coefficient for All Sectors).
Source: Authors' analysis.

Looking at the extremes (see Table 6.6) once again reveals some interesting patterns. The industry for which common official language was most important was leisure and entertainment, which is unsurprising given the sense that culture is particularly important in such industries. For colonial linkage, the highest

Table 6.6 *Highest, Lowest, and Smallest (Absolute Value) Coefficients for Each of the Distance Variables for Sectors in PPML Gravity Models of Announced Greenfield FDI*

	Sector with Highest Coefficient	Coefficient	(S.E.)
Common official language	Leisure and entertainment	1.198*	(0.652)
Colonial linkage	Minerals[†]	1.350	(0.915)
Regional bloc	Business services	2.734***	(0.941)
Common border	Business machines and equipment	1.383***	(0.417)
Physical distance (logged)	Space and defense	0.482	(0.421)
Ratio of per capita income (max/min, logged)	Semiconductors	0.616*	(0.337)
	Sector with Lowest coefficient	**Coefficient**	**(S.E.)**
Common official language	Minerals	−0.603	(0.890)
Colonial linkage	Semiconductors	−1.438***	(0.514)
Regional bloc	Business machines and equipment	−1.859***	(0.531)
Common border	Textiles	−0.638*	(0.342)
Physical distance (logged)	Wood products	−1.487***	(0.374)
Ratio of per capita income (max/min, logged)	Space and defense[‡]	−1.193	(1.012)
	Sector with Smallest coefficient (absolute value)	**Coefficient**	**(S.E.)**
Common official language	Business services	−0.003	(0.441)
Colonial linkage	Wood products	−0.031	(0.473)
Regional bloc	Coal, oil, and natural gas	−0.077	(0.413)
Common border	Communications	0.004	(0.195)
Physical distance (logged)	Automotive components	−0.008	(0.140)
Ratio of per capita income (max/min, logged)	Automotive components	0.022	(0.114)

Robust standard errors in parentheses, clustered by country pair.

*** $p<0.01$, ** $p<0.05$, * $p<0.1$.

† The highest statistically significant coefficient for colonial linkage was for business services.

‡ The lowest statistically significant coefficient for ratio of GDP per capita was for rubber.

statistically significant coefficient was for business services, which may reflect the benefits of similar legal and political systems for such services. The lowest coefficient was for semiconductors, an industry dominated by a small number of countries that, for the most part, do not have colonial linkages with each other.

The spread of coefficients for regional trade bloc was particularly interesting. In the histogram, the distribution is single-peaked and centered around zero. Yet there are significant negative *and* positive coefficients. This pattern is probably reflective of heterogeneity across industries in terms of the prevalence

Table 6.7 *Sectors with Best and Worst Model Fit in PPML Gravity Models of Announced Greenfield FDI*

Highest R-squared	R-squared	Lowest R-squared	R-squared
Software and IT services	0.970	Wood products	0.327
Leisure and entertainment	0.921	Minerals	0.342
Automotive components	0.917	Building and construction materials	0.434
Business machines and equipment	0.891	Coal, oil, and natural gas	0.476
Semiconductors	0.887	Paper, printing, and packaging	0.499
Beverages	0.876	Warehousing and storage	0.520
Medical devices	0.874	Ceramics and glass	0.525
Industrial machinery, equipment, and tools	0.868	Metals	0.549
		Healthcare	0.569
Automotive OEM	0.851	Textiles	0.570
Financial services	0.847		

of horizontal FDI (substituting for trade) and vertical FDI (motivated by trade). Baltagi, Egger, and Pfaffermayr (2008) discuss the complex relationship between regional trade agreements and FDI.

The industry where physical distance has the largest negative effect is wood products, although it is worth adding that wood products had an R-squared of only 0.33, the lowest among the industries analyzed (see Table 6.7). The ratio of GDP per capita does not show the same double-peaked distribution for greenfield FDI as it did for merchandise trade. Generally speaking, the negative coefficients are significant – seventeen industries have significant negative coefficients, whereas only two of the positive coefficients are significant (paralleling the results in Chapter 5).

Table 6.7 and Figure 6.4 indicate that the R-squared values are significantly worse for greenfield FDI by sector than for merchandise trade at the two-digit HS level. This presumably reflects the smaller sample size, the pooling of years, and the greater volatility of greenfield FDI announcements. Nevertheless, the top ten (out of thirty-nine) sectors have R-squared levels above 0.8, and only for five does R-squared drop below 0.5.

The analysis presented in this section has provided empirical support for the law of distance at the industry level. It also illustrated the heterogeneous effects that the individual types of distance highlighted by the CAGE Framework have across industries. This is consistent with the guidance in Ghemawat (2001) that managers should customize their CAGE distance analyses to the industry on which they are focused.

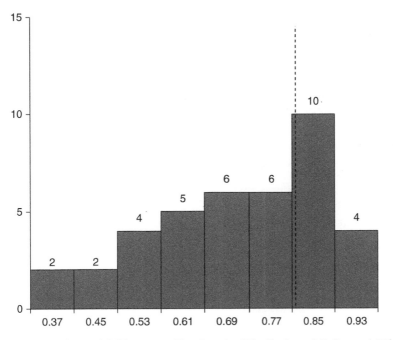

Figure 6.4 Histogram Showing the Distribution of R-Squared Values for Sectors in PPML Gravity Models of Announced Greenfield FDI.
Source: Authors' analysis.

The Law of Distance at the Firm Level

The country-level evidence presented in Chapter 5 and the industry-level evidence presented in the previous section already provide strong hints that the law of distance should hold at the firm level. Recall that an estimated 80 percent of trade takes place within the value chains of multinational firms (UNCTAD 2013, iii), and FDI is, of course, required for firms to become multinational, according to typical definitions.[6] However, rather than relying on such inferences, this section turns to the calibration of distance effects directly from firm-level data. The estimation of gravity models at the firm level is still a nascent research area, but one with the potential to generate new insights as it brings one of the most powerful tools from international economics to bear on the primary units of analysis in international business, the multinational firm and its subsidiaries.

Until recently, data availability constraints precluded firm-level analysis analogous to the country-level analysis presented in Chapter 5 since firms typically try to protect the confidentiality of detailed data on the geographic distribution of their international activities.[7] Gravity models of multinational activity, for example, Hejazi (2007), still tend to rely on data aggregated across firms by country. In light of these constraints, firm-level evidence for the law of distance has traditionally been based on analysis of single-country samples, for which it is easier to access the required data. The following subsection discusses such single-country evidence, after which we turn to more recent multicountry evidence and gravity models.

Single-Country Evidence

Single-country studies were responsible for the observation that firms operate much more intensively in proximate and similar countries, a major theme in the international business literature. The most cited paper in the history of the *Journal of International Business Studies* (Johanson and Vahlne 1977) drew on a sample of Swedish firms to argue that the order in which firms establish themselves in foreign markets reflects the psychic distance between the home and host countries. The second most cited paper in the same journal also featured single-country evidence of distance effects. Kogut and Singh (1988) used a sample of entries into the United States to relate entry mode to cultural distance.

Updated and expanded single-country evidence at the firm level for the law of distance is provided by data supplied to one of us (Ghemawat) by Jim Fetzer of the US Department of Commerce covering the foreign countries where US multinationals have established subsidiaries, segmented according to the number of foreign countries in which the firms operate. The median US multinational in 2012 operated in three foreign countries and the modal multinational in only one. The map in the top panel of Figure 6.5 reflects the location choices of US multinationals with a foreign subsidiary in just one country, and the bottom panel their counterparts that are present in more than twenty foreign countries.

Where do US firms go to establish their only foreign operation? Canada is their most frequent destination – almost exactly a third of the time. A somewhat smaller cohort of US companies choose to go to the UK. No other country reaches the 10 percent mark, and Canada, the UK, and Mexico combine to account for more than 60 percent of these US-company forays abroad, even though those three countries represent only about 10 percent of non-US world GDP.

In the bottom panel of Figure 6.5, if we look at firms that are present in more than twenty foreign countries, we find that the proportion of foreign investments in Canada, the UK, and Mexico does, of course, decline.[8] However, the pattern is still not the one that would be expected if distance had no impact at all. The UK and Canada are still the top ranked countries, even though they are only the world's sixth and eleventh largest economies. The other countries in the top five are European countries with close historical ties to the United States.

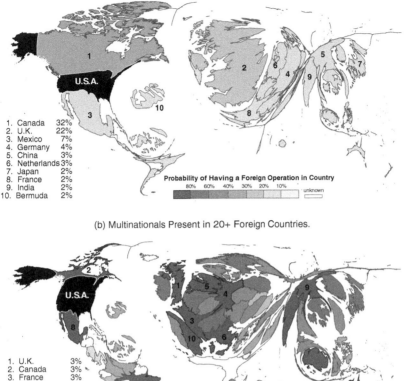

(a) Multinationals Present in One Foreign Country.

1. Canada   32%
2. U.K.   22%
3. Mexico   7%
4. Germany   4%
5. China   3%
6. Netherlands 3%
7. Japan   2%
8. France   2%
9. India   2%
10. Bermuda   2%

Probability of Having a Foreign Operation in Country
80% 60% 40% 30% 20% 10%   unknown

(b) Multinationals Present in 20+ Foreign Countries.

1. U.K.   3%
2. Canada   3%
3. France   3%
4. Germany   3%
5. Netherlands 3%
6. Italy   3%
7. Australia   2%
8. Mexico   2%
9. China   2%
10. Spain   2%

Probability of Having a Foreign Operation in Country
80% 60% 40% 30% 20% 10%   unknown

Figure 6.5 Foreign Operations of US Multinationals.
Source: Generated based on data provided by the US Department of Commerce.

At the firm level, one can also look at the impact of distance on a broader range of managerially relevant dependent variables, including performance metrics as well as aggregate volumes. Ghemawat (2007, 36), for example, showed that Wal-Mart's profitability declined sharply with physical distance from its US home base. Data from 2015 show that the same pattern also applies to Wal-Mart's market share in foreign markets (see Figure 6.6). This

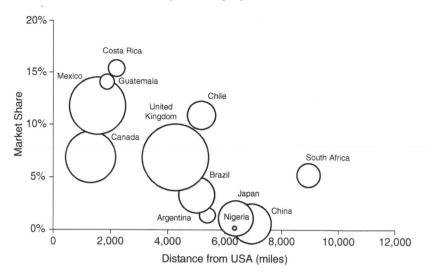

Figure 6.6 Wal-Mart's Share of Store-based Retail versus Distance from the United States (Bubbles Proportional to Wal-Mart Retail Sales Excluding Tax by Country).
Note: Ghana, Kenya, Uganda, Tanzania, Mozambique, Malawi, Zambia, Namibia, Botswana, Swaziland, Lesotho, El Salvador, Honduras, Nicaragua, and India are omitted from the figure due to lack of data on those countries.
Source: Generated based on data from Euromonitor Passport and CEPII.

analysis provides a firm-level analogue to the analysis of the intensity of Germany's merchandise exports relative to physical distance from Germany in Chapter 5.

Larger studies suggest that the relationship between distance and firm performance is complicated by dependence on the quality of firms' resources and capabilities as well as the extent to which managers anticipate and make efforts to adjust to or mitigate the effects of distance. Several studies do associate intraregional expansion with better results than interregional expansion (Qian et al. 2010; Rugman and Oh 2010). Oh and Contractor (2012) also find similar main effects for a sample of US firms, but report that interactions with product diversification can significantly shift the relationship between geographic scope and performance. Banalieva and Dhanaraj (2013), using a sample of Triad[9] based firms, discern a relationship between regionalization and performance in which higher performance reduces home region orientation, but home region orientation does not itself have a significant effect on performance. Almodóvar (2012), relying on a sample of Spanish firms, reports different performance patterns depending on firms' strategies of product standardization or customization/adaptation. Given the many factors that can affect firm performance as well as empirical problems with most work on the multinationality-performance relationship (Verbeke 2012), it is not surprising that the relationship between distance and performance remains murkier than the relationship between distance and the scope of business activity itself.

Multicountry Evidence

Moving beyond single-country evidence of firm-level distance effects, one of the data sources that has opened the way for new firm-level analysis using gravity models is the fDi Markets database, which we used in the previous section to analyze announced greenfield FDI at the industry level. Using fDi Markets data, Castellani, Jimenez, and Zanfei (2013) employ a gravity-like specification to analyze announced greenfield FDI in R&D relative to manufacturing, and find that R&D is less sensitive to physical distance than manufacturing. They also report that R&D investment is highly sensitive to institutional distance, and that after controlling for institutional distance, the effect of physical distance becomes insignificant for R&D (but not for manufacturing).

A promising source of new insights when shifting from calibrating distance effects at the country level to the firm level lies in the possibility of analyzing characteristics that are associated with some firms operating across more distance than others. Some single-country studies have already done so. Thus, Cho and Padmanabhan (2005, 307) find that "higher levels of experience, particularly decision-specific experience (prior experience with a particular ownership structure mode), mitigates potential impacts of uncertainty and costs caused by the high level of cultural distance."

Here, we analyze multiple dimensions of distance with a multicountry sample by estimating a gravity model of the foreign subsidiaries of the Fortune Global 500. One reason for choosing to focus on the world's largest firms by revenue is the pattern, discussed in Chapter 4, that multinationality is positively related to firm size. If the world's largest firms are significantly deterred by multiple dimensions of distance, this would provide stronger evidence for the law of distance than if the analysis were conducted using a sample of smaller firms. Focusing on the Fortune Global 500 also permits us to relate our analysis to prior research on the regionalization of that sample of firms (Rugman and Verbeke 2004, Oh and Rugman 2014), which we return to and update in Chapter 10.

We analyze the distances across which Fortune Global 500 firms operate using a dataset we assembled with Niccolò Pisani of the University of Amsterdam. The number of majority-owned subsidiaries a firm has in each foreign country is extracted from the Orbis database. We focus on simple counts of numbers of subsidiaries by country in order to sidestep concerns about nested subsidiary structures that sometimes lead to double counting (or worse) of revenues. The dataset covers the years 2013 and 2014, and shows that on average, 40 percent of foreign subsidiaries were intraregional in both years (based on the "broad triad" regions discussed in Chapter 10). This is roughly consistent with the 37–39 percent reported between 2000 and 2007 by Rugman and Oh (2013).[10]

In addition to the standard country-level CAGE variables that were used in the gravity models reported in Chapter 5, we add three firm characteristics to the dataset that we hypothesize could be associated with firms operating across greater distances. The R&D and advertising intensity of industries have long been recognized as markers of multinationality (see, e.g., Caves 1971),[11] prompting us to hypothesize that they may also be associated with reduced sensitivity to distance. We also add top management team (TMT) non-nativity (the proportion of the firm's top management team members who are not from the firm's home country), in line with the discussion in Chapter 8 on national diversity. Data on these variables were compiled from annual reports, company websites, and the Orbis database.

Prior to adding these firm-level explanatory variables to the analysis, we ran a set of baseline models using only the typical country-level gravity variables employed in Chapter 5. These baseline models were estimated both at the country level (aggregating up from firms) and at the firm level (see Table 6.8). The country-level model represents a standard gravity specification, and incorporates home country and host country fixed effects. At the firm level, firm fixed effects are included in place of home country fixed effects. For the same reasons as in the industry-level models, we again use the PPML estimator. At least one distance variable along each of the CAGE dimensions (common official language, colonial linkage, physical distance, ratio of per capita income) is significant in the firm-level model, and the results are generally stable across the two levels of analysis. The law of distance clearly applies to the locations of foreign subsidiaries of the Fortune Global 500.

In order to analyze how firm characteristics affect subsidiary locations, we need to add them to the model. However, simply adding them to the regressions as independent variables does not show the effect of these characteristics on sensitivity to distance. Instead, we insert them as interaction terms, running separate regressions in which we test each firm characteristic as a moderator of each distance variable (with those regressions containing all distance variables, the selected moderator, and the interaction of the selected moderator with the selected distance variable). Thus, for example, to test R&D intensity as a moderator of physical distance effects, we add into the baseline regression R&D

Table 6.8 *Fortune Global 500 Gravity Models at Country and Firm Levels*

	(1)	(2)
Dependent variable	Number of subsidiaries by country	
Level of analysis	Firm	Country
Independent variables		
Common official language	0.383***	0.378***
	(0.0651)	(0.105)
Colonial linkage	0.253***	0.250**
	(0.0747)	(0.123)
Regional bloc	0.0194	0.0226
	(0.0868)	(0.128)
Physical distance (logged)	−0.387***	−0.385***
	(0.0373)	(0.0614)
Common border	−0.0163	−0.0212
	(0.0983)	(0.121)
Ratio of per capita income (max/min, logged)	−0.119**	−0.122
	(0.0512)	(0.0799)
Product of GDPs (logged)	0.106*	0.0542
	(0.0645)	(0.119)
Home country fixed effects		Included
Partner country fixed effects	Included	Included
Firm fixed effects	Included	
Year fixed effects	Included	Included
Constant	1.260**	2.282***
	(0.513)	(0.780)
Observations	76,128	6,528
R-squared	0.520	0.913

Robust standard errors in parentheses, clustered by country pair.
*** $p<0.01$, ** $p<0.05$, * $p<0.1$.

intensity and the interaction of R&D Intensity with physical distance. The new (general) regression equation is then:

$$F_{fdt} = \beta_0 + \beta_1(\text{Common language})_{od} + \beta_2(\text{Colonial linkage})_{od} + \beta_3(\text{Regional bloc})_{odt} + \beta_4 \log(\text{Physical distance})_{od} + \beta_5(\text{Common border})_{od} + \beta_6 \log(\text{Income disparities})_{odt} + \beta_7(\text{Firm characteristic})_{ft} * (\text{Selected distance variable})_{odt} + \beta_8(\text{Firm characteristic})_{ft} + \beta_9 \log(\text{Product of GDPs})_{odt} + \varphi_f + \varphi_d + \varphi_t + u_{fdt}$$

Since we expect less distance sensitivity for firms with higher values of R&D intensity, advertising intensity, and TMT non-nativity, the coefficients on

Table 6.9 *Fortune Global 500 Gravity Models at Firm Level, Interactions of R&D Intensity, Advertising Intensity, and TMT Non-nativity with Distance Variables*

Distance variables	Common official language	Colonial linkage	Regional bloc	Physical distance (logged)	Common border	GDP per capita ratio (max/min, logged)
Hypothesized signs	−	−	−	+	−	+
Interaction terms						
R&D intensity	−2.470***	−3.025***	−5.021***	1.411***	−5.701***	−0.0037
	(0.870)	(1.154)	(1.226)	(0.368)	(1.396)	(0.334)
Advertising intensity	−1.918**	−3.118**	−5.068***	1.977***	−0.741	1.600***
	(0.911)	(1.255)	(1.283)	(0.362)	(1.011)	(0.292)
Top management team non-nativity	−0.579***	−0.115	−0.857***	0.436***	−0.763***	0.295***
	(0.179)	(0.282)	(0.176)	(0.0600)	(0.223)	(0.0554)

Robust standard errors in parentheses, clustered by country pair.
*** $p<0.01$, ** $p<0.05$, * $p<0.1$.

the interactions with the binary distance/similarity variables (common official language, colonial linkage, regional bloc, and common border) are hypothesized to be negative. The opposite holds for the continuous distance variables (physical distance and per capita income ratio), as a higher value of these variables means that two countries are more distant.

The interaction terms from these regressions are summarized in Table 6.9, and the full regression results are available in the online appendix at www. ghemawat.com/laws. Remarkably, for all of the significant interaction terms, the signs on the coefficients fit with our hypotheses, and almost all of the coefficients were significant. The only insignificant coefficients were: GDP per capita ratio interacted with R&D intensity, common border interacted with advertising intensity, and colonial linkage interacted with top management team non-nativity.

This analysis, in addition to providing evidence for the law of distance at the firm level, hints at the still untapped potential for gravity-based research on distance effects using firm-level data. Further research is needed to examine in more detail *how* these firm characteristics (and others) relate to the multiple dimensions of distance across which firms operate. Such research could also be expanded to incorporate other dependent variables, such as performance metrics. We return to the international business research agenda in Chapter 7. The remainder of this chapter discusses – very briefly – some of the implications for practice.

Distance Analysis and Business Strategy

This section begins the discussion of practical business applications of the law of distance, starting with the CAGE Distance Framework itself and then briefly recapping a set of complementary tools and frameworks meant to be used with it. And the final section discusses ways in which firms can become more "distance-capable": that is, boost their capacity to operate across multiple dimensions of distance. This material draws heavily on prior Ghemawat publications, most notably *Redefining Global Strategy* (Ghemawat 2007).

The CAGE Distance Framework in Business Analysis

The CAGE Distance Framework can be used in firm-level analysis both qualitatively and quantitatively to examine distances and differences between countries and elucidate their business implications. This type of examination should inform decisions about which trajectory of international expansion to follow, what strategy and sources of value creation to emphasize (discussed in the next subsection) and how to configure activities and which organizational coordination mechanisms to employ (discussed in the next section of this chapter). It is important to note that distance does not become irrelevant for firms that are already operating in a large number of countries. Rather, what becomes increasingly important for such firms is distance analysis that accounts for experience the firm has already gained abroad as well as capabilities rooted in those countries. For firms with broad footprints, the salience of *internal distance* within the firm may rise relative to external distance between the firm and its customers, suppliers, partners, and so on.

Turning to applications, one of the most basic uses of the CAGE Distance Framework is to help make key differences visible. While this application may seem too obvious to be worth belaboring, many notable international business debacles can be traced back to a failure to appreciate some relevant dimensions along which countries differ. In a world within which countries differ along many (different) dimensions, managers cannot simply rely on personal experience to ensure adequate sensitivity to differences.

A somewhat more sophisticated application involves pinpointing differences across countries that might handicap multinational companies relative to local competitors – drivers of the liability of foreignness – or, more generally, alter their relative positions. This can be a useful exercise for both multinationals and their local competitors. When there are substantial liabilities of foreignness, multinationals may look, among other expedients, to acquire or set up joint ventures with local firms to overcome these barriers.

Third, even if multinationals can be confident that they will be well-positioned relative to local competitors in a particular market, the CAGE Framework can be used at a finer level of resolution to shed light on the relative positions of multinationals from different countries. For example, CAGE analysis can help explain the strength of Spanish firms in many industries across Latin America, and also the fact that in Mexico, US firms have outperformed even Spanish firms in terms of their rate and scope of success there (Rangan and Sengul 2004). Again, this analysis is often most valuable when conducted at the industry level, although the application at the end of Chapter 5 should have indicated that some insights can be derived even at the aggregate country (or bloc) level. Also, note that "natural ownership" advantages can be trumped by other factors – for example, particularly good or bad international strategies.

In practice, the types of CAGE analysis described thus far are typically performed qualitatively. However, Ghemawat (2007) argued that even simple quantification, such as dividing the sizes of foreign markets by their physical distances from a firm's home country, can be a very useful heuristic. Such rough assessments can also be adjusted to reflect bridges – commonalities with particular countries – that might expand potential relative to that implied by size/distance quotients. Such simple analytics can also be performed at the industry level by, for instance, dividing industry-specific measures of market size instead of country-level measures such as GDP by physical distance.

The gravity-based distance effect calibrations that have been emphasized in this book can facilitate more sophisticated quantitative applications of the CAGE Framework. In Box 7.1 in Chapter 7, we describe the calculation of composite CAGE Distance scores based on gravity model coefficients. The multipliers described therein that are used to calculate CAGE Distance can also be used to "discount" foreign market opportunities according to distance. To cite a simple example, if gravity modeling indicates that a common language is expected to double the intensity of interactions, indicators of market attractiveness (size, growth, etc.) pertaining to opportunities in countries with a common language might be doubled relative to those in countries without a common language to factor in that effect. Taking advantage of the multiplicative specification of the gravity models used here and in Chapter 5, the effects of each of the individual CAGE variables can be multiplied together to generate multidimensional adjustment factors for assessments of foreign market opportunities. The CAGE Comparator™ online tool (www.ghemawat.com/cage) provides a convenient user interface to help practitioners perform this type of analysis.[12]

Robert Salomon's "Global Acumen" represents another technique for the quantitative incorporation of distance measures into firms' analyses of international business opportunities (Salomon 2016). Global Acumen translates data on cultural, administrative, and economic distances and differences into risk measures for incorporation into Net Present Value (NPV) calculations. This is accomplished by scaling cross-country difference and distance data between

0 and 30 percent, an upper bound that was selected based on venture-capital practices and payback analysis techniques. The resultant score is added to the domestic discount rate to produce a country-specific risk-adjusted discount rate.

Distance analysis, whether performed qualitatively or using quantitative techniques such as those incorporated into the CAGE Comparator™, enables firms to analyze how the value of a given international opportunity depends on where a particular firm is coming from. Furthermore, analysis at the level of individual dimensions of distance can help set an agenda for bridging distance in markets where a firm does choose to operate, with dimensions of distance that are particularly salient for a particular firm requiring special attention. The next subsection briefly describes a set of complementary tools and frameworks that are designed to be used with the CAGE Distance Framework.

Complementary Tools and Frameworks

We begin by discussing rooted maps that help sharpen managers' perceptions of the impact of distance. We then turn to the AAA strategies of *adaptation*, *aggregation*, and *arbitrage*, briefly introduced in Part I, which represent different ways of dealing with distance, and the ADDING Value Scorecard for assessing value creation – or destruction – through cross-border activity. The AAA strategies and ADDING Value Scorecard are described at length in Ghemawat (2007), and so will be discussed only briefly here.

These three kinds of tools can be associated with a three-step analytical process. First, determine which of a range of international differences – cultural, administrative, geographic, and economic – matter in a given situation. In other words, identify the most important differences that a firm's international strategy must address. Then, think systematically about what might be done to address those differences in terms of the AAA strategies. Finally, evaluate specific strategic options using the ADDING Value Scorecard.

Rooted Maps. Rooted maps (Ghemawat "Remapping" 2011) correct the misperception that the world looks the same regardless of the viewer's vantage point or purpose. They do so by adjusting the sizes of countries or regions in relation to a specific home country or firm, while otherwise maintaining familiar shapes and spatial relationships, which helps managers relate these maps to their existing mental models. Several rooted maps have appeared in earlier chapters: firm-level maps based on BMW's operations in Figure 4.3 and the country-level trade, capital, information, and people flow maps in Figures 5.3, 5.4, and 5.5.

It is typically useful to begin with a "reference map" that depicts a firm's industry environment by mapping the total sales of a given product by country or region. Coloring such a map based on the market share of foreign firms or based on imports as a percentage of sales can help provide a first impression of the difference between the overall size of a market and the part of it that might be accessible to a foreign competitor. Resizing countries based on sales of foreign firms or imports can make this point even more vividly, and is particularly useful in industries that are subject to large impediments to internationalization (i.e., exhibit low depth or intensity of globalization).

Such reference maps can be contrasted with rooted maps drawn from the perspective of a particular firm – and its major competitors. Rooted maps with areas colored based on firms' national or regional market shares often yield interesting insights by blending size-based and share-based perspectives. Comparisons between rooted maps and reference maps and across rooted maps for different competitors help inform qualitative CAGE analyses. Furthermore, such comparative mapping can also help highlight internal distance within firms. For example, in many multinationals, the stark contrast between maps based on the national origins of the firm's leadership team and its targeted growth markets highlights the need to boost national diversity, as discussed further in Chapter 8.

AAA Strategies. After developing a clear understanding of the dimensions of distance that matter in a given situation, it is natural to consider the strategies that can create value across them. The AAA strategies (Ghemawat 2007) identify three broad avenues for creating value across borders and distances: *adaptation* to adjust to the constraints imposed by differences, *aggregation* to overcome some differences and thereby achieve more scale or scope economies than country-level adaptation would allow, and *arbitrage* to exploit (selected) differences instead of treating them all as constraints on value creation.[13]

Although adaptation and aggregation have long been objects of attention in international business, the addition of arbitrage to the strategy set is more novel (Ghemawat 2003). Also novel is the articulation of a rich array of substrategies and levers summarized under each of these headings in Table 6.10. Although these may strike the reader as nothing more than checklists, it is worth reminding ourselves that checklists have recently attracted considerable attention in a number of fields as a way of helping practitioners dealing with complex environments to avoid errors due to forgetfulness, cognitive overload, and so on (Gawande 2010).

Some awareness of and attention to each of the three broad AAA strategies is generally necessary in global competition. It is also worth noting, however, that there are inherent tensions among them. They tend, for example, to align with different organizational structures: adaptation requires vesting more authority with local decision makers, aggregation implies greater centralization of authority in global business units, regional structures, global account teams and the like, and arbitrage is often facilitated by vertical or functional structures that help track the flow of products or work through the organization. As a

Table 6.10 *AAA Strategies and Substrategies/Levers*

Adaptation	Aggregation	Arbitrage
Variation (across locations)	Regions (geographic aggregation)	Cultural
• Products		• Product/service country
• Policies		of origin effects (e.g.
• Repositioning	Other country groupings	French wine)
• Metrics	• Cultural (e.g., IberoAmerica)	• Creativity (via culturally diverse teams)
Focus (to reduce need for variation)	• Administrative (e.g., by free trade agreement)	
• Products	• Economic (e.g., advanced vs. emerging economies)	Administrative
• Geographies		• Taxation
• Verticals		• Regulation
• Segments	Noncountry bases of aggregation	• Institutional protections
		• Policy incentives
Externalization (to reduce burden of variation)	• Products or industries (global business units)	Geographic
• Strategic alliances	• Customers (key global accounts)	• Climate differences (e.g., in agriculture)
• Franchising		• Time zone differences
• User adaptation	• Client industries	(e.g., accelerating
• Networking	• Functions	projects by employing
	• Competences (centers of excellence)	offshore teams working
Design (to reduce cost of variation)		during nighttime at firm's home)
• Flexibility		
• Partitioning		Economic
• Platforms		• Price levels (labor,
• Modularity		capital, other inputs)
		• Knowledge/skills
Innovation (to improve the effectiveness of variation)		
• Transfer		
• Localization		
• Recombination		
• Transformation		

Source: Adapted from Ghemawat (2007).

result, firms need to understand the relevant trade-offs and agree internally about how they are to be managed.[14]

ADDING Value Scorecard. Ghemawat (2007)'s ADDING Value Scorecard is a template for value analysis that adapts basic competitive logic of the sort discussed in strategy textbooks (e.g., Ghemawat 2009) to an international context in a way that stresses, in particular, how certain factors loom larger internationally than they would in the context of a purely domestic discussion (see Figure 6.7). It will be discussed in slightly greater detail than the AAA

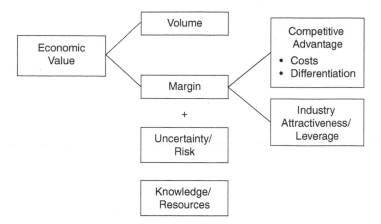

Figure 6.7 Components of ADDING Value.
Source: Ghemawat (2007, figure 3.7, p. 80).

strategies because it occupies only one chapter of Ghemawat (2007), versus four chapters, all told, for the AAA strategies – although again, that book chapter contains much more detail on how to operationalize what follows.[15]

The ADDING Value Scorecard is meant to force the strategist to go beyond thinking about cross-border moves in purely scalar terms. Although sizeism has long been a problem with strategy in general, global strategy provides extra scope for the operation of this bias because, global markets are, by definition, larger than individual national markets. For a summary of some of the evidence suggesting that this potential problem is actually a matter of practical importance, see pp. 149–151 of Ghemawat (2009).

Looking beyond volume to the other components of the ADDING Value Scorecard, the next two, competitive advantage and industry attractiveness, are staples of competitive strategy. Michael Porter (*Competitive Strategy* 1980, 1985) related them directly to the margin earned by business i in industry j as follows:

> Business i's margin = average margin in industry j + business i's competitive advantage

While this might be dismissed as just an accounting identity, the first term on the right hand side of the equation usefully reminds the strategist that industry effects often matter a great deal. Porter's five-forces framework for the structural analysis of industries has explored the strategic determinants of industry profitability in a single-country context (Porter "Industry Structure" 1980). In a cross-country context, there are also country-level effects that need to be recognized. Thus, McGahan and Victer (2010)'s data on 4,551 firms from 43 countries indicates an average return on assets of 5 percent over 1993–2003 that masked a wide dispersion of average profitability across countries: 12 percent for the top quartile versus –2 percent for the bottom quartile. And even if one strips out country-level effects by focusing on the rank order of performance of industries by country, analysis by Khanna and Rivkin (2001) shows that that varies quite drastically from country to country: ranks are positively and significantly correlated across less than 15 percent of country pairs.

The second term on the right hand side of the equation, competitive advantage, has been parsed by Porter and other strategists, notably Adam Brandenburger and Harborne Stuart (1996), into relative costs and differentiation, or more technically, comparisons across competitors of the gap between buyers' willingness-to-pay and (suppliers' opportunity) costs. The logic can be illustrated by considering a situation in which there are just two competitors, indexed 1 and 2:

> Business 1's competitive advantage = [willingness-to-pay – cost] for business 1– [willingness-to-pay – cost] for business 2
> = business 1's relative willingness-to-pay – business 1's relative cost.

In words, a company is said to have created competitive advantage over its rivals if it has driven a wider wedge between willingness-to-pay and cost than its competitors have done.

In a cross-border context, comparisons with more than one kind of reference competitor, and at multiple levels of aggregation, often make sense. Thus, a multinational might benchmark itself at a country level against other multinationals and against local competitors, as well as undertaking some comparisons at the regional or global level.

It usually makes sense to start with a rough assessment of current competitive position by looking at how a business's prices and costs compare with its competitors'. This links directly to their financial statements, but the analysis itself must go beyond conventional financial statement analysis: saying that one competitor has a higher level of profitability, however measured, doesn't specify whether that advantage is achieved through higher relative prices or lower relative costs (or even both).

What needs additional emphasis in a cross-border context is the adjustment of assessments of costs and willingness-to-pay to reflect consideration of distances and how they are dealt with (the topic of the discussions earlier of the CAGE Distance Framework and the AAA strategies respectively). This is different from the usual focus in international business on whether an advantage is location-specific or not as in Rugman's (1981) FSA/CSA matrix: in line with the law of distance, the ADDING Value Scorecard adopts the perspective that there is almost always some degree of location-specificity to an advantage and how much it matters depends on how far one is trying to redeploy it. The assessments of how a strategic initiative is likely to affect costs and prices helps quantify the potential for value creation (or destruction). And the final two components of the scorecard augment the standard competitive strategy template with two types of considerations – uncertainty/risk and the generation of knowledge and other resources – that, due to differences/distances, seem to loom larger internationally than they would in the context of a purely domestic discussion. Such considerations can sometimes be folded into the strategic analysis of margins described in this section. But especially when they resist such treatment, these two categories provide placeholders to help prevent them from being overlooked.

Finally, the emphasis on calculation of product market payoffs in the ADDING Value Scorecard should not be allowed to obscure the general strategic supposition that superior product market positions themselves depend on superior assets/capabilities/bundles that are (somewhat) durable, specialized, and untradeable[16] – and, as discussed in Chapter 3, increasingly intangible. The importance of improving these underlying determinants of competitive position is amplified, in a cross-border context, by two kinds of considerations. First, the average firm that competes domestically brings, by definition, assets of average quality to bear. But success overseas, especially through (horizontal) FDI, generally requires, according to a broad array of theoretical and empirical analysis, exceptional assets.[17] Second, globalization, or any other new source of competition, creates additional pressure to upgrade such assets if they are to retain any value over time (Sutton 2012).[18]

Managing across Distance

The previous section focused on distance analysis from the standpoint of environmental assessment and strategy setting. Most of the emphasis there was external: on the "objective" distance across which firms tap into international markets, supply chains, and so on. But firms also seem to vary in terms of how effectively they bridge external distances: compare a firm going abroad for the first time with, say, IBM. In this section, we shift our focus to the internal: we look at how firms can become better at bridging external distances, that is, more "distance-capable." One can often think of such capabilities as shrinking "effective distance," in an isotropic or anisotropic way.[19] Note the direct links to the previous section, in that firms' heterogeneous capabilities at dealing with particular types of distance condition the feasibility of international value creation strategies and so must be factored into the evaluation of strategy options in the ADDING Value Scorecard. And recall that it is often useful to start any diagnostic by contrasting internal and external maps.

There are a very wide variety of ways in which firms can deal more effectively internally with "external" distance. Rather than attempting to be comprehensive, we discuss four broad arenas of action: Configuration, Coordination,

Culture, and Cosmopolitanism. The configuration of a multinational's architecture builds closely on the discussion of trajectory in the previous section and its message that, other things being equal, priority should usually be given to countries that are close along various dimensions (except in the case of arbitrage strategies). Coordination encompasses formal organizational structure as well as other types of organizational linkages, formal and informal; the discussion here is focused on aspects that are critical to coordinating across national borders and international distances. Culture is discussed here in organizational terms: national culture is addressed in Chapter 8. And, finally, cosmopolitanism, while clearly related to organizational culture, focuses attention on the individuals who populate organizations and discusses what can be done to boost their capacity to operate across multiple dimensions of distance.

Configuration

The configuration or architecture of the value adding activities within a multinational firm affects both the amount of internal distance across which coordination must take place as well as the ease or difficulty of that coordination. In many instances, explicit consideration of trade-offs between internal and external distance can be helpful in getting such choices right. For example, locating R&D in a major foreign market may be advantageous from the standpoint of reducing external distance to customers – but entails costs associated with stretching a strategically important function across greater internal distance.

There is a large literature on the optimal location of activities and even attempts to articulate step-by-step processes for determining their configuration across (and within) countries. Thus, Collis (2014) has elaborated a process that involves disaggregating the activities that lie within the firm, filtering out the ones that are location-bound, and optimizing the ones that are footloose across possible locations in terms of current costs and future competitiveness, with total number of locations around the world and the degree of standardization/centralization also endogenous to the optimization procedure (and, one would hope, recognition of linkages across different activities). Although there are many useful practical tips embedded in Collis's detailed discussion, the overall process seems to us to be a bit too mechanical, not to mention complex, as it does to Collis who adds that it usually makes sense to work with a few "live" configurational options rather than consider the full spectrum of possibilities.

What can we say about configuration decisions beyond citing the determinants above and perhaps calculating their implications?

- Rather than going activity by activity in equal depth, it often makes sense to stipulate that some decisions will be highly centralized/coordinated (e.g., IT platforms and global R&D networks for high R&D spenders – the back-end activities in the front-back model) and others (typically front-end activities) will be decentralized, with more deliberation reserved for the ones that fall in between.

- Even when an activity is highly centralized, it need not always be located in the firm's home country. Wal-Mart, for example, secured the benefits of both arbitrage and aggregation by locating its global procurement headquarters in Shenzhen, China.

- There is no presumption that the optimal configuration will involve symmetry across locations, or even all the locations where an activity is performed (if it is dispersed at all). Some R&D or manufacturing units may have regional or global mandates, for example, while others have a purely local remit. More broadly, effective integration does not necessarily imply identical roles.

- Most speculatively, changes, many associated with IT (increasingly software-driven assets, ever richer streams of data, developments in the internet of things and machine intelligence, the induction of millennials – many of them "digital natives" – into the workforce) may be tilting more activities toward centralization. The rapid globalization of Airbnb, Uber, and so on has stirred great interest in platforms that instead of residing at the back-end can be taken to market globally.[20]

These examples and others hark back to some of the AAA substrategies/levers summarized in Table 6.10. Explicitly considering them can provide further input into the trade-offs among alternative strategies and also suggest ways of relaxing them to facilitate operation across greater distance.

Coordination

Given a particular configuration of activities across locations, there are several ways that firms can strengthen their ability to coordinate effectively over distance. The importance of technology was already discussed in the organizational section of Chapter 4. Although the potential of new technologies to overcome distance is often overhyped, most firms have yet to take full advantage of technology that is already available. In terms of the CAGE Distance Framework, it is worth adding that technology is often far more useful for reducing sensitivity to geographic distance than to other dimensions of distance, to which attention must continue to be paid.

In addition, technology does not eliminate the need for careful attention to coordination via formal organizational reporting structures and informal systems, routines, and relationships, as well as the interplay between formal and informal coordination. If putting in a front-back organization of the sort discussed in Chapter 4, for example, it is important to make sure that the managers in the middle are appropriately connected to both ends. If adopting a matrix, firms also need to ensure they have enough cross-linking devices. Given the results in Chapter 5 on how well physical distance predicts international interactions (as well as correlations between geographic and CAGE distance in Chapter 10), many firms should explicitly build geography into their coordination mechanisms as well.[21]

Geography, of course, is the dimension of distance that organization scholars have most often considered as a basis for aggregation. Stopford and Wells (1972) propose that firms with high levels of foreign sales (and in their model, by extension, geographic diversification) would adopt area (regional) structures, either on their own or matrixed with product divisions. Regional structures can improve information flows between countries and headquarters and help manage the complexity of a global enterprise. Lasserre (1996) enumerates a list of functions that can be performed by regional headquarters, which will be discussed in Chapter 10.

Firms have also structured themselves around other dimensions of the CAGE Framework, for example, IberoAmerica (linking Spain and Portugal with Latin America to take advantage of linguistic and other cultural commonalities) and the British Commonwealth (across which many countries share similar administrative/political systems). The distance dimension across which many established multinationals have recently attempted to straddle greater distance to tap into growth in emerging economies is economic distance. The examples that follow illustrate how some firms are attempting greater organizational coordination along the economic dimension of the CAGE Framework:

- General Electric's attempts to move production quickly to low-cost countries have been aided by mechanisms such as "pitcher-catcher": a "pitching team" at the existing site working closely with a "catching team" at the new site until the latter's performance met or exceeded the former's (Ghemawat 2003).
- IBM has created a growth markets unit and GE the post of a chief globalization officer, both based in Shanghai.
- Schneider Electric and KPMG based their CEO and Global Chairman respectively in Hong Kong.
- Royal Philips Electronics, Europe's largest maker of consumer electronics, moved the headquarters of its domestic appliances business to Shanghai (Ghemawat and Vantrappen 2015, 73).
- Starwood Hotels adopted a practice of relocating its top management team to a key emerging economy for one month every other year: to Shanghai in 2011, Dubai in 2013, and to Delhi and Mumbai in 2015.

Coordination mechanisms should also account for countries' different sizes and levels of strategic importance. GE, for example, groups some countries into regions while having others report directly to headquarters. Australia, Canada, China, Germany, India, and Russia were selected for direct reporting, while Africa, Europe, Japan/Korea, Latin/South America, the Middle East, and Southeast Asia were aggregated above the country level (General Electric 2010).

The discussion of economic distance here has emphasized the perspective of multinationals from advanced economies, but their counterparts from emerging economies also face special coordination challenges. Guillén and García-Canal (2012) argue that multinationals from emerging economies have more organizational flexibility since they are building new structures abroad rather than forcing change upon established ones. However, their heavier use of informal governance mechanisms at home rather than relying on more transparent formal structures can become a stumbling block. In particular, governance in emerging markets is "often relationship-based, which may be poorly perceived by foreign stakeholders as lacking accountability, transparency, and trustworthiness" (Cuervo-Cazurra, Newburry, and Park 2016, 148). For such firms, a key organizational challenge may entail closing gaps between formal structure and informal coordination mechanisms.

Culture

A strong corporate culture can serve as a bridge across national cultural differences. Investment banks, management consulting firms, and other kinds of far-flung professional services firms tend to place particular emphasis on culture as a unifier. Such firms often have to assemble teams from multiple locations and send them out at short notice to work with high levels of autonomy. Alignment along a set of cultural values helps their teams to get up to speed quickly and reassures clients about the consistency of the services they are receiving.

Such emphasis on culture as a unifier is not limited to professional services. Johnson & Johnson's sixty-plus-year-old *credo* speaks to commitments that apply across the company's diverse array of geographic markets and business units. "We believe our first responsibility is to the doctors, nurses, and patients, to mothers and fathers and all others who use our products."[22] Google's culture is also unmistakable around the world: "We hire people who are smart and determined, and we favor ability over experience ... We strive to maintain the open culture often associated with startups, in which everyone is a hands-on contributor and feels comfortable sharing ideas and opinions."[23] When two "Googlers" meet for the first time to collaborate on a project, the company's culture (from its recruitment process through to its office design) helps ease the way. They know there's a great deal they have in common, in spite of their potentially very different backgrounds.

A common corporate language can also help facilitate communication (and cultural integration). Mexico's Cemex, for example, implemented a single global operating language: in Cemex's case, English rather than the Spanish of its headquarters country in order to support its ambitions beyond its home region. Moving to a common language must be done with care, though, to avoid losing the valuable perspectives of people who struggle with the selected language. Interestingly, some research indicates that language barriers pose less of a problem for those providing information than for those receiving it. It may be easier for a manager for whom English is not a native language to make a comprehensible presentation in English than to get people listening to it to invest in comprehension: people tend to tune out on accents they have trouble understanding (Neeley 2011). Another cautionary perspective is provided by Schomaker and Zaheer (2014), who find linguistic relatedness to be positively related to knowledge communication but negatively related to knowledge understanding. They see in this result a parallel to the "psychic distance paradox" (O'Grady and Lane 1996) in which similarity may "lead to a sense of complacency and an underappreciation of critical – if subtle – differences" (Schomaker and Zaheer 2014, 71).

Having emphasized the benefits of a strong corporate culture, it is worth mentioning that every strong culture is not necessarily a culture that fosters openness to diverse ideas and people. A strong corporate culture that is too closely aligned with the national culture of a firm's home country may reduce the firm's capacity to bridge distance by signaling a lack of openness to perspectives from abroad. In contrast, Google's emphasis on meritocracy combines strength and openness.

Cosmopolitanism

Corporate cosmopolitanism (Ghemawat "Cosmopolitan" 2011) encompasses some of the ideas already discussed – including the cultivation of a culture that emphasizes openness to people and ideas from abroad. Here, we focus on the individual level, on the people who lead multinational firms. Chapter 4 highlighted the limited national diversity of the top management teams of the world's largest corporations. Among the 2013 Fortune Global 500, 87 percent of firms were led by a native CEO, and 85 percent of top management team members (direct reports to CEOs) were natives. And the law of distance applies here as well: foreign top management team members came disproportionately from the firm's home region (Ghemawat and Vantrappen 2015).

There is some evidence that boosting national diversity has the potential to unlock large benefits. As discussed in Chapter 4, Nielsen and Nielsen report that "TMT nationality diversity is among the few diversity attributes that help increase firm performance" and "the effects of international experience and functional diversity diminish over time, whereas the impact of nationality diversity becomes stronger" (2013, 377–378, 380). Barta, Kleiner, and Neumann (2012) find that "for companies ranking in the top quartile of executive-board diversity, ROEs were 53 percent higher, on average, than they were for those in the bottom quartile. At the same time, EBIT margins at the most diverse companies were 14 percent higher, on average, than those of the least diverse companies" (65).

In addition to such direct effects of national diversity on performance, there is another indirect but presumably powerful effect due to signaling. If a large share of a global company's assets, sales, and employees are located outside its home country, but it continues to choose native leaders, it signals limited long-term career prospects for foreign middle managers already in the company as well as potential hires, making it hard to hire or retain the right people. Conversely, selecting a non-native can serve as a very powerful signal as well. Thus, when Satya Nadella, born in India, was appointed Microsoft's CEO, the move was significant partly because of the assurance it provided about the absence of glass ceilings at the company – presumably particularly valuable to the one-third or more of Microsoft's workforce that is estimated to be of Indian ethnic origin (see, for instance, Ghosh 2014).

Other research on this topic reminds us that diversity must be supported by appropriate structures and processes for it to have positive effects. Given the difficulties of working across divides, diverse groups *can* perform worse than homogenous groups (see, for instance, Williams and O'Reilly 1998). Boards with foreign members tend to have weaker meeting attendance, their companies are more likely to pay their executives excessively, and they are more prone to restating financials (Masulis, Wang, and Xie 2012). Potential downsides of diversity, thus, lead Kaczmarek and Ruigrok (2013) to conclude that top management team national diversity becomes advantageous only in firms with a high degree of internationalization.

A strong corporate culture that encourages openness can help to strengthen the benefits of national diversity and mitigate its potential pitfalls. Boosting the cosmopolitanism of people within an organization – wherever they are from – can also help in this regard, and represents a complementary approach to reducing distance sensitivity. Chapter 15 of Ghemawat's *World 3.0* (2011) is devoted to this topic. It builds on Appiah's (1997) notion of "rooted cosmopolitanism" to recommend an approach to cosmopolitanism that reflects the effects of borders and distance that have been emphasized throughout this book.

Given the levels of globaloney reported in Chapter 2, an essential starting point for most business leaders to become more distance-capable at an individual level is to gain a better understanding of actual levels of globalization. Doing so helps to remind us that we all have strong roots, usually just in one part of the world but at most in two or three. These roots condition both how we see the world as well as how we are seen by others. A greater individual-level appreciation for the differences that persist in our semiglobalized world helps highlight how much one can learn from others. And the law of distance also implies a need for individuals to focus: differences and distances are too great to permit one to become equally competent at operating anywhere in the world.

Education and experience represent complementary levers for boosting cosmopolitanism. We will briefly return to the topic of education in Chapter 7 in the context of implications of the research in this book for business schools. Here, we note that firms have some advantages relative to universities for cultivating cosmopolitanism. Frameworks such as those discussed in this chapter can be incorporated into corporate training programs – and such training can be more tightly integrated with an executive's work content than is feasible in an MBA program. Mobility programs can incorporate longer and deeper immersion in light of research showing that it takes at least three months to really appreciate how business works in a new country (Bisoux 2007). Firms can also structure projects and relationships to shape the experiences executives gain abroad, and can build cosmopolitanism into their leadership assessment programs.

Becoming more distance-capable at both individual and firm levels represents an ongoing journey, rather than a box that can be checked off. It involves an evolution, but should be guided in the sense of being shaped and pushed by initiatives with strong top management support. Chapter 8 returns to this topic in the context of boosting firms' global leadership capacity.

Conclusion

This chapter concludes the exposition of empirical evidence for the law of distance. Together with the previous chapter, it has shown how international interactions at the country, industry, and firm levels all tend to be dampened by cultural, administrative, and geographic distance, and are often shaped in more complex ways by economic distance as well.

We also provided a more extended treatment here of implications for business practitioners than we did for public policymakers in Chapter 5. This reflects the primary emphasis of this book on globalization in business rather than in other spheres. We discussed ways in which firms can heighten their understanding of the relevant types of distance in their industries and its strategy implications. The final section shifted focus from external to internal distance and looked at ways firms can strengthen their capacity to operate across multiple dimensions of distance.

The discussion of implications of the law of distance for business practice highlighted a variety of topics that are also of interest to international business researchers. In Chapter 7, we turn directly to implications for international business research. We step back and relate the law of distance to international business theory and then discuss a variety of contemporary issues in this research stream.

Notes

1 In particular, PPML returns a single coefficient for each variable that can be interpreted in the same way as a double-logged OLS coefficient. In addition, fixed effects can be used in the same way they are used in OLS, which is an unusual property for nonlinear estimators. Other alternative models, such as the Heckman selection model, have been used in trade analysis; however, because the Heckman model is a two-stage model, it is not as well suited to the type of comparisons we present in this chapter.

2 PPML results paralleling the OLS results in Chapter 5 are reported in Ghemawat and de la Mata (2015) and in the online appendix to Chapter 5 at www.ghemawat.com/laws. In addition to the use of PPML rather than OLS, the merchandise trade analysis in this chapter also differs from that in Chapter 5 in that the data source used here was UN Comtrade (rather than primary reliance on IMF Direction of Trade Statistics in Chapter 5), and that the trade model in this chapter was estimated based on data covering the period 2005–2013 (instead of only 2005–2012 in Chapter 5).

3 The Law of Gravity web page (http://personal.lse.ac.uk/tenreyro/LGW.html), maintained by Santos Silva and Tenreyro, advises that the R-squared for PPML estimations is calculated by predicting fitted values using the regression equation, which are then correlated with the actual values and the result is squared. This is equivalent to the standard R-squared used in OLS regression analysis. However, it is important to note that in this volume, we report the adjusted R-squared for OLS-based gravity models, a standard practice that takes into account the increase or decrease in degrees of freedom from changing the number of variables in the regression equation. Thus, the PPML and OLS levels are not directly comparable.

4 There is a services trade database as well, but unfortunately, it has relatively limited coverage.

5 In all of the histograms in this chapter, values shown on the horizontal axes correspond to the midpoints of the "bins" in order to align properly with the vertical lines (coefficient values).

6 Buckley and Casson (1976, p. 1) define the multinational enterprise as "an enterprise which owns and controls activities in different countries." Whereas FDI is normally defined as requiring a minimum 10 percent ownership stake, statistics on multinational enterprise subsidiaries often set the even higher threshold of requiring a majority stake.

7 In that context, it was a major advance when Rugman and Verbeke (2004) took advantage of new disclosure requirements to quantify the intraregional share of sales of the Fortune Global 500.

8 For purely arithmetic reasons, now that we are looking at firms that are present in twenty plus countries, these values cannot exceed 15 percent.

9 Note that this is a multicountry study, but it is discussed here rather than in the next section due to its focus on performance.

10 Using the region classifications employed in the *DHL Global Connectedness Index* (detailed in Chapter 10), 36 percent of subsidiaries were intraregional in 2013 and 37 percent in 2014.

11 Helpman, Melitz, and Yeaple (2004) also incorporate R&D intensity into their analysis of exports versus FDI with heterogeneous firms. Note that both R&D intensity and advertising intensity are viewed here as proxies for related types of capabilities. Given the limited international reach of most brands and advertising (as discussed in Chapter 4), the implication of advertising intensity moderating distance effects is not that firms can simply spend more on advertising in order to become less constrained by distance. Rather, high levels of advertising intensity are to be viewed as a proxy for the development of marketing capabilities that can be applied across borders.

12 As discussed in Chapter 7, this multiplicative approach to calculating CAGE distance accounts for what Rugman, Verbeke, and Nguyen (2011) refer to as compounded distance.

13 In Ghemawat (2007), chapters 4 through 6 cover Adaptation, Aggregation, and Arbitrage, respectively. Note that some international business researchers have regarded these strategies as simply a relabeling of mainstream international strategy concepts. Ghemawat (2008) explained why this view is incorrect.

14 Chapter 7 of Ghemawat (2007) addresses the AAA strategies in relation to each other.

15 The ADDING Value Scorecard is the subject of chapter 3 of Ghemawat (2007).

16 See Ghemawat (1991), particularly chapters 2 and 6.

17 Note that conditions are less stringent for other types of globalization: nearly any firm can learn from abroad, and one must also recognize globalization moves that are motivated by acquiring strategically important resources abroad (as in Dunning's [1998] strategic-asset seeking FDI).

18 Sutton's model is discussed in some detail in Chapter 11 within the sections entitled "Will the Big Shift Lead to a Big Shakeup?" and "A Case Study of Competition within China."

19 In other words, sometimes effective distance is shrunk uniformly whereas in other cases the change may be dependent on the flow direction or other aspects of its orientation (e.g., may help information flow from headquarters to subsidiaries but not vice versa).

20 For a cautionary perspective, refer to Pankaj Ghemawat, "What Uber's China Deal Says About the Limits of Platforms," *Harvard Business Review*, August 10, 2016, available at https://hbr.org/2016/08/what-ubers-china-deal-says-about-the-limits-of-platforms.

21 Blending considerations of configuration and coordination, Lessard, Teece, and Leih (2016), with a focus on dynamic capabilities, see the emergence of a new kind of MNE which they call a meta-MNE, "a hybrid concept that encompasses the complex integration and coordination to orchestrate activities across multiple geographies."

22 For Johnson & Johnson's full credo, refer to the company's website (accessed February 2016) at http://www.jnj.com/sites/default/files/pdf/jnj_ourcredo_english_us_8.5x11_cmyk.pdf.

23 This description of Google's culture was quoted from its company website (accessed February 2016) at https://www.google.com/about/company/facts/culture/.

References

Almodóvar, Paloma. 2012. "The International Performance of Standardizing and Customizing Spanish Firms: The M Curve Relationships." *Multinational Business Review* 20 (4):306–330.

Appiah, Kwame Anthony. 1997. "Cosmopolitan Patriots." *Critical Inquiry* 23 (3):617–639.

Baltagi, Badi H., Peter Egger, and Michael Pfaffermayr. 2008. "Estimating Regional Trade Agreement Effects on FDI in an Interdependent World." *Journal of Econometrics* 145 (1–2):194–208. doi: 10.1016/j.jeconom.2008.05.017.

Banalieva, Elitsa R, and Charles Dhanaraj. 2013. "Home-Region Orientation in International Expansion Strategies." *Journal of International Business Studies* 44 (2):89–116.

Barta, Thomas, Markus Kleiner, and Tilo Neumann. 2012. "Is There a Payoff from Top-Team Diversity?" *McKinsey Quarterly* 2012 (12):65–66. www.mckinsey.com/insights/organization/is_there_a_payoff_from_top-team_diversity.

Bisoux, Tricia. 2007. "Global Immersion." *BizEd* 6 (4):44–49. www.e-digitaleditions.com/i/58060-julyaugust2007/45.

Brandenburger, Adam M., and Harborne W. Stuart. 1996. "Value-Based Business Strategy." *Journal of Economics & Management Strategy* 5 (1): 5–24.

Buckley, Peter J., and Mark Casson. 1976. *The Future of the Multinational Enterprise.* London: Macmillan.

Castellani, Davide, Alfredo Jimenez, and Antonello Zanfei. 2013. "How Remote Are R&D Labs Distance Factors and International Innovative Activities." *Journal of International Business Studies* 44 (7):649–675. doi: 10.1057/jibs.2013.30.

Caves, Richard E. 1971. "International Corporations: The Industrial Economics of Foreign Investment." *Economica* 38 (149):1–27. doi: 10.2307/2551748.

Cho, Kang Rae, and Prasad Padmanabhan. 2005. "Revisiting the Role of Cultural Distance in Mnc's Foreign Ownership Mode Choice: The Moderating Effect of Experience Attributes." *International Business Review* 14 (3):307–324. doi: http://dx.doi.org/10.1016/j.ibusrev.2005.01.001.

Collis, David J. 2014. *International Strategy: Context, Concepts and Implications.* West Sussex: John Wiley and Sons, Inc.

Cuervo-Cazurra, Alvaro, William Newburry, and Seung Ho Park. 2016. *Emerging Market Multinationals: Managing Operational Challenges for Sustained International Growth.* New York; Cambridge, UK: Cambridge University Press.

de Mooij, Marieke K. 2010. *Global Marketing and Advertising: Understanding Cultural Paradoxes.* 3rd ed. Los Angeles: SAGE.

Dunning, John H. 1998. "Location and the Multinational Enterprise: A Neglected Factor?" *Journal of International Business Studies* 29 (1):45–66.

Gawande, Atul. 2010. *The Checklist Manifesto: How to Get Things Right.* New York: Metropolitan Books.

General Electric. 2010. "GE Names Vice Chairman John Rice to Lead GE Global Growth & Operations." Last Modified November 8, 2010. www.genewsroom.com/press-releases/ge-names-vice-chairman-john-rice-lead-ge-global-growth-operations-225373.

Ghemawat, Pankaj. 1991. *Commitment: The Dynamic of Strategy.* New York; Toronto: Free Press; Maxwell Macmillan Canada.

2001. "Distance Still Matters: The Hard Reality of Global Expansion." *Harvard Business Review* 79 (8):137–147.

2003. "The Forgotten Strategy." *Harvard Business Review* 81 (11):76–84.

2007. *Redefining Global Strategy: Crossing Borders in a World Where Differences Still Matter*. Boston, MA: Harvard Business School Press.

2008. "Reconceptualizing International Strategy and Organization." *Strategic Organization* 6(2): 195–206.

2009. *Strategy and the Business Landscape*. 3rd ed. Boston: Prentice Hall.

2011. "The Cosmopolitan Corporation." *Harvard Business Review* 89 (5):92–99.

2011. "Remapping Your Strategic Mind-Set." *McKinsey Quarterly* (3):56–58.

2011. *World 3.0: Global Prosperity and How to Achieve It*. Boston, MA: Harvard Business Review Press.

Ghemawat, Pankaj, and Tamara de la Mata. "Globalization and Gravity." Unpublished working paper, IESE Business School 2015.

Ghemawat, Pankaj, and Rajiv Mallick. "The Industry-Level Structure of International Trade Networks: A Gravity-Based Approach." Harvard Business School Working Paper Feb. 2003 version, Boston, MA.

Ghemawat, Pankaj, and Herman Vantrappen. 2015. "How Global Is Your C-Suite?" *MIT Sloan Management Review* 56 (4):73–82.

Ghosh, Palash. 2014. "Microsoft's (MSFT) New CEO Satya Nadella Underscores Rise of Indians in U.S. High Tech." *International Business Times*. www.ibtimes.com/microsofts-msft-new-ceo-satya-nadella-underscores-rise-indians-us-high-tech-1552687.

Guillén, Mauro, and Esteban García-Canal. 2012. *Emerging Markets Rule: Growth Strategies of the New Global Giants*: McGraw Hill Professional.

Hejazi, Walid. 2007. "The Regional Nature of MNE Activities and the Gravity Model." In *Regional Aspects of Multinationality and Performance*, edited by Alan M. Rugman. Oxford: Elsevier JAI.

Helpman, Elhanan, Marc J. Melitz, and Stephen R. Yeaple. 2004. "Export Versus FDI with Heterogeneous Firms." *American Economic Review* 94 (1):300–316. doi: 10.1257/000282804322970814.

Johanson, Jan, and Jan-Erik Vahlne. 1977. "The Internationalization Process of the Firm-a Model of Knowledge Development and Increasing Foreign Market Commitments." *Journal of International Business Studies* 8 (1):23–32.

Kaczmarek, Szymon, and Winfried Ruigrok. 2013. "In at the Deep End of Firm Internationalization." *Management International Review* 53 (4):513–534. doi: 10.1007/s11575-012-0159-7.

Khanna, Tarun, and Jan Rivkin. "The Structure of Profitability around the World." Harvard Business School Working Paper 01-056, April 2001. www.hbs.edu/faculty/Pages/item.aspx?num=12419.

Kogut, Bruce, and Harbir Singh. 1988. "The Effect of National Culture on the Choice of Entry Mode." *Journal of International Business Studies* 19 (3):411–432. doi: 10.1057/palgrave.jibs.8490394.

Lasserre, Philippe. 1996. "Regional Headquarters: The Spearhead for Asia Pacific Markets." *Long Range Planning* 29 (1):30–37.

Lessard, Donald, David Teece, and Sohvi Leih, 2016. "The Dynamic Capabilities of Meta-Multinationals." Working Paper, August 15. (Forthcoming in *Global Strategy Journal*).

Masulis, Ronald W., Cong Wang, and Fei Xie. 2012. "Globalizing the Boardroom – the Effects of Foreign Directors on Corporate Governance and Firm Performance." *Journal of Accounting and Economics* 53 (3):527–554. doi: http://dx.doi.org/10.1016/j.jacceco.2011.12.003.

McGahan, Anita M., and Rogerio Victer. 2010. "How Much Does Home Country Matter to Corporate Profitability?" *Journal of International Business Studies* 41 (1):142–165.

Neeley, Tsedal B. "Language and Globalization: 'Englishnization' at Rakuten (A)." Case #412002, Harvard Business Publishing, Boston, MA, August 29, 2011.

Nielsen, Bo Bernhard, and Sabina Nielsen. 2013. "Top Management Team Nationality Diversity and Firm Performance: A Multilevel Study." *Strategic Management Journal* 34 (3):373–382. doi: 10.1002/smj.2021.

O'Grady, Shawna, and Henry W. Lane. 1996. "The Psychic Distance Paradox." *Journal of International Business Studies* 27 (2):309–333.

Oh, Chang Hoon, and Farok J. Contractor. 2012. "The Role of Territorial Coverage and Product Diversification in the Multinationality-Performance Relationship." *Global Strategy Journal* 2 (2):122. doi: 10.1002/gsj.1031.

Oh, Chang Hoon, and Alan M. Rugman. 2014. "The Dynamics of Regional and Global Multinationals, 1999-2008." *Multinational Business Review* 22 (2):108–117. doi: 10.1108/MBR-04-2014-0015.

Porter, Michael E. 1980. *Competitive Strategy: Techniques for Analyzing Industries and Competitors*. New York: Free Press.

   1980. "Industry Structure and Competitive Strategy: Keys to Profitability." *Financial Analysts Journal* 36 (4):30–41.

   1985. *Competitive Advantage: Creating and Sustaining Superior Performance*. New York: Free Press.

Qian, Gongming, Theodore A. Khoury, Mike W. Peng, and Zhengming Qian. 2010. "The Performance Implications of Intra-and Inter-Regional Geographic Diversification." *Strategic Management Journal* 31 (9):1018–1030.

Rangan, Subramanian, and Metin Sengul. 2004. "Institutional Similarities and MNE Relative Performance Abroad: A Study of Foreign Multinationals in Six Host Markets." Working paper, Cedex, France, October, 2004.

Rugman, Alan M. 1981. *Inside the Multinationals: The Economics of Internal Markets*. London Croom Helm.

Rugman, Alan M., and Chang Hoon Oh. 2013. "Why the Home Region Matters: Location and Regional Multinationals." British Journal of Management. 24 (4): 463–479. Multinationals." *British Journal of Management.* 24 (4): 463–479.

   2010. "Does the Regional Nature of Multinationals Affect the Multinationality and Performance Relationship?" *International Business Review* 19 (5):479–488.

Rugman, Alan M., and Alain Verbeke. 2004. "A Perspective on Regional and Global Strategies of Multinational Enterprises." *Journal of International Business Studies* 35 (1):3–18.

Rugman, Alan M., Alain Verbeke, and Quyen T. K. Nguyen. 2011. "Fifty Years of International Business Theory and Beyond." *Management International Review* 51 (6):755–786. doi: 10.1007/s11575-011-0102-3.

Salomon, Robert M. 2016. *Global Vision: How Companies Can Overcome the Pitfalls of Globalization*. New York: Palgrave Macmillan.

Santos Silva, J. M. C., and Silvana Tenreyro. 2006. "The Log of Gravity." *Review of Economics and Statistics* 88 (4):641–658.

Schomaker, Margaret Spring, and Srilata Zaheer. 2014. "The Role of Language in Knowledge Transfer to Geographically Dispersed Manufacturing Operations." *Journal of International Management* 20(1): 55–72.

Shepherd, Ben. 2013. "The Gravity Model of International Trade: A User Guide." *ARTNeT Books and Research Reports*.

Stopford, John M., and Louis T. Wells. 1972. *Managing the Multinational Enterprise: Organization of the Firm and Ownership of the Subsidiaries*, The Harvard Multinational Enterprise Series. New York: Basic Books.

Sutton, John. 2012. *Competing in Capabilities: The Globalization Process*, Clarendon Lectures in Economics. Oxford: Oxford University Press.

UNCTAD. 2013. "Global Value Chains and Development: Investment and Value Added Trade in the Global Economy." http://unctad.org/en/PublicationsLibrary/diae2013d1_en.pdf.

United Nations (UN). 2015. "UN Comtrade Database." http://comtrade.un.org/.

Verbeke, Alain. 2012. "How Good Are Multinationality–Performance (M-P) Empirical Studies?" *Global Strategy Journal* 2 (4):332. doi: 10.1111/j.2042-5805.2012.01040.x.

Williams, Katherine Y., and Charles A. O'Reilly, III. 1998. "Demography and Diversity in Organizations: A Review of 40 Years of Research." In *Research in Organizational Behavior*, edited by Barry M. Staw, and L. L. Cummings, 77–140. Greenwich, CT: JAI Press.

Distance and International Business Research

Pankaj Ghemawat and Steven A. Altman

Chapters 5 and 6 provided empirical evidence for the law of distance at the country, industry, and firm levels, and related patterns of international interactions to Ghemawat (2001)'s CAGE (cultural, administrative, geographic, and economic) Distance Framework. Those chapters also highlighted some of the ways that public and business policymakers can use the CAGE Distance Framework and complementary tools as inputs to their decision making. This chapter turns to the implications of the law of distance for international research, with a focus on research in international business in particular.

We begin this chapter by reviewing the utility of distance, highlighting evidence of its empirical value and practical relevance from elsewhere in this volume, and then pointing to the growth of distance-driven research as further evidence of its power to generate valuable insights. In the second section, we shift focus from empirics to theory, discussing distance's linkages with leading schools of international business theory as well as its broader bases in other disciplines. This discussion points to a focus on distance as a powerful comparative advantage for international business research. And in the third section, we discuss prominent critiques that have been leveled against distance and counters to them.

In the final and longest section of this chapter, we turn to future directions for distance-driven research, proposing six areas where we see promising opportunities. First, a substantial amount of research on distance still focuses on a single dimension of the CAGE Distance Framework, whereas the previous two chapters imply that such a narrow focus represents a fundamental specification error in many contexts. Second, while this book has made strenuous efforts to map the (rugged) landscape of globalization – with more analysis still to come in Part III – there are a number of ways in which the present lines of analysis could be extended empirically. Third, the heterogeneity in distance sensitivity across industries discussed in Chapter 6 suggests large research opportunities in addressing interindustry variation. Fourth, research on internal distance within firms and moderators that might help them become more distance-capable remains in its infancy. Fifth, while Part II of this book has mostly focused on objective indicators of distance, the evidence suggests that researchers should continue devoting attention to subjective (psychic) distance as well. Sixth, there are opportunities to improve the data employed that can strengthen future empirical research.

The Empirical and Practical Utility of Distance

Two of the major attractions of distance for international business research – its empirical utility and its practical relevance, which can be thought of, respectively, as its descriptive and prescriptive value – should already be apparent to readers of this book. To begin with the former, Chapters 5 and 6 provided empirical evidence for the law of distance at the country, industry, and firm levels. Those chapters relied heavily on gravity models, which, as already noted, are recognized for their success at producing "some of the clearest and most robust findings in economics" (Leamer and Levinsohn 1995, 1384). Each of the eleven types of trade, capital, information, and people flows (and stocks) analyzed at the country level in Chapter 5 was negatively and significantly related to geographic distance, as were industry-level trade flows for ninety-five out of ninety-seven product categories and company-level counts of Fortune Global 500 foreign subsidiaries, as reported in Chapter 6. The gravity models also consistently – though not quite as uniformly – showed that international interactions diminish with cultural and administrative distance, and are shaped by economic distance.

Part III of this book will further expand the empirical base of the law of distance and connect it more closely to international business research. Chapters 8 and 9 will augment, respectively, the cultural and administrative/institutional distance measures in the standard gravity model – common official language for cultural similarity and colony/colonizer ties as well as membership in a common regional bloc or trade agreement for administrative linkages – with measures and modes of analysis that are more prominent in the international business literature, for example, Kogut and Singh (1988)'s cultural distance index and regulative, cognitive, and normative measures of institutional distance based on Scott (1995). In Chapter 10, we will relate geographic distance to the large literature in international business on regionalization, and Chapter 11 will examine correlates of the economic distance between advanced and emerging economies and the likely implications of the big shift in the relative importance of the former versus the latter.

The practical relevance of the law of distance for business and public policy has also been highlighted in the previous chapters, which additionally discussed several tools that have been developed to help managers incorporate distance analysis into their decision making. Practical applications will be discussed further, in the context of specific dimensions of distance, in Part III. Additional indirect evidence of the practical relevance of distance can be derived from management education curricula. In 2009, one of us (Ghemawat) collaborated with Bernard Yeung under the auspices of AACSB International's taskforce on the Globalization of Management Education to survey eighty-four academic thought leaders across ten functional business disciplines about what globalization-related content should be incorporated into MBA curricula (Ghemawat "Curricular Content" 2011). The responses clearly highlighted the importance of cultural, legal/regulatory, political, economic, financial, and other aspects of distance.[1]

Given the amount written about the empirical utility and practical relevance of distance elsewhere in this book – and the literature – we will not expand on those arguments in favor of distance-based research. Rather, we will devote the remainder of this section to summarizing the growth of distance-driven research. The rapid growth of this research stream supplies further evidence of the utility of distance in international business research via researchers' revealed preferences.

Beugelsdijk and Mudambi (2013) report that the rise in publications on distance in the *Journal of International Business Studies* (JIBS) followed Dunning's (1998) article, "Location and the multinational enterprise: a neglected factor?" and Ghemawat's (2001) introduction of the CAGE Distance Framework.[2] Dow (2014) also documents substantial growth in publications on distance in the broader *Web of Science* database since 2003. To put the expansion of distance-based research in perspective, it is useful to compare the number of publications mentioning distance to those mentioning other central concepts in international business. Internalization theory is arguably the best benchmark. Peter Buckley and Pervez Ghauri (2015) assert that "The dominant paradigm in research on the multinational firm is the internalization approach" (8). Jean-Francois Hennart (2009) deemed internalization and transaction cost theories more generally the "dominant theories of the MNE" (126). Over the period covered in Figure 7.1 (from 1990 to 2014), 543 JIBS publications mentioned distance, as compared to 261 including the term internalization (and 387 mentioning transaction cost(s)). On this basis, distance research seems to be at least as vibrant as work on internalization.

In order to focus the majority of this chapter on theory and on directions for future research, we do not review this large literature here. For a recent review, readers may wish to refer to Hutzschenreuter, Kleindienst, and Lange (2015), which covers 216 articles published in 21 peer-reviewed journals since 1977, is organized based on the CAGE Distance Framework, and summarizes findings about the effects of distance on market selection, entry mode, performance, and knowledge transfer/interorganizational relationships.

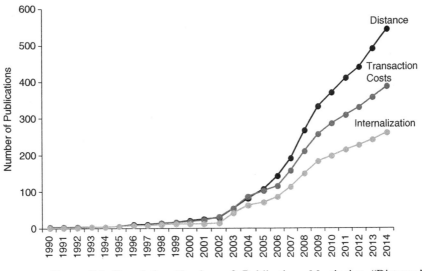

Figure 7.1 Cumulative Number of Publications Mentioning "Distance," "Internalization," and "Transaction Cost(s)" in the *Journal of International Business Studies*, 1990–2014.
Source: Generated by the authors based on data from the JIBS website (www.palgrave-journals.com/jibs/index.html).

The Theoretical Case for Distance-Driven Research

Among the papers on distance covered in the Hutzschenreuter et al. (2015) review, 86 percent were classified as either quantitative or qualitative empirical studies; only 14 percent were theoretical. The majority of this book has also been empirical, prompting an extended treatment in this section of the theoretical underpinnings and implications of the law of distance. We begin with distance's theoretical connections to international economics and business before exploring its broader bases in other disciplines, most notably in social psychology. Although the latter discussion reflects our commitment to interdisciplinary learning, in the spirit of Dunning (1989), we are also sensitive to the gains available from specialization by discipline. We therefore conclude our theoretical case for distance with an appeal to comparative advantage, in the sense of distance providing a distinct source of insight for international business relative to single-country business research.

Theoretical Connections to International Economics and Business

The law of distance is rooted in the empirical success of the gravity models discussed in Chapters 5 and 6. Despite – or perhaps because of – their empirical success, gravity models were criticized early on by international economists for lacking a theoretical foundation. More recent work allays such concerns. Thus, gravity-like specifications can be derived in the context of the Heckscher-Ohlin-Vanek (H-O-V) model of homogeneous products under constant-returns-to-scale technology, and the Helpman-Krugman (H-K) model of differentiated goods and increasing-returns-to-scale in production in the face of variety-loving utility, to cite just two prominent lines of theoretical modeling. Frankel, Stein, and Wei (1997) conclude, "the [gravity] equation has thus apparently gone from an embarrassing poverty of theoretical foundations to an embarrassment of riches!" (53).

Given the number of theoretical models that give rise to gravity-like speci-fications, it has been suggested that the success of such specifications tells us something about what happens in international trade but not why, that is, helps summarize patterns but does not, by itself, identify any particular theoretical model of behavior (Deardorff 1984). And although there has been significantly less theoretical work on how distance affects other types of international inter-actions, papers such as Helpman, Melitz, and Yeaple (2004) on exports versus FDI by heterogeneous firms permit one to deduce distance effects in the con-text of (horizontal) FDI as well.

To turn from international economics to international business, mainstream research does incorporate distance as a relevant concept, but in very varied ways. Distance, particularly psychic distance, received early prominence in the literature on the Uppsala internationalization process model. Johanson and Vahlne (1977) observed that the order in which firms established them-selves in foreign markets "seems to be related to the psychic distance between the home and import/host countries." The original Uppsala internationaliza-tion process model drew upon Cyert and March (1963), Penrose (1959), and Aharoni (1966). Its origins in behavioral theory and emphasis on uncertainty and bounded rationality are very different from the theoretical foundations tapped in the international economics literature to derive gravity equations. Knowledge, in particular, is emphasized as a distance-sensitive constraint, drawing attention to how experience as a source of knowledge influences commitments to foreign markets. The Uppsala school, thus, can be viewed as reflecting a theoretical basis for the law of distance rooted in informational imperfections, especially the location-specificity of knowledge.[3]

When Johanson and Vahlne later revised the Uppsala internationalization process model to reflect the "importance of networks in the internationalization of firms," they shifted emphasis from the liability of foreignness to the liability of being an outsider but continued to maintain that "the larger the psychic distance, other things being equal, the more difficult it is to build new relationships" (2009, 1413, 1412). Their revised model also locates psychic distance at the level of the decision maker within a firm rather than the firm itself. If a key executive has, for example, lived and worked in a country objectively distant from the firm's home base, entry into that country may involve low rather than high psychic distance. Although the revised model generally retains alignment with the law of distance, it does contain statements (e.g., "As networks are borderless") that suggest that it may underestimate the extent to which networks themselves are shaped by distance.

Distance is accorded less emphasis in internalization theory (Buckley and Casson 1976; Rugman 1980; Hennart 1982), but is recognized in that theoretical tradition as well, primarily as a driver of transaction costs. Buckley and Casson discuss costs of internalization (which must be weighed against its benefits), and argue that "the additional communication cost attributable to internalization…is greater, the greater the geographical distance between the regions linked by the market, and the greater the 'social distance,' i.e. the dissimilarities in language and social business environment" (1976, 44). Hennart makes a similar point: "the costs of firm governance rise dramatically with cultural, institutional, and geographic distance…this explains the noted preference of MNEs for investments that are geographically, institutionally, and culturally close to their home country" (2007, 430).[4]

Rugman and Verbeke build on internalization theory by relating distance to the reach of firm-specific advantages (FSAs):

High distance simply means that the MNE must make substantial investments to develop or access resources that will complement its present FSA bundles, and will allow the profitable exploitation thereof in the host region environment … it is distance, with its geographic, economic, institutional, and cultural components, that determines the reach of FSAs. Here, it is the decay in value across space that determines empirically the extent to which an FSA should be called location-bound or non-location-bound. (Rugman and Verbeke 2008, 330)

While distance is not incorporated as one of the three legs of Dunning's OLI (ownership, location, internalization) eclectic framework, it is included in its location (L) leg. One of the footnotes in Dunning's 1980 paper on the eclectic framework states, "distance from foreign markets is treated as a negative location-specific endowment" (Dunning 1980, 28). Note that this reflects both a limited emphasis on distance as well as a narrow conception of it – allowing only for negative rather than positive effects.[5]

Internalization theory and the OLI eclectic framework have jointly been regarded as economic theories of international business, in contrast to the Uppsala school's behavioral approach. The emphasis on distance-sensitive transaction costs in these streams of international business literature aligns more closely to the "trade costs" in the traditional derivations of gravity models of international trade. Although internalization theory emphasizes how transaction costs vary across potential modes of participation in foreign markets, the law of distance highlights how major sources of trade costs also affect alternative modes such as licensing and FDI. Recall from Chapter 5 that transportation costs and tariffs account for less than half of distance-driven trade costs (Head and Mayer 2013), and that recent trade literature emphasizes "trade-reducing factors such as differences in legal systems, administrative practices, market structures, networks, languages, and monetary regimes" (Fratianni 2009, 84).

This view of transaction costs, which is supported by the empirical work reported in Chapters 5 and 6, provides a useful reminder that distance effects – while entirely consistent with internalization theory from a conceptual standpoint – do substantially limit the scope within which whether to internalize or not arises as a relevant question. As Rugman and Verbeke conclude from their work on the regionalization of the Fortune Global 500, in distant locations where customers attach limited value to firms' FSAs, "the internalization question of optimal entry mode choice becomes redundant" (2004, 12).

Broader Bases

Rising emphasis in international business on subjective distance effects at the individual level (see, e.g., Sousa and Bradley 2006; Håkanson and Ambos 2010; Dow 2014; Nebus and Chai 2014) also suggests attention to foundations from other disciplines that have delved more deeply into how the human mind deals with distance. Such themes have been contemplated for far longer than international business has been a field of inquiry. The debate about whether similarity or difference makes for better friendships, for example, extends at least as far back as Plato. Although he ultimately straddled the fence on this question, there are antecedents to the law of distance in some of his writings, such as his observation that "similarity begets friendship" (McPherson, Smith-Lovin, and Cook 2001, 416). And the aphorism "out of sight, out of mind" dates back to the sixteenth century, if not earlier.[6]

Modern scholarship in psychology and sociology incorporates several lines of research that relate to the law of distance. At the individual level, the construal-level theory of psychological distance (Trope and Liberman 2010) provides an interesting analogue to our multidimensional treatment of distance. This stream of work addresses how people think across spatial, social, temporal, and hypothetical dimensions of distance and suggests important commonalities across them, including reduced sensitivity to distance from a distal as opposed to proximate perspective, and reliance on abstractions to permit planning about something that is not part of the "here-and-now" (Liberman and Trope 2014; Maglio, Trope, and Liberman 2013).

Layering on interpersonal interactions, the propinquity effect was first identified by psychologists Leon Festinger, Stanley Schachter, and Kurt Back (1950) who found physical proximity – and hence frequent contact – to be a strong predictor of friendships. Recent research finds that even e-mail exchanges diminish with the distance between desks on the same floor within an office (Waber, 2013). And work on homophily (Lazarsfeld and Merton 1954) broadens beyond physical distance to other aspects of similarity that are associated with stronger social ties, particularly status (incorporating factors such as religion and ethnicity) and values.

Chapter 8 adds such cultural variables to the baseline gravity models in Chapter 5 and concludes that some of them do boost international interactions. Particularly robust in its effects is common religion, which, based on the results of an ambitious experimental study of diverse communities from around the world, can be rationalized in terms of "the hypothesis that beliefs in moralistic, punitive, and knowing gods increase impartial behavior towards distant co-religionists" (Purzycki et al. 2016, 327). A similar argument can be made about common ethnicity, which also sometimes boosts interactions, although the enforcement mechanism that has been stressed in that case runs through tightly knit ethnic networks that cross national borders (Greif 1994).

Another relevant stream of research in social psychology derives from Bibb Latané's (1981) theory of social impact, which incorporates distance into a model of the effects of external influences on an individual. Empirical work testing this theory also seems to fit well with our gravity model results. Latané et al. (1995) analyzes social influence based on memorable interactions and finds that "the relationship between distance and interaction frequency was well described by an inverse power function with a slope of approximately −1" (795).

The extent to which people are influenced more strongly by those who are close to them along multiple dimensions may help to explain the persistence of distance effects over time, a perspective that is also consistent with Head and Mayer's (2013) view that historically determined differences in tastes may provide the most promising explanation for why distance continues to have such a strong negative effect on trade. Head and Mayer also observe that this view suggests shifting emphasis from distance as a trade cost to viewing it as a source of limits on the potential gains from trade.

Sociologists as well as psychologists have explored the distinction between objective and subjective distance, examined it empirically (accounting for asymmetry/directionality), and posited multiple dimensions of distance. Simmel (1908) conceived of the "stranger" as physically close but socially distant. Bogardus (1925) created a "social distance scale" that ranges from openness to becoming relatives by marriage to wishing to exclude someone from entry to the respondent's country.[7] And Rummel (1976) wrote of eleven types of distance and grouped them into four categories: material, psychological, social, and cultural. For a very helpful review of this literature, refer to Lewandowski and Lisk (2012).

More speculatively, recent research also suggests the possibility of a biological basis for distance effects. Iacoboni (2009) sees a convergence between social psychology and neuroscience and argues that "neural mirroring solves the 'problem of other minds' (how we can access and understand the minds of others) and makes intersubjectivity possible, thus facilitating social behavior." This line of research has started to pick up hints of distance effects, at least based on work with monkeys. Caggiano et al. (2009) perform a series of actions at varying distances from their subjects, and report evidence of two sets of spatially selective mirror neurons: one that is active more vigorously when the action happens in the closer peripersonal space (and diminishes with distance) and another that responds more in the farther extrapersonal space (and increases with distance).

Evolutionary biology suggests another possible biological basis for distance effects. Xenophobia has been linked to disease avoidance based on the observation that outsiders were more likely to carry pathogens to which a given population lacked antibodies (Navarrete and Fessler 2006).[8] Such findings lead some to theorize that genetic factors contribute to fear and hostility toward people who are different (McEvoy 1995). This perspective is consistent with the line of reasoning in Ghemawat (*World 3.0* 2011) that humanity's long history of living in small groups surrounded by external threats may have contributed to levels of mental distance sensitivity that are no longer adaptive.

By now, we have obviously ventured far beyond our areas of expertise and so must be very cautious in drawing conclusions. However, the pervasiveness of distance effects in social psychology and potentially even in neuroscience and evolutionary biology, and articulations of the mechanisms underlying them, suggest that the law of distance does have a far more profound basis than is typically recognized in international business and economics.

Comparative Advantage

Thus far, our case for distance-driven international research has focused on distance's absolute attractions in terms of empirical utility, practical relevance, and theoretical linkages with a wide range of disciplines. This subsection will argue that there is also a relative or comparative advantage for international business in studying distance, which therefore merits (even) more attention than would be implied by the absolute attractions already discussed.

The comparative advantage argument is different, in terms of its thrust, than the more expansive visions of international business research sometimes offered by scholars, particularly internalization theorists. Thus, as Mark Casson put it nearly thirty years ago,

Table 7.1 *Strategy Domains*

Focus		Increasing Attention to Business-Specificity/Nonspecificity	
		Single Business	Multiple Businesses
Increasing Attention to Location-Specificity/ Nonspecificity	Single Country/ Location	1. (Mainstream) Business Strategy	2. (Mainstream) Corporate Strategy
	Multiple Countries/ Locations	3. International Business Strategy	4. International Corporate Strategy

Source: Reprinted by permission from Macmillan Publishers Ltd. Ghemawat, Pankaj. 2003. "Semiglobalization and International Business Strategy." *Journal of International Business Studies* 34 (2), Table 5, p. 146.

> The modern theory of multinational enterprise has the potential to become a general theory of the enterprise in space, and as such, to encompass theories of the multiregional and multiplant firm. The theory of the uninational single plant firm under perfect competition – a theory that used to be known quite simply as "the theory of the firm" – turns out to be a quite trivial, special case. (Casson 1987, 1).

To clarify the ambitiousness of this research program, consider the matrix in Table 7.1, which is based on Ghemawat ("Semiglobalization" 2003). Domain 1, mainstream (single country) business strategy, effectively focuses attention on firms involved in a single line of business in a single location, that is, allots the least attention to understanding either business/usage-specificity or location-specificity. Domain 2, mainstream corporate strategy, allows for variation in the extent to which key firm activities, resources, or knowledge are business-specific as opposed to generic in the sense of being fungible across businesses. Domain 3, international business strategy, brings in variations in the extent to which activities, resources, knowledge, and so on are location-specific as opposed to generic in the sense of being fungible across locations. And domain 4, international corporate strategy, combines considerations of business/usage-specificity and location-specificity. With this representation, Casson's intent can be framed in terms of moving beyond domain 1 by advancing thinking about, arguably, domains 2, 3, and 4.

Internalization theory's achievements are generally reckoned to have been narrower than this ambitious intent. Thus, Dunning (1998) concluded,

> the internalization school has done more to explain the existence and growth of the multi-activity firm than that of the MNE per se. This is because, with relatively few exceptions, the transaction and coordination costs identified with arm's-length intermediate product markets have not, in general, been specific to cross-border markets, or, indeed, to traversing space (46).

So by his reading, internalization theory has done more to advance analysis in domain 2 than in domains 3 or 4 – which is where international business is involved! The obvious remedy – and this is the comparative advantage argument – is that instead of taking the broad approach of simultaneously trying to theorize about multibusiness and multinational enterprises, it may make more sense for internationally minded researchers to focus on the international border and distance effects that are manifestations of location-specificity and for corporate strategy researchers to concentrate on business/usage-specificity and what might be called interindustry distance.[9]

A final thought in this regard is that international distance is not only a logical focus for international business researchers; it also seems to exert more effect as a focusing and constraining force on firms' scope choices than interindustry distance. Consider some evidence on diversification across countries versus across industries. The United States has, according to the Commerce Department, about 3,800 multinationals (defined as firms with FDI in at least one country) representing about 0.01 percent of all US firms. There are many, many more establishments in the United States that operate in five-plus product markets, and, obviously, the horizontal diversification level of multiestablishment enterprises is even higher (Collis, Anand, and Cheng forthcoming. See especially Tables 1 and 2). US firms' significantly lower propensity to engage in international as opposed to horizontal diversification suggests a sense in which international distance matters more than interindustry distance, further enhancing the former's research appeal.

Critiques and Counters

We emphasized in the previous section how differences and distances between countries provide a logical focus for international business research. Some scholars – particularly those focused on culture – have accepted that differences are central to international business, but have objected to thinking of them in terms of distances. The classic critique of this sort is Shenkar (2001), which alleges several irremediable flaws with cultural distance and proposes friction as an alternative. Harzing (2003) also critiques studies of cultural distance, and recommends more focus on home and/or host country characteristics.

Shenkar (2001)'s critiques sparked a great deal of reflection about cultural distance research (Tihanyi, Griffith, and Russell 2005; Shenkar, Luo, and Yeheskel 2008; Tung and Verbeke 2010), and have also been related more broadly to other dimensions of distance (Zaheer, Schomaker, and Nachum 2012). Shenkar divided his critiques into the methodological and the conceptual. In terms of methodologies, progress is ongoing and we find it efficient to return to some of his methodological points in our discussion of future directions for distance research. We will focus here on the conceptual critiques since they are the ones that allegedly undermine the validity of distance-based research. Shenkar argued that distance has five problematic conceptual properties: symmetry, stability, linearity, causality, and discordance. We find none of these to be intrinsic to the concept itself, and will briefly point to ways in which each of these supposedly irremediable problems has been addressed.

To start with *symmetry*, while the great circle distance between two points is indeed symmetric, the conception of distance employed in this book is far broader and does not require symmetry. Håkanson and Ambos (2010), for example, do report asymmetric psychic distance scores, which we incorporate into gravity models in the next section. Symmetry is also not a necessary assumption in gravity models – in fact, there are reasons to estimate separate gravity equations for, say, imports and exports – and applied work (e.g., our *DHL Global Connectedness Index*) often pays explicit attention to the directionality of interactions.

Stability also need not be assumed within our broader conception of distance, and indeed the gravity models in Chapter 5 incorporate changing administrative and economic distance over time (driven by the implementation of new trade agreements and changes in countries' levels of per capita income). Time-variant measures of cultural and geographic distance could, in principle, also be employed. However, there is evidence that distance effects along those two dimensions may be more stable than often assumed. The penultimate section of Chapter 5 reviewed studies of how the effects of geographic distance have evolved over time. That work exemplified how dynamic insights can be obtained by estimating gravity models at different points in time. One can also think of more sophisticated approaches to analyzing panel data. Chapter 8 will provide a short discussion of the stability of cultural distance effects.

Linearity is not really a critique that applies to gravity models that customarily invoke power laws and multiplicative specifications rather than linear ones – and that can, in any case, be addressed by working with different functional forms. Henderson and Millimet (2008) focus specifically on probing linearity in gravity models. Gallego and Llano (2014) estimate separate effects of geographic distance on trade for distinct "stretches" of distance, and we also incorporate this approach in our analysis of regionalization in Chapter 10. Furthermore, the law of distance itself involves no specific assumptions about the functional form of the (typically negative) relationship between distance and international interactions.

Shenkar's concern about *causality* focuses on "the connotation that culture is the only determinant of distance with relevance to FDI" (2001, 524). We, of course, agree that other dimensions of distance also matter, as elaborated in

Ghemawat (2001)'s CAGE Distance Framework and demonstrated empirically in Chapter 5. Therefore, we must view Shenkar's point as addressing only narrowly scoped cultural research, without raising any fundamental issue with distance as a concept.

Discordance represents yet another critique that reflects a narrower conception of distance effects than the one adopted in this book. Shenkar argues that "the implicit assumption that differences in cultures produce lack of 'fit' and hence an obstacle to transaction is questionable" (Shenkar 2001, 524). Ghemawat ("Forgotten Strategy" 2003) highlighted arbitrage strategies motivated by differences, and Chapter 6 showed that economic distance has positive effects on trade in some products and negative effects on trade in others. That analysis, however, focused specifically on economic distance and trade because it represents an unusual case: the empirical work in Chapters 5 and 6 clearly showed that distance tends to dampen interactions far more often than it intensifies them.

Having discussed Shenkar's critiques, it is convenient also to address his recommended replacement for distance. We do not see how replacing distance as a central metaphor with friction, as he proposes, would improve matters. Indeed, it might create new problems. While Luo and Shenkar (2011) identify the possibility of positive friction effects (arbitrage), standard usage of the friction metaphor does tend to imply a focus on negative rather than positive effects. And publication data suggest that as a descriptive matter, the distance concept remains far more widely used by international business researchers than friction. Between 2002 (after Shenkar's classic article) and 2015, 561 articles in the *Journal of International Business Studies* have mentioned distance and 24 included distance as a keyword, as compared to only 66 articles mentioning friction and 2 including it as a keyword (one of which was authored by Shenkar himself).

Shenkar is not the only scholar to have recommended discarding distance. Harzing and Pudelko (2016) is titled, "Do we need to distance ourselves from the distance concept? Why home and host country context might matter more than (cultural) distance." The authors find that cultural distance becomes insignificant in regressions predicting entry mode after home and host country dummy variables are added, and note that the home and host country dummies boost explanatory power far more than does cultural distance. Although their study does raise important questions about prior research relating cultural distance to entry modes, it has been customary in gravity modeling to incorporate home and host country fixed effects since Anderson and van Wincoop (2003) highlighted the salience of multilateral resistance. Thus, the models in Chapters 5 and 6 all incorporated home and host country fixed effects, and still identified significant distance effects. Furthermore, we must disagree with Harzing and Pudelko's lament that "it is regrettable that in International Business research country-specific knowledge appears to be considered subordinate to 'universal theories' these days" (2016, 23). Although deep contextualization is valuable, it would be a costly error for the international business field not to devote substantial attention to regularities that are broadly generalizable – which is the spirit in which this book offers its two laws of globalization.

Thus, our review does not, for reasons we have explained, indicate any irremediable flaws with the concept of distance that offset the advantages discussed earlier in this chapter. That said, actual research on distance does have its limitations, which future work can strive to address. Zaheer et al. (2012) offers several useful recommendations in this regard, including the importance of distinguishing between distance and "tendency toward a particular characteristic" (18), a concern to which we return when analyzing institutional distance variables in Chapter 9. We also aim to strengthen future distance-driven research by proposing six research directions in the next section.

Six Directions for Distance-Driven Research

We begin our discussion of proposed future research directions by discussing multidimensionality, in response to the disproportionate focus of prior research on cultural or other isolated dimensions of distance.[10] Then, we turn to opportunities to map distance landscapes in even more detail and from different perspectives. Next, we argue for greater attention to interindustry variation and also proceed to the firm level to discuss the need for greater attention to intrafirm distance and its moderators. We recommend openness to both subjective and objective measures of distance. And, finally, we draw attention to still untapped opportunities for researchers to improve the data with which they work.

Accounting for Multiple Facets of Distance

Most research on distance in international business – like the scholars who produce it – focuses on only a single dimension of distance. Only one-third of the articles covered in the Hutzschenreuter et al. (2015) review addressed multiple types of distance and the majority even of that subset still focused on only one or two dimensions of the CAGE Framework.[11] While some degree of specialization is efficient, limited attention to distance's multidimensionality risks a state of affairs resembling the parable of the blind men and the elephant, in which each of the men examines only part of the animal and the result is loud disagreement about its nature rather than progress toward understanding its totality.

Looking beyond international business, an even higher proportion of research in other fields seems to treat distance in a narrow, unidimensional way. Geographers tend to focus only on geographic distance, sociologists on institutional distance, anthropologists on cultural distance, and so on. The evidence presented here and in Chapter 5 suggests that such single facet research, no matter how well executed *en soi*, is subject to a basic specification error.[12] Note that there is also a class of work that appears to focus on two dimensions but effectively collapses one into the other. Thus, work on institutional voids in emerging markets (Khanna and Palepu 1997) collapses economic distance into a particular kind of administrative difference, specifically a vertical measure of institutional quality.[13]

The multidimensionality of distance increases the complexity that firms face when doing business far from home, and also poses additional challenges for researchers. The empirical evidence already discussed in this volume provides some support for the view that the effort required for researchers to analyze distance multidimensionally is worthwhile.[14] When adopting a multidimensional design, the phenomenon being studied and the theory being tested should guide the selection of distance dimensions to be analyzed. Multidimensional frameworks such as CAGE help ensure a holistic perspective, and the country and industry level detail provided in Tables 5.1 and 6.1 respectively can help with hypothesis development. Another multidimensional structure proposed by Berry, Guillén, and Zhou (2010) incorporates nine dimensions of distance, although these can roughly be collapsed into the four CAGE categories. While the choice of how many dimensions to use is partly a matter of taste, theories of subitizing (Kaufman et al. 1949), at least, would seem to favor four over nine.

Whether to consolidate multiple dimensions or subdimensions of distance into indexes is another important research question. While it is useful, for heuristic purposes, to group individual dimensions of differences into broader aggregates (e.g., "cultural distance"), the consequential relationships being asserted should usually be interpreted to operate through more granular types of differences (e.g., language, religion, ethnicity, etc.) rather than at the aggregate level. In this regard, we strongly support Zaheer et al.'s (2012) strictures against oversimplifying distance.

If a researcher does decide to aggregate distance dimensions or subdimensions into indexes, several issues merit consideration. First, recall Shenkar (2001)'s methodological critique of the assumption of *equivalence* in response to Kogut and Singh (1988)'s cultural distance index, which treats each of the dimensions of national culture as equally important. Consistent with findings from other research, Chapter 8 will provide additional evidence of nonequivalent effects of the Hofstede dimensions on international interactions. Another concern about Kogut and Singh (1988)'s cultural distance index has been raised by Berry, Guillén, and Zhou (2010), who note that indices computed using Euclidean distance can give extra weight to characteristics measured by correlated variables and are sensitive to the scale of measurement. As a remedy, they propose Mahalanobis distance, which is "equivalent to the Euclidian distance calculated with the standardized values of the principal components" Berry et al. (2010, 1469). We test Mahalanobis-based cultural distance measures in Chapter 8 and report the results in the online appendix at www.ghemawat.com/laws.

Also relevant when combining effects across multiple dimensions of distance is Rugman, Verbeke, and Nguyen's (2011) argument in their discussion of "compounded distance" that distance effects are multiplicative rather than additive.[15] Multiplicative distance effects are reflected in the gravity specification described in Chapter 5, our treatment of directional psychic distance in this section, as well as in the CAGE Comparator™ (www.ghemawat.com/cage).[16] The CAGE Distance calculations generated for the CAGE Comparator™ can also be incorporated into other research studies as a gravity-based alternative to traditional distance measures (see Box 7.1 on page 225).

Mapping Distance Landscapes in More Detail

Dealing with multiple dimensions of distance is just one of the complexities that arises in mapping distance. While the (logged) multiplicative specification typically used in gravity models – and followed in Chapters 5 and 6 – is very specific, the law of distance itself, as articulated in this book, does not impose this or any specific functional form on the relationship between measures of international interactions and measures of distance beyond insisting that distance-dependence is usually negative rather than positive. According to Head and Mayer (2014) "the main reason to insist on the multiplicative form in the definition of gravity is historical usage. It is therefore possible that future work would abandon the multiplicative form and redefine gravity to allow other functional forms" (138). Since much international business research is still focused on understanding the types of outcomes that are affected by distance and whether the effects are negative or positive, this may not be an immediate priority, but the analysis of the possible non-loglinearity of the effects of physical distance in Chapter 10 suggests that some research along these lines is worth pursuing.

Shenkar's (2001) critique regarding spatial homogeneity has suggested another kind of extension as well: Beugelsdijk and Mudambi (2013) recommend that within-country distance effects be incorporated into international business research because of significant internal variation relative to country-level measures that are typically used. And Ghemawat (2015) argues that intranational distance effects imply that international business research has a great deal to contribute to domestic business about how to deal with distance. Intranational and international interactions should indeed ideally both be accounted for, but the dearth of data on the former often gets in the way. Given such practical constraints, it is helpful to note that given the two laws of globalization and how they have been operationalized empirically, international business research that focuses only on international distance effects – and folds intranational distance into country fixed effects – retains its logic.

Another limitation of most distance-based research is that it does not fully account for international network effects. Although gravity models now typically do incorporate multilateral resistance terms based on country fixed effects, they still focus on modeling interactions on a dyadic basis. Moving from a dyadic conception of global flows to consider how countries are connected to each other indirectly as well as directly offers the potential to better grasp their interdependence. Ongoing work by Pankaj Ghemawat, Fabrizio Ferraro, and Jordi Torrents discussed in Chapter 5 attempts to deal with this critique by calculating measures of countries' network centrality in various types of international interactions. Such centrality does, however, turn out to be highly correlated with the size of international flows, suggesting that future research should focus not just on network analysis but also on how conclusions derived from it differ from those based on traditional methods. Further network-theoretic research on trade flows should also benefit from new trade data based on value added rather than gross revenues – one of the areas where better data seem to offer significant room for research progress, as discussed in the final part of this section.

Building on the emphasis on multidimensionality in the previous subsection, our mapping of distance landscapes could also be greatly enhanced by identifying interdependencies across different types of international interactions. Interdependencies between trade and FDI are particularly salient for international busines research. Some horizontal FDI is motivated by avoiding transportation and other trade costs and so substitutes for trade. However, it is important to note that such substitution can take place even as both are separately subject to significant negative distance effects. Indeed, several empirical studies provide support for this sense of the relationship between trade and FDI. Helpman et al. (2004) find that "firms tend to substitute FDI sales for exports when transport costs are large and plant-level returns to scale are small" (300–301). Oldenski (2012) reports that distance has a significant negative relationship with the ratio of exports relative to foreign affiliate sales. In addition, similar substitution effects seem to show up between types of FDI. Kleinert and Toubal (2013) analyze data on the establishment of distribution versus manufacturing affiliates abroad by German MNEs and find that the probability of producing abroad rises with distance.

Broadening beyond only trade and FDI, the gravity models in Chapter 5 – consistent with other studies – support the view that substitution effects are usually outweighed by the shrinkage effects of distance: they do not generally lead to the observation of positive signs on strongly significant distance variables.[17] This is also consistent with the points noted in Chapter 1 that people flows have been found to stimulate trade[18] and information flows (Perkins and Neumayer 2013) and information flows are positively associated with capital flows (Portes and Rey 2005). But given common underlying factors – the CAGE variables in the baseline gravity models in Chapter 5 – sorting through what drives what remains challenging.

Finally, also of empirical interest is the emerging body of work in international economics on dynamic gravity models that posit that the intensity of trade between country pairs depends on past as well as current trade costs.[19] Continuing the development of such methodologies and extending them to other types of international interactions – and to firm-level analyses as well – seems to have intriguing potential to bring fixed/sunk cost investments into the picture.

Recognizing Interindustry Variation

Variation across industries – as well as firms, as discussed in the next subsection – can shed additional light on the contours of multidimensional distance landscapes. The first section of Chapter 6 focused on evidence for the law of distance at the industry level, and showed that the sensitivity of merchandise trade and foreign direct investment to multiple dimensions of distance does vary significantly across industries. This suggests a need, at minimum, for distance-driven research to control for interindustry variation. Even more ambitiously, research could strengthen our understanding of what makes some industries more sensitive to particular dimensions of distance than others. Table 6.1 provided a qualitative characterization, but quantitative research in this area remains lacking.

At least with regard to merchandise trade, high value-to-weight and value-to-bulk ratios are already well recognized as reducing sensitivity to geographic distance. And the firm-level analysis presented in the second section of Chapter 6 suggests the hypotheses that high versus low R&D and advertising intensity at the industry level may also be associated with different levels of sensitivity to particular dimensions of distance. One can readily think of other testable hypotheses such as an association specifically between R&D intensity and administrative distance (related, for example, to protection of intellectual property), and between labor intensity and economic distance (due to larger possibilities for labor cost arbitrage). Research on these and other potential relationships has the potential to yield a clearer taxonomy of industries based on their sensitivity to particular distance dimensions.

Interindustry variation is, of course, not the only predictable source of variation that is worth exploring. Think, for instance, of variation across functions to complement the earlier discussions of variation across dimensions of distance, types of international interactions, and industry resource-intensity. In Chapter 6, we cited research by Castellani, Jimenez, and Zanfei (2013) showing announced greenfield FDI to be less sensitive to geographic distance when it pertains to R&D as compared to manufacturing. And Rugman and Verbeke (2004) observed that large MNEs can more easily disperse upstream (sourcing/ production) than downstream (sales) activities across regions.

Exploring Intrafirm Distance and Its Moderators

Another promising new direction for distance research, as discussed in Chapter 6, involves the application of analytical techniques that have traditionally been used primarily at the country level – such as the gravity model – to the analysis of firms and their subsidiaries. In this subsection, we highlight three such opportunities in firm-level distance research that we view as having particular promise: the distinction between internal and external distance, moderators of distance effects that highlight possibilities for firms to become more distance-capable, and dynamic models of firm-level distance effects.

Internal distance refers to distance within a firm, typically between organizational units but also between individuals, whereas external distance refers to the distance between a firm and other market participants and relevant nonmarket actors in the firm's environment. We introduced the distinction between internal and external distance in Chapter 6, in the context of the configuration of value adding activities within multinational firms.

Internal distance has not been emphasized much in the international business literature, which typically pays more attention to border effects rather than distance effects within firms, but it does have several points of connection with prior research. In Chapter 6, we discussed trade-offs between external and internal distance. In order to get closer to external opportunities (e.g., foreign markets), a firm may stretch itself over greater internal distance. One can also think in terms of broader alignment requirements between a firm's approaches to internal and external distance and the AAA strategies. A strategy that emphasizes adaptation to large external market differences, for example, will likely require a substantial amount of internal adaptation.

To turn to moderators of firm-level distance effects, some firms are clearly better able to manage across distance than others are. Of particular interest are firm characteristics that can be shaped by managers to make their firms more distance-capable.[20] Prior research in this vein, however, has focused mainly on experience as a moderator of distance effects. Cho and Padmanabhan (2005) find that several types of experience reduce cultural distance effects, and that among them decision-specific experience pertaining to a particular ownership mode has the most powerful effect. Dikova (2009) reports that market-specific experience negates the effects of psychic distance on performance. For further references as well as discussion of distance as a contingency factor, refer to Hutzschenreuter et al. (2015).

In Chapter 6, we also presented preliminary findings on how Fortune Global 500 firms with greater R&D intensity, advertising intensity, and top management team national diversity operate across greater cultural, administrative, geographic, and economic distances. These are only three among many possible firm characteristics that could potentially moderate multidimensional distance effects. Much more work is still required to provide robust empirical support for a set of managerially relevant characteristics that make some firms more distance-capable than others.

One can also think of dynamic analysis of firms' expansion trajectories as treating their footprints as moderators. The need for more such analysis suggests a call for greater attention to experience and capabilities that a firm has already amassed abroad and hence the reference point from which distance is measured. The simplest method is to measure from the firm's home country, and this method does gain some support from the law of semiglobalization. As discussed in Ghemawat ("Cosmopolitan" 2011), most firms do still have very clear home bases. Nonetheless, for firms with large current footprints abroad, measuring distance *only* from the firm's headquarters can result in an incomplete and potentially misleading perspective. The Hutzschenreuter et al. (2015) review incorporates studies recommending several alternatives: all countries where a firm operates, its home region or cluster, and the closest existing subsidiary. Some of the techniques for dynamic gravity modeling referenced earlier in this chapter may also prove useful in this context. More generally, greater attention to dynamics suggests a need for distance research to rely more on longitudinal data.[21]

Finally, further research is needed to confirm whether more global managerial mindsets help with globalization, as stressed by the international business literature. Linking managerial mindsets to firms' capabilities to bridge distance, however, requires further work that takes account of subjective as well as objective distance, as discussed next.

Considering Subjective as well as Objective Distance

The multidimensional treatment of distance in the gravity models in Chapters 5 and 6, consistent with standard gravity modeling practice, used only objective distance variables, such as kilometers of physical distance and the presence or absence of a common language. However, the focus of international business research on firms and the people who lead them provides a reason to consider subjective or perceptual distance measures alongside objective ones. As noted in the discussion of distance's broader theoretical bases, there has been increasing interest among international business scholars in individual-level subjective distance effects. The incidence and implications of globaloney – the exaggerated perceptions of the depth of globalization discussed in Chapter 2 – suggests that significant discrepancies between perceived and actual distance may indeed affect managers' international business decisions, a concern that also draws support from research on the "psychic distance paradox" (O'Grady and Lane 1996) mentioned in Chapter 6.

When Johanson and Vahlne (1977, 24) appropriated Beckerman's (1956) term "psychic distance" and positioned it as central to the Uppsala internationalization process model, they defined psychic distance as "the sum of factors preventing the flow of information from and to the market. Examples are differences in language, education, business practices, culture, and industrial development." Johanson and Vahlne's description of psychic distance recognizes that perceptions are shaped at least in part by objective distance factors, a perspective that would later be operationalized in Dow and Karunaratna's (2006) distinction between (subjective) perceived psychic distance (PPD) and (objective) psychic distance stimuli (PDS), which parallels Håkanson and Ambos's (2010) antecedents of psychic distance.

Conceptually, both objective and subjective distance can usefully be thought of in multidimensional CAGE terms. Along each of the CAGE dimensions, individual-level perceived distance can vary relative to objective distance. However, we also recognize that the paucity of subjective psychic distance data implies that empirical research will seldom be able to draw upon managers' separate perceptions of individual distance dimensions. Verbeke and Kano (2012, 142) propose that psychic distance is "somewhat similar to the four distance dimensions between the home and host country – cultural, administrative (or institutional), geographic (or spatial) and economic (Ghemawat, 2001)." This is true to the extent that all four CAGE dimensions can shape perceived psychic distance. However, our emphasis in this section and elsewhere on multidimensionality – as well as the importance of the distinction between subjective and objective distance discussed here – suggests that the two should still be treated as distinct.

In order to examine how psychic distance relates to the evidence for the law of distance, we incorporate psychic distance scores from Håkanson and Ambos (2010) into the standard gravity model of eleven types of international interactions that was described in Chapter 5. Håkanson and Ambos (2010) assembled a team of collaborators to collect perceptual psychic distance data in the world's twenty-five largest economies. Respondents were asked to rate countries based on the "sum of factors (cultural or language differences, geographical distance, etc.) that affect the flow and interpretation of information to and from a foreign country." The responses were aggregated to produce directional (i.e., asymmetric) psychic distance scores for each country pair. While the limited availability of psychic distance data reduced the average number of observations from 22,763 to

Table 7.2 *Adjusted R-squared of Gravity Models Using Psychic Distance*

Dependent variables	(0) Unrestricted Baseline (Chapter 5)	(1) Baseline Restr. to Countries with Psychic Distance Available	(2) Add Psychic Distance From Country 1 to 2 * from 2 to 1	(3) Add Psychic Distance from Country 1 to 2	(4) Add Psychic Distance from Country 2 to 1
Merchandise exports	0.777	0.874	0.883	0.882	0.881
Services exports	0.881	0.872	0.886	0.884	0.884
FDI outward stocks	0.751	0.801	0.810	0.808	0.808
Portfolio equity assets stocks	0.766	0.871	0.874	0.873	0.873
Portfolio long-term debt stocks	0.762	0.848	0.851	0.850	0.851
Outgoing phone calls	0.893	0.835	0.858	0.856	0.852
Printed publications exports	0.701	0.835	0.858	0.856	0.852
Patent applications	0.820	0.894	0.902	0.901	0.901
Emigrant stocks	0.802	0.769	0.804	0.797	0.800
Tertiary students inbound	0.715	0.832	0.854	0.847	0.854
Tourist arrivals	0.879	0.938	0.944	0.942	0.944
Average Adjusted R-squared	*0.795*	*0.852*	*0.866*	*0.863*	*0.864*
Average Observations	*22,763*	*3363*	*3363*	*3363*	*3363*

only 3,363, psychic distance (when added into the model together with all of the explanatory variables described in Chapter 5) was significant with the expected negative sign for all eleven types of international interactions!

Table 7.2 summarizes the adjusted R-squared values obtained across the various psychic distance models described in this subsection. Column 0, for reference, reports the adjusted R-squared values of the models reported in Chapter 5. Column 1 repeats the same models with the restricted sample of countries for which psychic distance data are available, to provide a baseline for the comparisons that follow. Column 2 adds psychic distance to the baseline model using the product of the directional psychic distance scores in order to capture subjective distance as it is perceived at both origin and destination.

Columns 3 and 4 present the adjusted R-squared values from models that add single direction psychic distance scores alone to the baseline model (column 1). Psychic distance from the reporting country (e.g., the exporter for merchandise exports) is used in Column 3 and the partner country (e.g., the importer) is in Column 4. The adjusted R-squared of these models is typically quite similar across the two directions. It makes intuitive sense, for example, that for both trade and FDI, perspectives from both sides of the interaction are relevant. A notable exception is international students where the adjusted R-squared is higher from the perspective of the student's origin country. In addition, the general pattern that both perspectives matter is consistent with the observation that models using the product of the directional psychic distance scores (column 2) perform better than (or at least as well as) those based on scores for a single direction (columns 3 and 4).

While these results show that subjective psychic distance measures can help explain international interactions alongside objective distance measures, special care is in order when using such indicators. The evidentiary basis for the performance of psychic distance in explaining international flows is still limited. And the focus on large economies in this analysis is likely to result in some upward bias of the predictive power of psychic distance due to survey respondents' greater familiarity with these countries. If asked about all countries, respondents might be unable to differentiate among smaller countries, except neighboring ones and those that feature particularly prominently in the news. While evidentiary standards should presumably be higher for subjective than objective measures, the evidentiary basis for the former remains much more limited.

In spite of the large resource and coordination challenges involved, expanding and validating subjective distance measures should, given the results presented here, be an important research priority. In addition to the promising results obtained with currently available measures, subjective distance measures may prove particularly helpful for advancing our understanding of benefits firms can gain from changing managerial mindsets. There is a natural linkage between subjective distance and the discussions, in Chapters 6 and 8 respectively, of helping organizations and their leaders become more distance-capable.

Improving Data

Investing to broaden and validate psychic distance measures is just one of several areas where there are opportunities to strengthen empirical research by improving the data employed. Major advances in research on distance in international business have often required enterprising researchers to push the boundaries of existing data sources. The largest data collection effort in the field's history remains the Harvard Multinational Enterprise Project (1965–1977), led by Raymond Vernon. A team of 40+ research assistants compiled data on the activities of each operating unit of some 400 multinationals, drawing on public sources as well as questionnaires. The project's datasets had underpinned 17 books, 151 articles, and 28 doctoral theses as of its 10-year mark, as well as many more since its completion (Vernon 1969, 1994). On a more modest scale, Rugman and Verbeke's (2004) landmark study on the regionalization of the Fortune Global 500 was based on data collected from annual reports. Our update of this analysis with Niccolò Pisani of the University of Amsterdam was similarly labor-intensive, but yielded, in contrast with earlier work, evidence of deregionalization as reported in Chapter 10. And Ghemawat and Vantrappen's (2015) analysis of the national origins of the top management teams of the Fortune Global 500 (discussed in Chapter 4) required two research assistants to spend several months reading executive biographies to manually assign home countries to every senior executive.

Fortunately, many of the present opportunities for improving data are less labor-intensive for the researcher than those highlighted in the previous paragraph. We will briefly discuss several examples in this vein: improvements in trade and FDI data, data sources that directly track the activities of foreign affiliates of multinational firms, and longer-run opportunities afforded by the explosion of geospatial data.

Dyadic data on merchandise trade extend back decades, providing the most comprehensive available coverage of international interactions. However, as discussed in Chapter 2, traditional ("gross") trade data double-count (or more) goods that cross national borders more than once. The joint OECD-WTO initiative on measuring trade in value added[22] has made substantial progress toward untangling the effects of multicountry value chains to provide a clearer picture of trade patterns. Given the central role played by firms in shaping these value chains, analysis that incorporates these new data will likely prove highly relevant for the international business field.

The emphasis of international business research on multinational firms has also led to a strong reliance on FDI data, despite known problems with it. Here too, there are some improvements in the data available, for example, the fDi Markets database used in Chapter 6, which provides dyadic data on announced greenfield FDI broken out by industry, activity, and so on. Another interesting characteristic of this source is that it pinpoints origins and destinations at the city level. And at the official level, efforts are underway to capture ultimate rather than immediate sources and destinations in order to deal with problems associated with tax havens. Some countries, including the United States, France, Austria, and Finland already produce inward FDI statistics based on the ultimate source of the investment (Eurostat 2014), and the US Bureau of

Economic Analysis is working on the development of a parallel set of outward FDI statistics.[23]

Improvements to FDI statistics, however, only represent partial remedies since FDI stocks have been found to provide incomplete – and biased – perspectives on the activity of multinational firms. One simple indicator of the magnitude of the problem is the fact that the assets of foreign affiliates worldwide are roughly four times as large as the total global stock of FDI (UNCTAD 2015, 18). In addition to the obvious problems associated with tax havens, the fact that FDI data do not reflect funds raised locally in host countries causes FDI data to underestimate MNE activity in countries with more advanced financial markets. Similarly, FDI data underestimate affiliate activity in countries with higher labor productivity (Beugelsdijk et al. 2010).

The limitations of FDI data suggest that international business researchers should place more emphasis on datasets that directly track the activities of multinational firms and their foreign affiliates. This is probably the motivation behind roughly two-thirds of empirical studies in international business restricting themselves to single-country samples and gathering data via primary surveys (Yang, Wang, and Su 2006). However, this creates its own problems, particularly when distance is a research focus. As Harzing and Pudelko (2016) point out, in a study with just one home country, supposed home-host distance effects may actually capture differences across host countries instead.[24]

Another (still fragmented) set of data is related to the fact that several countries, including the United States and Japan, have long reported detailed data on the activities of home country multinationals abroad and foreign multinationals in their domestic markets. An important step forward came in 2007, when EU legislation mandated harmonized collection of foreign affiliate activity data, which are now available in Eurostat's FATS dataset. Together with additional datasets from the OECD, South Korea, and China, data are available on a substantial portion of multinational activity around the world, and these data cover several variables not addressed by FDI statistics: sales, trade, value added, employment, and so on. Fukui and Lakatos (2012) estimate a global database of foreign affiliate sales drawing primarily from Eurostat FATS. Further work on integration across datasets covering foreign affiliate activity seems likely to provide another important source of insight for international business research.

Moving beyond only trade and capital flows, the explosion of geospatially encoded data also offers promise to improve research on information and people flows. Geospatial data is one of the major drivers of the "big data" revolution (Sui, Goodchild, and Elwood 2013) and is changing how data are stored, analyzed, and visualized (Schwartz 2012; Pitts 2013). The potential applications to international business research are myriad. Think, for example, of the field's longstanding interest in information/knowledge flows within multinational firms (Egelhoff 1982; Gupta and Govindarajan 1991; Minbaeva 2007). The rising proportion of those flows that take place in digital form with geographic metadata suggests large opportunities for novel empirical analysis. More precise locational data also afford the possibility of greater integration with related fields such as economic geography, which would not have been possible when limited to country- or even region-level data.[25]

Progress at improving and expanding data sources can also pave the way for advances in how data are analyzed. The firm-level gravity models presented in Chapter 6, for example, required data on Fortune Global 500 subsidiary footprints by country, whereas prior analyses of the footprints of this sample of firms had to work within the limits of region-level data. Given the complexity of datasets on international interactions as well as their inherent spatiality, it is worth adding that advanced data visualization techniques can help guide data analysis and strengthen how results are communicated. Several flexible data visualization tools (as well as a simple gravity modeling tool) that can be applied to most of the datasets used in this book (as well as others) can be found at www.ghemawat. com, along with CAGE Distance measures of the sort described in Box 7.1.

Box 7.1. Incorporating CAGE Distance into Quantitative Studies

Chapter 5 briefly mentioned composite distance metrics based on gravity model coefficients, which were generated using the methodology developed for the CAGE Comparator™ online distance analysis tool. International business researchers may wish to consider incorporating these metrics into their models as an alternative to geographic distance or to popular indexes such as Kogut and Singh's (1988) cultural distance. Therefore, we release CAGE Distance Scores and provide supporting documentation at www. ghemawat.com/cage.

One advantage of distance scores based on gravity model coefficients is that researchers can select scores that were calibrated based on data for the most relevant types of international interactions. For example, models of knowledge flows may perform better with distance measures calibrated based on telephone calls than those based on trade or FDI. Customization can also be accomplished at the industry level, as illustrated in Chapter 6. Another advantage is that the multiplicative gravity model specification generates a form of "compounded distance" in the sense proposed by Rugman, Verbeke, and Nguyen (2011).

These composite (compounded) distances are calibrated for each type of interaction based on all of the distance-related coefficients included in a given gravity model. We convert each coefficient into an effect multiplier, taking into account how each of the underlying variables entered into the gravity equation. One of the benefits of this approach is that it facilitates customization. Suppose that a researcher wishes to conduct an analysis of an unfamiliar flow type or industry, on which gravity model coefficients are not available. In this case, the researcher may find it helpful to adjust the effects implied by flow multipliers for other similar types of interactions, and then conduct sensitivity analysis. In addition, the use of multipliers facilitates the explanation of the model assumptions to nonacademic audiences. Practitioners, naturally, tend to be cautious about trusting outputs from any "black box" model, and can usually grasp multipliers more easily than gravity model coefficients themselves.

Once a set of effect multipliers has been generated from gravity model coefficients – customized as appropriate by the researcher – the effects for each country are calculated by taking the products of the multipliers and the relevant country pair data. For continuous variables, multipliers are converted back to coefficients (taking into account any customization) to maintain consistency with the original gravity specification. In order to make the results more intuitive as distance scores, they are then rescaled so that the sum of the composite distance scores from a given home country to all foreign countries is equal to the sum of the physical distance (in kilometers) from the focal country to all other countries covered in the analysis.

Conclusion

This chapter has made the case for placing distance at the center of international business research. The empirical utility and practical value of distance are themes that extend throughout this volume and were summarized briefly in this chapter. More attention was devoted to the theoretical bases of distance in international business, economics, and in other disciplines. We also explained why focusing on distance affords international business research a comparative advantage.

We then turned to some of the critiques of distance-driven research in international business. Much of this has taken the form of debates about methodological points, which should help improve the quality of empirical work over time. However, distance has also faced a set of conceptual critiques, which scholars – most notably Shenkar (2001) – have argued are intrinsic to distance and compromise its use. We responded directly to these critiques, showing that many have in fact already been addressed and that none represent irremediable weaknesses of distance that offset its empirical and theoretical attractions.

The last substantive section of this chapter moved on to propose six directions for distance-driven research in the future. Clearly, there are many opportunities to further increase our understanding of distance and how it affects international business. Part III pushes forward in some of these respects as it examines applications of each of the four dimensions of the CAGE Distance Framework.

Notes

1 This led to the design a CAGE-based course on globalization at a "micro" level, which is discussed briefly in Chapter 8. For additional information as well as course materials, refer to www.ghemawat.com/globecourse or www.aacsb.edu/knowledge/resources/course%20materials/globe.

2 Beugelsdijk and Mudambi term this a "**Dunning Effect**" (expressed primarily in rising use of the term distance itself) and a "**Ghemawat Effect**" (expressed primarily in an increasing number of papers on cultural and psychic distance, with rising work on geographic, economic, and administrative/institutional distance showing up only several years later).

3 Penrose (1959) wrote of the "receding managerial limit," and the distance construct as employed here helps to understand how it actually recedes: from close to far.

4 Newer work in this research stream places somewhat greater emphasis on distance. It highlights the complexity involved with managing across multiple dimensions of "compounded distance," (Rugman, Verbeke, and Nguyen 2011) and recognizes how problems associated with bounded rationality and bounded reliability (Verbeke and Greidanus 2009) tend to rise with distance (Verbeke and Kano 2016).

5 Other streams of international business research also address distance. Institutional theory has given rise to a large body of research on institutional distance – which is discussed in Chapter 9. Distance also appears in research grounded in the knowledge-based view of the firm, in which "distance impedes the capacity to absorb new knowledge, and even more importantly, to impede the application of already existing knowledge" (Hutzschenreuter et al. 2015, 7).

6 See www.phrases.org.uk/meanings/274400.html.

7 Bogardus's intermediate categories mention neighbors and citizens of the same country, recalling Hierocles's circles of identity, which are discussed in Ghemawat (*World 3.0* 2011, 316–317).

8 Note that further support for this view is reflected in the finding that in-group favoritism is heightened among women in the first trimester of pregnancy, when immune responses are suppressed, as described in Navarrete, Fessler, and Eng (2007).

9 While the primary focus of this chapter (and Part II in general) is on distance, border effects are also mentioned here both because of the wider applicability of the argument and because this is the only chapter of this book focused on theory and research implications (it has no counterpart in Part I).

10 Since 2000, more than three times as many JIBS articles have mentioned cultural distance as compared to the second most mentioned type, psychic distance.

11 Among the 216 total articles covered in the Hutzschenreuter et al. (2015) review, 204 dealt with specific types of distance, and among those 49 dealt with multiple

types (counting as multiple any article listing multiple types of distance even if they were closely related, e.g., formal and informal institutional distance).

12 The industry- and firm-level models in Chapter 6 provide additional support for this point.

13 Chapter 9 reports results of incorporating several administrative or institutional variables into gravity models. In that analysis, measures of vertical institutional quality underperform the alternatives tested.

14 A multidimensional perspective on distance can also help tease out positive (arbitrage) effects that would otherwise remain hidden. Malhotra, Sivakumar, and Zhu (2009) report that cross-border acquisitions by emerging market firms are negatively related to cultural and geographic distance but positively related to administrative and economic distance, and Cuervo-Cazurra and Genc (2011) disaggregate administrative distance into subdimensions with directionally different impacts on multinationals from advanced versus emerging economies. Multidimensionality may also take on additional salience in dynamic studies of international expansion, as suggested by Hutzschenreuter, Kleindienst, and Lange (2014)'s finding that added governance (administrative) distance had the largest effect on the performance of German MNEs, followed by cultural and geographic distance.

15 While they assert that Ghemawat's approach to the multiple dimensions of distance has been "largely additive," Ghemawat (*World 3.0* 2011 58) explicitly describes the multiplicative aggregation of distance effects in relation to the many sources of intense ties between the United States and Canada.

16 Consistent with our shared view of multiplicative distance effects, the multiplicative method of combining directional psychic distance scores outperformed an alternative specification (not reported) in which the directional psychic distance scores were summed rather than multiplied.

17 Economic distance, as discussed in Chapters 5 and 6, does sometimes have positive effects. Part of the purpose of the empirical analysis in those chapters was to explore such relationships where theory offers no clear guidance – and reality is clearly a mix of the two different types of trade – to figure out which, at least, predominates.

18 Doubling the number of immigrants from a particular country is associated with 9% higher imports from that country according to Hatzigeorgiou (2010). See also Lin (2011).

19 See, for example, Olivero and Yotov (2012).

20 The concept of distance capability discussed here is related to but distinct from that of location capabilities as discussed in Zaheer and Nachum (2011). We focus on capabilities for traversing distance, whereas Zaheer and Nachum focus on those required to build locational capital abroad.

21 Several recent studies illustrate the potential of research that looks at distance from more than just the perspective of a firm's home country. Hutzschenreuter, Voll, and Verbeke (2011) relate incremental ("added") cultural distance (relative to the closest existing subsidiary) to the pace of international expansion, and find support for the hypothesis that "higher added cultural distance associated with the MNE's international expansion in one period will reduce the rate of international expansion in the subsequent period" (311). Zhou and Guillén (2015) take into account all countries where a firm operates, but weight them based on how long the firm has operated there to calculate distance from the firm's evolving "home base," which they find outperforms static distance from the home country as a predictor of market entry.

Nachum and Song (2011) also consider all of the countries where a firm operates, but emphasize thinking about multinational firms as evolving portfolios, drawing attention to the importance of "fit" between new and existing units.

22 See www.oecd.org/sti/ind/measuringtradeinvalue-addedanoecd-wtojointinitiative.htm.

23 Several researchers have also worked on cleaning up the official Chinese FDI data. See, for example, Casanova, Garcia-Herrero, and Xia (2015) which adjusts China's outward FDI data to account for round-tripping and offshoring.

24 For additional discussion of this problem and evidence supporting the use of (at least) two-country samples, refer to Brouthers, Marshall, and Keig (2016).

25 An interesting example of the value afforded by pinning down locational data more precisely is Hillberry and Hummels (2008) research on trade patterns within the United States by zip (postal) code. They found that shipments within zip codes (with a median radius of just four miles) were three times larger than shipments across zip code boundaries.

References

Aharoni, Yair. 1966. "The Foreign Investment Decision Process." *The International Executive* 8 (4):13–14. doi: 10.1002/tie.5060080407.

Anderson, James E., and Eric van Wincoop. 2003. "Gravity with Gravitas: A Solution to the Border Puzzle." *American Economic Review* 93 (1):170–192.

Beckerman, W. 1956. "Distance and the Pattern of Intra-European Trade." *Review of Economics and Statistics* 38 (1):31–40. doi: 10.2307/1925556.

Berry, Heather, Mauro F. Guillén, and Nan Zhou. 2010. "An Institutional Approach to Cross-National Distance." *Journal of International Business Studies* 41 (9):1460–1480. doi: 10.1057/jibs.2010.28.

Beugelsdijk, Sjoerd, Jean-François Hennart, Arjen Slangen, and Roger Smeets. 2010. "Why and How FDI Stocks Are a Biased Measure of MNE Affiliate Activity." *Journal of International Business Studies* 41 (9):1444–1459.

Beugelsdijk, Sjoerd, and Ram Mudambi. 2013. "MNEs as Border-Crossing Multi-Location Enterprises: The Role of Discontinuities in Geographic Space." *Journal of International Business Studies* 44 (5):413–426.

Bogardus, Emory S. 1925. "Measuring Social Distance." *Journal of Applied Sociology* 9 (2): 299–308.

Brouthers, Lance Eliot, Victor B. Marshall, and Dawn L. Keig. 2016. "Solving the Single-Country Sample Problem in Cultural Distance Studies." *Journal of International Business Studies* 47: 471–479. doi:10.1057/jibs.2016.15

Buckley, Peter J., and Mark Casson. 1976. *The Future of the Multinational Enterprise*. London: Macmillan.

Buckley, Peter J., and Pervez N. Ghauri. 2015. *International Business Strategy: Theory and Practice*. London: Routledge.

Caggiano, Vittorio, Leonardo Fogassi, Giacomo Rizzolatti, Peter Thier, and Antonino Casile. 2009. "Mirror Neurons Differentially Encode the Peripersonal and Extrapersonal Space of Monkeys." *Science* 324 (5925):403–406.

Casanova, Carlos, Alicia Garcia-Herrero, and Le Xia. 2015. "Chinese Outbound Foreign Direct Investment: How Much Goes Where after Roundtripping and Offshoring?"

www.bbvaresearch.com/wp-content/uploads/2015/07/15_17_Working-Paper_ ODI.pdf

Casson, Mark. 1987. *The Firm and the Market: Studies on Multinational Enterprise and the Scope of the Firm.* Cambridge, MA: MIT Press.

Castellani, Davide, Alfredo Jimenez, and Antonello Zanfei. 2013. "How Remote Are R&D Labs? Distance Factors and International Innovative Activities." *Journal of International Business Studies* 44 (7):649–675. doi: 10.1057/jibs.2013.30.

Cho, Kang Rae, and Prasad Padmanabhan. 2005. "Revisiting the Role of Cultural Distance in Mnc's Foreign Ownership Mode Choice: The Moderating Effect of Experience Attributes." *International Business Review* 14 (3):307–324. doi: http://dx.doi.org/10.1016/j.ibusrev.2005.01.001.

Collis, David J., Bharat N. Anand, and J. Yo-Jud Cheng. forthcoming. "Business Groups in the USA since 1960." In *Business Groups in the West* edited by Asli M. Colpan, and Takashi Hikino. Oxford: Oxford University Press.

Cuervo-Cazurra, Alvaro, and Mehmet Erdem Genc. 2011. "Obligating, Pressuring, and Supporting Dimensions of the Environment and the Non-Market Advantages of Developing-Country Multinational Companies." *Journal of Management Studies* 48 (2):441–455. doi: 10.1111/j.1467-6486.2010.00964.x.

Cyert, Richard Michael, and James G. March. 1963. *A Behavioral Theory of the Firm.* Englewood Cliffs, N.J.,: Prentice-Hall.

Dahlgren, Peter. 2005. "The Internet, Public Spheres, and Political Communication: Dispersion and Deliberation." *Political Communication* 22 (2):147–162. doi: 10.1080/10584600590933160.

Deardorff, Alan V. 1984. "Testing Trade Theories and Predicting Trade Flows." In *Handbook of International Economics,* edited by Ronald W. Jones, and Peter B. Kenen, 467–517. Amsterdam; New York: North Holland.

Dikova, Desislava. 2009. "Performance of Foreign Subsidiaries: Does Psychic Distance Matter?" *International Business Review* 18 (1):38–49. doi: 10.1016/j.ibusrev.2008.11.001.

Dow, Douglas. 2014. "Distance in International Business Research: Are We Really Making Any Progress?" In *Contributions to International Business: Essays in Honour of Professor Jorma Larimo,* edited by Martti Laaksonen, Ahmad Arslan, and Minnie Kontkanen, 119–140. Vaasa, Finland: University of Vaasa.

Dow, Douglas, and Amal Karunaratna. 2006. "Developing a Multidimensional Instrument to Measure Psychic Distance Stimuli." *Journal of International Business Studies* 37 (5):578–602. doi: 10.2307/4540370.

Dunning, John H. 1980. "Toward an Eclectic Theory of International Production: Some Empirical Tests." *Journal of International Business Studies* 11 (1):9–31.

1989. "The Study of International Business: A Plea for a More Interdisciplinary Approach." *Journal of International Business Studies* 20 (3):411–436. doi: 10.2307/155185.

1998. "Location and the Multinational Enterprise: A Neglected Factor?" *Journal of International Business Studies* 29 (1):45–66.

Egelhoff, William G. 1982. "Strategy and Structure in Multinational Corporations: An Information-Processing Approach." *Administrative Science Quarterly* 27 (3):435–458.

Eurostat. 2014. "Paper on FDI by Ultimate Host/Ultimate Investing Country." International Conference on Measurement of Trade and Economic Globalization, Aguascalientes, Mexico, September 29–October 1, 2014. http://unstats.un.org/unsd/trade/events/2014/mexico/documents/session2/Paper%20on%20FDI%20by%20ultimate%20counterpart.pdf.

Festinger, Leon, Kurt W. Back, and Stanley Schachter. 1950. *Social Pressures in Informal Groups: A Study of Human Factors in Housing*: Stanford University Press.

Fiedler, Klaus. 2007. "Construal Level Theory as an Integrative Framework for Behavioral Decision-Making Research and Consumer Psychology." *Journal of Consumer Psychology (Lawrence Erlbaum Associates)* 17 (2):101–106. doi: 10.1080/10577400701242607.

Frankel, Jeffrey A., Ernesto Stein, and Shang-Jin Wei. 1997. *Regional Trading Blocs in the World Economic System*. Washington, DC: Institute for International Economics.

Fratianni, Michele. 2009. "The Gravity Model in International Trade." In *The Oxford Handbook of International Business*, edited by Alan M. Rugman, 72–89. 2nd ed. Oxford; New York: Oxford University Press.

Fukui, Tani, and Csilla Lakatos. 2012. "A Global Database of Foreign Affiliate Sales."

Gallego, Nuria, and Carlos Llano. "On the Non-Linear Relation between Trade and Distance: New Results for the Border Effect Using Region-to-Region National and Inter-National Flows." *Economic Analysis Working Paper Series* 6/2014, Universidad Autónoma de Madrid, Madrid.

Ghemawat, Pankaj. 2001. "Distance Still Matters: The Hard Reality of Global Expansion." *Harvard Business Review* 79 (8):137–147.

2003. "The Forgotten Strategy." *Harvard Business Review* 81 (11):76–84.

2003. "Semiglobalization and International Business Strategy." *Journal of International Business Studies* 34 (2):138–152. doi: 10.1057/PALGRAVE.JIBS.8400013.

2011. "The Cosmopolitan Corporation." *Harvard Business Review* 89 (5):92–99.

2011. "Responses to Forces of Change: A Focus on Curricular Content." In *Globalization of Management Education: Changing International Structures, Adaptive Strategies, and the Impact on Institutions: Report of the AACSB International Globalization of Management Education Task Force*, 105–156. Bingley: Emerald.

2011. *World 3.0: Global Prosperity and How to Achieve It*. Boston, MA: Harvard Business Review Press.

2015. "From International Business to Intranational Business." In *Emerging Economies and Multinational Enterprises*, edited by Laszlo Tihanyi, Elitsa R. Banalieva, Timothy M. Devinney, and Torben Pedersen, 5–28: Emerald Group Publishing Limited.

Ghemawat, Pankaj, and Herman Vantrappen. 2015. "How Global Is Your C-Suite?" *MIT Sloan Management Review* 56 (4):73–82.

Greif, Avner. 1994. "Cultural Beliefs and the Organization of Society: A Historical and Theoretical Reflection on Collectivist and Individualist Societies." *Journal of Political Economy* 102 (5):912–950. doi: 10.1086/261959.

Gupta, Anil K., and Vijay Govindarajan. 1991. "Knowledge Flows and the Structure of Control within Multinational Corporations." *Academy of Management Review* 16 (4):768–792.

Håkanson, Lars, and Björn Ambos. 2010. "The Antecedents of Psychic Distance." *Journal of International Management* 16 (3):195–210. doi: 10.1016/ j.intman.2010.06.001.

Harzing, Anne-Wil. 2003. "The Role of Culture in Entry-Mode Studies: From Neglect to Myopia?" In *Managing Multinationals in a Knowledge Economy: Economics, Culture, and Human Resources*, edited by Joseph L. C. Cheng, and Michael A. Hitt, 75–127. Bingley: Emerald Group Publishing Limited.

Harzing, Anne-Wil, and Markus Pudelko. 2016. "Do We Need to Distance Ourselves from the Distance Concept? Why Home and Host Country Context Might Matter More Than (Cultural) Distance." *Management International Review* 56 (1):1–34. doi: 10.1007/s11575-015-0265-4.

Hatzigeorgiou, Andreas. 2010. "Migration as Trade Facilitation: Assessing the Links between International Trade and Migration." *The B.E. Journal of Economic Analysis & Policy* 10 (1). doi: 10.2202/1935-1682.2100.

Head, Keith, and Thierry Mayer. 2013. "What Separates Us? Sources of Resistance to Globalization." *Canadian Journal of Economics/Revue canadienne d'économique* 46 (4):1196–1231. doi: 10.1111/caje.12055.

2014. "Gravity Equations: Workhorse, Toolkit, and Cookbook." In *Handbook of International Economics*, edited by Gita Gopinath, Elhanan Helpman, and Kenneth S. Rogoff, 131–195. Oxford: North-Holland.

Helpman, Elhanan, Marc J. Melitz, and Stephen R. Yeaple. 2004. "Export Versus FDI with Heterogeneous Firms." *American Economic Review* 94 (1):300–316. doi: 10.1257/000282804322970814.

Henderson, Daniel J., and Daniel L. Millimet. 2008. "Is Gravity Linear?" *Journal of Applied Econometrics* 23 (2):137–172. doi: 10.1002/jae.974.

Hennart, Jean-François. 1982. *A Theory of Multinational Enterprise*. Ann Arbor: University of Michigan Press.

2007. "The Theoretical Rationale for a Multinationality-Performance Relationship." *Management International Review* 47 (3):423–452.

2009. "The Theories of the Multinational Enterprise." In *The Oxford Handbook of International Business*, edited by Alan M. Rugman, 125–145. 2nd ed. Oxford: Oxford University Press.

Hillberry, Russell, and David Hummels. 2008. "Trade Responses to Geographic Frictions: A Decomposition Using Micro-Data." *European Economic Review* 52 (3):527–550. doi: 10.1016/j.euroecorev.2007.03.003.

Hutzschenreuter, Thomas, Ingo Kleindienst, and Sandra Lange. 2014. "Added Psychic Distance Stimuli and MNE Performance: Performance Effects of Added Cultural, Governance, Geographic, and Economic Distance in Mnes' International Expansion." *Journal of International Management* 20 (1):38–54. doi: 10.1016/ j.intman.2013.02.003.

2015. "The Concept of Distance in International Business Research: A Review and Research Agenda." *International Journal of Management Reviews*. http://dx.doi. org/10.1111/ijmr.12065.

Hutzschenreuter, Thomas, Johannes C. Voll, and Alain Verbeke. 2011. "The Impact of Added Cultural Distance and Cultural Diversity on International Expansion Patterns: A Penrosean Perspective." *Journal of Management Studies* 48 (2):305–329. doi: 10.1111/j.1467-6486.2010.00966.x.

Iacoboni, Marco. 2009. "Imitation, Empathy, and Mirror Neurons." *Annual Review of Psychology* 60 (1):653–670. doi: 10.1146/annurev.psych.60.110707.163604.

Johanson, Jan, and Jan-Erik Vahlne. 1977. "The Internationalization Process of the Firm-a Model of Knowledge Development and Increasing Foreign Market Commitments." *Journal of International Business Studies* 8 (1):23–32.

⸻. 2009. "The Uppsala Internationalization Process Model Revisited: From Liability of Foreignness to Liability of Outsidership." *Journal Of International Business Studies* 40 (9):1411–1431. doi: 10.1057/jibs.2009.24.

Kaufman, E. L., M. W. Lord, T. W. Reese, and J. Volkmann. 1949. "The Discrimination of Visual Number." *American Journal of Psychology* 62 (4):498–525. doi: 10.2307/1418556.

Khanna, Tarun, and Krishna Palepu. 1997. "Why Focused Strategies May Be Wrong for Emerging Markets." *Harvard Business Review* 75 (4):41–51.

Kleinert, Jörn, and Farid Toubal. 2013. "Production Versus Distribution-Oriented FDI." *Review of World Economics* 149 (3):423–442.

Kogut, Bruce, and Harbir Singh. 1988. "The Effect of National Culture on the Choice of Entry Mode." *Journal of International Business Studies* 19 (3):411–432. doi: 10.1057/palgrave.jibs.8490394.

Latané, Bibb. 1981. "The Psychology of Social Impact." *American Psychologist* 36 (4):343–356. doi: 10.1037/0003-066X.36.4.343.

Latané, Bibb, James H. Liu, Andrzej Nowak, Michael Bonevento, and Long Zheng. 1995. "Distance Matters: Physical Space and Social Impact." *Personality and Social Psychology Bulletin* 21 (8):795–805. doi: 10.1177/0146167295218002.

Lazarsfeld, P. F., and R. K. Merton. 1954. "Friendship as a Social Process: A Substantive and Methodological Analysis." In *Freedom and Control in Modern Society*, edited by M. Berger, T. Abel, and C. Page, 18–66: Van Nostrand.

Leamer, Edward E., and James Levinsohn. 1995. "International Trade Theory: The Evidence." In *Handbook of International Economics*, edited by Gene M. Grossman, and Kenneth Rogoff, 1339–1394. Amsterdam: Elsevier Science.

Lewandowski, Joshua, and Timothy C. Lisk. 2012 "Foundations of Distance." In *Exploring Distance in Leader-Follower Relationships: When Near Is Far and Far Is Near*, edited by Michelle C. Bligh and Ronald E. Riggio. Routledge.

Liberman, Nira, and Yaacov Trope. 2014. "Traversing Psychological Distance." *Trends in Cognitive Sciences* 18 (7): 364–369.

Lin, Faqin. 2011. "The Pro-Trade Impacts of Immigrants: A Meta-Analysis of Network Effects." *Journal of Chinese Economic and Foreign Trade Studies* 4 (1):17–27. doi: 10.1108/17544401111106789.

Luo, Yadong, and Oded Shenkar. 2011. "Toward a Perspective of Cultural Friction in International Business." *Journal of International Management* 17 (1):1–14. doi: 10.1016/j.intman.2010.09.001.

Maglio, Sam J., Yaacov Trope, and Nira Liberman. 2013. "Distance from a Distance: Psychological Distance Reduces Sensitivity to Any Further Psychological Distance." *Journal of Experimental Psychology: General* 142 (3): 644.

Malhotra, Shavin, K. Sivakumar, and PengCheng Zhu. 2009. "Distance Factors and Target Market Selection: The Moderating Effect of Market Potential." *International Marketing Review* 26 (6):651–673. doi: 10.1108/02651330911001332.

McEvoy, Chad Joseph. 1995. "A Consideration of the Sociobiological Dimensions of Human Xenophobia and Ethnocentrism." Social Science Information System, Last Modified September 13, 2013 www.sociosite.net/topics/xenophobia.php.

McPherson, Miller, Lynn Smith-Lovin, and James M. Cook. 2001. "Birds of a Feather: Homophily in Social Networks." *Annual Review of Sociology* 27:415–444.

Minbaeva, Dana B. 2007. "Knowledge Transfer in Multinational Corporations." *Management International Review* 47 (4):567–593.

Nachum, Lilach, and Sangyoung Song. 2011. "The MNE as a Portfolio: Interdependencies in MNE Growth Trajectory." *Journal of International Business Studies* 42 (3): 381–405.

Navarrete, Carlos David, and Daniel M. T. Fessler. 2006. "Disease Avoidance and Ethnocentrism: The Effects of Disease Vulnerability and Disgust Sensitivity on Intergroup Attitudes." *Evolution and Human Behavior* 27 (4):270–282. doi: 10.1016/j.evolhumbehav.2005.12.001.

Navarrete, Carlos David, Daniel M. T. Fessler, and Serena J. Eng. 2007 "Elevated Ethnocentrism in the First Trimester of Pregnancy." *Evolution and Human Behavior* 28 (1):60–65. doi: 10.1016/j.evolhumbehav.2006.06.002.

Nebus, James, and Kah Hin Chai. 2014. "Putting the "Psychic" Back in Psychic Distance: Awareness, Perceptions, and Understanding as Dimensions of Psychic Distance." *Journal of International Management* 20 (1):8–24. doi: 10.1016/j.intman.2013.01.001.

O'Grady, Shawna, and Henry W. Lane. 1996. "The Psychic Distance Paradox." *Journal of International Business Studies* 27 (2):309–333.

Oldenski, Lindsay. 2012. "Export Versus FDI and the Communication of Complex Information." *Journal of International Economics* 87 (2):312–322.

Olivero, María Pía, and Yoto V. Yotov. 2012. "Dynamic Gravity: Endogenous Country Size and Asset Accumulation." *Canadian Journal of Economics* 45 (1):64–92. doi: 10.1111/j.1540-5982.2011.01687.x.

Penrose, Edith Tilton. 1959. *The Theory of the Growth of the Firm.* Oxford: Basil Blackwell.

Perkins, Richard, and Eric Neumayer. 2013. "The Ties That Bind: The Role of Migrants in the Uneven Geography of International Telephone Traffic." *Global Networks* 13 (1):79–100. doi: 10.1111/j.1471-0374.2012.00366.x.

Pitts, Robert. 2013. "Geospatial Data Integration Challenges and Considerations." *Sensors & Systems.* V1 Media. http://sensorsandsystems.com/geospatial-data-integration-challenges-and-considerations/.

Portes, Richard, and Hélène Rey. 2005. "The Determinants of Cross-Border Equity Flows." *Journal of International Economics* 65 (2):269–296. doi: 10.1016/j.jinteco.2004.05.002.

Purzycki, Benjamin Grant, Coren Apicella, Quentin D. Atkinson, Emma Cohen, Rita Anne McNamara, Aiyana K. Willard, Dimitris Xygalatas, Ara Norenzayan, and Joseph Henrich. 2016. "Moralistic Gods, Supernatural Punishment and the Expansion of Human Sociality." *Nature* 530 (7590):327–330. doi: 10.1038/nature16980.

Rugman, Alan M. 1980. "Internalization as a General Theory of Foreign Direct Investment: A Re-Appraisal of the Literature." *Weltwirtschaftliches Archiv* 116 (2):365–379.

Rugman, Alan M., and Alain Verbeke. 2004. "A Perspective on Regional and Global Strategies of Multinational Enterprises." *Journal of International Business Studies* 35 (1):3–18.

2008. "The Theory and Practice of Regional Strategy: A Response to Osegowitsch and Sammartino." *Journal of International Business Studies* 39 (2):326–332.

Rugman, Alan M., Alain Verbeke, and Quyen T. K. Nguyen. 2011. "Fifty Years of International Business Theory and Beyond." *Management International Review* 51 (6):755–786. doi: 10.1007/s11575-011-0102-3.

Rummel, R. J. 1976. *Understanding Conflict and War, Volume 2: The Conflict Helix.* Beverly Hills.

Schwartz, Karen D. 2012. "Gis Data: A Storage Puzzle." *BizTech.* www.biztechmagazine.com/article/2012/04/gis-data-storage-puzzle.

Scott, W. Richard. 1995. *Institutions and Organizations.* Thousand Oaks: SAGE.

Shenkar, Oded. 2001. "Cultural Distance Revisited: Towards a More Rigorous Conceptualization and Measurement of Cultural Differences." *Journal of International Business Studies* 32 (3):519–535. doi: 10.2307/3069495.

Shenkar, Oded, Yadong Luo, and Orly Yeheskel. 2008. "From "Distance" to "Friction": Substituting Metaphors and Redirecting Intercultural Research." *Academy of Management Review* 33 (4):905–923.

Simmel, Georg. 1908. *Soziologie: untersuchungen über die formen der vergesellschaftung.* Duncker & Humblot.

Sousa, Carlos M. P., and Frank Bradley. 2006. "Cultural Distance and Psychic Distance: Two Peas in a Pod?" *Journal of International Marketing* 14 (1):49–70. doi: 10.1509/jimk.14.1.49.

Sui, Daniel Z., Michael F. Goodchild, and Sarah Elwood. 2013. "Volunteered Geographic Information, the Exaflood, and the Growing Digital Divide." In *Crowdsourcing Geographic Knowledge: Volunteered Geographic Information (Vgi) in Theory and Practice,* edited by Daniel Z. Sui, Sarah Elwood, and Michael F. Goodchild, 1–12. Dordrecht; New York: Springer.

Tihanyi, Laszlo, David A. Griffith, and Craig J. Russell. 2005. "The Effect of Cultural Distance on Entry Mode Choice, International Diversification, and MNE Performance: A Meta-Analysis." *Journal of International Business Studies* 36 (3):270–283.

Trope, Yaacov, and Nira Liberman. 2010. "Construal-Level Theory of Psychological Distance." *Psychological Review* 117 (2):440–463. doi: 10.1037/a0018963.

Tung, Rosalie L., and Alain Verbeke. 2010. "Beyond Hofstede and Globe: Improving the Quality of Cross-Cultural Research." *Journal of International Business Studies* 41 (8):1259–1274. doi: 10.1057/jibs.2010.41.

UNCTAD. 2015. "World Investment Report 2015: Reforming International Investment Governance." United Nations. http://unctad.org/en/PublicationsLibrary/wir2015_en.pdf.

Verbeke, Alain, and Nathan S. Greidanus. 2009. "The End of the Opportunism vs Trust Debate: Bounded Reliability as a New Envelope Concept in Research on MNE Governance." *Journal of International Business Studies* 40 (9): 1471–1495.

Verbeke, Alain, and Liena Kano. 2012. "An Internalization Theory Rationale for MNE Regional Strategy." *Multinational Business Review* 20 (2):135–152. doi: 10.1108/15253831211238212.

2016. "An internalization theory perspective on the global and regional strategies of multinational enterprises." *Journal of World Business.* 51 (1): 83–92. doi:10.1016/j.jwb.2015.08.014.

Vernon, Raymond. 1969. "Multinational Enterprise and the Nation State Project Report from the Harvard Business School." *Journal of Common Market Studies* 8 (2):160–168.

———. 1994. "Contributing to an International Business Curriculum: An Approach from the Flank." *Journal of International Business Studies* 25 (2):215–227. doi: 10.1057/palgrave.jibs.8490198.

Waber, Ben. 2013. *People Analytics: How Social Sensing Technology Will Transform Business and What It Tells Us about the Future of Work.* FT Press.

Yang, Zhilin, Xuehua Wang, and Chenting Su. 2006. "A Review of Research Methodologies in International Business." *International Business Review* 15 (6):601–617.

Zaheer, Srilata, and Lilach Nachum. 2011. "Sense of Place: From Location Resources to MNE Locational Capital." *Global Strategy Journal* 1 (1–2): 96–108.

Zaheer, Srilata, Margaret Spring Schomaker, and Lilach Nachum. 2012. "Distance without Direction: Restoring Credibility to a Much-Loved Construct." *Journal of International Business Studies* 43 (1):18–27. doi: 10.1057/jibs.2011.43.

Zhou, Nan, and Mauro F. Guillén. 2015. "From Home Country to Home Base: A Dynamic Approach to the Liability of Foreignness." *Strategic Management Journal* 36 (6): 907–917.

Part III

Business Applications

8   Cultural Distance and National
       Cultural Differences

Pankaj Ghemawat and B. Sebastian Reiche

Dutch psychologist and culture expert Geert Hofstede interviewed unsuccessfully for an engineering job with a US company early in his career. Later, he wrote of the cross-cultural misunderstandings that crop up when US managers interview Dutch recruits and vice versa:

> American applicants, to Dutch eyes, oversell themselves. Their CVs are worded in superlatives...during the interview they try to behave assertively, promising things they are very unlikely to realize...Dutch applicants in American eyes undersell themselves. They write modest and usually short CVs, counting on the interviewer to find out by asking how good they really are...To an uninitiated American interviewer an uninitiated Dutch applicant comes across as a sucker. To an uninitiated Dutch interviewer an uninitiated American applicant comes across as a braggart. (Hofstede 1991, 79)[1]

The salience of cultural distance in business extends well beyond obvious areas such as human resources to virtually every function within a multinational firm. Whenever customers, colleagues, suppliers, partners, or competitors from multiple backgrounds are involved, cultural distance matters. And misdirected cultural diversity training can sometimes do more harm than good.

International business research has directed a great deal of attention to cultural differences and their implications. As noted in Chapter 7, there are more publications in major journals on cultural distance than on any other dimension of distance (Hutzschenreuter, Kleindienst, and Lange 2015).[2] Nonetheless, results of prior empirical work – particularly that using Kogut and Singh (1988)'s "ubiquitous" cultural distance index based on Hofstede's (1980) dimensions of national cultural values – have been inconsistent (Shenkar 2001; Zaheer, Schomaker, and Nachum 2012; Dow 2014; Harzing and Pudelko 2015). Critiques of this body of research that also apply to other distance dimensions were already discussed in Chapter 7. Here, we focus on issues that are unique to culture as a phenomenon that comprises both observable characteristics as well as underlying values and beliefs.

The authors wish to thank Steven A. Altman for his assistance with analyzing and writing up the second section of this chapter.

We should also clarify up front that we do not equate cultural distance with psychic distance, contrary to Kogut and Singh (1988, 430)'s assertion that they are similar in most respects. As discussed in Chapter 7, we follow Beckerman (1956)'s original framing of psychic distance as perceptual or subjective, shaped only in part by actual objective distance and subject to biases. We also view psychic distance as relating to all four dimensions of the CAGE Distance Framework (cultural, administrative/institutional, geographic, and economic) (Ghemawat 2001), rather than being exclusively or even primarily associated with culture. In spite of the widespread tendency of researchers to equate cultural distance with psychic distance, Håkanson and Ambos (2010) find that geographic distance is more than three times as strong as the usual measures of cultural distance as a predictor of psychic distance.

In the first section of this chapter, we define culture, distinguish aspects of culture that are directly observable from underlying values and beliefs, and introduce several ways of measuring cultural distance. In the second section, we analyze country-level implications of national cultural differences by incorporating cultural distance measures from the previous section into the gravity models of trade, capital, information, and people flows that were presented in Chapter 5. In the third section, we illustrate firm-level implications of culture on a function-by-function basis. Finally, we devote the fourth section to challenges that cultural and other types of distance impose on global leaders and actions that firms can take to address them.

Defining and Measuring Cultural Distance

We define culture, for the purposes of this chapter, *as a set of shared values, assumptions, beliefs, morals, customs, and other habits that are learned through membership in a group, and that influence the attitudes and behaviors of group members* (Kluckhohn 1954; Hofstede 1980). Note three implications of this definition. First, culture is a group-level phenomenon. From this perspective, cultures exist at many different levels, including organizational functions or business units, organizations, industries, regions, and nations (Leung et al. 2005). We focus in this chapter in particular on national culture and the role of cultural differences across countries rather than other cultural groups, because this level of culture is particularly relevant for international businesses.[3] (Some considerations regarding corporate culture have already been discussed in Chapter 6.) Second, the definition implies that culture is acquired through a process of socialization instead of being innate. Shared values, assumptions, and beliefs are learned through interactions with family, teachers, officials, experiences, and society-at-large. Third, culture delineates what is considered acceptable or attractive behavior. In other words, cultural values provide preferences or priorities for one behavior over another.

Also implicit in this group-level definition of culture is that such attempts to characterize behavior are necessarily approximate since they abstract away from individual-level factors that also matter. As a result, it is important not to treat cultural characterizations as fully explaining or determining behavior. Rather, the operational criterion for assessing the usefulness of cultural characterizations is whether they offer more insight into behavior than would be obtained if one were to ignore them.

With that caveat in mind, however, cultural differences do seem to drive large variations in behavior across countries. Consider the following high-stakes example. You are riding in a car with a close friend, who hits a pedestrian. "You know that he was going at least 35 miles per hour in an area of the city where the maximum allowed speed is 20 miles per hour. There are no other witnesses. His lawyer says that if you testify under oath that he was only driving 20 miles per hour it may save him from serious consequences" (Trompenaars and Hampden-Turner 1998, 33). More than 90 percent of managers in Switzerland, the United States, Canada, Ireland, Sweden, Australia, and the UK report that they would *not* testify falsely under oath to help their close friend. In contrast, fewer than half of managers in Venezuela (32 percent), Nepal (36 percent), South Korea (37 percent), Russia (44 percent), and China (47 percent) say they would refuse to testify falsely in this hypothetical situation (Trompenaars and Hampden-Turner 1998, 35).

To embed such considerations into a more general perspective, it is useful to start with Edward T. Hall's likening of a culture to an iceberg, with a visible tip and a larger portion hidden below (1990). The observable parts of a culture include elements such as language, music, food, and behaviors. A deeper understanding of a culture also involves looking at the submerged portion – larger according to the iceberg analogy – at the values expressed by the members of a culture and, underlying them, the basic assumptions that they take for granted. In the hypothetical situation described earlier, differences in willingness to testify falsely under oath represent the visible tip of the iceberg that may be explained, in part, by unstated differences in cultural values. While honesty and loyalty are probably both viewed as laudable everywhere, some cultures put more emphasis on *universal* commitments (like honesty) while others put more weight on loyalty to *particular* people and relationships.[4]

On the basis of this conceptualization, cultural distance measures should ideally focus on the totality of the cultural iceberg, visible and invisible. The next subsection focuses on cultural distance measures based on the visible or observable cultural characteristics emphasized by economists, and the following subsection looks at cultural distance measures based on frameworks from psychology and sociology that try to capture the values that underpin behavioral differences across cultures.

Cultural Distance based on Observable Characteristics

Economists have tended to focus on aspects of culture, such as language and religion, that are directly observable and that may also capture some important unobservable characteristics. Language, according to some researchers, offers a window into deeper beliefs and thought processes. Spanish-speaking cultures, for example, tend to be more hierarchical than English-speaking cultures,[5] and Spanish is one of several languages with distinct formal (usted) and informal (tu) forms of the English "you." This hierarchical emphasis also appears in speech patterns such as the tendency in Mexico to introduce an engineer as "ingeniero" or a lawyer as "licenciado" whereas both would just be called "mister" in English (West and Graham 2004, 246).

Research on the implications of linguistic differences for thought patterns across cultures dates back at least to early work by Edward Sapir (1921) and Benjamin Whorf (1940). One scholar provides the following description of language's deeper impact: "Language carries with it patterns of seeing, knowing, talking, and acting ... patterns that mark the easier trails for thought and perception and action" (Agar 1994, 71). Later scholars such as Noam Chomsky moved away from this view to focus on universal patterns across languages, but more recent research again shows an "appreciation of how interpretive differences can be rooted as much in systematic uses of language as in its structure" (Gumperz and Levinson 1996, 2–3).

One way to summarize the extent of linguistic differences is to note that among a sample of 163 countries, in only 10 percent of the country pairs do 20 percent or more of the populations of both countries speak a common language (based on the Mayer and Zignago 2011 dataset). The genealogical classification of languages permits more nuanced characterizations of linguistic distance based on whether two languages have common ancestors or not. Table 8.1 presents a table of linguistic distance from the United States on this basis.

Religion, even more explicitly than language, connects expressed values and basic assumptions to observable behaviors. Most research using religion as a marker of differences in national culture focuses on whether or not countries share a common religion. According to the *World Christian Encyclopedia*, "there are 19 major world religions, which are subdivided into 270 large religious groups, and many smaller ones" (quoted in Robinson 2011), with Christianity (33 percent of the world population in 2000), Islam (20 percent), and Hinduism (13 percent) being the largest high-level groupings. On the basis of a sample of 163 countries, 51 percent of country pairs have at least 30 percent or more of both populations practicing the same major religion.[6] More nuanced characterizations treat commonalities at the level of denomination or sect as closest (e.g., Methodist), then consider matches at broader levels of aggregation within a single religion (e.g., Protestant), then at the level of a

Table 8.1 *Linguistic Distance from the United States, Twenty-Five Largest Economies*

Linguistic Distance from United States	Countries
1 Same language	Australia, Canada, India, Nigeria, UK
2 Same subbranch at the first level but different at the second level	Belgium, Germany, Netherlands, Switzerland
3 Same branch but different at the first subbranch level	Sweden
4 Same family but different branches	Argentina, Brazil, France, Italy, Mexico, Poland, Russia, Spain
5 Different families	China, Indonesia, Japan, Korea, Saudi Arabia, Taiwan, Turkey

Note: This table is based on the distance between the two closest major languages for each pair of countries.
Source: "L1" Variable from Dow and Karunaratna (2006).

religion (e.g., Christianity), and then most broadly combine groups of religions with a similar origin and some common beliefs (e.g., "monotheistic religions of a common Middle-Eastern origin," the category that encompasses Judaism, Christianity, and Islam) (Dow and Karunaratna 2006, 600).

Ethnic groups – like religious groups – can embody cultural traditions, making the extent to which countries share common ethnicities another observable characteristic on which to base measures of cultural distance. Prior research on ethnicities as an enabler of trade flows has highlighted the effects of international ethnic networks forged by migration (see, for example, Rauch 2001). This provides a useful reminder of the complementarity across types of international interactions discussed briefly in Chapter 2. It is also important to note, however, that it seems even more difficult to objectively discern ethnic commonalities than religious or linguistic ones. Thus, Ellingsen (2000)'s ethnicity dataset, based on *Britannica Book of the Year*, reports that the largest ethnic group in both the United States and the UK is "European," whereas the largest in France is "French" and in Canada it is "English-Canadian," implying that the United States and UK share a common ethnicity, but (oddly) that neither of these countries does so with Canada.[7] Later in this chapter, we use a set of gravity models based on those reported in Chapter 5 to test the effects of linguistic, religious, and ethnic commonalities on international trade, capital, information, and people flows.[8]

Cultural Distance based on Underlying Value Dimensions

Psychologists and sociologists have developed frameworks that attempt to generalize about differences in cultural values that lie beneath the surface in the iceberg analogy. The most widely used framework for categorizing national cultures is the one developed by Geert Hofstede, a Dutch social psychologist (Hofstede 1980). On the basis of surveys of more than 100,000 IBM employees in more than 50 countries between 1967 and 1973, Hofstede argues that national cultures differ systematically across four dimensions: *power distance, individualism/collectivism, uncertainty avoidance*, and *masculinity/ femininity*.[9]

Power distance concerns the degree to which a culture accepts and reinforces the uneven distribution of power in society. Members of high *power distance* cultures such as Malaysia are expected to accept status differences and show proper respect to their superiors. Status differences may reflect organizational hierarchy, but they may also be based on age, social class, or family role. Low *power distance* cultures such as Denmark are less comfortable with differences in organizational rank or social class; they share more participation in decision making and frequently disregard hierarchical levels. Correlations between power distance and selected aspects of countries' institutional configurations will be discussed in Chapter 9.

A second dimension Hofstede identifies is *individualism/collectivism*. Members of *individualist* cultures such as the UK maintain loose social structures marked by independence, the importance of individuals' rights, and the recognition of personal initiative and achievement. In contrast, *collectivist* cultures such as Guatemala place more emphasis on the overall good of and loyalty to the group. Members of *collectivist* societies distinguish more clearly between in-groups and out-groups, and are expected to subordinate their individual interests to those of their in-groups (e.g., family, or organization). Hofstede's research also suggests a strong correlation with *power distance: individualist* cultures tend to exhibit lower *power distance*, although there are exceptions (e.g., France).

Uncertainty avoidance concerns the degree to which cultural members are willing to accept and deal with ambiguous situations. Cultures with high levels of *uncertainty avoidance* such as Greece prefer structure and predictability, which results in explicit rules of behavior and strict laws. Members of such cultures tend to be relatively averse to changing employers, embracing new approaches, or engaging in entrepreneurship. Societies with low *uncertainty avoidance* such as Singapore have greater acceptance of unstructured situations and ambiguity, favoring risk taking, innovation, and the acceptance of different views.

The fourth dimension Hofstede identifies is *masculinity/femininity*. Masculine cultures such as Japan are generally supposed to reflect a dominance of "tough" values such as achievement, assertiveness, competition, and material success, which are stereotypically associated with male roles. In contrast, *feminine* cultures tend to focus on "tender" values such as personal relationships, care

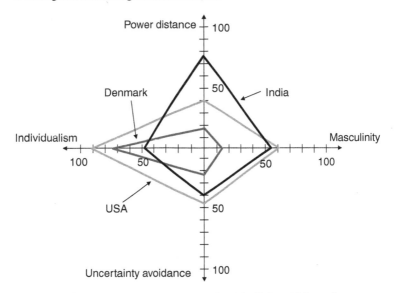

Figure 8.1 Cultural Profiles Based on Hofstede's Cultural Dimensions.
Source: Generated by the authors based on data from Hofstede, Geert. 2001. *Culture's Consequences: Comparing Values, Behaviors, Institutions, and Organizations across Nations*. 2nd ed. Thousand Oaks, CA: Sage Publications.

for others, and quality of life. In addition, *feminine* cultures such as Sweden also present less distinct gender roles. Firms in feminine cultures are predicted to place a stronger emphasis on overall employee well-being than on bottom-line performance.

Hofstede's research has been replicated by other scholars and extended to more than eighty countries. Table 8.2 lists the scores along each dimension for thirty of them. Using these scores, Hofstede develops national cultural profiles to compare cultures and highlight cultural differences (see Figure 8.1). Other research has clustered national cultures based on similarity and dissimilarity in work-related attitudes, examining the combined role of culture, language, religion, and geography (see Figure 8.2). It is important to note that a culture's position along a certain cultural dimension is not an evaluation of whether members of that culture approach situations better or worse than in other cultures. Instead, the cultural dimensions simply demonstrate different preferences, priorities, or approaches to social issues.

Although Hofstede's framework remains the most widely used approach to classify and compare national cultures, it has several limitations. The data are relatively old and, despite attempts at replication, may not fully capture recent changes in the political environment (e.g., the end of the Cold War and the decline

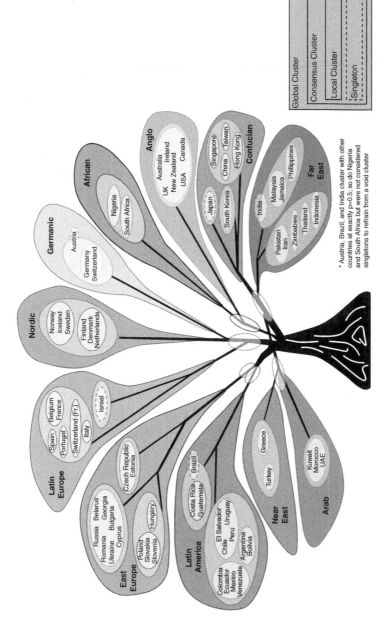

Figure 8.2 Clusters of National Cultures from Ronen and Shenkar (2013).

Source: Reprinted by permission from Macmillan Publishers Ltd: *Journal of International Business Studies,* Ronen, Simcha, and Oded Shenkar, "Mapping World Cultures: Cluster Formation, Sources and Implications," 44 (9), Figure 2, pg. 881.

Table 8.2 *Hofstede's Cultural Value Scores for Thirty Countries*

Country	Power Distance	Individualism/ Collectivism	Uncertainty Avoidance	Masculinity/ Femininity
Argentina	49	46	86	56
Australia	36	90	51	61
Brazil	69	38	76	49
Canada[a]	39	80	48	52
Chile	63	23	86	28
China	80	20	30	66
Colombia	67	13	80	64
Denmark	18	74	23	16
France	68	71	86	43
Germany	35	67	65	66
Greece	60	35	112	57
Indonesia	78	14	48	46
India	77	48	40	56
Iran	58	41	59	43
Israel	13	54	81	47
Italy	50	76	75	70
Japan	54	46	92	95
Korea (South)	60	18	85	39
Malaysia	104	26	36	50
Mexico	81	30	82	69
Netherlands	38	80	53	14
Philippines	94	32	44	64
Poland	68	60	93	64
Portugal	63	27	104	31
Russia	93	39	95	36
Singapore	74	20	8	48
Spain	57	51	86	42
Sweden	31	71	29	5
UK	35	89	35	66
United States	40	91	46	62

Source: Adapted from Hofstede (2001, Exhibit A5.1 pg. 500, Exhibit A5.3 pg. 502).

[a] English-speaking part.

of communism) or the work place (a stronger focus on cooperation, knowledge sharing, and empowerment). Second, the reliance on data from employees of a single organization, IBM, offers a narrow – and arguably biased – basis for generalizing about national cultural characteristics (McSweeney 2002). Third, a later study that Hofstede conducted using a Chinese equivalent of his original survey developed by Chinese social scientists challenges the dimension of *uncertainty avoidance* (Hofstede and Bond 1988). Using data from twenty-three countries, including twenty from Hofstede's original study, the scholars identify a different fourth dimension representing Chinese values, originally termed Confucian Work Dynamism and later relabeled *long-term/short-term orientation.* Fourth, some challenge the content of the *masculinity/femininity* dimension. It is also less clear what exactly this dimension involves. For example, the high masculinity score for Japan appears to contradict the high levels of concern and care that Japanese organizations usually show toward their employees, which would seem to be more indicative of a *feminine* culture as defined by Hofstede.

Critiques of Hofstede's cultural dimensions have prompted researchers to develop several alternative cultural value frameworks, and some of the popular ones are summarized in Box 8.1.[10] While the focal dimensions vary considerably from one cultural framework to the other, together it seems to be useful to group them into five fundamental questions related to social interaction and management practices in a global environment. Specifically, the questions concern (1) how power and authority are distributed in a society; (2) the extent to which the individual versus the group constitute a society's main building block; (3) how people perceive their relationship with the surrounding natural environment; (4) how people in a society organize their time in performing certain activities; and (5) how societies reduce uncertainties and control behavior of individual members (Steers, Nardon, and Sánchez-Runde 2013).

Box 8.1 Some Alternative Cultural Frameworks

In addition to the cultural dimensions identified by Hofstede, there is a range of other cultural frameworks that aim to classify national cultures along various value dimensions. While some dimensions match or overlap with the ones proposed by Hofstede, the following well-known frameworks also include other dimensions:

- Fons Trompenaars, another Dutch researcher, collected more recent data in over forty countries. Out of the seven dimensions identified in his study, five focus on relationships between people (e.g., the relative importance of applying universal and standardized rules as reflected in the earlier example of whether or not to testify against a friend, or the extent to which people are free to express their emotions in public), whereas the remaining two dimensions concern time management and a culture's relationship with nature (Trompenaars and Hampden-Turner 1998).
- Shalom Schwartz, an Israeli psychologist, provided yet another approach to describe and classify national cultures. Schwartz argues that cultural values reflect three basic issues that confront societies: the nature of the relation between the individual and the group, how to guarantee responsible behavior, and how to regulate the relation

of people to the natural and social world. Using data from school-teachers and university students in over sixty countries, Schwartz derived three dimensions that represent solutions to the above issues (Schwartz 2014).

- Robert House, along with an international team of researchers, engaged in an ambitious effort to characterize cultures; they mainly focused on cultural differences in leadership. Termed the GLOBE study (Global Leadership and Organizational Behavior Effectiveness), this research derived nine cultural dimensions that addressed both previously identified value dimensions (e.g., power distance and individualism/collectivism) and new ones (e.g., gender egalitarianism and performance orientation) (House et al. 2004).

Turning from classification to distance measurement, Kogut and Singh (1988), in the second most cited paper in the history of the *Journal of International Business Studies*,[11] introduce a cultural distance measure based on Hofstede's four (original) dimensions of national culture. This measure has been subjected to substantial criticism (see, for example, Shenkar 2001), but as Zaheer et al. (2012) observe, many of the critiques leveled against it, for example, symmetry and homogeneity, also apply to other distance measures, and so were discussed in Chapter 7 and will not be repeated here.

What should be mentioned here, however, is that some of the distance scores generated based on this measure do, on casual observation, raise concern. Perhaps because Kogut and Singh limited their analysis to distance from the United States, the results they obtained did not seem particularly counterintuitive. But when we apply their formula to all pairs of countries Hofstede covers, the most distant pair of countries in the world is Denmark and Slovakia, while the most proximate are Peru and South Korea. Although nearby cultures can be quite different and faraway lands might have similar cultures, it still seems concerning that the world's most culturally similar countries would be 16,307 km[12] apart, while the most distant are separated by only 961 km.[13] Concerns such as these notwithstanding, the Kogut and Singh cultural distance measure remains "ubiquitous" in the international business literature as the "dominant instrument for measuring abstract forms of distance" (Dow 2014, 121) and so will be included in the gravity models presented in the next section.

National Culture and International Interactions

Chapter 5 used a gravity model to calibrate the effects of cultural, administrative, geographic, and economic distance on eleven types of trade, capital, information, and people flows. In that analysis, culture is captured by a single binary variable indicating whether or not two countries share a common official language. As the previous section illustrates, however, language is only one of several indicators that have been used to classify cultures and measure the differences or distances between them. This section examines the extent to which alternative or additional cultural variables could improve the baseline analysis presented in Chapter 5.

This section will proceed in three parts. The analysis will begin by incorporating binary variables indicating shared religion and ethnicity alongside a common language (three observable cultural characteristics). It will then examine the use of continuous instead of binary variables corresponding to the same observable aspects of national culture. And, finally, it will look at the Kogut and Singh (1988) cultural distance index based on Hofstede's (1980) cultural value dimensions.

Binary Variables based on Observable Cultural Characteristics

The use of a binary variable for common official language[14] in Chapter 5 was based on that variable's inclusion in the standard set of gravity variables that Head and Mayer (2014) identify in their review of 2,508 gravity models. Common language was the third most frequently used explanatory variable in the gravity models of trade reviewed there, behind only geographic distance and contiguity (common border).

Religion and ethnicity have also been used as cultural variables in gravity models (see, for example, Felbermayr and Toubal 2010), although far less frequently than common language. Table 8.3 summarizes the results of the incorporation of binary religious and ethnic commonality variables into the same set of gravity models that were described in Chapter 5. The religious commonality variable ("Religion Dummy") is based on Dow and Karunaratna (2006). Dow and Karunaratna's "R1" variable assesses religious distance on a five-point scale,[15] which we collapse here into a binary variable that takes value 1 if the closest major religions across a country pair are the same or part of the same religion family and takes value 0 otherwise. The ethnic commonality variable ("ethnicity dummy") was constructed by using data Ellingsen (2000) assembled for a study on multiethnicity and domestic conflict. Among the three ethnicity datasets she compiled, we selected the one sourced from *Britannica Book of the Year* for this analysis, as it is the most complete.[16] The ethnicity dummy variable takes value 1 if two countries have the same ethnic background (with respect to the largest ethnic group in those countries) and 0 otherwise.

The top row of Table 8.3 (Model 0) summarizes relevant results from the models reported in Chapter 5. Across the eleven flows analyzed there, a common official language was significant[17] with the expected positive sign for ten

Table 8.3 *Summary Comparison of Gravity Models across Binary Cultural Variables*

		Number of significant focal coefficients and signs				
		Common official language	D&K religion dummy	Ellingsen ethnicity dummy	Average number of observations	Average adjusted R-squared
Language baseline	0. Common official language - full sample	10+			22,763	0.795
	1. Common official language - restricted sample	10+			13,255	0.804
Religion	2. D&K religion dummy		6+		13,255	0.798
	3. Common official language + D&K religion dummy	10+	5+		13,255	0.805
Ethnicity	4. Ellingsen ethnicity dummy			7+	13,255	0.797
	5. Common official language + Ellingsen ethnicity dummy	10+		3+	13,255	0.804
All combined	6. Common official language + D&K religion dummy + Ellingsen ethnicity dummy	10+	5+	3+	13,255	0.805

of the eleven flows, and the average adjusted R-squared across those eleven regressions was 0.795. Since data availability on the religion and ethnicity variables is more limited and results can vary due to changes in the sample of observations across which the models are run, the comparisons that follow were all run on the common set of observations for which all of the variables of interest were available (reducing the average number of observations from 22,763 to 13,255).[18] (An alternative version of this analysis in which all available observations were used in each regression is provided in the online appendix at www.ghemawat.com/laws.)

Model 1 repeats the baseline model from Chapter 5 but utilizes the restricted set of observations across which the religion and ethnicity data are available. This results in a small increase in R-squared, and common official language remains significant for all types of international flows (and stocks) except portfolio long-term debt (consistent with the unrestricted baseline). When introduced without common language, the religion and ethnicity binary variables are significant for six and seven flows respectively, and the models attain average R-squared slightly below that of the baseline model. (Note that R-squared is consistently high across all of these models due to the use of origin and destination fixed effects as described in Chapter 5, making it unsurprising that the changes in cultural variables discussed here produce only small changes in R-squared). When both the religion and ethnicity variables are added together with common language, religion remains significant across five flows (merchandise trade, phone calls, tertiary students, emigration, and tourist arrivals), and ethnicity retains significance for three (merchandise trade, trade in printed publications, and tourist arrivals). To summarize, binary religion and ethnicity variables can achieve significance and add to explanatory power alongside language, but neither by itself outperforms the common official language binary variable.

Continuous Variables based on Observable Cultural Characteristics

Binary variables, of course, provide very coarse characterizations of the variation in degrees of cultural commonality across countries. Table 8.4 repeats the analysis substituting continuous linguistic, religious, and ethnic distance variables. The continuous language variable was developed by Melitz and Toubal and is a "summary index of common language" (2014, 358) obtained by pooling binary Common Official Language[19] and Common Native Language[20] variables together with data on Linguistic Proximity.[21] The continuous religion and ethnicity variables were newly constructed for this analysis. The continuous religion variable, based on data from the World Christian Database, sums the absolute value of the difference of the share that each religion represents in each country across the country pairs included.[22] The continuous ethnicity variable, based on the *Britannica Book of the Year* data compiled in Ellingsen (2000), reflects the proportion of each country pair's population comprising people sharing a common ethnicity, based on the first and second largest ethnicities in each country.[23]

Table 8.4 *Summary Comparison of Gravity Models across Continuous Cultural Variables*

		Number of significant focal coefficients and signs					
		Common official language	M&T continuous language	WCD continuous religion	Ellingsen continuous ethnicity	Average number of observations	Average adjusted R-squared
Language	1. M&T continuous language		10+			13,255	0.805
Religion	2. WCD continuous religion			9+		13,255	0.799
	3. Common official language + WCD continuous religion	10+		9+		13,255	0.806
Ethnicity	4. Ellingsen continuous ethnicity				7+	13,255	0.797
	5. Common official language + Ellingsen continuous ethnicity	10+			3+	13,255	0.805
All combined	6a. Common official language + WCD continuous religion + Ellingsen continuous ethnicity	10+		9+	3+, 1-	13,255	0.806
	6b. M&T continuous language + WCD continuous religion + Ellingsen continuous ethnicity		10+	6+	3+, 1-	13,255	0.806

Comparing Table 8.4 with Table 8.3 provides a rough assessment of the gains from using the selected continuous rather than binary variables. Comparison of Model 1 across the two tables indicates that switching from a dummy variable for common official language to the continuous language variable provided by Melitz and Toubal (2014) results in the same ten significant coefficients and slightly increases the average adjusted R-squared. We test the continuous religion variable in Model 2. Here, the number of significant coefficients increases from six to nine and the average adjusted R-squared remains roughly the same. When religion is included in the model along with Common Official Language, in Model 3, the latter variable retains its significance for the same ten flows, and religion remains significant for nine out of eleven. Model 4 tests the continuous ethnicity variable without common official language and obtains results comparable to the corresponding binary model. Model 5, with continuous ethnicity and common official language, again obtains roughly equivalent results to the binary version. When both the religion and ethnicity variables are included together with Common Official Language in Model 6a, the continuous religion variable remains significant in the same nine flows as in Model 2, which is a substantial improvement over Model 6 from Table 8.3. However, the continuous ethnicity variable remains positive and significant for only three flows and becomes negative and significant for one. Finally, Model 6b uses all three continuous variables together and obtains better results for continuous religion but worse results for ethnicity compared to the parallel model using all three binary variables, with a slightly improved average adjusted R-squared.

This effort at replacing binary variables with parallel continuous variables has yielded mixed results. The continuous religion variable clearly outperformed its binary counterpart, but the continuous language and ethnicity variables did not. Since, a priori, one would expect that continuous variables should generally outperform binary variables in these types of models, researchers may wish to work on generating better continuous variables for language and ethnicity, in addition to developing and testing variables pertaining to other types of observable national cultural differences.[24]

Multidimensional Cultural Distance Based on Underlying Value Dimensions

Finally, we turn to the cultural distance measures based on underlying value dimensions that have greater prominence in the international business, rather than the international economics, literature. Table 8.5 compares the baseline model from Chapter 5 with an alternative model using Kogut and Singh's cultural distance measure. As before, the sample has been restricted to those country pairs for which all required data are available, in this case a reduction

Table 8.5 *Kogut and Singh Cultural Distance*

		Number of significant focal coefficients and signs			
		Common official language	K&S cultural distance	Average number of observations	Average Adjusted R-squared
Language baseline	0. Common official language - restricted sample	11+		13,036	0.823
Cultural distance	1. K&S cultural distance		10–	13,036	0.818
	2. Common official language + K&S cultural distance	11+	5–	13,036	0.824

takes place to an average of 13,036 observations. With this restricted sample, the baseline model's average adjusted R-squared is higher than before, 0.823, and common official language becomes significant for all eleven flows. Switching from a model where cultural distance is measured by a binary common official language variable to one where Kogut and Singh's cultural distance measure is used reduces the number of significant coefficients from 11 to 10, and is accompanied by a decline in average R-squared. Moreover, when the two measures are combined, the number of significant coefficients remains the same for common official language, while it drops from 10 to 5 for Kogut and Singh's cultural distance.

The results presented in Table 8.5 do not provide convincing evidence that international business research, via its widespread adoption of cultural distance indexes such as Kogut and Singh's, has improved upon the standard practice in international economics of focusing on observable cultural characteristics such as language and religion. Note that others have reported even more perplexing results using the Kogut and Singh index, for example, the finding by Linders et al. (2005), that cultural distance increases bilateral trade. Nor do newer cultural distance indexes based on the same Hofstede (1980) cultural dimensions perform significantly better in our models. Berry, Guillén, and Zhou (2010) critiqued Kogut and Singh's index, and provided a cultural distance measure calculated using Mahalanobis[25] distance based on data from the World Values Survey.[26] While the results varied across regressions we ran using Berry, Guillén, and Zhou (2010)'s cultural distance and our own Mahalanobis-adjusted version of Kogut and Singh, the general pattern of a lack of significant improvement relative to our baseline model persisted. The results of these regressions are summarized in the online appendix at www.ghemawat.com/laws.

The somewhat unconvincing results obtained with cultural distance indexes based on Hofstede's cultural dimensions, however, do not imply that cultural frameworks such as Hofstede's should be disregarded in this type of research. Table 8.6 summarizes the results of a parallel set of models to those reported in Table 8.5 with distance along each of Hofstede's original four dimensions of national culture entered separately (distance, here, was computed based on absolute values of differences). What stands out as particularly striking from Model 1, in which language is excluded, is that Uncertainty Avoidance is significant with the expected negative sign for all eleven flows, the only variable apart from language that achieved this, albeit with a lower average R-squared. In Model 2, even when common official language is added, Uncertainty Avoidance achieves significance for ten out of eleven flows, as compared to nine for common official language. Shenkar (2001) cites Hofstede (1989) in support of the view that "differences in uncertainty avoidance are potentially the most problematic for international cooperation due to their correlates in terms of differential tolerances towards risk, formalization, and the like" (525). Masculinity-femininity also achieves significance with the expected negative sign for six flows in Model 1 and five flows in Model 2. Power distance and individualism-collectivism, on the other hand, when significant, enter these models more often with positive signs.

A first general inference from across the models tested in this section – both those that used binary and continuous language, religion, and ethnicity measures and those that drew upon Hofstede's cultural value dimensions – is that this analysis provides support for the baseline model presented in Chapter 5. The Melitz and Toubal continuous language variable and Hofstede's Uncertainty Avoidance at best very modestly outperformed the binary common official language variable, and all of the other variables tested were shown to have significance for a more limited range of international activity.

This analysis also indicates that observable cultural characteristics generally seem to do at least an equivalent if not a superior job of explaining international interactions than measures that attempt to capture underlying cultural values. However, it would be a mistake to interpret this analysis as implying that cultural value dimensions such as those identified by Hofstede are unimportant. Recall that the gravity model employs country fixed effects, which capture unilateral characteristics – including culture – that boost or suppress interactions with all partner countries. While the salience of these characteristics of a given country A do not depend on whether one is approaching that country from country B or country C, they may still be highly relevant to a firm that contemplates doing business in country A. The next section will return to the business implications of unilateral variation along Hofstede's dimensions of national cultural values.

Table 8.6 *Hofstede's Original Four Dimensions of National Culture*

		Number of significant focal coefficients and signs					
		Common official language	Power distance	Individualism-collectivism	Masculinity-femininity	Uncertainty avoidance	Average number of observations	Average adjusted R-squared
Language baseline	0. Common official language - restricted sample	11+					13,036	0.823
Cultural distance	1. Hofstede cultural dimensions		3+, 1-	4+, 1-	6-	11-	13,036	0.821
	2. Common official language + Hofstede cultural dimensions	9+	3+, 1-	6+, 1-	5-	10-	13,036	0.826

Nonetheless, this analysis does suggest that cultural distance indexes such as Kogut and Singh's should be approached with particular caution. Our results support Zaheer, Schomaker, and Nachum's contention that "objective, lower-order distance constructs such as time, space and perhaps even language and religion may in fact provide more powerful tools of investigation than complex higher-order distance constructs whose multidimensionality has been reduced" (2012, 20). The value of using more narrowly tailored cultural distance indicators is also likely to rise further for the analysis of particular industries or business functions. Regarding alcoholic beverages, religion is particularly relevant since its consumption is prohibited in some (e.g., Islam) while it is used in the rituals of others (e.g., Christianity), and trade in printed publications is, unsurprisingly, especially sensitive to language. Uncertainty avoidance might be crucial in the negotiation of long-term contracts, whereas individualism/collectivism might matter more in performance management.

Another important result is that all of the variables tested here were able to achieve significance and add to explanatory power alongside common language for at least some types of international activity. This suggests that researchers should select aspects of culture to measure based on the specific context of the analysis of interest and proposed mechanisms via which cultural distance is hypothesized to influence phenomena under investigation.

Finally, the analysis presented in this section also broadens the empirical support for the cultural dimension of the law of distance. While some cultural distance measures achieved significance for more flows than others did, when these measures were significant, they almost always entered into our models with the expected signs. Trade, capital, information, and people flows do tend to be dampened by a wide variety of cultural differences. Nonetheless, it is important to remember that when focusing on specific industries or functions, arbitrage across cultural differences can also boost international interactions. French wines represent a classic example. The possibility of cultural arbitrage is another reason why it is advisable to select cultural distance measures based on specific hypotheses about their potential effects rather than resorting to composite cultural distance indexes.

Business Implications of Cultural Variation

The variety of cultural distance measures that achieved significance in the gravity models described in the previous section highlights the multifaceted nature of the challenges culture can impose on firms. This section expands upon that inference by summarizing some of the concrete ways in which culture affects multinational firms. We focus here on unilateral attributes corresponding to Hofstede's dimensions of national culture. The most obvious application of cultural analysis at the firm level reflects the idea that improving

Table 8.7 *Summary of Business Implications of Power Distance*

Area	Implications of High Power Distance (Relative to Low)
Marketing and sales	• Consumers more likely to buy based on emotion rather than information • Public relations focuses more on building relationships rather than disseminating information • Online marketing less interactive • Humor less prevalent in advertising
Innovation and new product development	• Innovation more centralized • More demand for products that demonstrate status • Weaker innovation capabilities
Manufacturing and supply chain	• Formal quality management systems can be implemented without external market pressure
Human resources and organization	• Employee selection gives more emphasis to social class (over education) • Training emphasizes conformity (versus autonomy) • Evaluations focus on compliance or trustworthiness (over performance) • Wage differences between managers and workers are larger • Leadership is more authoritarian (versus participative) • Motivation is more coercive (instead of rewards based) • Organizations are more hierarchical
Negotiations	• Seniority of negotiator and size of negotiating team send important signals • Negotiators less attuned to joint gains

the alignment between management practices and cultural contexts yields tangible business benefits. Consider some examples (drawn from Newman and Nollen 1996):

- Participative management can improve profitability in low *power distance* cultures but worsen it in high *power distance* cultures.
- Quick fixes can improve profitability in more *short-term oriented* cultures but worsen it in more *long-term oriented* cultures.
- Merit-based pay and promotion policies can improve profitability in more *masculine* cultures and reduce it in more *feminine* cultures.
- Emphasizing individual contributions can improve profitability in more *individualistic* cultures and worsen it in more *collectivistic* cultures.

To provide a more systematic treatment, this section summarizes some of the implications that have been asserted in the literature for Hofstede's cultural dimensions, particularly power distance (see Table 8.7), across a range of business functions or activities.

Begin with marketing. Evidence that using humor in advertising is more prevalent in countries with lower *power distance* as well as low *uncertainty avoidance* (de Mooij 2010, Figure 7.4, p. 172), provides one example of how Hofstede's cultural dimensions affect marketing communications. In addition, according to another study, 63 percent of humorous television advertisements in Thailand and Korea (countries with high *power distance*) contain characters of unequal status, versus only 29 percent in the United States and Germany (countries with low *power distance*) (Alden, Hoyer, and Chol 1993). High *power distance* often indicates a tendency for consumers to make purchase decisions based on emotion rather than information. Moreover, in countries with high *power distance* and *collectivism*, public relations focuses more on building and maintaining relationships whereas in low *power distance* and *individualistic* cultures, it entails more explicit dissemination of information. In addition, consider online marketing where the larger gap between marketers and consumers in high *power distance* cultures entails less consumer-marketer interactivity. There also tend to be higher service expectations in high *power distance* cultures, and even the organization of products in retail stores may vary according to this dimension of culture (based on material in Chapter 7 in de Mooij 2010).

The link between marketing and innovation/new product development seems to work better when managed in a centralized way in cultures with high *power distance* (Garrett, Buisson, and Yap 2006). Furthermore, looking at innovation more broadly, studies indicate that countries with low *power distance* tend to have stronger innovation capabilities, which might affect a company's decisions about where to locate its innovative activities. Low *uncertainty avoidance* and high *individualism* also correlate with innovation capability (Hongyi 2009). In cultures with high *power distance*, consumers are more likely to want products that help them demonstrate their status.

National culture also has an impact on manufacturing and supply chain practices, which can be useful to consider in a variety of contexts: analyzing manufacturing footprints, managing multiplant operations, assessing competitors and suppliers in different countries, and so on. Consider the adoption of quality management practices. One European study indicates that in cultures with low *power distance* and low *uncertainty avoidance*, implementation of formal quality management systems may require external market pressure (Mathews et al. 2001).[27]

There are also important organizational or human resources implications of national culture. In countries with high (versus low) *power distance*, employee selection tends to give more emphasis to social class (over education), training tends to emphasize conformity (versus autonomy), evaluations focus on compliance or trustworthiness (over performance), wage differences between managers and workers are larger, leadership is more authoritarian (instead of participative), motivation is based on the assumption that subordinates dislike work and hence is more coercive (instead of reward-based), and organizations are more hierarchical (versus flat).[28] Achieving significant change in high *power distance* cultures requires putting senior staff front and center in communication efforts, using legitimate authority, and "tell[ing] subordinates what to do." In lower *power distance* cultures, it is more important to explain the reasons for change, "allow for questions and challenges" and involve employees in figuring out how to implement the desired change (Bing 2004, 85).

The implications of *power distance* for human resources also reach beyond individual firms to affect the design of institutions and governance structures. Chapter 9 presents data showing that high *power distance* is associated with more stringent employment protection legislation. The protections afforded to labor in such cultures also correlate with less external equity financing and a greater degree of family ownership. Hofstede also asserts a link between *power distance* and accounting: "In large *power distance* countries, the accounting system will be used more frequently to justify the decisions of the top power holder(s); in fact it usually is their tool to present the desired image, and figures will be twisted to this end" (Hofstede 1987, 8). Subsequent research casts doubt on the impact of *power distance* on accounting disclosure, but does indicate that high levels of *uncertainty avoidance* fit with low disclosure and conservatism in accounting (Finch 2010).

Entire books have been written on cross-cultural negotiations. A typical observation is that in higher *power distance* cultures, the seniority of the negotiator (and size of the negotiating team) sends important signals. Companies from low *power distance* cultures can run into trouble by sending a junior negotiator (who might be better versed in the content) or by trying to save money by limiting the size of the negotiating team. There are also indications that negotiators from high *power distance* cultures may be less attuned to joint gains, as they may be more accustomed to power differences simply determining outcomes.

In addition to these country-level characterizations, studies of cross-border phenomena such as the choice of entry mode and level of international diversification also reveal variation along Hofstede's dimensions of national culture. A survey article reports that "firms from countries with high *power distance* prefer subsidiary and equity JV entry modes whereas firms from countries high in *uncertainty avoidance* prefer contract agreements and export entry modes" (Kirkman, Lowe, and Gibson 2006, 301). The same summary article also cites various studies analyzing the effects of overall cultural distance – typically calculated using Kogut and Singh's index – on entry modes:

As the cultural distance between countries increased, the tendency to choose a joint venture (JV) over an acquisition increased. Also, as cultural distance increased, Japanese firms were more likely to choose greenfields or wholly owned subsidiaries over shared ownership; the tendency to choose licensing over JVs or wholly owned subsidiaries increased; the tendency to choose a greenfield over an acquisition increased; wholly owned subsidiaries were less preferred than either shared-equity ventures or technology licensing; [and] the tendency to choose management-service contracts over franchising increased. (Kirkman et al. 2006, 299)

In addition, others show that "cultural distance is a significant deterrent to Foreign Portfolio Investment" (Aggarwal, Kearney, and Lucey 2009, 4).

Global Leadership for Bridging Cultural Distance

The importance of cultural differences across functions within firms illustrated in the previous section hints at the complexity with which global leaders in multinational enterprises must contend. Global leaders face challenges associated with their task and relationship environments that impose heightened demands for physical and psychological mobility. This section will elaborate the global leadership challenge and then point to organizational responses in the areas of hiring and promotion, development, socialization, and broader education of talent within global organizations.

Challenges of Global Leadership

Evidence suggests that a growing number of people take on roles and responsibilities that reach beyond the domestic work context and do so in an increasing range of host countries (Brookfield Global Relocation Services 2015), and that global work assignments will increase significantly over the coming years (PwC 2012; Santa Fe Group 2014). However, industry surveys indicate that companies struggle to adequately prepare their employees to take on global leadership responsibilities (Ernst & Young 2012). Further, training for cultural diversity does not necessarily deliver the levels of proficiency required (Buchtel 2014).[29]

The challenges associated with global leadership may be summarized in terms of task-related and relationship-related challenges. The task-related challenges derive from the complexity global leaders face due to greater degrees of variety, interdependence, and flux (Lane, Maznevski, and Mendenhall 2004; Reiche et al. 2015).[30] *Variety* concerns the diversity in approaches of organizing, competing, and governing along with their attendant actors. Leaders in multinational firms constantly face different optimal solutions across different business lines, countries, and tasks. *Interdependence* is reflected in multifaceted interconnections with the external task environment, as in the case of global leaders dealing with multipoint competition and global clients that require strategic responses as an integrated whole. *Flux* concerns the degree to which change in the task environment is destabilizing. Global leaders experience more frequent and more intense changes in their task environment because these changes occur at different times across different locations, often at different velocities and in different directions (Osland 2013).

These three facets of complexity are also reflected in the changing nature of multinational companies themselves. While multinationals traditionally follow a hub-and-spoke model that centers around relationships between HQ and its subsidiaries, global competitive pressures have gradually led multinationals toward an integrated network model that not only involves greater direct interactions among national subsidiaries, but increasingly disaggregates country subsidiaries into functionally specific and discrete value-adding units, such as a sales unit or an R&D center (Birkinshaw 2001; Piekkari and Westney forthcoming). This greatly increases coordination challenges, and implies that cross-border interactions are not limited to the executive suite but involve middle management and even front-line staff such as R&D scientists or sales employees. Furthermore, while international relocations used to be a single career event, more and more employees seem to engage in repeated transfers and relocations to a larger number of different destinations, thereby increasing the intensity of global mobility over the course of their careers.

To turn to relationship-related challenges, global leaders are involved in substantial boundary spanning activities, which result in several relational challenges. Boundary spanning concerns an individual's integration and coordination activities through allocating ideas, information, decisions, talent, and resources (Beechler et al. 2004). Given the increased coordination challenges and denser cross-unit interactions in multinational companies, boundary-crossing activities have risen substantially. Leaders span boundaries not only across functions, business units, and divisions within their organizations, but they also deal with numerous external stakeholders, including industry consortia, government agencies, regulators, customers, suppliers, nongovernmental organizations, the media, and other business partners.

Particular relationship challenges derive from the structural and content-related characteristics of leaders' stakeholder interactions. For example, communication is likely more virtual and asynchronous when leaders spend less contact time with each respective actor given the wide geographical dispersion of their constituents and task responsibilities. The sharing of relevant information that can be accessed asynchronously, according to each actor's time zone and work schedule, may support decision-making processes and improve decision-making quality. However, certain types of resources such as the development of trust and the sharing of context-specific information require face-to-face interaction (Jarvenpaa and Leidner 1999). This is particularly relevant for interactions across organizational boundaries, as in the case of cross-border joint ventures, which are subject to greater potential differences in strategic interests, organizational values and mindsets, and management systems, thereby placing a greater burden on the development and maintenance of high-quality relationships.

Leading across nonproximate locations also entails a variety of social frictions that not only affect the structure but also the content of interaction. These frictions may have negative effects on the level of global leadership an individual can exert, for example, due to cultural misunderstandings, stereotypes, or other biases that impair effective interactions. Consistent with the material presented in the previous section, studies have consistently shown cultural differences in negotiation, conflict management, reciprocation, and cooperative behaviors (Morris et al. 1998; Adair and Brett 2005; Chen and Li 2005; Reiche et al. 2014). The variety of cultural stimuli that characterize the wider task context in which global leaders operate also have a bearing on how individuals socially construct meaning and develop or resist shared identities and, by extension, relate to each other (Ashforth and Mael 1989). This is particularly relevant given the prevalence of multicultural, as opposed to single-cultural encounters, as in the case of global teams, cross-border task forces, or alliances with other multinationals.

These task and relationship challenges imply that global leadership requires both physical and psychological mobility. Physical mobility is necessary because despite advances in communication technology, virtual means cannot fulfil all necessary boundary-spanning activities. Arguably, exchanging the most relevant resources such as tacit and contextual knowledge, for example, about how to deal with a particular customer, as well as trust requires face-to-face contact (Reiche, Harzing, and Kraimer 2008).

Psychological mobility refers to the perception of one's capacity to make transitions and entails both cognitive and affective flexibility. Cognitive flexibility concerns the extent to which global leaders can adjust their thought patterns and behaviors to effectively interact with people and adapt to situational demands across cultures (Shaffer et al. 2012). Cognitive flexibility also reflects the demands resulting from exposure to different sources of identification, such as those of the HQ, the local subsidiary or a joint venture partner (Butler et al. 2012). Affective flexibility, and empathy in particular, entails the need to adapt one's affective responses toward cultural others. This is particularly relevant when operating in a context of increased diversity, higher pace, more complexity, and more virtual forms of communication that limit face-to-face contact time. Neuroscience research indicates that people are less able to experience empathy and compassion when they are distracted or mentally overloaded (Immordino-Yang et al. 2009).

Management Practices to Strengthen Global Leadership

What can firms do to boost their leaders' ability to bridge cultural and other types of international distance? Simply providing cross-cultural training is not enough because teaching people to place individuals from different countries into a handful of different cultural buckets may just lead to sophisticated stereotyping (Osland and Bird 2000), and in fact *increase* the use of stereotyping (Buchtel 2014). Rather, firms can employ a broader set practices, which we will organize here into four categories: hiring and promotion, development, socialization, and education practices (summarized in Table 8.8). These practices have natural synergies and some overlap with the content on boosting corporate cosmopolitanism covered in Chapter 6.

Given the many task- and relationship-related challenges that individuals face when operating across borders, a first set of *hiring and promotion* levers concerns building a more diverse pool of global leaders. Hiring and promoting people from diverse backgrounds may sound simple, yet many companies continue to favor parent country nationals, not only at the top but also for many lower-level managerial positions at foreign operations (Ghemawat and Vantrappen 2015). To signal willingness to increase their staff diversity, companies will need to start at the top – but they should also focus on diversity at lower levels. Firms can also embrace self-initiated expatriates, that is, individuals who expatriate themselves from their home country without the support of an employing company (Tharenou and Caulfield 2010). A second way to increase the repertoire of dealing with increased complexity and boundary-spanning activities is to hire – and then continue to develop and promote – bicultural or multicultural individuals who, through their upbringing and experience, have internalized the norms and behavioral sets that are appropriate in different cultural, ethnic, and linguistic environments and can easily shift between them.[31]

Development of global leadership talent within an organization requires (1) selecting *which* types of competencies are necessary; (2) deciding *how* they are to be identified and developed; and (3) identifying *who* is eligible for competency development. Social scientists have identified more than 160 competencies relevant for global leadership effectiveness, yet many of these competencies are conceptually overlapping and often separated only by semantic differences. These competencies can, however, be grouped into three broad categories: intrapersonal competencies (associated with the internal psychological/emotional sphere of the leader), interpersonal (concerned with management of people and relationships), and business acumen (directed at the understanding of and ability to act within business and organizational realities) (Jokinen 2005; Bird 2013). It is also important to account for the tremendous variation in global leadership roles and responsibilities and

Table 8.8 *Managerial Practices to Strengthen Global Leadership*

Talent function	Managerial practice	Time horizon	Limitations and blind spots
1. Hiring and promotion	Develop and promote foreign nationals for country-manager and senior HQ positions	Medium-term	Overreliance on language-sensitive recruitment and promotion
	Inpatriation of foreign talent to HQ	Medium-term	Potentially limited career opportunities upon return to foreign subsidiary
	Hire and develop multi-cultural individuals	Short-/ medium-term	Insufficient attention to how monoculturals can learn from their multicultural colleagues to improve cross-cultural effectiveness
	Hire self-initiated expatriates	Short-/ medium-term	Self-initiated expatriates proactively manage their own assignment tenure, which makes retention more difficult to manage
2. Development	Adopt clear and manageable competency model	Short-/ medium-term	Overly long competency lists complicate measurement and development interventions
	Customize intervention and career paths according to individual requirements	Short-term	Customization needs to be evaluated against overall consistency of competency model
	Establish pool of opportunities for and forms of international exposure	Short-/ medium-term	Overreliance on short-term postings with limited developmental value
	Create and maintain central roster of global talent in organization	Medium-term	Preference/politicking for historically grown and regionally different talent systems
	Systematically plan repatriation and career paths	Medium-/ long-term	Difficulty to foresee vacancies especially for long-term international assignments
	Incentivize global travel, for example, through leisure travel policies (i.e., link business and leisure travel)	Short-term	Potential for adverse selection of talent; growth of "unattractive" assignment destinations
	Offer regular and repeated cultural mentoring and training	Short-/ medium-term	Insufficient involvement of local nationals, who regularly interact with global leaders/ employees, in training
	Provide support for common language learning	Short-/ medium-term	Overreliance on language-sensitive recruitment and promotion

Table 8.8 (cont.)

Talent function	Managerial practice	Time horizon	Limitations and blind spots
3. Socialization	Develop a common corporate culture	Long-term	Overreliance on HQ national cultural values as source of identification
	Assess value fit at selection stage and through regular developmental appraisals	Short-/ medium-term	Value congruence needs to be evaluated against required competencies and expertise
	Offer standardized induction programs	Short-term	Value depends on clarity of established corporate culture
	Offer formalized coaching and mentoring	Short-term	Value depends on clarity of established corporate culture
	Combine multiple face-to-face and virtual contact points for collaboration	Short-/ medium-term	Overreliance on virtual means of interaction
4. Education	Make use of available data sources about levels of globalization and cultural differences	Short-term	Risk of sophisticated stereotyping
	Formalize the transfer of experiences and best practices	Short-/ medium-term	Experiences and best practices are insufficiently tracked and archived
	Provide financial support, for example, through public-private partnerships	Short-/ medium-term	May require coordination with other external stakeholders

customize competence development, as well as intervention paths, according to actual needs (Ghemawat 2012).

Several interventions exist to identify and facilitate the development of the necessary competencies. A first step is to provide staff simply with international exposure (Jokinen 2005), and there are many different ways to achieve this. Beyond more traditional long-term expatriation, there is a wealth of other forms of global work assignments including inpatriation, short-term postings, global virtual teamwork, often combined with international business travel, cross-border project work and task forces, or commuter assignments.

There are also other tools to grow one's cultural and broader contextual repertoire. Cultural training and mentoring, especially if they accompany an individual's international assignment, are useful for learning and retaining newly learned experiences. In cross-cultural training, it is important to beware of simplistic approaches that may lead to more rigid use of stereotypes. While such generalizations may serve as a useful initial guide about a particular cultural context when more detailed knowledge is missing, the main problem with stereotypes, including sophisticated stereotypes about general cultural dimensions, lies in their stickiness and their resistance to revision in light of new information (Ratiu 1983).

A critical additional skillset for global leadership is proficiency in a common language. This can be achieved either by developing proficiency in a firm-wide common language or by individuals learning the native language of another country unit. Although the latter may be more difficult to achieve, especially with regard to multiple country units, job rotations and face-to-face interactions in the form of regular meetings, conferences or cross-border project teamwork may help to improve foreign language fluency for key talent. There are also perils associated with implementing a firm-wide common language, as illustrated vividly by "Englishnization" at Rakuten, Japan's largest online retailer. A common language provokes immediate changes in the status of native and nonnative speakers that can impact performance (Neeley 2013).

Turning to who is eligible for competency assessment and development, it is useful to think beyond individuals who are expected to fulfill global leadership and boundary-spanning responsibilities. While such leaders ought to be the primary target of global leadership development activities, it is also valuable to involve local nationals in foreign operations, especially those who regularly interact with global leaders and expatriates (Toh and DeNisi 2007).

Socialization focuses on commonalities that bind an organization together rather than the internal differences within it. Especially in diverse contexts, we may simply fail to identify with people because we are focusing on how different they are and because we are thinking about them in terms that are too specific and narrow. One way of binding organizational members together without privileging home country nationals is through a common corporate culture. A growing number of organizations are recognizing the importance of cultural fit of their employees, and explicitly assessing value congruence both at the selection stage and on an ongoing basis during development. Job rotations, regular meetings – and the creation of multiple points of contact across dispersed organizational units more broadly – are equally powerful as they help break silos and fault lines along national, ethnic, or gender markers, and increase organizational members' mutual knowledge of their counterparts' local contexts (Cramton 2001). Finally, as briefly touched upon earlier, a common corporate language can also facilitate an overarching identity. Indeed, shared language not only facilitates the exchange of information but has also been demonstrated to foster solidarity and social identification (Reiche, Harzing, and Pudelko 2015).

Broader *education* about globalization is a final lever for strengthening global leadership. This is particularly important because individuals across all hierarchical levels in organizations tend to overestimate how global the world is (recall the discussion of "globaloney" in Chapter 2) – while also underestimating the scope of cultural differences (Ghemawat 2007). Relevant education can occur through widely available sources of data and information as well as experience-based sharing of knowledge and best practices in multinationals. For example, data sources such as the *DHL Global Connectedness Index* (Ghemawat and Altman 2014) provide data on levels of cross-border integration along trade, capital, information, and people flows that can be looked at from the vantage point of a particular country or region. Ghemawat ("Focus on Curricular Content" 2011), in the report of the AACSB's task force on the globalization of management education, discusses the incorporation of such content into business school curricula and has followed up by developing a course organized, as the report recommended, around the two laws of globalization, disseminating its core materials electronically through the AACSB and offering it as a MOOC on the Coursera platform.[32]

Experience is, of course, an essential complement to education. There are limits to how much a global leader can expect to figure out ahead of time about a new foreign context along cultural or for that matter other dimensions. Immersion in a foreign context for long enough to develop a meaningful level of experience can be the starting point of an experiential learning cycle which, in Kolb's influential model, also encompasses reflection, conceptualization, and experimentation (Kolb 1984), to which we would simply add the reminder that there is a higher-level complementarity between experiential learning and education to be exploited as well. We make this point because of the sense, expressed in the AACSB task force report, that at least in the context of business education, "Too often, classroom diversity, treks abroad, special projects and similar elements are relied upon in lieu of attention to course of program content" (Ghemawat 2011, 140).

Although cultural and other forms of distance impose a unique set of challenges on global leaders, as discussed in the previous subsection, firms do have a wide array of management practices at their disposal to strengthen global leadership. Hiring and promotion, development, socialization, and education all represent complementary levers, which used in combination can powerfully accelerate the growth of a firm's global leadership capacity.

Conclusion

Cultural distance – contrary to prominent worries by those who fear globalization might lead to homogenization[33] – is a persistent feature of the international business environment. Sources such as the World Values Survey, a study of sixty-five countries covering 75 percent of the world's population, suggest that national cultural traits have, at a deep level, remained fairly stable despite superficial evidence of some convergence in cultural habits, artifacts, and symbols, for example, the spread of American consumer culture (Inglehart and Baker 2000).[34]

Therefore, this chapter began by defining culture and identifying several ways to measure it, before incorporating several cultural distance measures into gravity models and obtaining results that fit with the law of distance. Gravity modeling also suggested that observable indicators – in particular, the presence or absence of a common language – do at least an equivalent if not a better job of explaining international interactions than Hofstede's influential measures of underlying cultural values. This casts some doubt on the sense from the iceberg analogy that the hidden (submerged) elements of culture are more important than its observable aspects when it comes to explaining the international inter-actions studied in this chapter – especially when the submerged elements are collapsed into indexes of cultural distance.

The discussion of business implications of cultural variation that followed, however, reaffirmed the relevance of underlying cultural values in understanding individual countries (unilateral effects) even if they do not always perform as well as distance measures (bilateral effects). The final section illustrated some of the many practical implications of a deeper understanding of cultural distance for global leadership by highlighting task and relationship challenges and actions firms can take in hiring and promotion, development, socialization, and education to boost their leaders' capacity to bridge cultural distance.

Notes

1 Hofstede relates this pattern to his masculinity/femininity dimension of national culture: the United States ranks in the upper third of national cultures on masculinity whereas only two others rank as more feminine than the Netherlands (out of sixty-six).

2 Unfortunately, the international business field's focus on cultural distance sometimes comes at the expense of any attention at all to other dimensions of distance. Among the articles covered in the Hutzschenreuter, Kleindienst, and Lange (2015) review that incorporated cultural distance, only one-quarter also incorporated other distance dimensions.

3 One can also point to attempts to analyze cultures at levels more aggregated than the national level, for example, Nisbett (2003) on differences between Eastern and Western ways of thinking and the Huntington (1993, 1996) thesis of a clash of civilizations.

4 Universalism and Particularism are discussed at length in chapter 2 of Hampden-Turner and Trompenaars (2000).

5 On Hofstede's Power Distance scale, which we introduce in the next subsection, Spanish-speaking countries average 69, and English-speaking countries average 32.

6 Calculation based on subset of 163 countries using data from Mayer and Zignago (2011).

7 In another example of seemingly mismatched levels of aggregation, Zimbabwe's largest ethnic group is reported as "Shona" whereas Zambia's is "African."

8 In the gravity model analysis presented later in this chapter, we use Ellingsen (2000)'s ethnicity dataset (based on *Britannica Book of the Year*), despite the anomalies described here, because it outperformed available alternatives in our models, including a genetic distance measure from Spolaore and Wacziarg (2009). We could not use migrant stocks as a proxy for ethnic commonalities because migration itself is one of our dependent variables.

9 Hofstede's later work incorporates two more dimensions: Long-Term Orientation and Indulgence.

10 Another framework worth mentioning, developed recently by Michele Gelfand and coauthors, provides insight into variations within as well as across thirty-three countries by classifying them in terms of their "tightness" (Gelfand et al. 2011). *Tight cultures* such as India or Korea have many strong behavioral norms across everyday situations (e.g., in classrooms, libraries, public parks) and low tolerance for deviations from them, whereas *loose cultures* such as Ukraine or the Netherlands have weaker social norms and higher tolerance of deviant behavior. Individuals in tight cultures are supposed to focus on avoiding mistakes and behaving properly; they are to have higher self-regulatory strength (higher impulse control) and a greater need for structure. The tightness-looseness distinction is related to, yet somewhat distinct from, the value dimensions that we have already discussed. For example, tightness is positively but only partially correlated with collectivism and power distance. It also has some other interesting correlates. Thus, tight cultures tend to have less open media and a higher incidence of religious observance by their members. Members of tight cultures also seem more likely to perceive their own culture to be superior to members of loose cultures.

11 www.palgrave-journals.com/jibs/most-cited.html.

12 Note that the circumference of the earth is 40,075 km, so the maximum distance between two places is 20,038 km. Thus, Peru and South Korea are 81% as far from each other as is geographically possible.

13 The original four dimensions used in Kogut and Singh's calculations were uncertainty avoidance, individuality, tolerance of power distance, and masculinity-femininity. Adding long-term orientation and indulgence as dimensions makes Australia and the United States the most culturally similar, as Peru and South Korea are particularly distant on long-term orientation and not nearly as similar on indulgence. While the United States and Australia are 14,802 km from each other, their common language and similar history at least make them a sensible closest pair. Nevertheless, Denmark and Slovakia remain the most distant. Other non-geographic comparisons substantiate these concerns. Douglas Dow and Amal Karunaratna proposed a set of measures of psychic distance stimuli, which have their basis in societal attributes. Denmark and Slovakia are more like each other on all of these attributes than Peru and South Korea (Dow and Karunaratna 2006, 592–593).

14 Several types of binary common language variables have been used in the gravity modeling literature, and Melitz and Toubal report that "the usual measure of common language is a binary one based on official status" (2014, 351).

15 1 – Same denomination or sect; 2 – Same division but different denomination or sect; 3 – Same religion but different division; 4 – Same family but different religions; 5 – Different families of religion.

16 Ellingsen (2000) provided three datasets of ethnic composition that she derived from *Handbook of the Nations, Demographic Yearbook,* and *Britannica Book of the Year.*

17 In Tables 8.3 through 8.6, all variables significant at the 0.1 level or higher are counted as significant. In the case of common official language discussed here, all were significant at the 0.01 level.

18 The sample was restricted based on availability of both the binary variables used in this subsection and the continuous variables used in the next subsection in order to ensure comparable results across the two.

19 Melitz and Toubal (2014) generated this using CIA World Factbook as their main source, and filling gaps with other sources.

20 Sourced primarily from the Special Eurobarometer 243 with gaps were filled from Ethnologue and CIA World Factbook.

21 The authors actually created two measures of Linguistic Proximity: LP1 and LP2. LP1 calculates linguistic proximity following the description and repartition of language trees "between trees, branches and sub-branches" (Melitz and Toubal 2014, 355). LP2, which is the measure included in the index of continuous linguistic distance, has been derived from an analysis of "lexical similarity between 200 words in a list (first) compiled by Swadesh in 1952" (355).

22 The continuous religious distance variable was calculated by Tamara de la Mata, who compared the share of a set of religions for each pair of countries. The absolute value of the difference of the share that each religion represents in each country is obtained and summed across religions by each country pair. The list of religions considered are the ones defined as major religions in the World Christian Database: Bahais, Buddhists, Chinese folk-religionists, Christians, Confucianists, Daoists (Taoism), Hindus, Jains, Jews, Muslims, Pagans, Shintoists, Sikhs, Spiritists, Zoroastrians, and Atheists and Agnostics.

$$religion\_similarity_{ij} = \sum_{r=1}^{R} 1 - \left| \frac{pop_{ri}}{\sum pop_i} - \frac{pop_{rj}}{\sum pop_j} \right|$$

The source database is at www.worldchristiandatabase.org/wcd/.

23 More precisely, for each common first or second ethnicity in a country pair, we construct the variable by summing the ethnicity's share of population in the country where its share is smaller. The result is a variable ranging between 0 (no shared first or second ethnicity) and 100 (the full population across the country pair shares a common ethnicity). We enter the variable into the regression without taking the natural logarithm in order to preserve 0 values.

24 We also tried Spolaore and Wacziarg's (2009) genetic distance as an additional continuous variable, but models using that variable substantially underperformed the baseline. The methodology followed by Spolaore and Wacziarg (2009) is based on

previous work by Cavalli-Sforza, Menozzi, and Piazza (1994) and their main focus is on the set of 42 world populations for which all bilateral distances, computed from 120 alleles, were available.

25 Berry, Guillén, and Zhou pointed out several shortcomings of Kogut and Singh's index in this context, in particular the fact that it does not account for partial collinearity of Hofstede's dimensions, as well as the assumption that the scale of each dimension is of equal importance. Mahalanobis distance addresses these concerns "because it takes into account the information contained in the variance-covariance matrix and is scale-invariant" (2010, 1469). There is an obvious link here to principal-component analysis: Mahalanobis distance is "equivalent to the Euclidian distance calculated with the standardized values of the principal components" (2010, 1469).

26 www.worldvaluessurvey.org/wvs.jsp.

27 Note that this study is based on research conducted only in the UK, Finland, and Portugal.

28 We draw this paragraph from Cullen and Parboteeah's Exhibit 2.2 (2014, 55). We quote some material directly, and paraphrase other material (not marked to improve readability).

29 For a general critique of cross-cultural training research and practice, see Reiche, Lee, and Quintanilla (2014).

30 See also Lane, Maznevski, and Mendenhall (2004).

31 While our focus here is on national and cultural diversity, it often makes sense to take an integrated approach to diversity that also accounts for other aspects such as gender.

32 Materials for this course, "Globalization of Business Enterprise (GLOBE)" are available for download at www.aacsb.edu/knowledge/resources/course%20 materials/globe as well as www.ghemawat.com/globecourse. For the MOOC version offered on Coursera, refer to www.coursera.org/course/globe.

33 Chapter 11 of Ghemawat's (2011) book, *World 3.0*, is devoted to assessing and addressing this concern.

34 Shalom Schwartz found similar levels of stability over time in his own research (see Schwartz 2014).

References

Adair, Wendi L., and Jeanne M. Brett. 2005. "The Negotiation Dance: Time, Culture, and Behavioral Sequences in Negotiation." *Organization Science* 16 (1):33–51. doi: 10.1287/orsc.1040.0102.

Agar, Michael. 1994. *Language Shock: Understanding the Culture of Conversation*. New York: Wm. Morrow.

Aggarwal, Raj, Colm Kearney, and Brian Lucey. 2009. "Is Gravity a Cultural Artefact? Culture and Distance in Foreign Portfolio Investment." FMA Annual Meeting. www.efmaefm.org/0EFMAMEETINGS/EFMA%20ANNUAL%20MEETINGS/ 2009-Milan/papers/EFMA2009_0455_fullpaper.pdf.

Alden, Dana L., Wayne D. Hoyer, and Lee Chol. 1993. "Identifying Global and Culture-Specific Dimensions of Humor in Advertising: A Multinational Analysis." *Journal of Marketing* 57 (2):64–75.

Ashforth, Blake E., and Fred Mael. 1989. "Social Identity Theory and the Organization." *Academy of Management Review* 14 (1):20–39. doi: 10.5465/AMR.1989.4278999.

Beckerman, W. 1956. "Distance and the Pattern of Intra-European Trade." *Review of Economics and Statistics* 38 (1):31–40. doi: 10.2307/1925556.

Beechler, Schon, Mikael Söndergaard, Edwin L. Miller, and Allan Bird. 2004. "Boundary Spanning." In *The Blackwell Handbook of Global Management a Guide to Managing Complexity*, edited by Henry W. Lane, Martha L. Maznevski, Mark E. Mendenhall, and Jeanne McNett, 121–133. Oxford, UK: Blackwell.

Berry, Heather, Mauro F Guillén, and Nan Zhou. 2010. "An Institutional Approach to Cross-National Distance." *Journal of International Business Studies* 41 (9):1460–1480.

Bing, John W. 2004. "Hofstede's Consequences: The Impact of His Work on Consulting and Business Practices." *Academy of Management Executive* 18 (1):80–87. doi: 10.5465/ame.2004.12689609.

Bird, Allan. 2013. "Mapping the Content Domain of Global Leadership Competencies." In *Global Leadership: Research, Practice, and Development*, edited by Mark E. Mendenhall, 80–96. 2nd ed. New York: Routledge.

Birkinshaw, Julian. 2001. "Strategy and Management in MNE Subsidiaries." In *The Oxford Handbook of International Business*, edited by Alan M. Rugman and Thomas L. Brewer, 380–401. New York: Oxford University Press. www.oxfordscholarship.com/view/10.1093/0199241821.001.0001/acprof -9780199241828-chapter-14.

Brookfield Global Relocation Services. 2015. "2015 Global Mobility Trends Survey: Mindful Mobility." http://globalmobilitytrends.brookfieldgrs.com/#?q=5.

Buchtel, Emma E. 2014. "Cultural Sensitivity or Cultural Stereotyping? Positive and Negative Effects of a Cultural Psychology Class." *International Journal of Intercultural Relations* 39:40–52. doi: 10.1016/j.ijintrel.2013.09.003.

Butler, Christina L., Lena Zander, Audra Mockaitis, and Ciara Sutton. 2012. "The Global Leader as Boundary Spanner, Bridge Maker, and Blender." *Industrial & Organizational Psychology: Perspectives on Science and Practice* 5 (2):240–243. doi: 10.1111/j.1754-9434.2012.01439.x.

Cavalli-Sforza, L. L., Paolo Menozzi, and Alberto Piazza. 1994. *The History and Geography of Human Genes*. Princeton: Princeton University Press.

Chen, Xiao-Ping, and Shu Li. 2005. "Cross-National Differences in Cooperative Decision-Making in Mixed-Motive Business Contexts: The Mediating Effect of Vertical and Horizontal Individualism." *Journal of International Business Studies* 36 (6):622–636. doi: 10.1057/palgrave.jibs.8400169.

Cramton, Catherine Durnell. 2001. "The Mutual Knowledge Problem and Its Consequences for Dispersed Collaboration." *Organization Science* 12 (3):346–371. doi: 10.1287/orsc.12.3.346.10098.

Cullen, John B., and K. Praveen Parboteeah. 2014. *Multinational Management: A Strategic Approach*. 6th edn. Mason, OH: South-Western Cengage Learning.

de Mooij, Marieke K. 2010. *Global Marketing and Advertising: Understanding Cultural Paradoxes*. 3rd edn. Los Angeles: SAGE.

Dow, Douglas. 2014. "Distance in International Business Research: Are We Really Making Any Progress?" In *Contributions to International Business: Essays in Honour of Professor Jorma Larimo*, edited by Martti Laaksonen, Ahmad Arslan, and Minnie Kontkanen, 119–140. Vaasa, Finland: University of Vaasa.

Dow, Douglas, and Amal Karunaratna. 2006. "Developing a Multidimensional Instrument to Measure Psychic Distance Stimuli." *Journal of International Business Studies* 37 (5):578–602. doi: 10.2307/4540370.

Ellingsen, Tanja. 2000. "Colorful Community or Ethnic Witches' Brew? Multiethnicity and Domestic Conflict During and after the Cold War." *Journal of Conflict Resolution* 44 (2):228–249. doi: 10.2307/174664.

Ernst & Young. 2012. "Paradigm Shift: Building a New Talent Management Model to Boost Growth." Ernst & Young. www.ey.com/GL/en/Issues/Driving-growth/ Growing-Beyond–Paradigm-Shift–Overview#.VnrWCVmSbfA.

Felbermayr, Gabriel J., and Farid Toubal. 2010. "Cultural Proximity and Trade." *European Economic Review* 54 (2):279–293.

Finch, Nigel. 2010. "Towards an Understanding of Cultural Influence on the International Practice of Accounting." *Journal of International Business and Cultural Studies* 2 (February). Academic and Business Research Institute. www.aabri.com/manu- scripts/09175.pdf.

Garrett, Tony C., David H. Buisson, and Chee Meng Yap. 2006. "National Culture and R&D and Marketing Integration Mechanisms in New Product Development: A Cross-Cultural Study between Singapore and New Zealand." *Industrial Marketing Management* 35 (3):293–307. doi: 10.1016/j.indmarman.2005.09.007.

Gelfand, Michele J., Jana L. Raver, Lisa Nishii, Lisa M. Leslie, Janetta Lun, Beng Chong Lim, et al. 2011. "Differences between Tight and Loose Cultures: A 33- Nation Study." *Science* 332 (6033):1100–1104. doi: 10.1126/science.1197754.

Ghemawat, Pankaj. 2001. "Distance Still Matters: The Hard Reality of Global Expansion." *Harvard Business Review* 79 (8):137–147.

2007. *Redefining Global Strategy: Crossing Borders in a World Where Differences Still Matter*. Boston, MA: Harvard Business School Press.

2011. "Responses to Forces of Change: A Focus on Curricular Content." In *Globalization of Management Education: Changing International Structures, Adaptive Strategies, and the Impact on Institutions: Report of the AACSB International Globalization of Management Education Task Force*, 105–156. Bingley: Emerald.

2011. *World 3.0: Global Prosperity and How to Achieve It*. Boston, MA: Harvard Business Review Press.

2012. "Developing Global Leaders." *McKinsey Quarterly* (3):100–109.

Ghemawat, Pankaj, and Steven A. Altman. 2014. "DHL Global Connectedness Index 2014: Analyzing Global Flows and Their Power to Increase Prosperity." Deutsche Post DHL. www.dhl.com/gci.

Ghemawat, Pankaj, and Herman Vantrappen. 2015. "How Global Is Your C-Suite?" *MIT Sloan Management Review* 56 (4):73–82.

Gumperz, John J., and Stephen C. Levinson. 1996. "Introduction: Linguistic Relativity Re-Examined." In *Rethinking Linguistic Relativity*, edited by John J. Gumperz, and Stephen C. Levinson, 1–18. Cambridge, England: Cambridge University Press.

Håkanson, Lars, and Björn Ambos. 2010. "The Antecedents of Psychic Distance." *Journal of International Management* 16 (3):195–210. doi: 10.1016/j.intman.2010.06.001.

Hall, Edward T. 1990. *The Silent Language*. New York: Anchor Books.

Hampden-Turner, Charles, and Alfons Trompenaars. 2000. *Building Cross-Cultural Competence: How to Create Wealth from Conflicting Values*. New Haven, CT: Yale University Press.

Harzing, Anne-Wil, and Markus Pudelko. 2015. "Do We Need to Distance Ourselves from the Distance Concept? Why Home and Host Country Context Might Matter More Than (Cultural) Distance." *Management International Review.*

Head, Keith, and Thierry Mayer. 2014. "Gravity Equations: Workhorse, Toolkit, and Cookbook." In *Handbook of International Economics*, edited by Gita Gopinath, Elhanan Helpman, and Kenneth S. Rogoff, 131–195. Oxford: North-Holland.

Hofstede, Geert. 1980. *Culture's Consequences: International Differences in Work-Related Values.* Vol. 5, Cross Cultural Research and Methodology. Beverly Hills, CA: Sage Publications.

    1987. "The Cultural Context of Accounting." In *Accounting and Culture: Plenary Session Papers and Discussants' Comments from the 1986 Annual Meeting of the American Accounting Association*, edited by Barry E. Cushing, 1–11. Sarasota, FL: American Accounting Association.

    1989. "Organising for Cultural Diversity." *European Management Journal* 7 (4):390–397. doi: 10.1016/0263-2373(89)90075-3.

    1991. *Cultures and Organizations: Software of the Mind.* London; New York: McGraw-Hill.

    2001. *Culture's Consequences: Comparing Values, Behaviors, Institutions, and Organizations across Nations.* 2nd edn. Thousand Oaks, CA: Sage Publications.

Hofstede, Geert, and Michael Harris Bond. 1988. "The Confucius Connection: From Cultural Roots to Economic Growth." *Organizational Dynamics* 16 (4):5–21. doi: 10.1016/0090-2616(88)90009-5.

Hongyi, Sun. 2009. "A Meta-Analysis on the Influence of National Culture on Innovation Capability." *International Journal of Entrepreneurship and Innovation Management* 10 (3/4):353–360. doi: 10.1504/ijeim.2009.025678.

House, Robert J., Paul J. Hanges, Mansour Javidan, Peter W. Dorfman, and Vipin Gupta, eds. 2004. *Culture, Leadership, and Organizations: The Globe Study of 62 Societies.* Thousand Oaks, CA: Sage Publications.

Huntington, Samuel P. 1993. "The Clash of Civilizations?" *Foreign Affairs* 72 (3):22–49.

    1996. *The Clash of Civilizations and the Remaking of World Order.* New York: Simon & Schuster.

Hutzschenreuter, Thomas, Ingo Kleindienst, and Sandra Lange. 2015. "The Concept of Distance in International Business Research: A Review and Research Agenda." *International Journal of Management Reviews.* http://dx.doi.org/10.1111/ijmr.12065.

Immordino-Yang, Mary Helen, Andrea McColl, Hanna Damasio, and Antonio Damasio. 2009. "Neural Correlates of Admiration and Compassion." *Proceedings of the National Academy of Sciences* 106 (19):8021–8026. doi: 10.1073/pnas.0810363106.

Inglehart, Ronald, and Wayne E. Baker. 2000. "Modernization, Cultural Change, and the Persistence of Traditional Values." *American Sociological Review* 65 (1):19–51.

Jarvenpaa, Sirkka L., and Dorothy E. Leidner. 1999. "Communication and Trust in Global Virtual Teams." *Organization Science* 10 (6):791–815. doi: 10.1287/orsc.10.6.791.

Jokinen, Tiina. 2005. "Global Leadership Competencies: A Review and Discussion." *Journal of European Industrial Training* 29 (2/3):199–216.

Kirkman, Bradley L., Kevin B. Lowe, and Cristina B. Gibson. 2006. "A Quarter Century of 'Culture's Consequences': A Review of Empirical Research Incorporating

Hofstede's Cultural Values Framework." *Journal of International Business Studies* 37 (3):285–320. doi: 10.1057/palgrave.jibs.8400202.

Kluckhohn, Clyde. 1954. "Culture and Behavior." In *Handbook of Social Psychology*, edited by Gardner Lindzey, 921–976. Cambridge, MA: Addison-Wesley.

Kogut, Bruce, and Harbir Singh. 1988. "The Effect of National Culture on the Choice of Entry Mode." *Journal of International Business Studies* 19 (3):411–432. doi: 10.1057/palgrave.jibs.8490394.

Kolb, David A. 1984. *Experiential Learning: Experience as the Source of Learning and Development.* Englewood Cliffs, NJ: Prentice-Hall.

Lane, Henry W., Martha L. Maznevski, and Mark E. Mendenhall. 2004. "Globalization: Hercules Meets Buddha." In *The Blackwell Handbook of Global Management a Guide to Managing Complexity*, edited by Henry W. Lane, Martha L. Maznevski, Mark E. Mendenhall, and Jeanne McNett, 3–25. Oxford, UK: Blackwell.

Leung, Kwok, Rabi S. Bhagat, Nancy R. Buchan, Miriam Erez, and Christina B. Gibson. 2005. "Culture and International Business: Recent Advances and Their Implications for Future Research." *Journal of International Business Studies* 36 (4):357–378. doi: 10.1057/palgrave.jibs.8400150.

Linders, Gert-Jan, Arjen Slangen, Henri L.F. De Groot, and Sjoerd Beugelsdijk. 2005. "Cultural and Institutional Determinants of Bilateral Trade Flows." Tinbergen Institute Discussion Paper 05-074/3, July 2005. http://ssrn.com/abstract=775504.

Mathews, Brian P., Akiko Ueno, Tauno Kekäle, Mikko Repka, Zulema Lopes Pereira, and Graça Silva. 2001. "European Quality Management Practices: The Impact of National Culture." *International Journal of Quality & Reliability Management* 18 (7):692–707. doi: 10.1108/EUM0000000005776.

Mayer, Thierry, and Soledad Zignago. 2011. "Geodist Dataset." CEPII, Last Modified December 12, 2011. www.cepii.fr/CEPII/fr/bdd_modele/download.asp?id=6.

McSweeney, Brendan. 2002. "Hofstede's Model of National Cultural Differences and Their Consequences: A Triumph of Faith – a Failure of Analysis." *Human Relations* 55 (1):89–118. doi: 10.1177/0018726702551004.

Melitz, Jacques, and Farid Toubal. 2014. "Native Language, Spoken Language, Translation and Trade." *Journal of International Economics* 93 (2):351–363. doi: 10.1016/j.jinteco.2014.04.004.

Morris, Michael W., Katherine Y. Williams, Kwok Leung, Richard Larrick, M. Teresa Mendoza, Deepti Bhatnagar, Jianfeng Li, Mari Kondo, Jin-Lian Luo, and Jun-Chen Hu. 1998. "Conflict Management Style: Accounting for Cross-National Differences." *Journal of International Business Studies* 29 (4):729–747. doi: 10.1057/palgrave.jibs.8490050.

Neeley, Tsedal B. 2013. "Language Matters: Status Loss and Achieved Status Distinctions in Global Organizations." *Organization Science* 24 (2):476–497. doi: 10.1287/orsc.1120.0739.

Newman, Karen L., and Stanley D. Nollen. 1996. "Culture and Congruence: The Fit between Management Practices and National Culture." *Journal of International Business Studies* 27 (4):753–779. doi: 10.1057/palgrave.jibs.8490152.

Nisbett, Richard E. 2003. *The Geography of Thought: How Asians and Westerners Think Differently – and Why.* New York: Free Press.

Osland, Joyce S. 2013. "Leading Global Change." In *Global Leadership: Research, Practice, and Development*, edited by Mark E. Mendenhall, Joyce S. Osland, Allan

Bird, Gary R. Oddou, Martha L. Maznevski, Michael Stevens, and Günther K. Stahl, 183–214. 2nd edn. New York: Routledge.

Osland, Joyce S., and Allan Bird. 2000. "Beyond Sophisticated Stereotyping: Cultural Sensemaking in Context." *Academy of Management Executive* 14 (1):65–77. doi: 10.5465/AME.2000.2909840.

Piekkari, Rebecca, and D. Eleanor Westney. forthcoming. "Language as Meeting Ground for Research on the MNC and Organization Theory." In *Multinational Corporations and Organization Theory*, edited by Christoph Dörrenbächer, and Mike Geppert.

PwC. 2012. "Talent Mobility 2020: The Next Generation of International Assignments." PricewaterhouseCoopers. www.pwc.com/gx/en/issues/talent/future-of-work/global-mobility-map.html.

Ratiu, Indrei. 1983. "Thinking Internationally." *International Studies of Management & Organization* 13 (1/2):139–50.

Rauch, James E. 2001. "Business and Social Networks in International Trade." *Journal of Economic Literature* : 1177–1203.

Reiche, B. Sebastian, Anne-Wil Harzing, and Markus Pudelko. 2015. "Why and How Does Shared Language Affect Subsidiary Knowledge Inflows? A Social Identity Perspective." *Journal of International Business Studies* 46 (5):528–551. doi: 10.1057/jibs.2015.3.

Reiche, B. Sebastian, Allan Bird, Mark E. Mendenhall, and Joyce Osland. 2015. "The Conceptual Basis for a Global Leadership Typology." *Academy of Management Proceedings* 2015 (1):10907 (Meeting Abstract Supplement).

Reiche, B. Sebastian, Pablo Cardona, Yih-Teen Lee, Miguel Ángel Canela, Esther Akinnukawe, Jon P. Briscoe, et al. 2014. "Why Do Managers Engage in Trustworthy Behavior? A Multilevel Cross-Cultural Study in 18 Countries." *Personnel Psychology* 67 (1):61–98. do\i: 10.1111/peps.12038.

Reiche, B. Sebastian, Anne-Wil Harzing, and Maria L. Kraimer. 2008. "The Role of International Assignees' Social Capital in Creating Inter-Unit Intellectual Capital: A Cross-Level Model." *Journal of International Business Studies* 40 (3):509–526. doi: 10.1057/jibs.2008.86.

Reiche, B. Sebastian, Yih-teen Lee, and Javier Quintanilla. 2014. "Cross-Cultural Training and Support Practices of International Assignees." In *The Routledge Companion to International Human Resource Management*, edited by David G. Collings, Geoffrey T. Wood, and Paula M. Caligiuri, 308–323. London: Routledge.

Robinson, B. A. 2011. "Religions of the World: Numbers of Adherents of Major Religions, Their Geographical Distribution, Date Founded, and Sacred Texts." Last Modified, September 28, 2011. www.religioustolerance.org/worldrel.htm.

Ronen, Simcha, and Oded Shenkar. 2013. "Mapping World Cultures: Cluster Formation, Sources and Implications." *Journal of International Business Studies* 44 (9):867–897. doi: 10.1057/jibs.2013.42.

Santa Fe Group. 2014. "Global Mobility Survey." www.globalmobilitysurvey.com.

Sapir, Edward. 1921. *Language: An Introduction to the Study of Speech.* New York: Harcourt, Brace, and Company.

Schwartz, Shalom H. 2014. "National Culture as Value Orientations: Consequences of Value Differences and Cultural Distance." In *Handbook of the Economics of Art and Culture*, edited by Victor A. Ginsburgh and David Throsby, 547–586. Oxford: Elsevier; North-Holland.

Shaffer, Margaret A., Maria L. Kraimer, Yu-Ping Chen, and Mark C. Bolino. 2012. "Choices, Challenges, and Career Consequences of Global Work Experiences: A Review and Future Agenda." *Journal of Management* 38 (4):1282–1327. doi: 10.1177/0149206312441834.

Shenkar, Oded. 2001. "Cultural Distance Revisited: Towards a More Rigorous Conceptualization and Measurement of Cultural Differences." *Journal of International Business Studies* 32 (3):519–535. doi: 10.2307/3069495.

Spolaore, Enrico, and Romain Wacziarg. 2009. "The Diffusion of Development." *The Quarterly Journal of Economics* 124 (2):469–529. doi: 10.1162/qjec.2009.124.2.469.

Steers, Richard M., Luciara Nardon, and Carlos Sánchez-Runde. 2013. *Management across Cultures: Developing Global Competencies.* 2nd edn. Cambridge; New York: Cambridge University Press.

Tharenou, Phyllis, and Natasha Caulfield. 2010. "Will I Stay or Will I Go? Explaining Repatriation by Self-Initiated Expatriates." *Academy of Management Journal* 53 (5):1009–1028. doi: 10.5465/AMJ.2010.54533183.

Toh, Soo Min, and Angelo S. DeNisi. 2007. "Host Country Nationals as Socializing Agents: A Social Identity Approach." *Journal of Organizational Behavior* 28 (3):281–301. doi: 10.1002/job.421.

Trompenaars, Alfons, and Charles Hampden-Turner. 1998. *Riding the Waves of Culture: Understanding Cultural Diversity in Global Business.* 2nd edn. New York: McGraw Hill.

West, Joel, and John L. Graham. 2004. "A Linguistic-Based Measure of Cultural Distance and Its Relationship to Managerial Values." *MIR: Management International Review* 44 (3):239–260. doi: 10.2307/40835991.

Whorf, Benjamin Lee. 1940. "Science and Linguistics." *Technology Review* 42 (6):229–248.

Zaheer, Srilata, Margaret Spring Schomaker, and Lilach Nachum. 2012. "Distance without Direction: Restoring Credibility to a Much-Loved Construct." *Journal of International Business Studies* 43 (1):18–27. doi: 10.1057/jibs.2011.43.

9   Administrative Distance and Institutional Variety

Pankaj Ghemawat and Thomas M. Hout

Administrative (or institutional) differences can seem more abstruse than cultural differences. Since both of us teach on multiple continents, we sometimes highlight administrative distance by asking students from one location, say New York, about what might be different about setting up a business in another, say Abu Dhabi. While the students in New York do point out some of the differences between Abu Dhabi – or the United Arab Emirates (UAE), of which it forms part – and the United States, (e.g., oil wealth, zero taxes, heavy reliance on foreign labor, etc.), they usually miss out on many other relevant elements, especially administrative ones, as the students in Abu Dhabi are quick to note.

To highlight just some of the relevant administrative differences, noncitizens can own businesses outright only in free zones: majority local ownership is required "onshore" to afford Emiratis, especially well-connected ones, some of the rents from ownership. Emirati workers generally enjoy protected employment status. The broader legal system is a mix of continental civil law and Sharia law and given the former, requires businesses to be licensed, and to apply for renewal of that license every year. Bureaucratic approvals are slow, opaque, and subject to a lack of clear separation between governmental and personal interests. Fees payable to obtain approvals are often high and can be seen as akin to taxation. Local equity markets are not very vibrant and financing from financial institutions is often hard to obtain (a consequence of there being no security law allowing assets to be pledged), so firms, even large ones, often resort to using postdated checks as security. Prison looms in store in the event of inability to pay them off: debtors of various stripes are estimated to account for 70 percent of Abu Dhabi's prisoners, and imprisonment does not discharge debts. Unsurprisingly, these arrangements seem to influence cultural attitudes as well, for example, a strong aversion to business failure.

While some in the United States might simply conclude that Abu Dhabi is idiosyncratic, it is worth pointing out that administratively, the United States is perhaps even more unusual. Thus, in terms of ownership structure, the widely

The authors wish to thank Steven A. Altman for his assistance with analyzing and writing up the first section of this chapter.

held large corporation controlled by professional managers is most common (among large economies) in the United States and the UK. Elsewhere, more concentrated ownership, group interlocks, and owner involvement in management tend to be more frequent. US tax rates on corporate income are the highest among OECD members, which is why US corporations hold perhaps two trillion dollars of cash overseas instead of repatriating it. And in terms of labor relations, the United States is the only developed country with employment at will; other developed countries, in contrast, require cause for termination of workers or notice or both. Such US exceptionalism adds to the importance of broadening awareness of the variety of administrative arrangements around the world more than if the United States really were some kind of "base case" – which is how it is treated in much of the discourse about business.

It is time to be more precise about what we mean by administrative/institutional variation. Douglass North, who won the Nobel Prize in economics for his work on institutions, defines them as "the rules of the game in a society or, more formally ... the humanly devised constraints that shape human interaction" (North 1990, 3). North also emphasizes that they "consist of both informal constraints (sanctions, taboos, customs, traditions, and codes of conduct), and formal rules (constitutions, laws, property rights)" (1991, 97). Note the large degree of overlap between such informal constraints and the cultural considerations covered in the previous chapter. We try to avoid going over ground that has already been covered – we do not, for instance, reclassify language as an institution, as some institutionalists suggest – but will return to the linkages between cultural and administrative differences in the final section of this chapter.

It is also worth noting that this chapter focuses on country-level institutions. While supranational institutions clearly matter for business behavior (e.g., the discussion of accounting in Chapter 4), their impact seems, in keeping with the law of semiglobalization, to be limited. One crude indicator: the total employees of international organizations (including the United Nations, European Union, World Bank, etc.) add up to less than 0.1 percent of the total number of people employed by governments around the world (even after excluding employees of state-owned enterprises).[1] And even in the European Union, where more supranational governance has been attempted than anywhere else, the EU budget is about 1 percent of member countries' combined GDP, as compared to average government budgets across EU countries of 49 percent of their GDPs (European Commission 2015).

The first section of this chapter relates the administrative dimension of the CAGE distance framework to the large literature on institutions and undertakes additional regressions to plumb which of the many variables cited in this literature might be most worth adding to the ones included in the standard gravity model in Chapter 5. This exercise ends up focusing attention on the ownership of business firms and their relationships with the suppliers of the two key factors of production: capital and labor.

These topics are discussed in more detail in the sections that follow in order to provide a deeper sense of administrative/institutional variation than can be gleaned from gravity regressions that group all unilateral country-specific influences into one fixed effect per country. The second and third sections of this chapter examine, respectively, differences in who owns large businesses and the outlook for different modes of ownership. The two sections that follow look, respectively, at businesses' relationships with external suppliers of capital, and at how labor laws shape their relationships with labor. The final substantive section explores the links among ownership, external finance, and labor regulations as well as some of the cultural differences discussed in Chapter 8.

Administrative Distance, Institutions, and International Interactions

There is more than one stream of research within international business that examines institutional variation across countries and its implications for multinational firms (Bae and Salomon 2010; Hotho and Pedersen 2012). Thus, Kostova (1997, 1999) draws upon the work of sociologist W. Richard Scott and proposes measuring institutional distance based on regulative, cognitive, and normative pillars (Scott 1995). And Henisz and Williamson (1999) extend single-country work on transaction cost economics and the hazards faced by firms to incorporate institutional differences and firm multinationality.

The contrast between these two research streams suggests, among other things, the usefulness of distinguishing between "horizontal institutional distance," which refers to a situation in which countries differ but cannot be ranked as better or worse, and "vertical institutional distance," which implies that they *can* be ranked.[2] The next two subsections incorporate, in turn, horizontal and vertical institutional distance measures associated with these two streams into the standard gravity model from Chapter 5.

A third subsection draws on yet another stream of research, on comparative capitalism, that has received less attention in international business. This approach, associated with work such as Richard Whitley's *Business Systems* and Hall and Soskice's *Varieties of Capitalism*, examines the path-dependent development of interrelated systems of economic coordination and how business practices vary with them. The distances analyzed under this rubric may also be thought of as horizontal, since there is no single business system or variety of capitalism that is generally agreed to outperform all others. However, we treat this research stream separately from the others due to its distinct theoretical underpinnings and the different measurement issues that it raises.

Horizontal Institutional Distance

The gravity modeling in Chapter 5 covered two kinds of administrative variables that are commonly used in international economics: (1) a binary variable indicating whether or not one country in a pair ever colonized the other and (2) a binary variable indicating whether or not two countries are members of the same regional bloc or otherwise linked by a free trade agreement. In this subsection, we add in horizontal institutional distance variables corresponding to Scott's regulative, normative, and cognitive pillars. For each pillar, we tested several variables cited in the literature. We summarize the results with the additional variables that performed the best.[3]

For the regulative pillar, we use a binary variable that takes the value 1 when two countries share a common legal origin, based on data from La Porta, Lopez-de-Silanes, and Shleifer (1999).[4] For normative distance, we use the metric reported in Xu, Pan, and Beamish (2004), which was constructed based on variables covering product design, customer orientation, staff training, willingness to delegate, performance-related pay, professional managers, and effectiveness of corporate boards from the World Economic Forum's *Global Competitiveness Report*.[5] Finally, we construct a measure of cognitive distance based on indicators drawn from IMD's *World Competitiveness Yearbook* that seem to us to correspond most closely to Kostova's (2009) discussion of cognitive distance.[6]

It is important to recognize the significant overlap between the normative and cognitive pillars and the cultural indicators discussed in Chapter 8, particularly Kogut and Singh's (1988) cultural distance index and the underlying Hofstede (1980) dimensions of national culture, which, as Kostova (2009) notes, have been used as measures for both of these pillars. This also points to the ambiguous boundary between cognitive and normative. Gaur and Lu (2007) actually combine these pillars, aligning the regulative pillar with North's formal institutions and the combined normative and cognitive pillar with North's informal institutions.

The results of rerunning the standard gravity model with these additional variables are summarized in Table 9.1.[7] The "unrestricted baseline" repeats the results from Chapter 5, and the "restricted baseline" is based on rerunning the same model as in Chapter 5 on the restricted sample of countries for which all of the horizontal institutional distance variables are available. This time, the average number of observations is reduced from 22,763 to 8,610.

The most striking result from Table 9.1 is that the measure we select for the regulative pillar, common legal origin, is significant with the expected positive sign across all eleven types of interactions. This is particularly noteworthy because these models already incorporate the colonial linkages that

Table 9.1 *Summary Comparison of Gravity Models across Horizontal Institutional Distance Variables*

	Number of significant focal coefficients and signs					Average number of observations	Average adjusted R-squared
	Colony/ colonizer	Regional bloc/trade agreement	Regulative: common legal origin	Normative distance	Cognitive distance		
Unrestricted baseline	10+	4+, 2–				22,763	0.795
Restricted baseline	8+	4+, 1–				8,610	0.829
1. Common legal origin	8+	4+, 1–	11+			8,610	0.832
2. Normative distance	8+	3+, 1–		5–		8,610	0.830
3. Cognitive distance	9+	4+, 1–			7–	8,610	0.829
4. Common legal origin + Normative distance + Cognitive distance	8+	4+, 1–	11+	4–	3–	8,610	0.832

appear to underlie many legal commonalities, and indeed common legal origin achieves significance for more flows, though when it is significant, colonial linkage always has a larger coefficient. Normative distance is significant for only five of the eleven interactions, but those five include the three that are most closely associated with firms' cross-border activities: merchandise trade, services trade, and FDI stocks (as well as patent applications and trade in printed publications). Cognitive distance achieves significance for seven flows (services trade, portfolio equity stocks, portfolio long-term debt, tertiary students, emigration, phone calls, and patent applications) but when regulative and normative measures are also included, it retains its significance only for three (services trade, FDI stocks, and emigration).

It is also worth noting that the signs we obtain on the significant horizontal institutional distance variables are all consistent with the law of distance. Common legal origin (an indicator of similarity rather than difference) always enters with a positive sign while normative and cognitive distance (indicators of difference), when significant, always enter with negative signs. These results favor the selective incorporation of measures of horizontal institutional distance into gravity models.

Vertical Institutional Distance

Table 9.2 adds three measures of vertical institutional distance to the standard gravity model. The first additional variable is the political constraints index (POLCON), which captures "the number of independent veto points over policy outcomes and the distribution of preferences of the actors that inhabit them" (Henisz 2000, 5).[8] The logic behind this is that political systems with power distributed across multiple actors with potentially different policy preferences will likely provide greater policy stability for firms and investors. The second additional variable is an index[9] based on six variables from the Worldwide Governance Indicators (WGI) database (Kaufman, Kraay, and Mastruzzi 2007): voice and accountability, political stability, government effectiveness, regulatory quality, rule of law, and control of corruption. As Bae and Salomon (2010) explain: "beyond the stability of governments, governmental policies and the effectiveness of checks and balances, the Kaufman et al. (2007) metric captures the extent to which the government and the country's citizens respect extant legal and political institutions" (331). Third, we look at the control of corruption indicator from Kaufman et al. (2007)[10] by itself because of the intense interest in the impact of this variable on firms and economies.[11]

The results we report in Table 9.2 using these measures of vertical institutional distance are generally weaker than the results in Table 9.1 based on horizontal institutional distance. None of the variables added in Table 9.2 achieve significance with the expected negative sign for more than half of the flows

Table 9.2 Summary Comparison of Gravity Models across Vertical Institutional Distance Variables

			Number of significant focal coefficients and signs			Average number of observations	Average adjusted R-squared
	Colony / colonizer	Regional bloc / trade agreement	POLCON	WGI (6 variables)	WGI (corruption only)		
Restricted Baseline	10+	4+, 2–				18,840	0.801
1. POLCON	10+	4+, 2–	4+, 2–			18,840	0.801
2. WGI (6 variables)	10+	4+, 2–		4+, 3–		18,840	0.801
3. WGI (corruption only)	10+	5+, 2–			2+, 5–	18,840	0.801
4. POLCON + WGI (6 variables)	10+	4+, 2–	5+, 2–	3+, 3–		18,840	0.801

analyzed, and both POLCON and the 6-variable WGI index achieve more positive than negative significant coefficients.

One plausible inference from these results is that the differences analyzed here dampen a narrower set of international interactions than the ones tested in the previous subsection. It is unsurprising that flows vary in their sensitivity to particular types of distance. For example, there are strong reasons to expect the policy stability on which POLCON focuses to matter for FDI, and indeed, there is a strong negative relationship (significant at the 0.05 level). A firm with a stable regulatory environment at home is likely to be particularly unwilling to invest in a volatile host country. However, it is harder to conceive of how POLCON would affect international telephone calls (a flow for which it was significant with a positive sign).

In addition, the weaker performance of the vertical institutional distance variables tested here relates to one of the critiques of distance-based research discussed in Chapter 7. Zaheer, Schomaker, and Nachum (2012, 22–23) caution against the use of distance measures when the "cultural or institutional attribute makes the focal process easier, while its converse renders the process more difficult." Vertical institutional distance measures have this characteristic, since higher institutional quality generally reduces transaction costs, uncertainty, and so on. There are, however, known counterexamples, such as Cuervo-Cazurra and Genc's finding that "having a home country with poor institutions…can become a relative advantage when the firm moves into other countries with even more difficult governance conditions" (2008, 976). Consistent with their research, differences in the control of corruption have a significant negative effect on FDI in our model.

Comparative Capitalism

The Comparative Capitalism literature on interrelated systems of economic coordination has tended to emphasize rich qualitative work rather than quantitative measurement. For example, Jackson and Deeg (2008) contrast the typically "thin" operationalization of institutional analysis in international business based on unidimensional variables with the "thick" description and case studies in Comparative Capitalism. Thus, Whitley (1999) identifies six *business systems*[12] and relates them to four key institutions: state, financial system, skill development and control system, and trust and authority relations. And work by Hall and Soskice (2001) on *varieties of capitalism* groups advanced economies into two broader categories – Liberal Market Economies (e.g., the United States) and Coordinated Market Economies (e.g., Germany) – and elaborates them in terms of "five spheres in which firms must develop relationships to resolve coordination problems central to their core competencies" (6–7). These are industrial relations (often involving bargaining with unions), vocational training and education, corporate governance, relationships with other firms (addressing interactions with suppliers, customers, competitors), and relationships with employees (agency issues).

The multidimensionality of these constructs implies that simple unidimensional indicators will not fully capture the richness of how business works in particular economies. However, both the *business systems* and the *varieties of capitalism* literatures do emphasize the ownership and governance of business firms and their relationships with suppliers of capital and labor.[13] The rest of this section adds measures related to these three aspects of economic systems to the standard gravity model to analyze quantitatively their influence on international flows, and the sections that follow provide a richer, qualitative treatment of each of the three.

The first additional distance variable is derived from the proportion of the ten largest domestic conglomerates in a country that are under family control, based on the employee-weighted measure that Fogel reports (2006). The second variable, which relates to both capital markets and ownership, captures variation in the market capitalization of listed companies as a percentage of a country's GDP (obtained from the World Bank's World Development Indicators). Finally, as an indicator of differences in labor market regulation, we use the Heritage Foundation's *Labor Freedom Index*, which measures (the absence of) regulations concerning minimum wages, laws inhibiting layoffs, severance requirements, and measurable regulatory restraints on hiring and hours worked.[14] Since family ownership data are available for only forty countries, we compute separate (restricted) baselines in order to allow for the analysis of the other two new variables to be reported using a substantially larger sample of country pairs. Table 9.3 summarizes the results of adding these variables to the standard gravity model.[15]

The new variables related to Comparative Capitalism generally perform better than those based on vertical institutional distance but not those based on horizontal institutional distance (or at least not as well as common legal origins). Stock market capitalization as a percentage of GDP performs best when added by itself, achieving significance with the expected negative sign for seven out of eleven flows, including all of the capital and information flows that we analyze, as well as services trade (but none of the three people flows). Labor freedom, when added alone, is significant with a negative sign for five out of eleven flows (merchandise trade, FDI stocks, portfolio equity, tertiary students, and patent applications). Family ownership, for which the number of observations is more limited, is significant with a negative sign when added alone only for printed publications exports, and significant with a positive sign for three (services trade, portfolio equity, and portfolio long-term debt). When all three of the new variables are added into the model together, stock market capitalization as a percentage of GDP continues to perform best (5 negative

Table 9.3 *Summary Comparison of Gravity Models across Institutional Distance Variables based on Comparative Institutionalism*

	Number of significant focal coefficients and signs					Average number of observations	Average adjusted R-squared
	Colony/ colonizer	Regional bloc/trade agreement	Family ownership	Mkt cap % of GDP	Labor freedom		
Restricted baseline (for family ownership)	10+	5+				7,349	0.822
1. Family ownership	11+	5+	3+, 1–			7,349	0.822
Restricted baseline (for other variables)	8+	5+				16,920	0.807
2. Stock market capitalization % of GDP	8+	5+		7–		16,920	0.808
3. Labor freedom	8+	5+			5–	16,920	0.807
4. Family ownership + Stock market capitalization % of GDP + Labor freedom	11+	4+	3+	5–	3–	7,286	0.825

and significant coefficients) followed by labor freedom (3 negative and significant coefficients), while family ownership returns 3 positive and significant
coefficients.

To put these results into perspective, recall that the Comparative
Capitalism literature stresses that the "rules of the game" vary across countries in ways that go well beyond such simple indicators. Since the simple
indicators nonetheless manage to achieve significance about one-half of
the time, that bolsters the case for a richer, qualitative examination of how
ownership and relationships with (other) suppliers of capital and with labor
vary around the world, and some of the implications of those patterns for
multinationals.

Ownership around the World

The widely held corporation, while widely studied in business schools around
the world, is not as common outside the classroom, even among large businesses. In many countries, large businesses[16] form part of larger, interconnected
sets of companies principally owned and controlled by a family or business
group or state. Table 9.4 identifies the owners of the twenty largest publicly
traded corporations (as measured by market capitalization) in each of twenty-
seven major economies with relatively well-developed public equity markets
(La Porta, Lopez-de-Silanes, and Shleifer 1999). Although there are problems
with the data presented – limited coverage of countries (including only two
emerging ones), sensitivity of the classifications to the cut-off points used, and
overlap across the categories of concentrated ownership – they do provide a
baseline for further analysis. La Porta et al. calculate that of the firms in their
sample, 30 percent are controlled by a family, 18 percent by the state, and
15 percent by another firm: a business group or a financial institution of some
kind (1999). The remaining 36 percent are the ones that they classify as widely
held. Looking at somewhat broader samples of large firms significantly boosts
the share of family-owned firms (Economist "To Have" 2015). And among
mid-sized firms, even in the United States, 85 percent are private, with roughly
equivalent numbers owned by families, by private equity firms, and by other
structures such as partnerships.[17] Furthermore, looking at a broader sample of
countries indicates that major corporations can also be controlled by political
parties, religious entities, and military organizations.

Vignettes from around the world will help illustrate the variation underlying these summary statistics as well as some of its implications. To begin with
advanced economies, Sweden presents an extreme example of dominance
by a few "spheres" of companies, most notably the one associated with the
Wallenberg family, which has been estimated to encompass companies that
account for up to one-half of total Swedish stock market capitalization (Morck

Table 9.4 *Who owns the 20 largest firms by market capitalization in 27 major economies, 1995*

Country	Widely Held	Family	State	Firms	Miscellaneous
Argentina	0%	65%	15%	20%	0%
Austria	5	15	70	0	10
Australia	65	5	5	25	0
Belgium	5	50	5	30	10
Canada	60	25	0	15	0
Denmark	40	35	15	0	10
Finland	35	10	35	10	10
France	60	20	15	5	0
Germany	50	10	25	15	0
Greece	10	50	30	10	0
Hong Kong	10	70	5	5	10
Ireland	65	10	0	10	15
Israel	5	50	40	5	0
Italy	20	15	40	15	10
Japan	90	5	5	0	0
South Korea	55	20	15	5	5
Mexico	0	100	0	0	0
Netherlands	30	20	5	10	35
New Zealand	30	25	25	20	0
Norway	25	25	35	5	10
Portugal	10	45	25	15	5
Singapore	15	30	45	10	0
Spain	35	15	30	20	0
Sweden	25	45	10	15	5
Switzerland	60	30	0	5	5
UK	100	0	0	0	0
United States	80	20	0	0	0
Sample Average	36	30	18	10	5

Note: Criteria for control is 20% or more ownership directly or indirectly.

Source: Republished with permission of Blackwell Publishing, Inc., from "Corporate Ownership around the World," Rafael La Porta, Florencio Lopez-de-Silanes, and Andrei Shleifer, volume 54, no. 2, Table II (selected columns), pg. 492 (April 1999).

2010). The lines of control mostly pass through Investor, an industrial holding firm, although the family interests also include another holding company that consolidates its stakes in unlisted companies and a private equity fund. Wallenberg family foundations own 23 percent of Investor's equity capital but 50 percent of the voting rights (Milne 2015). Investor, in turn, holds voting rights that substantially exceed its ownership share in a number of its core investments (e.g., 21.5 percent of the votes versus 5.3 percent of the capital in the case of Ericsson). This divergence reflects dual classes of shares: the Ericsson A shares held by Investor have 10 times the voting rights of the B

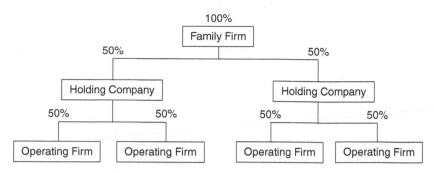

Figure 9.1 Schematic of Pyramid Ownership

Pyramid works as follows:

- Family firm owns 50 percent or less, i.e., just as much as necessary to control the holding companies underneath it. Presence of other friendly shareholders (other families, banks, etc.) permit family to lower stake and still control.
- Holding companies own 50 percent or less of first tier operating companies, again depending on presence of other friendly shareholders. Thus is this example, family owns 25 percent of each of 4 operating companies. Consequently, the assets it controls (i.e., all four companies) are 4 times its total cash flow interest.
- The more tiers to the pyramid and the lower ownership percentage required to retain control, the larger this control-to-cash flow interest becomes.

Source: Based on Section 3.2 The Use of Control Pyramids from Morck et al. (2005, 661–666).

shares (although this is down from 1,000 times in 2004) (Economist 2006). The Wallenbergs effectively control Ericsson even though they own only 1.2 percent of its cash flow rights.

This is a classic example of a pyramid structure, in which an apex firm holds a controlling interest in one or more companies, which in turn hold controlling interests in companies one tier down, and so on. The greater the number of tiers, the lower the percentage of capital the owners of the apex firm have to contribute to maintain control of the bottom tier corporations. The controlling owners can further conserve capital by owning less than a majority of total shares but giving their own shares disproportionately high voting rights or by issuing nonvoting shares to outside shareholders. Figure 9.1 provides a schematic depiction.

South Korea is another example of an advanced economy dominated by family-based business groups, known as the *chaebol*. The Asian financial crisis at the end of the 1990s led to the collapse of eleven of the thirty largest chaebol because they were overly diversified and leveraged, but others have survived and even thrived. Thus, in 2014, Samsung had revenues equivalent to 20 percent of Korean GDP, with the four next largest – Hyundai, SK, LG, and Lotte – accounting for another 35 percent (Lee 2015 [based on data from Korea Fair Trade Commission]). To focus on Samsung, although it has taken significant interest in the longevity of the Wallenbergs' governance model, which is approaching its fifth generational transition, replicating it is infeasible because Korean law does not allow for dual classes of shares (Kim 2014). As a result, Samsung – like the other chaebol – is built around reciprocal cross-holdings among group member companies: a system that has been characterized as "circular" shareholdings (Kim 2014, 1). These arrangements allow, for example, the Lee family, which founded Samsung and remains directly involved in its management, to control it despite a combined ownership stake estimated to be less than 2 percent (Lee 2015).

Next door, Japan has a hybrid system that features both strong group roots and modern standalone influences. Japan's famous industrial giants like Toyota and Matsushita are widely held companies with group characteristics including cross-holdings of suppliers, distributors, and so on.[18] Japan's traditional *keiretsu* – Mitsubishi, Mitsui, and Sumitomo – are cross-held groups, the more decentralized residuals of Japan's pre-World War II *zaibatsu*, which were more like chaebols – that is, family-centered and family-managed. Their once-powerful main banks are now less dominant. In addition, Japan's mid-size globally dominant but lesser known component companies – Shin-etsu (semiconductor materials), Mabuchi (small electric motors), Murata (electronic components), and so on – are often single-business standalone companies.

In Germany, the ties between financial institutions and industrial companies, strengthened by the Nazi decree that transferred small shareholders' voting rights to their depository banks, seem to have remained stronger: one authority characterizes much of big business as "large diffuse business groups loosely controlled by major banks voting small investors' shares" (Morck 2010, 620). Daimler Benz illustrates both traditional patterns in German big business and how globalization has recently influenced them. Deutsche Bank had long been its controlling shareholder but after the disastrous merger with Chrysler and listing in the United States, a perception that such holdings by financial institutions were viewed unfavorably by US investors and pressures due to Deutsche Bank's involvement in diversification decisions at Daimler have led to that stake being unwound (Clarke 2007, 392). However, the former chairman of the supervisory board of Deutsche Bank, Clemens Börsig, still sits on the supervisory board of Daimler AG.

Belgium (and France) present even more complexity, with families and groups interlocked through reciprocal shareholdings and voting pacts. For example, Groupe Bruxelles Lambert is a listed holding company, one of Belgium's ten largest, and is controlled by two families – the Frères of Belgium and the Desmarais of Canada. The Group's holdings include a number of French companies such as GDF Suez, an energy-holding company itself and one-third owned by the French government, and LaFarge, one of the world's largest cement companies. As a result, ownership of French and Belgian industry is highly interlocked through this cross-national variant of family capitalism.

Shareholder capitalism in the United States (and the UK) seems far removed from these vignettes of family, group, or state control. The state owns only a few troubled companies and discourages group formation with its tax on inter-company dividends (introduced by Franklin Roosevelt in the 1930s). But a closer look at the US corporate sector does suggest significant departures even there from the stereotype of diffuse ownership. Family businesses account for about 33 percent of US companies that have achieved at least $1 billion in sales, versus 40 percent in France and Germany (BCG data as reported in Economist "To Have" 2015). Private equity firms also embody concentrated, if time-bound, ownership. Private equity activity fluctuates greatly, in line with broader market movements, but Collis, Anand, and Cheng (forthcoming) estimate that private equity firms have accounted, on average, for about 7 percent of US nonfinancial corporate assets since 2000. And dual classes of shares enable the concentration of control without (proportionate) owner-ship: Larry Page and Sergey Brin use them to bolster their control of Google, and many other tech companies have followed suit – including Alibaba, which listed in the United States rather than Hong Kong for that purpose. So the United States also features a fair amount of concentrated as opposed to diffuse ownership.

Turning to emerging economies, comparatively fewer large businesses are widely held, and family, group, and state ownership are more in evidence. Thus, in India, two families, the Tata-Pallonjis and the Ambanis, control close to one-half of the assets of private big business (Sarkar 2010).[19] The largest, the Tata Group, has recently gone through its fifth generational transition. Its apex company is the investment holding company, Tata Sons, controlled by the Tata family foundations. Tata Sons holds direct and indirect stakes in more than a hundred operating companies, which also have significant cross-holdings in each other. Ratan Tata's recent stint as chairman (1991–2012) was a period of strengthening rather than weakening intragroup ties: (cross-)ownership stakes that had dwindled away were rebuilt, operating companies were required to start paying a royalty to the group for the use of the Tata name, and the group attempted to improve management practices across the operating companies with initiatives such as the Tata Business Excellence Model.

That said, state-owned companies are much more evident in Indian big business than in the advanced countries discussed earlier. State-owned com-panies accounted for only 4 percent of advanced economy companies on the Fortune Global 500. In contrast, of the eight Indian companies in the Fortune

Global 500 in 2014, five – Indian Oil, State Bank of India, Bharat Petroleum, Hindustan Petroleum, and Oil and Natural Gas Corporation – are state-owned. Despite some moves at partial privatization and restructuring, especially in the 2000s, large-scale sell-offs do not seem imminent. And state-ownership of much of the financial sector remains intact.

China provides an even more extreme example of state dominance. Of the 92 mainland Chinese firms on the 2014 Fortune Global 500, 76 were state-owned, and state-owned firms also accounted for 78 percent of the revenues generated by China's top 500 business groups, down from 89 percent in 2000 (Lee and Kang 2010). Despite their relative decline, state-owned enterprises (SOEs) still dominate sectors like energy, natural resources, banking, telecommunications, and transportation and are still regarded as enjoying favored status in the eyes of the Chinese state. China's private sector companies have, however, been more dynamic, growing twice as fast between 2008 and 2014 and accounting for almost all new urban jobs created (Economist "China That Works" 2015). Some private firms have started to form pyramidal group structures (Fan, Wong, and Zhang 2006, 7–8). But even or especially for the very largest such firms, accommodations with state interest seem to be essential. Thus, Wang Jianlin, the property tycoon who founded the Wanda Group and is ranked as China's richest man, serves on the standing committee of the Chinese People's Political Consultative Congress, and counts relatives of some of China's most powerful politicians and their associates as significant shareholders in his company. In a country where access to long-term property rights must be secured from the state, which owns all the land, his self-described ability to do so for half the cost of his competitors would seem to be key (Forsythe 2015).

Other emerging economies exhibit somewhat similar patterns of highly concentrated ownership. The state-owned proportion, while variable, is generally high: in 2014, 59 percent of Fortune Global 500 companies from emerging economies other than China and India were state-owned. In terms of private ownership, pyramidal business groups, usually controlled by families, tend to be a staple. Southeast Asia has the highest share of large companies that are family owned compared to other regions of the world. Of the $1 billion-plus businesses in Southeast Asia, 80–90 percent of them are family-run (Björnberg, Elstrodt, and Pandit 2014). Networks of "overseas Chinese" are prominent as well. Diversified family-based groups also dominate many other emerging economies. The *grupos* of Latin America are typical examples: families control more than half of the twenty largest companies in countries as large as Mexico and Argentina, as well as fifteen of the twenty-four largest private domestic business groups in Brazil (Aldrighi and Postali 2010). Families also control 60–70 percent of large companies in Eastern Europe and the Middle East, as well as 30–40 percent in Africa (Björnberg et al. 2014).

Ownership Outlook

The previous section indicated that concentrated ownership – by a variety of owners – is the norm around the world, although widely held firms are also prevalent in some countries, most notably the United States and the UK. Are these patterns likely to persist, or is convergence to be expected? The answer to this question in economics and business have been heavily influenced by Berle and Means's (1932) landmark book on the emergence of a then-new form of ownership and control that separated the two: the widely held firm owned by dispersed shareholders but controlled by professional managers. There has since been a tendency, especially in the United States, to treat such firms as *the* modern corporate form, and other forms as inherently less efficient. On that basis, the widely held model might be expected, given the survivor principle, to become more widespread over time.

But a cross-country look at the evidence raises doubts about broad convergence: it suggests, instead, that neither family nor state ownership seems likely to fade away. To start with family-owned firms, it is far from obvious *a priori* that they should be expected to underperform. While they face distinctive issues, particularly around succession and the role of the family in management and governance, they also have some advantages, for example, the potential to reduce the principal-agent problems between shareholders and managers in the widely held model as well as the ability to rely on especially trustworthy family and kinship networks (see James 2008 for a discussion).[20]

The discussion of family ownership nonetheless seems to have been conditioned by what Harold James describes as:

A quite unique US structure, in which older family firms play a much less important role than anywhere else...Most American academics and analysts have in consequence assumed, following the work of Alfred Chandler, that there is a simple one way trajectory that leads from the infantile stage of the family firm to the mature managed corporation with a widely dispersed ownership. That is still the model that is taught in most American business schools. (2008, 6)

In assessing this model, it is useful to begin by noting that family-owned firms do not conspicuously underperform widely held ones. To the contrary, several studies have found evidence of superior performance by family-owned firms, at least under some conditions, across a variety of markets (Anderson and Reeb 2003; Maury 2006; Villalonga and Amit 2006; Martínez, Stöhr, and Quiroga 2007; Andres 2008). A recent BCG study (Kachaner, Stalk, and Bloch 2012) reports that family firms weathered the global financial crisis better than nonfamily firms, consistent with a pattern of lower profitability during boom times but far stronger results during economic downturns.[21] This emphasis on resilience is exactly one of the respects in which the objectives of a family-owned enterprise might be expected to differ from a widely held one – and, along with a longer-term outlook, is one of the self-characterizations that family owners themselves tend to offer (Economist "Virtues" 2015).

These possible differences in objective functions between family-owned and widely held businesses also serve to weaken the survivor principle in favor of, ironically, an emphasis on survival over strict value maximization. In other words, it is possible to imagine a situation in which family-owned firms earn average long-run returns lower than widely held firms, yet find it optimal to continue to operate as such instead of shifting ownership form.

Evidence on actual shifts in ownership form sheds further light on the limits to using the survivor principle to predict a broad increase in the incidence of widely held firms. It seems that only in certain kinds of countries do family-owned firms show a clear tendency to turn into widely held firms over time; in others they do not. Franks et al. (2012, 1678) find evidence of such a progression "in countries with strong investor protection, developed financial markets, and active markets for corporate control but not in other countries." These and other relevant attributes of the external environment will be elaborated in the sections that follow. But for now, what this suggests is that unless the differences in administrative arrangements, cultural values, or the other attributes responsible for such divergent outcomes change quickly, they are likely to check the cross-country spread of widely held enterprises.

In fact, treating current preferences for ownership forms as fixed has let the McKinsey Global Institute conduct some illustrative calculations suggesting an increased incidence of family-owned firms among the world's largest. Extrapolations driven primarily by the big shift of economic activity to Asia – a part of the world relatively partial to family ownership – lead to the projection that family-owned firms from emerging economies with more than $1 billion in revenues will increase from 16 percent of the total in 2010 to 37 percent of the total by 2025 (Björnberg et al. 2014). Whatever one thinks of those precise predictions, they do embody another reason to be cautious about assuming quick convergence toward the widely held model.

State-owned enterprises, while also embodying concentrated ownership, raise somewhat different issues. Once again, the discussion is probably affected by the exceptionalism of the United States, where the value of SOEs is estimated to account for less than 0.5 percent of GDP, versus an average of about 10 percent for the rest of a sample of dozen advanced economies (Australia and Canada come closest to matching the United States), and dominant shares, as noted above, in many emerging economies (OECD 2014). The minimal importance of SOEs in the United States (and other Anglo-American countries) probably contributes to summary dismissals of SOEs, as do reasons for thinking that they will indeed be significantly less efficient than privately owned firms.

Recognizing SOEs' salience across many other countries suggests taking them a bit more seriously. Governments can and do block the application of the survivor principle to SOEs through an array of measures that range from award-ing them monopolies to impeding competitors to providing financial support through a variety of mechanisms (Bremmer 2009). It is common, as a result, to model SOEs as facing soft budget constraints unless the government itself faces financial exigencies or is, for some other reason, intent on fundamental reforms.

Privatization revenues provide one indicator of activity aimed at reforming the state sector. The privatization wave launched by the Thatcher government in the UK in the early 1980s accelerated through the 1990s (Megginson and Netter 2001) but there has been significant year-to-year volatility since then, with privatization levels typically tending to be higher when stock markets are buoyant. And the years since the global financial crisis have been quite anomalous: while some years have seen record revenues from privatization, there have also been record levels of nationalizations and state investments, with the latter exceeding the former in several years (Megginson 2012). This postcrisis shift has been so palpable that it has even triggered proclamations that state capitalism has finally come of age (Bremmer 2009). One could probably also make a quantitative case for the increased salience of state ownership, along the lines proposed by the McKinsey Global Institute for family ownership, by pointing to emerging economies' greater proneness to state ownership plus their increasing weight in the world economy.

In addition to histories and extrapolations, it seems particularly important in this context to pay attention to governmental intent. Although this judgment is subjective, we do not presently seem to see the sort of political or popular fervor for large-scale privatization that prevailed in at least some circles 20–25 years ago. Thus, the partial privatization efforts in China and India briefly described earlier notwithstanding, most analysts do not see any commitment (yet) to more fundamental reconsideration of the role of SOEs in those two countries. That also seems to be the case for other major economies except oil exporters, who are engaging in privatizations to generate some revenues (e.g., Saudi Arabia's plans to sell a stake in Saudi Aramco). Some of the reservations about privatization may be related to the bungled – or artfully manipulated – processes used in previous privatization waves (e.g., in Russia). And some are intrinsic to the fact that state-ownership and, as a result, privatizations, have tended to be concentrated in the same sectors around the world (Pryor 1973). In addition to natural resources – the world's dozen largest oil companies are all state-owned – state ownership is common in several (overlapping) categories:

- Industries that raise concerns about market failures of various sorts, for example, network industries prone to small numbers problems and industries involving public goods such as national security and defense.
- Industries that provide widely used inputs that can affect the functioning of the rest of the economy, for example, finance and education as well as many network industries.

- Industries that, in private hands, would raise concerns about holdup by governments because of very high sunk costs (e.g., infrastructure), that produce mass-consumption staples that might even be considered entitlements (e.g., water), and that depend on the government as a buyer.

Privatizing an industry in one of these categories does not eliminate the underlying problems that may have promoted state ownership in the first place. Argentina privatized most of its water system in the 1990s, including, most visibly, the concession for Buenos Aires. But despite some obvious performance gains – for example, massive expansion of access to water and, apparently as a result, a significant drop in infant mortality – tariff increases proved politically unpalatable and Buenos Aires's water supply reverted to state control in 2006 (Galiani, Gertler, and Schargrodsky 2005; Rocca 2014).

That example and the typology that preceded it are reminders of not only the reasons that SOEs seem unlikely to fade away but also the range of functions states can demand SOEs to perform: the soft budget constraint typically comes with strings attached. Whether state demands can be aggregated even approximately into simple, coherent objective functions for SOEs is an open question. Hrnjic, Reeb, and Yeung (2015) suggest a higher-order objective of survival, à la family-owned firms, as opposed to value maximization. But the similarity between family-owned and state-owned firms in this respect should not be overstated: survival means something very different in the context of a soft budget constraint as opposed to a hard one. At least for the case of Chinese SOEs, we have good evidence that avoidance of large-scale layoffs is a key objective (Chen et al. 2015), and the preservation of employment levels or emoluments resonates more broadly as an explanation of many aspects of SOE behavior. But at the same time, other state objectives may supervene, so there may be significant departures from the pattern of behavior implied by any simple objective function.

This discussion of the objectives of state-owned firms can be put into broader perspective. Begin by comparing, *pace* Hrnjic et al. (2015), fragmented (widely-held) ownership and concentrated ownership. Widely-held ownership seems likely, subject to principal-agent problems and the possible limitations of the public equity markets, to harness a company to shareholder value maximization. Concentrated ownership leaves more room for entrenched owners to depart from strict value maximization in ways that embody significant discretion but also do seem to reflect systematic variation by ownership type, as summarized in Figure 9.2. Family-owned firms may emphasize survival rather than strict value maximization, state-owned firms jobs, private equity firms cashing out within 5–7 years, venture capitalists shorter, much riskier investments, and so on.[22] And when we turn to look at labor instead of capital, the list of ownership forms can be extended to cooperatives and partnerships, which have their own distinct orientations.

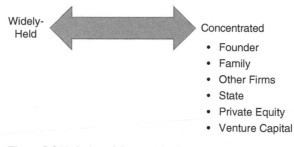

Figure 9.2 Varieties of Ownership Structures.

Figure 9.2 should also make it clear that we are *not* talking about a vertical continuum in which advanced (Anglo-American) economies are positioned at the top and emerging or otherwise deficient economies – as identified by the institutional voids literature (Khanna and Palepu 1997), for example – at the bottom. Even with access to vibrant public equity markets, concentrated ownership accounts for a significant fraction of US big business, mostly through family and private equity ownership. Elsewhere, of course, concentrated ownership generally dominates and seems unlikely to fade away, as already discussed. So the evidence contradicts impressions that the widely held firm will take over big business. An important corollary: instead of assuming that particular firms that one is interested in – as potential employers, partners, or competitors – are shareholder value maximizers, it is worth paying attention to what their actual objectives seem to be. For international business research, this also suggests some reservations regarding standard assumptions about firm objectives in work grounded in internalization theory, echoing concerns that Coase himself expressed late in life (2009) about his seminal early work on the theory of the firm (1937).

Having examined variations in the ownership of businesses, the next two sections cover, more briefly, variations in the external financing of businesses and in their relationships with labor. The objective is to look for patterns in how they vary because that would make the diversity of administrative arrangements across countries easier to apprehend and act upon.

External Capital

Our discussion of ownership highlighted some of the devices that families and other concentrated owners use to leverage the control afforded by their finite financial resources. But they nonetheless typically do seem to need to look externally for additional financing. The sources of external finance vary greatly from economy to economy, with the variations shedding additional light on the links between ownership and capital.

External financing through equity is directly related to the level of development of an economy's equity markets. A crude measure is provided by the ratio of total equity market capitalization to GDP, which varies greatly across countries. The market capitalizations of some countries with a British financial heritage (as well as a few others) have tended to exceed GDP, except during stock market crashes. Continental European market capitalizations are generally less than GDP, and emerging economies tend to have even less equity finance (the median ratio for emerging economies in 2014 was 37 percent, as compared to 73 percent among advanced economies).[23]

Two measurable correlates of levels of equity market development have to do with the availability of rich information about individual companies and ample protections for their minority shareholders. The former can be proxied for by the degree to which stock prices move up and down together based on overall market movement ("synchronicity"). Low synchronicity is indicative of reliable and revealing information about individual companies sufficient for investors to place different values on companies, while high synchronicity indicates absence of such information, leaving investors only aggregate data to work with (Morck, Yeung, and Yu 2000). And the levels of protection afforded minority shareholders, which can be characterized at least roughly based on certain specific criteria,[24] matter because with concentrated owners, the abuse/nonabuse of suppliers of external finance becomes a key issue, on par with the focus, in analyses of widely-held firms, on the problems between managers and shareholders in general.

The least synchronicity and best shareholder protection laws exist in the United States, Ireland, Canada, the UK, and Australia (Morck et al. 2000; World Bank 2008). The highest synchronicity resides in larger developing economies such as Poland, China, Turkey, and Malaysia that have considerable but not very sophisticated stock markets. Interestingly, economies with family-based groups range widely across the synchronicity scale. For example, Japan and Mexico rank high, while Sweden and Germany rank significantly lower.

Corporate earnings disclosure also varies systematically across economies, with significant implications. In the five less synchronous markets listed earlier, earnings do appear to reflect changes in company performance and to inform individual share prices. However, in economies where banks and groups are more important and trading in equity markets is thinner, earnings serve more to smooth financial performance over time and support the dividend payout decisions of the bankers and families controlling the groups. The broad use of reserves in accounting helps accomplish this. Not surprisingly, in the United States, Canada, and Australia, share price responsiveness to earnings disclosure is very high, but it is much lower in France, Germany, and Japan where companies are more dependent on banks that hold and vote their shares. There, the most important performance disclosure is done privately to banks and group members (Ball 2002). In addition, the most important investor protection in these economies is for creditors, not shareholders.

When equity markets are not well developed, neither are public bond markets: some of the same factors appear to underlie both forms of market-based financing. In such cases, bank financing dominates. As a crude proxy for the size of the banking sector, consider bank deposits: in 2014, they were nine times as large as stock market capitalization in Slovakia, but only one-third as large in the United States.[25] And although stock market capitalization is (still) larger than bank deposits in most economies, it would be wrong to conclude that equity dominates as a source of finance: market capitalization measures the amount of equity listed, rather than raised. The proportion of investments (proxied by gross fixed capital formation) that are funded through equity issues averages only 13 percent for a multicountry sample in 1999, about the same as immediately prior to World War I and World War II (with the latter being followed by several decades of low activity). Debt generally plays a much larger role, in absolute terms, in funding investments in the corporate sector (Beck and Levine 2002).

Banks are important elements of the corporate financial landscape in most countries. Sometimes banks as well as industrial corporations are controlled by families, often the same ones, as in Argentina, Belgium, the Philippines, Portugal, Israel, and Malaysia. But in other cases, family control of corporations does not extend to banks, as in Sweden and India. Companies in postwar Germany have had unusually strong relationships with banks that owned or otherwise voted significant share blocks. In contrast, if corporations are widely held, so too typically are the banks. Australia, the United States, the UK, Canada, Ireland, Japan, and Switzerland are cases in point.

The role and operation of banks varies broadly across major economies as well. In state-driven economies like China, the state banks' first task is to fund state-owned enterprises and state-sponsored infrastructure projects, so access to bank credit for small private Chinese companies is limited. Family-controlled banks inside pyramids presumably have the task of funding the corporations in the pyramid. So it is not surprising that state and family banks may not be profit-maximizers, and indeed do appear to financially underperform widely held independent banks (Shleifer and Vishny 1998; Rajan and Zingales 2004). And economic efficiency as measured by innovation rates, low nonperforming loan incidence, vitality of sectors unaffiliated with the banks' controlling interests, and so on, may be lower in economies served by banks tied to the state or to groups (Morck, Daniel, and Yeung 2005).

Financial systems across the world also vary in terms of how well they serve borrowers and creditors. Historically, good access to bank credit, as in North America, Europe, and developed Asia, has been associated with lower interest rates than in parts of Africa, the Middle East, and Eastern Europe where access is more limited. (Of course, the subprime mortgage crisis serves as a reminder that access can be extended too far.) The effectiveness of the credit process rests on institutions such as the availability of credit information to lenders, the rights of creditors to enforce repayment, and the efficiency of courts in settling credit disputes. These correlate positively with broad access to credit and deep markets, and negatively with the size of the underground economy (World Bank 2003, 12). In addition, market structure also matters: thus high concentration and muted competition (especially for corporate lending) among the major UK banks probably play a role in strengthening reliance on equity finance. Given the many proposals for reforming regulatory and competition policy in banking as well as potentially drastic technological changes, the future of banking remains highly uncertain.

Labor

The final piece of the comparative capitalism literature to be examined here – before turning to how the pieces fit together – has to do with firms' relationships to the suppliers of labor. In the first instance, this adds further to our list of concentrated ownership forms by suggesting ones in which provision of key labor services is fused with ownership. Thus, partnerships are a common way of expanding beyond sole proprietorships – and still characterize many professional services firms, so do not necessarily indicate backwardness. And workers' cooperatives, or cooperatives more generally, are supposed to exhibit more resilience than individual firms in addition to often having social objectives.

But rather than focusing on these particular organizational forms, we take a broad look at labor, for two reasons. First, it accounts for the largest share of national income, about one-half to two-thirds for most developed countries (but as low as one-third or even one-quarter for developing ones).[26] Second, the division of economic surplus between capital and labor has long been one of the most contested issues around the world and is receiving fresh attention with discussions about rising inequality and the future consequences of automation.

Interventions in labor markets are pervasive and "free" labor markets an idealization. Although labor systems have not been as extensively researched as financial systems, there *have* been some efforts to characterize and analyze differences in labor market institutions, particularly in labor laws. This section summarizes some of the cross-country variation around regulatory protections for labor: support for collective bargaining (e.g., unionization), other laws that affect the costs of adjusting employment levels, and mandated levels of social security. For brevity, nonregulatory institutions such as education and training systems will be omitted even though they also drive significant variation across countries: the German system, for instance, is supposed to encourage investments specific to particular companies and industries whereas the US system does not.

Labor unions supply the most obvious example of a labor institution authorized by governments – often as an exception to antitrust laws – to enhance labor's bargaining power vis-à-vis capital. Unionization levels vary from close to zero in some countries – mostly poorer ones – to nearly 80 percent in Sweden, and show large increases with per capita income. However, unionization levels have gone down in many developed countries in recent decades.[27] The United States exemplifies a particularly steep, sustained decline: unionization levels there dropped from 31 percent in 1960 to 12 percent in 2007. And yet at the same time, dispersion in average unionization levels across developed countries has actually increased.[28]

Unionization levels, however, offer only partial and sometimes misleading indications of labor's exercise of collective bargaining power. Thus, estimates of Russian unionization levels range from 50 to 75 percent, but the relatively inert Soviet-era legacy, the Federation of Independent Russian Trade Unions, accounts for an overwhelming share of union membership. At the other end of the spectrum, France has a unionization level of about 6–8 percent, lower than any other major developed economy, and yet its collective bargaining coverage is, at 90 percent, among the highest in the world. This reflects the fact that unlike the United States, France – and a number of other EU countries – extend collective bargaining contracts to all workers and firms in a sector, so that most workers are likely to be covered by collective bargaining whether they personally belong to a union or not.

Or compare two emerging economies, India and China. Indian unionization levels are, at an estimated 5 percent of the workforce, even lower than France's, and only about a tenth of Chinese levels. But the Chinese official union functions, like its erstwhile counterpart in the Soviet Union, as an instrument of the Communist Party and has historically not been very assertive about labor rights. And while unions are more assertive in India, its real disadvantage seems to be that it ranks among the top 10 percent of countries in terms of how much hiring and firing are regulated, whereas China falls in the bottom 20 percent – a difference that, at the margin, has tipped a significant number of multinationals toward China rather than India as a production base.[29]

All four country examples point to the need to assess the multiple determinants of collective bargaining power instead of collapsing them into a simple outcome such as unionization levels. This is the direction in which researchers have moved. Thus, Botero et al. (2004) analyzed labor protections across eighty-five countries based on four composite indices (labor union power, protection of workers during collective disputes, laws restricting employment contracts, and social security benefits) and reach the following conclusions:

There is some evidence that more protective collective relations laws (but not others) are associated with a larger unofficial economy, that more protective employment, collective relations, and social security laws lead to lower male (but not female) participation in the labor force, and that more protective employment laws lead to higher unemployment, especially of the young ... The evidence on the unemployment of the young is most consistent with the political view that the privileged and older incumbents support more stringent labor laws, a finding broadly consistent with ... Blanchflower and Freeman (2000). (Botero et al. 2004, 1375, 8)

Much of the other research on labor regulations also emphasizes their negative effects. For instance, there is evidence suggesting that employment protection legislation hurts the speed of adjustment to shocks and job churn, impairing productivity growth (see, for instance, Micco and Pagés 2006; Caballero et al. 2013). But other readings of the evidence *are* possible. As Richard Freeman puts it, "the evidence shows that labor institutions reduce the dispersion of earnings and income inequality, which alters incentives, but finds equivocal effects on other aggregate outcomes, such as employment and unemployment" (2008, 2).

This focus on formal regulations does, of course, gloss over variations in their enforcement. One indication of systematic variation in this regard is provided by Botero et al. (2004) who note that the patterns they described apply to the richer countries in their sample but not to the poorer ones, presumably because of poorer enforcement. More direct evidence, however, comes in the form of variations in the size of the shadow economy, which generally looms large even when defined narrowly to focus on the production of legal goods and services that is concealed from public authorities to evade taxes, social security levies, labor standards, and so on – that is, excluding crime and the informal household sector (see Schneider, Buehn, and Montenegro 2010). Thus, according to Schneider et al. (2010) the weighted average shadow economy has been estimated at 30–40 percent of official GDP for countries in sub-Saharan Africa, Central/South America, and post-Communist Eurasia, nearly 20 percent on average for East Asian/Pacific countries and about 13 percent for OECD member countries. The shadow economy tends, particularly in emerging economies, to be relatively employment-intensive, amplifying its impact on labor.

The extent to which the shadow economy is economically beneficial as opposed to harmful is more controversial. What is clear is that labor-related legislation in the formal economy, particularly legislation that increases tax and social security contributions, is the key diverter of jobs to the shadow economy, where the protections can be much weaker, verging on absent. Such diversion must therefore be reckoned with as a consequence of labor laws – but, of course, without necessarily rendering them unworthwhile.

Ownership, Capital, and Labor

How do the ownership of businesses, their external financing, and their relationships with labor covary? Looking for patterns requires choices about which measures to focus on. Here we return to the measures discussed in the first section of this chapter that are summarized in Table 9.3: the Heritage Foundation's *Labor Freedom Index* as an indicator of the lack of labor market regulation, *Stock Market Capitalization/GDP* as an indicator of the availability of external equity finance,[30] and the Fogel (2006) measure of *family ownership*.

Figure 9.3 summarizes the results of relating the indicator of labor market deregulation to the stock market capitalization-to-GDP ratio (Figure 9.3a) and to the degree of family control (Figure 9.3b). Figure 9.3a reveals a positive relationship between "labor freedom" and external equity finance. Switzerland, the United States, and Canada all score high on both, whereas the pattern is reversed for developing countries such as Turkey and Argentina as well as some developed ones such as Italy and Germany. Figure 9.3b shows a negative relationship between "labor freedom" and family control.

The trade-off in Figure 9.3a, in particular, reflects one of the bases upon which Hall and Soskice (2001) cluster countries into Liberal Market Economies (LMEs) and Coordinated Market Economies (CMEs). The former combine shareholder capitalism with limited legal protections for labor and considerable discretion for top management and the latter feature considerable labor protections and concentrated ownership, often by families who also tend to be directly involved in management. The LME/CME dichotomy is based on a chart like Figure 9.3a but uses narrower employment-related measures and focuses on advanced economies, so the expanded data we present here suggest, at a minimum, paying more attention to very high (formal) labor protection in some large emerging economies.

Other scholars seek to explain why different countries end up at the points that they have along the broad tradeoff we depict in Figure 9.3a instead of arguing whether the scatter of data naturally cluster into two, three, or more groups. Theirs is a search not just for patterns but also for common underlying factors. We cite three types of explanations here: one administrative and two cultural. For some data that will, in conjunction with earlier exhibits, shed light on them, see Table 9.5 on page 308.

Legal System. Some scholars argue for the criticality of legal systems, of which a small variety have been transplanted (e.g., through colonialism) around the world, a perspective supported by the strong performance of this variable in the first section of this chapter. These scholars particularly distinguish between countries that rely on civil law to translate government policy directly into elaborate laws and regulations, leaving little room for judicial discretion, and countries that rely on *common law* or the flow of precedent from the judiciary in which the body of court decisions over time shapes law and regulation. In common law then, a petitioner – say, an aspiring entrepreneur locked out of a business by legislation giving preferences to powerful incumbent firms – can argue unlawful exclusion on the basis of seemingly distant but actually relevant earlier cases, and common law judges have the latitude

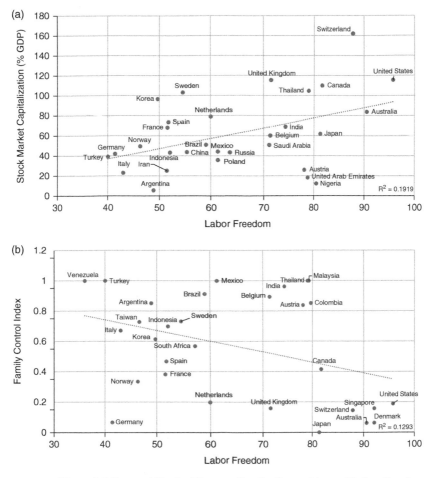

Figure 9.3 External Equity Finance, Family Ownership, and Labor Freedom
Sources: Standard & Poor's Global Stock Markets Factbook (2012) and S&P
data as reported in the World Bank World Development Indicators (2012);
The Heritage Foundation (2012); Variable Dv on Family Ownership from
Fogel (2006).

to apply them across such distance. Capitalist governance based on civil law
is, in comparison, more centralized and rigid and might be easier for powerful
incumbents to "capture" (Rajan and Zingales 2003, 42).[31] On the basis of such
reasoning, Andrei Shleifer and various coauthors argue that civil law systems
push countries toward the "coordinated market economies" at the left end of
the tradeoff in Figure 9.3a, and common law systems in the opposite direction,

Table 9.5 *Legal System, Primary Religion, and Power Distance Index (PDI) for Major Countries*

Country	Legal System	Primary Religion	PDI
Argentina	Civil/French	Catholic	49
Australia	Common	Protestant	36
Austria	Civil/German	Catholic	11
Belgium	Civil/French	Catholic	65
Brazil	Civil/French	Catholic	69
Canada	Common-Civil/French	Catholic	39
Chile	Civil/French	Catholic	63
Colombia	Civil/French	Catholic	67
Denmark	Civil/Scandinavian	Protestant	18
Ecuador	Civil/French	Catholic	78
Egypt	Civil/French	Muslim	n.a.
Finland	Civil/Scandinavian	Protestant	33
France	Civil/French	Catholic	68
Germany	Civil/German	Protestant	35
Greece	Civil/French	Greek Orthodox	60
Hong Kong	Common	Local beliefs	68
India	Common	Hindu	77
Indonesia	Civil/French	Muslim	78
Ireland	Common	Catholic	28
Israel	Common	Judaism	13
Italy	Civil/French	Catholic	50
Japan	Civil/German	Buddhist	54
Jordan	Civil/French	Muslim	n.a.
Kenya	Common	Protestant	n.a.
Malaysia	Common	Muslim	104
Mexico	Civil/French	Catholic	81
Netherlands	Civil/French	Catholic	38
New Zealand	Common	Protestant	22
Nigeria	Common	Muslim	n.a.
Norway	Civil/Scandinavian	Protestant	31
Pakistan	Common	Muslim	55
Peru	Civil/French	Catholic	64
Philippines	Civil/French	Catholic	94
Portugal	Civil/French	Catholic	63
Singapore	Common	Buddhist	74
South Korea	Civil/German	Protestant	60
South Africa	Common	Protestant	49
Spain	Civil/French	Catholic	57
Sri Lanka	Common	Buddhist	n.a.
Sweden	Civil/Scandinavian	Protestant	31
Switzerland	Civil/German	Catholic	34
Taiwan	Civil/German	Buddhist	58
Thailand	Common	Buddhist	64
Turkey	Civil/French	Muslim	66
UK	Common	Protestant	35

Table 9.5 (*cont.*)

Country	Legal System	Primary Religion	PDI
Uruguay	Civil/French	Catholic	61
United States	Common	Protestant	40
Venezuela	Civil/French	Catholic	81
Zimbabwe	Common	Syncretic	n.a.

Source: Reprinted from *Journal of Financial Economics* 70 (3):313–49. Stulz, René M., and Rohan Williamson. "Culture, Openness, and Finance." Table 1, Page No. 323 (2003).

toward the "liberal market economies." Thus, La Porta et al. (1999) make the case that common law economies tend to have more nonfamily and nonstate ownership, more independent banks, stronger shareholder rights, and a more active market for the control of corporate equity. In addition, Botero et al. (2004) make the parallel case that labor rights are likely to be weaker under common law than civil law.

Religion. The stronger presence of widely held ownership, strong equity markets, and shareholder rights in Protestant versus Catholic, Jewish, Muslim, and Buddhist countries suggests the possibility that the Reformation's challenge to hierarchy and emphasis on the individual's role in defining faith influenced the evolution of Protestant capitalism. Max Weber, the father of German sociology, famously wrote a book entitled *The Protestant Ethic and the Spirit of Capitalism*, arguing that the Reformation associated success in business and favor in the eyes of God in believers' minds, which would also explain why Protestant economies generally have less robust "safety nets." It might be more accurate, in the light of the diversity depicted earlier, to say that the Reformation shaped just one of many capitalisms. Of course, other religions have had important influences as well. Islam strongly shaped early capitalism in the eighth through twelfth centuries, originating practices such as bills of exchange and the management of stable currency later adopted by Europeans. In addition, Sharia or religious law essentially prohibits the payment of pure interest, so Islamic banking innovated profit sharing and equity partnerships to mobilize capital. Recall from Chapter 8 that a continuous variable capturing shared religions across pairs of countries is associated with significantly larger interactions between them for nine out of the eleven types of international interactions analyzed.

Power Distance Index. Geert Hofstede's *Power Distance Index* (PDI) is, as discussed in Chapter 8, a cultural measure of the extent to which the less powerful members of organizations and institutions (like the family) accept and expect that power is distributed unequally. While the PDI apparently has not previously been discussed in these terms as an alternative cultural

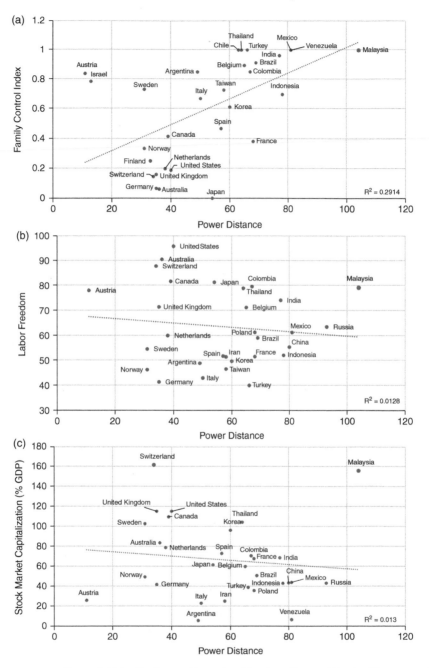

Figure 9.4 Family Ownership, Labor Freedom, External Equity Finance, and Power Distance.

explanation of ownership and governance arrangements, its antiegalitarianism suggests some obvious points of contact with the trade-off (at least in the short run) between capital and labor. Figure 9.4 indicates that higher PDI scores are strongly associated a greater degree of family ownership and weakly associated with more stringent labor market regulation and less (external) equity finance.

While the influence of these deep factors that change very slowly, if at all, appears to be substantial, the role of events such as wars, political cataclysms, and economic depressions should also be recognized. The strong post-World War II role of German banks in corporate ownership and governance took shape in the 1930s: the Nazis confiscated Jewish and other assets and nationalized banks, but let the banks be proxy voters for shares they held on behalf of surviving individual shareholders (Morck and Steier 2006, 30). Over in the United States, the populist Progressive Movement of more than a hundred years ago led to new legislation that penalized powerful nineteenth-century family trusts and pyramids and heavily taxed intercorporate dividends, laws that seem directly related to the distinctive ownership structure in that country. And one can only speculate about whether China would have become a capitalist instead of communist economy if it had not been for the colonialism-induced financial disasters of the 1920s and subsequent imperialist occupation.

The Chinese case also suggests, as do many other emerging economies, that the trade-off between capital and labor – as conventionally conceived in the literature and traced in Figure 9.3a – may be too narrow a way of thinking about the menu of governance systems. China has broad-ranging state or collective ownership of business and dominant state banking, both of which reflect a strong economic development role for the state. Business decisions with major political or military implications, for example, are (even) less likely to be reducible to a tug-of-war between suppliers of capital and of labor: the independent interests of the Chinese state are likely to supervene. Accounting for such possibilities would require adding a third axis to the two in Figure 9.3a.

Figure 9.4 (cont.)

Sources: Variable Dv on Family Ownership from Fogel (2006); The Heritage Foundation (2012); Geert Hofstede Dimension Data Matrix; Standard & Poor's Global Stock Markets Factbook (2012) and S&P data as reported in the World Bank World Development Indicators (2012).

Conclusions

A broad conclusion from the gravity modeling reported at the beginning of this chapter is that institutional distance, analyzed in particular based on horizontal measures – which indicate that countries are simply different rather than some doing better than others – tends to dampen international interactions. Although this is precisely what the law of distance predicts, it is worth pausing to consider how the opposite pattern was also plausible. In particular, Hall and Soskice (2001) couch their discussion of *varieties of capitalism* in terms of distinct "comparative institutional advantages" for LMEs and CMEs, which they argue help to explain patterns of specialization across countries. This framing might lead one to expect more interactions between LMEs and CMEs, that is, across greater institutional distances, with more activity aimed at taking advantage of institutional differences than not.

The pattern that institutional distance tends to dampen international interactions was established by testing several measures of institutional distance and reporting their performance across multiple types of international interactions. The exercise suggests that there is no single institutional distance measure that is appropriate for all studies. Rather, an understanding of how specific institutions are expected to relate to phenomena being studied should point toward the selection of appropriate distance measures.

Beyond formal distance modeling, this chapter has also unpacked key components identified by the comparative capitalism literature and has sought to understand how they covary. The examination of the ownership structures of big business around the world suggests that widely held firms are far more common in the United States than they are in most of the rest of the world, where concentrated ownership predominates. Concentrated owners can and do pursue objectives that diverge from shareholder value maximization in systematic ways. And since concentrated ownership seems unlikely to fade away, it is important to understand and account for such divergence. Specifically, classic competitor analysis, involving attention to goals, the personalities of the key decisionmakers, and so on, becomes even more important when the firms being analyzed have concentrated ownership instead of being widely held.

Bringing two additional key elements of the comparative capitalism literature, relationships with (external) suppliers of capital and of labor, into the picture yields some additional insights. Although there is a great deal of diversity, it does not seem to reflect random variation. Some kinds of institutions naturally go hand-in-hand with others (e.g., widely held firms and large public equity markets); others seem to be substitutes rather than complements (e.g., widely held firms and restrictive labor regulations). Clarifying the nexus of ownership structure, external financing, and labor relations – which the LME/ CME dichotomy attempted for a narrower range of countries and ownership structures – helps one understand the interlocking logic of the multiple elements of capitalist systems in a way that should facilitate broader, more integrative thinking about business ownership and governance as well as implications for firm behavior.

From a managerial perspective, while one cannot learn in advance the administrative intricacies of all of the countries where one might do business, the discussion in this chapter should help by identifying the major dimensions of difference and providing a sense of the range of such variation. That is, of course, ideally a complement to rather than a substitute for focused attempts to understand focal jurisdictions (e.g., Abu Dhabi, to return to the example with which this chapter began) as well as experience living and working there for an extended period to appreciate how institutions really function.

Notes

1 Calculation based on public sector employment data from the International Labour Organization (ILO) and the websites of various international organizations.
2 This distinction parallels the one in industrial economics between horizontal product differentiation, in which different people rank products differently, and vertical product differentiation, in which they agree on which product is better.
3 Kostova (2009) and Bae and Salomon (2010) both identified a wide range of variables that have been used in prior literature in this area, and thus provided a useful starting point for this exercise. From there, we selected variables to test based on data availability as well as our own views of the underlying concepts. Alternative variables tested for this subsection included regulative distance measures from Xu, Pan, and Beamish (2004) and Gaur and Lu (2007), as well as selected indicators of cognitive distance from Ionascu, Meyer, and Estrin (2004).
4 The variable used was extracted from CEPII's Gravity Dataset, downloaded from www.cepii.fr/CEPII/en/bdd_modele/presentation.asp?id=8.
5 The normative scores from Xu, Pan, and Beamish (2004) were converted into distances by taking the ratio (max/min) of the values for each country pair.
6 The specific variables extracted from the *World Competitiveness Yearbook* (www. imd.org/wcc/wcy-world-competitiveness-yearbook) are: Corporate values; Value system; Need for economic and social reforms; National culture; Image abroad or branding; Attitudes toward globalization. These variables were combined into an index following the methodology used by Kogut and Singh (1988) for their Cultural Distance index.
7 The normative and cognitive distance variables entered the model in logged form.
8 The specific POLCON measure used is POLCONV (Henisz 2000). As alternatives, we also tested POLCONIII (Henisz 2002) as well as the CHECKS indicator from Beck et al. (2001).
9 These variables were combined into an index following the methodology used by Kogut and Singh (1988) for their Cultural Distance index.

10 As an alternative, we also tested the Corruption Perceptions Index from Transparency International.

11 The POLCON and WGI Corruption data were converted into distances by taking the ratio (max/min) of the values for each country pair. All of the vertical institutional distance measures entered the model in logged form.

12 The 6 *business systems* are: fragmented, coordinated industrial district, compartmentalized, state organized, collaborative, and highly coordinated (Whitley 1999, 42).

13 Thus, four of the five spheres of coordination in *Varieties of Capitalism* deal specifically with capital (corporate governance) and labor (industrial relations, vocational training and education, and employees).

14 For details, refer to www.heritage.org/index/labor-freedom#fn-5. As an alternative, we also tested the Employment Protection Legislation indicators from the OECD.

15 The data for all of these measures were converted into distances by taking the ratio (max/min) of the values for each country pair, and they entered into the model in logged form.

16 Small businesses tend to be sole proprietorships that typically do not face complex governance issues, at least on the capital side: they tend to be self-financed.

17 Based on data provided by Thomas A. Stewart in an e-mail to Pankaj Ghemawat on June 6, 2016, drawing upon National Center for the Middle Market and Milken Institute, "Access to Capital: How Small and Mid-Size Businesses Are Funding Their Futures," 2015. In this context, mid-sized firms are defined as those with revenues between $10 million and $1 billion.

18 Many of these firms are, however, classified as widely held in Table 9.4 because the groups of firms invested in them contain no dominant members.

19 The Tata and Reliance groups accounted for 47 percent of the assets of the top 20 Indian business groups in 2006.

20 James also points out that the obverse of the trust-related advantage of family firms has a flip side: the "insiderism" that it perpetuates can and often has been described in terms of crony capitalism featuring socially excessive levels of business entrenchment.

21 The performance implications of different ownership forms, particularly business groups, are not elaborated here, partly for reasons of space, partly because consideration of the objectives of concentrated owners suggests caution in using exactly the same performance yardsticks for them, and partly because the variation within a category (e.g., family-owned firms) often seems larger and more interesting than cross-category variations in the averages (e.g., family-owned versus widely-held).

22 Another, narrower example pertains to regulated firms (e.g. utilities) that face incentives to inflate their capital bases (Averch and Johnson 1962).

23 Calculation based on data from the World Bank's World Development Indicators.

24 Rankings on the strength of investor protection across countries used in World Bank's "Doing Business 2009: Comparing Regulation in 181 Economies" are based on: (1) requirements on approval and disclosure of related-party transactions; (2) liability of CEO and board of directors in related-party transactions; and (3) type of evidence that can be collected before and during the trial.

25 The discussion in this paragraph and the next is based on Rajan and Zingales (2003).

26 The lower estimates are computed from OECD data and the higher estimates are based on Prados de la Escosura and Rosés (2003).

27 Developing countries do not exhibit a similarly clear trend in this regard.
28 In 2000, the five developed countries – out of a sample of twenty-four – with the highest unionization levels averaged 66 percent while the five with the lowest averaged 13 percent, versus figures of 68 percent and 19 percent respectively in 1980 (Visser 2006).
29 These calculations are based on measures compiled by Freeman (2010).
30 The focus on capital market outcomes instead of capital rights is dictated in part by the unavailability of satisfactory measures of capital rights. Most of the ones that have been used in the past focus on the rights of different kinds of capitalists relative to each other rather than on the rights of capitalists as a group.
31 Civil code-based legal systems are not all alike. For example, German judges have more latitude than French judges do.

References

"2015 Index of Economic Freedom." 2015. The Heritage Foundation and The *Wall Street Journal*. www.heritage.org/index

Aldrighi, Dante M., and Fernando A. S. Postali. 2010. "Business Groups in Brazil." In *The Oxford Handbook of Business Groups*, edited by Asli M. Colpan, Takashi Hikino, and James R. Lincoln. Oxford: Oxford Handbooks Online. www.oxfordhandbooks.com/view/10.1093/oxfordhb/9780199552863.001.0001/oxfordhb-9780199552863-e-13.

Anderson, Ronald C., and David M. Reeb. 2003. "Founding-Family Ownership and Firm Performance: Evidence from the S&P 500." *Journal of Finance* 58 (3):1301–1328. doi: 10.1111/1540–6261.00567.

Andres, Christian. 2008. "Large Shareholders and Firm Performance – an Empirical Examination of Founding-Family Ownership." *Journal of Corporate Finance* 14 (4):431–445. doi: 10.1016/j.jcorpfin.2008.05.003.

Averch, Harvey, and Leland L. Johnson. 1962. "Behavior of the Firm under Regulatory Constraint." *The American Economic Review* 52 (5): 1052–1069.

Bae, Jin-Hyun, and Robert M. Salomon. 2010. "Institutional Distance in International Business Research." In *The Past, Present and Future of International Business & Management*, edited by Timothy Devinney, Torben Pedersen, and Laszlo Tihanyi, 327–349. Bingley, UK: Emerald Group Publishing Limited.

Ball, Ray. 2002. "Globalization of Accounting Research." Harvard Business School Research Workshop on International Business.

Beck, Thorsten, George Clarke, Alberto Groff, Philip Keefer, and Patrick Walsh. 2001. "New Tools in Comparative Political Economy: The Database of Political Institutions." *World Bank Economic Review* 15 (1): 165–176.

Beck, Thorsten, and Ross Levine. 2002. "Industry Growth and Capital Allocation: Does Having a Market- or Bank-Based System Matter?" *Journal of Financial Economics* 64 (2):147–180. doi: http://dx.doi.org/10.1016/S0304-405X(02)00074-0.

Berle, Adolf A., and Gardiner C. Means. 1932. *Modern Corporation and Private Property*. New York, Chicago: Commerce Clearing House, Loose leaf service division of the Corporation Trust Company.

Björnberg, Åsa, Heinz-Peter Elstrodt, and Vivek Pandit. 2014. "The Family-Business Factor in Emerging Markets." *McKinsey Quarterly*. www.mckinsey.com/global-themes/winning-in-emerging-markets/the-family-business-factor-in-emerging-markets.

Blanchflower, David G., and Richard B. Freeman. 2000. "The Declining Economic Status of Young Workers in OECD Countries." In *Youth Employment and Joblessness in Advanced Countries*, 19–56. University of Chicago Press.

Botero, Juan C., Simeon Djankov, Rafael La Porta, Florencio Lopez-de-Silanes, and Andrei Shleifer. 2004. "The Regulation of Labor." *Quarterly Journal of Economics* 119 (4):1339–1382. doi: 10.1162/0033553042476215.

Bremmer, Ian. 2009. "State Capitalism Comes of Age: The End of the Free Market?" *Foreign Affairs* 88 (3):40–55.

Caballero, Ricardo J., Kevin N. Cowan, Eduardo M. R. A. Engel, and Alejandro Micco. 2013. "Effective Labor Regulation and Microeconomic Flexibility." *Journal of Development Economics* 101:92–104. doi: 10.1016/j.jdeveco.2012.08.009.

Chen, Donghua, Dequan Jiang, Alexander Ljungqvist, Haitian Lu, and Mingming Zhou. "State Capitalism Vs. Private Enterprise." National Bureau of Economic Research Working Paper Series 20930, February 2015. www.nber.org/papers/w20930.

Clarke, Thomas. 2007. *International Corporate Governance: A Comparative Approach*. New York: Routledge.

Coase, Ronald. "Markets, Firms and Property Rights." Markets, Firms and Property Rights: A Celebration of the Research of Ronald Coase, University of Chicago Law School, November 23, 2009. www.law.uchicago.edu/video/coase112309.

Coase, Ronald H. 1937. "The Nature of the Firm." *Economica* 4 (16):386–405. doi: 10.1111/j.1468-0335.1937.tb00002.x.

Collis, David J., Bharat N. Anand, and J. Yo-Jud Cheng. forthcoming. "Business Groups in the USA since 1960." In *Business Groups in the West* edited by Asli M. Colpan, and Takashi Hikino. Oxford: Oxford University Press.

Cuervo-Cazurra, Alvaro, and Mehmet Genc. 2008. "Transforming Disadvantages into Advantages: Developing-Country MNEs in the Least Developed Countries." *Journal of International Business Studies* 39 (6):957–979.

Economist. 2006. "Sweden's Enduring Business Dynasty." *Economist*. www.economist.com/node/8023389.

    2015. "The China That Works." *Economist*. www.economist.com/news/leaders/21664143-if-economic-miracle-continue-officials-must-give-private-sector-more-freedom.

    2015. "Old-Fashioned Virtues." *Economist*. www.economist.com/news/special-report/21648172-patience-distinctiveness-thrift-and-trust-still-count-old-fashioned-virtues.

    2015. "To Have and to Hold." *Economist*. www.economist.com/news/special-report/21648171-far-declining-family-firms-will-remain-important-feature-global-capitalism.

European Commission. 2015. "Myths and Facts: The EU Budget Is Enormous!" Last Modified March 5, 2015 Accessed July 13, 2015. http://ec.europa.eu/budget/explained/myths/myths_en.cfm#1of15.

Fan, Joseph P. H., T. J. Wong, and Tianyu Zhang. "The Emergence of Corporate Pyramids in China." CEI Working Paper Series 2006-3, Center for Economic Institutions, Institute of Economic Research, Hitotsubashi University. http://EconPapers.repec.org/RePEc:hit:hitcei:2006-3.

Fogel, Kathy. 2006. "Oligarchic Family Control, Social Economic Outcomes, and the Quality of Government." *Journal of International Business Studies* 37 (5):603–622. doi: 10.1057/palgrave.jibs.8400213.

Forsythe, Michael. 2015. "Wang Jianlin, a Billionaire at the Intersection of Business and Power in China." *New York Times*, April 28, 2015. www.nytimes.com/2015/04/29/world/asia/wang-jianlin-abillionaire-at-the-intersection-of-business-and-power-in-china.html?smprod=nytcore-ipad&smid=nytcore-ipad-share&_r=2.

Franks, Julian, Colin Mayer, Paolo Volpin, and Hannes F. Wagner. 2012. "The Life Cycle of Family Ownership: International Evidence." *Review of Financial Studies* 25 (6):1675–1712.

Freeman, Richard B. 2008. "Labor Market Institutions around the World." CEP Discussion Paper CEPDP0844, Centre for Economic Performance, London School of Economics and Political Science, January 2008. http://cep.lse.ac.uk/pubs/download/dp0844.pdf.

Freeman, Richard B. 2010. "Labor Regulations, Unions, and Social Protection in Developing Countries: Market Distortions or Efficient Institutions?" In *Handbook of Development Economics*, edited by Dani Rodrik, and Mark Rosenzweig, 4657–4702: Elsevier.

Galiani, Sebastian, Paul Gertler, and Ernesto Schargrodsky. 2005. "Water for Life: The Impact of the Privatization of Water Services on Child Mortality." *Journal of Political Economy* 113 (1):83–120. doi: 10.1086/426041.

Gaur, Ajai S., and Jane W Lu. 2007. "Ownership Strategies and Survival of Foreign Subsidiaries: Impacts of Institutional Distance and Experience." *Journal of Management* 33 (1):84–110.

Hall, Peter A., and David W. Soskice. 2001. "An Introduction to Varieties of Capitalism." In *Varieties of Capitalism: The Institutional Foundations of Comparative Advantage*, edited by Peter A. Hall, and David W. Soskice, 1–68. Oxford England; New York: Oxford University Press.

Henisz, W. J. 2000. "The Institutional Environment for Multinational Investment." *The Journal of Law, Economics, and Organization* 15 (2): 334–364.

Henisz, W. J. 2002. "The Institutional Environment for Infrastructure Investment." *Industrial And Corporate Change* 11 (2):355–389.

Henisz, Witold J., and Oliver E. Williamson. 1999. "Comparative Economic Organization – within and between Countries." *Business and Politics* 1 (3):261–278.

Hofstede, Geert. 1980. *Culture's Consequences: International Differences in Work-Related Values*. Vol. 5, Cross Cultural Research and Methodology. Beverly Hills, CA: Sage Publications.

Hofstede, Geert, and Gert Jan Hofstede. "Six Dimensions in 0–100 Range.Csv." www.geerthofstede.nl/dimension-data-matrix.

Hotho, Jasper J., and Torben Pedersen. 2012. "Beyond the 'Rules of the Game': Three Institutional Approaches and How They Matter for International Business." In *Handbook of Institutional Approaches to International Business*, edited by Geoffrey Wood, and Mehmet Demirbag, 236–73. Cheltenham: Edward Elgar.

Hrnjic, Emir, David M. Reeb, and Bernard Yeung. "Styles of Financial Management." Draft prepared for Workshop on Business Models for Speed and Scale, Center for Globalization of Education and Management (CGEM); Center for Global Enterprise (CGE), New York, March 2015.

Ionascu, Delia, Klaus E. Meyer, and Saul Estrin. 2004. "Institutional Distance and International Business Strategies in Emerging Economies." William Davidson Institute Working Paper Number 728, November 2004.

IMD. 2016. "World Competitiveness Yearbook." Lausanne, Switzerland: IMD World Competitiveness Center. www.imd.org/wcc/wcy-world-competitiveness-yearbook.

Jackson, Gregory, and Richard Deeg. 2008. "Comparing Capitalisms: Understanding Institutional Diversity and Its Implications for International Business." *Journal of International Business Studies* 39 (4):540–561.

James, Harold. 2008. "Family Values or Crony Capitalism?" *Capitalism and Society* 3 (1). www.degruyter.com/view/j/cas.2008.3.1/cas.2008.3.1.1031/cas.2008.3.1.1031. xml.

Kachaner, Nicolas, George Stalk, and Alain Bloch. 2012. "What You Can Learn from Family Business." *bcgperspectives.com*. Reprinted from: *Harvard Business Review*, November 2012. https://www.bcgperspectives.com/content/articles/strategic_planning_mergers_acquisitions_what_can_learn_from_family_business/; https://www.bcgperspectives.com/Images/BCG_R1211H-PDF-ENG_PDF.pdf.

Kaufman, Daniel, Art Kraay, and Massimo Mastruzzi. 2007. "Government Matters VI: Aggregate and Individual Governance Indicators for 1996–2006." World Bank Policy Research Working Paper 4280, Washington, DC, August 2007. http://elibrary.worldbank.org/doi/abs/10.1596/1813-9450-4280.

Khanna, Tarun, and Krishna Palepu. 1997. "Why Focused Strategies May Be Wrong for Emerging Markets." *Harvard Business Review* 75 (4):41–51.

Kim, Hwa-Jin. "Concentrated Ownership and Corporate Control: Wallenberg Sphere and Samsung Group." Law & Economics Working Papers 105, University of Michigan Law School, July 2014. http://repository.law.umich.edu/law_econ_current/105.

Kogut, Bruce, and Harbir Singh. 1988. "The Effect of National Culture on the Choice of Entry Mode." *Journal of International Business Studies* 19 (3):411–432. doi: 10.1057/palgrave.jibs.8490394.

Kostova, Tatiana. 1997. "Country Institutional Profiles: Concept and Measurement." *Academy of Management Best Papers Proceedings* (August):180–184. doi: 10.5465/AMBPP.1997.4981338.

1999. "Transnational Transfer of Strategic Organizational Practices: A Contextual Perspective." *Academy of management review* 24 (2):308–324.

2009. "Institutional Distance in International Business Research." AIB Frontiers Conference, Charleston, SC, December 5, 2009.

La Porta, Rafael, Florencio Lopez-de-Silanes, and Andrei Shleifer. 1999. "Corporate Ownership around the World." *Journal of Finance* 54 (2):471–517.

2008. "The Economic Consequences of Legal Origins." *Journal of Economic Literature* 46 (2):285–332. doi: doi: 10.1257/jel.46.2.285.

Lee, Jungah. 2015. "Samsung." *Bloomberg QuickTake*. www.bloombergview.com/quicktake/republic-samsung.

Lee, Keun, and Young-Sam Kang. 2010. "Business Groups in China." In *The Oxford Handbook of Business Groups*, edited by Asli M. Colpan, Takashi Hikino, and James R. Lincoln. Oxford: Oxford Handbooks Online. www.oxfordhandbooks.com.ezp-prod1.hul.harvard.edu/view/10.1093/oxfordhb/9780199552863.001.0001/oxfordhb-9780199552863-e-8.

Martínez, Jon I., Bernhard S. Stöhr, and Bernardo F. Quiroga. 2007. "Family Ownership and Firm Performance: Evidence from Public Companies in Chile." *Family Business Review* 20 (2):83–94.

Maury, Benjamin. 2006. "Family Ownership and Firm Performance: Empirical Evidence from Western European Corporations." *Journal of Corporate Finance* 12 (2):321–341. doi: 10.1016/j.jcorpfin.2005.02.002.

Megginson, William L. 2012. "Privatization Trends and Major Deals in 2012 and 1H2013" In *The PB Report 2012: A Surprisingly Strong Year*, 3–24. Milano, Italy: Privatization Barometer. https://www.kpmg.com/IT/it/IssuesAndInsights/ArticlesPublications/Documents/PBKPMGENI.pdf.

Megginson, William L., and Jeffry M. Netter. 2001. "From State to Market: A Survey of Empirical Studies on Privatization." *Journal of Economic Literature* 39 (2):321–389.

Micco, Alejandro, and Carmen Pagés. "The Economic Effects of Employment Protection: Evidence from International Industry-Level Data." Discussion paper series 2433, Forschungsinstitut zur Zukunft der Arbeit (IZA)/Institute for the Study of Labor, Bonn, November 2006.

Milne, Richard. 2015. "Meet the Wallenbergs." *FT Magazine*. Financial Times. www.ft.com/intl/cms/s/0/4f407796-0a35-11e5-a6a8-00144feabdc0.html.

Morck, Randall. 2010. "The Riddle of the Great Pyramids." In *The Oxford Handbook of Business Groups*, edited by Asli M. Colpan, Takashi Hikino, and James R. Lincoln, 602–628. Oxford: Oxford Handbooks Online. www.oxfordhandbooks.com/view/10.1093/oxfordhb/9780199552863.001.0001/oxfordhb-9780199552863-e-21.

Morck, Randall, Wolfenzon Daniel, and Bernard Yeung. 2005. "Corporate Governance, Economic Entrenchment, and Growth." *Journal of Economic Literature* 43 (3):655–720. doi: 10.1257/002205105774431252.

Morck, Randall K., and Lloyd Steier. 2006. "The Global History of Corporate Governance: An Introduction." In *A History of Corporate Governance around the World: Family Business Groups to Professional Managers*, edited by Randall K. Morck, 1–64. Chicago: University of Chicago Press. Original edition, This chapter first appeared as NBER working paper w11062. www.nber.org.ezp-prod1.hul.harvard.edu/chapters/c10267.pdf.

Morck, Randall, Bernard Yeung, and Wayne Yu. 2000. "The Information Content of Stock Markets: Why Do Emerging Markets Have Synchronous Stock Price Movements?" *Journal of Financial Economics* 58 (1–2):215–260. doi: 10.1016/S0304-405X(00)00071-4.

North, Douglass C. 1990. *Institutions, Institutional Change, and Economic Performance*, The Political Economy of Institutions and Decisions. Cambridge; New York: Cambridge University Press.

North, Douglass C. 1991. "Institutions." *Journal of Economic Perspectives* 5 (1):97–112. doi: 10.1257/jep.5.1.97.

OECD. 2014. "The Size and Sectoral Distribution of SOEs in OECD and Partner Countries." OECD Publishing. http://dx.doi.org/10.1787/9789264215610-en.

Prados de la Escosura, Leandro, and Joan R. Rosés. "Wages and Labor Income in History: A Survey." Working Papers in Economic History wh031006, Universidad Carlos III, Instituto Figuerola de Historia y Ciencias Sociales, Madrid, February 2003. https://ideas.repec.org/p/cte/whrepe/wh031006.html.

Pryor, Frederic L. 1973. *Property and Industrial Organization in Communist and Capitalist Nations*, Studies in Development No. 7. Bloomington: Indiana University Press.

Rajan, Raghuram G., and Luigi Zingales. 2003. "The Great Reversals: The Politics of Financial Development in the Twentieth Century." *Journal of Financial Economics* 69 (1):5–50. doi: http://dx.doi.org/10.1016/S0304-405X(03)00125-9.

2004. *Saving Capitalism from the Capitalists: Unleashing the Power of Financial Markets to Create Wealth and Spread Opportunity*. Princeton: Princeton University Press. Original edition, 2003. Reprint, with a new preface by the authors.

Rocca, Mariela Verónica. 2014. "Water Services in the Buenos Aires Metropolitan Area: How Does State Regulation Work?" *Brazilian Political Science Review* 8 (2):31–46.

Sarkar, Jayati. 2010. "Business Groups in India." In *The Oxford Handbook of Business Groups*, edited by Asli M. Colpan, Takashi Hikino, and James R. Lincoln. Oxford: Oxford Handbooks Online. www.oxfordhandbooks.com/view/10.1093/oxfordhb/9780199552863.001.0001/oxfordhb-9780199552863-e-11?rskey=EisciD&result=2.

Shleifer, Andrei, and Robert W. Vishny. 1998. *The Grabbing Hand: Government Pathologies and Their Cures*. Cambridge, MA: Harvard University Press.

Schneider, Friedrich, Andreas Buehn, and Claudio E. Montenegro. 2010. "New Estimates for the Shadow Economies All over the World." *International Economic Journal* 24 (4):443–461. doi: 10.1080/10168737.2010.525974.

Scott, W. Richard. 1995. *Institutions and Organizations*. Thousand Oaks: SAGE.

Stulz, René M., and Rohan Williamson. 2003. "Culture, Openness, and Finance." *Journal of Financial Economics* 70 (3):313–349. doi: 10.1016/S0304-405X(03)00173-9.

Villalonga, Belen, and Raphael Amit. 2006. "How Do Family Ownership, Control and Management Affect Firm Value?" *Journal of Financial Economics* 80 (2):385–417. doi: 10.1016/j.jfineco.2004.12.005.

Visser, Jelle. 2006. "Union Membership Statistics in 24 Countries." *Monthly Labor Review* (January):38–49.

Weber, Max. 2002. *The Protestant Ethic and the Spirit of Capitalism: And Other Writings*. Penguin.

Whitley, Richard. 1999. *Divergent Capitalisms: The Social Structuring and Change of Business Systems: The Social Structuring and Change of Business Systems*: Oxford University Press.

World Bank. 2003. "Doing Business 2004: Understanding Regulations." Washington, DC: World Bank Group. www.doingbusiness.org/reports/global-reports/doing-business-2004.

2008. "Doing Business 2009: Comparing Regulation in 181 Economies." Washington, DC: World Bank Group. www.doingbusiness.org/reports/global-reports/doing-business-2009.

Xu, Dean, Yigang Pan, and Paul W Beamish. 2004. "The Effect of Regulative and Normative Distances on MNE Ownership and Expatriate Strategies." *MIR: Management International Review*:285–307.

Zaheer, Srilata, Margaret Spring Schomaker, and Lilach Nachum. 2012. "Distance without Direction: Restoring Credibility to a Much-Loved Construct." *Journal of International Business Studies* 43 (1):18–27. doi: 10.1057/jibs.2011.43.

10 Geographic Distance and Regionalization

Pankaj Ghemawat and Steven A. Altman

In contrast to its cultural and administrative counterparts discussed in Chapters 8 and 9, geographic distance is more tangible, so there is broader agreement on what geography is. While the international business literature has paid less attention to geographic distance than to its cultural and administrative counterparts (Hutzschenreuter, Kleindienst, and Lange 2015), regionalization – with its obvious correspondence to geography – has been a central theme in international business since the publication of Rugman and Verbeke (2004). International business scholars have argued strongly that regions matter and have accorded primary emphasis to region definitions based on the "triad" introduced by Ohmae (1985). This chapter relates regionalization to the law of distance to examine the relevance of regions to international interactions, explores possible explanations for those patterns, highlights some of their managerial implications, and closes with a discussion of what current trends suggest about the future of regionalization.

It has already been documented elsewhere that the bulk of international interactions take place within rather than between roughly continent-sized regions (see, for example, Ghemawat and Altman 2014). Therefore, after briefly reviewing levels of regionalization, we devote the first section of this chapter to relating regionalization to the distance effects on which we have focused elsewhere in this volume. We begin by analyzing whether regionalization is simply a manifestation of distance effects or if intraregional interactions are even more intense than standard distance effects imply they should be. Given a lack of consensus about how regions should be defined, we use six different classification schemes to analyze this issue. This analysis indicates that most types of international interactions *are* more intense within regions than predicted by the baseline gravity models, at least using the seven-region classification employed in the *DHL Global Connectedness Index* (other classifications yield varying results). Then, we consider possible explanations for this greater intensity of international interactions within regions. International business scholars have proposed that substantial discontinuities arise at the region boundary (Aguilera, Flores, and Kim 2015; Verbeke and Asmussen 2016). Probing this issue further, we conclude that it is probably better – as a general rule – to think in terms of continuous distance effects that are not perfectly captured by a single logged physical distance coefficient than in terms of discontinuities at the regional boundary.

The second section turns to why geography – whether conceived of in terms of distance or regionalization – matters so much. It does so by examining how geography correlates with the other dimensions of the CAGE Framework. There is greater similarity within regions than between them across all four CAGE dimensions. The third section shifts the focus from understanding regionalization to thinking about its managerial implications, and discusses a range of regional business strategies. The final substantive section takes a longitudinal perspective to analyze changes in the regionalization of international interactions. This section concludes that the rise of emerging economies – the theme of Chapter 11 – is behind the recent reversal of a longstanding trend toward more regionalization.

Before zooming in on regionalization, however, we should briefly comment on other aspects of geography that will not be emphasized in this chapter. Table 10.1 follows the template from Chapters 8 and 9 to summarize the effects of adding geographic distance variables based on time zones, precipitation, temperature, and population density to the baseline gravity model in Chapter 5. These results show that all four variables achieve significance for at least four out of the eleven flows analyzed, but their signs are mixed. Time zone[1] and precipitation differences,[2] when significant, typically enter the models with negative signs, indicating that distance along these dimensions dampens international interactions. In contrast, differences in temperature[3] and population density[4] are more often significant with positive signs, suggesting a preponderance of arbitrage-driven interactions, e.g., tourism and agricultural trade motivated by climate differences.

Distance Effects and Regionalization[5]

International business scholars have emphasized how most international activity takes place inside regions. Figure 10.1 utilizes the seven-region classification scheme[6] from the *DHL Global Connectedness Index* (GCI) to compare levels of regionalization across several types of trade, capital, information, and people flows. Tourism is the most regionalized, with more than 70 percent of international tourists remaining within their home regions, as compared to a population-based frictionless benchmark of 14 percent.[7] Roughly 55 percent of merchandise exports and 50 percent of outward FDI stocks are intraregional, compared to a GDP-based frictionless benchmark of 17 percent. At the other end of the spectrum, the majority of international portfolio equity assets and

Table 10.1 *Summary Comparison of Gravity Models across Additional Geographic Variables*

	Number of significant focal coefficients and signs						Average number of observations	Average adjusted R-squared
	Physical distance	Common border	Time zone differences	Precipitation	Temperature	Population density		
0. Unrestricted baseline	11–	6+					22,763	0.795
1. Restricted baseline	11–	7+					21,649	0.793
2. Time zone differences	11–	8+	7–				21,649	0.794
3. Precipitation	11–	6+		5–, 1+			21,649	0.794
4. Temperature	11–	7+			3+,1–		21,649	0.794
5. Population density	11–	6+				4+,1–	21,649	0.794

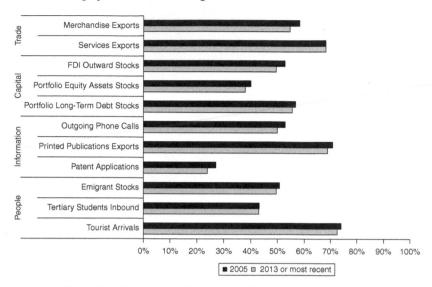

Figure 10.1 Intraregional Proportion of International Interactions by Type.
Source: Authors' analysis.

international university students do cross regional boundaries, but approximately 40 percent of those interactions are intraregional.[8] The least regionalized flow is patent applications, only 24 percent of which are intraregional, but these are concentrated in a very small number of countries.[9]

The business activity of multinational firms is also highly regionalized. Oh and Rugman (2014), in an update of Rugman and Verbeke (2004), report that the Fortune Global 500 earned an average of 70 percent of their revenue and deployed 72 percent of their assets in their home regions between 1999 and 2008 (based on the "broad triad" regions of Europe, North America, and Asia-Pacific). We will analyze more recent trends for this sample of firms in the final section of this chapter. Asmussen et al. (2015), utilizing a metric introduced in Asmussen (2009), find intraregional market penetration almost three times as high as interregional market penetration for the world's 2000 largest firms by revenue in 2005.

International interactions – at both the country and the firm levels – are therefore far more intense within than between regions, consistent with the law of distance. But are intraregional interactions *even more intense* (relative to interregional interactions) than one would expect based on the distance variables already captured in standard gravity models? In the words of Sammartino and Osegowitsch (2013), is regionalization simply "a parsimonious way of saying country-to-country distance matters" or is it "a meaningful concept above and beyond simply capturing distance"? The remainder of this section focuses

Table 10.2 *Attributes of Six Regional Classification Schemes Used in This Chapter*

	M49 Minor	GCI Region	Continent	M49 Major	Broad Triad	Complete Triad
Number of regions	22	7	6	5	3	3
Average countries per region	9.9	31.1	36.3	43.6	49.7	72.7
Average physical distance within regions (km)	1,488	3,145	3,108	3,282	5,008	4,503
Maximum physical distance within regions (km)	6,947	13,096	9,772	13,156	18,490	17,643

on answering this fundamental question, first by adding regional dummies to standard gravity models and then by testing alternative geographic explanations for the phenomenon of regionalization.

Adding Regions to Standard Gravity Models

The most straightforward technique for testing whether regions matter above and beyond the distance effects already captured in the standard gravity model is to add in a binary variable capturing whether or not both members of a country pair are in the same region.[10] This is the method employed by Hejazi (2005, 2007), which took a similar tack but was restricted to a more limited sample of countries and international flows. Hejazi (2005) found that trade among OECD countries is more regionalized than predicted by his baseline gravity model, and that FDI in Europe is also more regionalized than predicted.

Adding binary region variables to our gravity models requires selecting region classification scheme(s) to be employed. We have already mentioned our own GCI regions as well as the broad triad regions used in Rugman and Verbeke (2004), but those are just two of several possibilities. A good part of the literature relies on United Nations classification schemes, but region classification systems vary across different UN agencies. At least one interagency report includes aggregates using six different schemes in its annex tables (World Health Organization [WHO], UNICEF, UNFPA et al. 2015). (For a brief discussion of the some of the challenges associated with classifying countries into regions, see Box 10.1 on page 335.)

Given this state of affairs, we look across six different classification schemes in the analyses presented in this section. Table 10.2 summarizes their major attributes, with the alternatives arrayed from smallest to largest based on the average number of countries per region. The GCI regions have already been discussed. Continents follow standard geographic definitions.[11] The

M49 regions, widely used in UN publications, are defined at two levels of aggregation (United Nations 2013). The higher level, which we refer to as the "M49 Major" scheme, is very similar to continental classifications, although North and South America are combined into a single region ("The Americas") (United Nations 2013). The lower level, which we refer to as the "M49 Minor" scheme, comprises twenty-two country groupings, each of which is a subregion of an M49 Major region. The "Broad Triad" (so named in Rugman and Verbeke [2004] to distinguish it from original triad of the United States, the EU, and Japan proposed by Ohmae) has already been introduced. Here, it is defined as the countries of NAFTA, the continent of Europe, and Asia-Pacific, including both continental Asia and the East Asia and the Pacific region, but excluding Russia (which is included in the European region). Since this is the only classification used here that does not cover the whole world,[12] we also add a "Complete Triad," adapted from the GCI Regions: EMEA (Europe and the Middle East and Africa), the Americas (North and South), and Asia-Pacific (South Asia and East Asia and the Pacific).

Returning to the gravity models from Chapter 5,[13] we add a dummy variable that is coded 1 if a particular pair of countries is in the same region given the region classification scheme being used. The coefficients on this variable are shown in Table 10.3.[14] If the hypothesis that flows within regions are greater than predicted by the baseline gravity model holds, we should find positive and significant coefficients. The bottom two rows of the table summarize the signs of the significant coefficients, and indicate greatest support for this hypothesis when using the GCI regions, which achieved a significant and positive coefficient for eight flows (out of eleven), while obtaining a significant and negative coefficient for only one. The smaller M49 minor regions are significant for only four flows (all positive), and all of the larger groupings obtain more negative coefficients that are significant than the GCI regions. The broad triad, in particular, seems to be too broad in this context, with only three positive coefficients and five negative ones.

This result is particularly surprising given the emphasis the international business literature has placed on the regionalization of multinational firms. We follow up on it by undertaking parallel analyses of three other datasets on foreign investment by multinational firms: FDI flows,[15] announced greenfield FDI,[16] and counts of majority-owned foreign subsidiaries of the Fortune Global 500.[17]

Owing to the greater proportion of zero values in these additional datasets, as well as for consistency with the analyses reported in Chapter 6, all of the models with these additional variables were estimated using PPML rather than the OLS estimates on which Table 10.3 is based. As a result, the magnitudes of the coefficients reported in Table 10.4 should not be compared

Table 10.3 *Coefficients of a Binary Variable Coded 1 When Flows are Intraregional Using Each of the Six Regional Classifications*

	M49 Minor	GCI Region	Continent	M49 Major	Broad Triad	Complete Triad
Merchandise exports	0.527***	0.152**	0.141**	0.107*	−0.281***	0.242***
Services exports	−0.0518	0.496***	0.358***	−0.312**	0.315**	0.134
FDI outward stocks	−0.0176	−0.549***	−0.396**	−0.337**	−0.648***	−0.129
Portfolio equity assets stocks	0.279	0.653***	0.195	0.0909	−0.510***	−0.342**
Portfolio long-term debt stocks	−0.0950	0.541***	0.272*	0.273*	0.0957	−0.375***
Outgoing phone calls	0.150*	0.157	0.318***	0.0968	0.103	0.0861
Printed publications exports	0.404***	1.032***	0.541***	0.715***	−0.0293	0.452***
Patent applications	0.428***	−0.000312	−0.189**	−0.258***	−0.375***	−0.0745
Emigrant stocks	0.182	0.402***	0.557***	0.434***	−0.187**	0.298***
Tourist arrivals	−0.107	0.606***	0.773***	0.567***	0.374**	0.392***
Tertiary students inbound	−0.159	0.363***	0.319***	0.287***	0.205**	0.0938
Count *positive* and significant	4	8	8	6	3	4
Count *negative* and significant	0	1	2	3	5	2

*** $p<0.01$, ** $p<0.05$, * $p<0.1$.

directly to those in Table 10.3. That said, the results using the new FDI-related variables do provide some evidence of regional effects, as was the case (with GCI regions) for all the significant interactions except outward FDI stocks in Table 10.3. For FDI flows and Fortune Global 500 subsidiaries, there are positive and significant coefficients for all region classifications except M49 minor. In both cases, the largest coefficients are obtained with the GCI regions. In contrast, for announced greenfield FDI, we obtain a significant and positive coefficient only for GCI regions.

In light of the contrast between these results and the original FDI stocks analysis, we also performed several robustness tests, the results of which are

Table 10.4 *PPML Coefficients of a Binary Variable Coded 1 When Flows Are Intraregional Using Each of the Six Regional Classifications (Additional Indicators of Foreign Investment by Multinational Firms)*

	M49 Minor	GCI Region	Continent	M49 Major	Broad Triad	Complete Triad
FDI Flows (PPML)	−0.0943	1.049***	0.928***	0.413*	0.848***	0.542**
Announced Greenfield FDI (PPML)	0.0526	0.371**	0.00642	−0.0984	0.0429	−0.136
Fortune Global 500 Subsidiaries (PPML)	0.00412	0.554***	0.422***	0.294***	0.427***	0.435***
Count *positive* and significant	0	3	2	2	2	2
Count *negative* and significant	0	0	0	0	0	0

*** p<0.01, ** p<0.05, * p<0.1.

reported in the online appendix at www.ghemawat.com/laws. First, all of the OLS regressions reported in Table 10.3 were repeated with PPML, resulting in a similar pattern of many significant and positive coefficients, especially for the specifications that included 6–7 regions. There were, however, some changes to which coefficients were positive and significant. With this change, the coefficient for FDI stocks became insignificant across all region classifications (and positive except for M49 Minor). Second, we ran another set of regressions on FDI stocks using all available country pairs (rather than only the 97 covered in the baseline model) and the PPML estimator, resulting in positive coefficients for the intraregional dummy that were significant at the 0.05 level for GCI regions and continents and at the 0.1 level for the broad triad. Third, to address concerns that the number of subsidiaries of the Fortune Global 500 might be a noisy indicator of investment because firms may establish additional subsidiaries in a country for purely legal or tax advantages, we generated binary variables reflecting the simple presence or absence of one or more subsidiaries in a given country. Logit and probit regressions with this dependent variable produced roughly similar results to the PPML regression reported in Table 10.4.

Region Boundary Discontinuities or Other Proximity Effects?

The results reported in the previous subsection are certainly compatible with the view expressed by several international business scholars that region boundaries matter in a way that is roughly analogous to that of national borders: as the locus of significant discontinuities in distance effects. Aguilera et al. (2015) argue that "regional borders constitute points of discrete discontinuities" and add that a "spike in cost of doing business arises when firms cross regional boundaries" (378–379). Verbeke and Asmussen (2016) concur, stating that "the distance between countries forming a region and those outside of it represents a quantum leap or 'spike' as compared to intraregional distance" (5–6). But the mechanism by which intraregional interactions are intensified beyond standard distance effects merits further examination, especially because of the multiplicity of region classification schemes. If there is really a "quantum leap" in the distance effects faced by firms at regional boundaries, there should presumably be wider agreement about where those boundaries are located. A somewhat more analytical perspective is provided by adapting our gravity models to try to make such discontinuities visible. If distance effects spike at region boundaries, we should be able to pick up these spikes by replacing the physical distance variable in our standard model with a series of binary variables corresponding to stretches of physical distance (e.g., a binary variable for physical distance between 0 and 100 km, etc.), with separate series for interregional and intraregional physical distances.[18]

Figure 10.2 presents the results of such an analysis for merchandise trade, segmenting interregional and intraregional flows based on GCI regions. The physical distance stretches were defined using quantiles to ensure that each stretch (within the intra- and inter- series) is based on the same number of observations. The pattern we observe here is that there is a great deal of intermingling among the intraregional and interregional distance effects, without any obvious discontinuities. Furthermore, the logarithmic trend lines fitted to these points provide further support for the logged specification in the traditional gravity model. We also ran similar analyses for each of the other flows and region classifications covered in the previous subsection and while the results vary (as reported in the online appendix at www.ghemawat.com/laws), they do all feature substantial intermingling among the intraregional and interregional distance effects.

These results suggest that the region variables in the previous subsection may be picking up geographic proximity effects that are not fully captured in the standard gravity specification rather than actual discontinuities at the region boundary. If so, we should be able to improve upon at least some of those models by using alternative proximity measures. Of the many such possibilities, we test two simple ones: (1) a binary variable corresponding to a maximum physical distance within which interactions are expected to be more intense (i.e., a dummy variable coded 1 if the country pair is within n km of each other) and (2) a binary variable corresponding to a maximum physical distance rank from the perspective of the reporting country (i.e., a

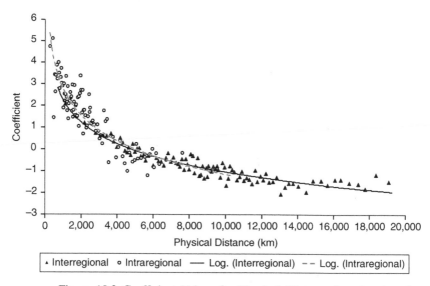

Figure 10.2 Coefficient Values for Physical Distance Stretches based on Merchandise Trade.
Source: Authors' analysis.

dummy variable coded 1 if the partner country is one of the *n* nearest countries to the reporter). In order to be as comprehensive as possible, we test physical distance-based proximity in increments of 100 km and closest rank based proximity for every rank.[19]

In Figure 10.3, we compare physical distance-based proximity versus GCI regions for merchandise exports.[20] Moving along the horizontal axis, the varying dots show where a coefficient is significant at the 0.1, 0.05, and 0.01 levels. Setting the physical distance-based binary variable between 2,000 km and 4,000 km results in a coefficient that is significant at the 0.01 level and larger than the intraregional binary variable, even with the (correlated) logged physical distance and trade agreement variables included in the regression equation. Also, at points between 2,300 km and 4,400 km, the intraregional binary variable loses statistical significance at conventional levels (although it remains positive). These results provide further support for the inference that the regional effect observed in the previous subsection for merchandise trade is better explained by geographic proximity effects above and beyond those captured in the baseline model than by spikes at region boundaries. Note also that beyond a radius of 11,300 km, the physical distance-based proximity variable becomes statistically significant again, and this time it is negative. This implies

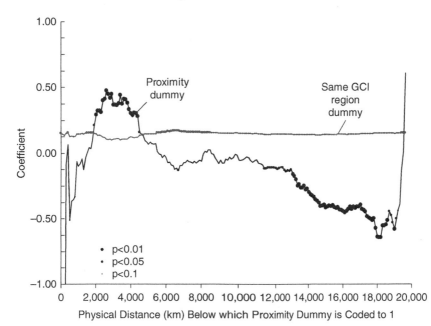

Figure 10.3 Regression Coefficients for the Gravity Model of Merchandise Trade, Adding Dummy Variables Coded 1 If Countries Are In the Same Region (Intraregional) and Within a Certain Physical Distance of Each Other (Proximity). *Source:* Authors' analysis.

that – at least for merchandise trade – the logged specification is not quite perfect. While it works well for country pairs in the 5,000–11,000 km range, it is not an ideal predictor for country pairs that are closer together or farther apart.

Replacing the physical distance-based proximity variable with a closest (n) countries (rank-based) binary proximity variable (that is, if $n = 10$, the nearest 10 countries to each exporting country will be coded 1 and all others 0) reveals a similar pattern. When the closest 5–19 countries are included, the coefficient is positive and significant at the 0.01 level; the intraregional coefficient loses significance when the proximity variable is included and n is between 13 and 20. Beyond n of 71, the coefficient becomes negative and significant. These results are broadly consistent with the physical distance-based proximity results, a pattern that generally holds across the flows analyzed. Owing to space constraints, the detailed results with both types of proximity for all of the flows are reported in the online appendix rather than here.

We summarize the results across both this subsection and the previous one in Table 10.5. Within and across each of the three approaches employed – regions,

Table 10.5 *Summary of Gravity Models using Regions versus Other Proximity Indicators*

	Region classification				Proximity (kilometers)				Proximity (ranks)			
	Region Classification with Maximum Coefficient	Maximum coefficient	S.E. at Maximum	R-squared at Maximum	Distance with Maximum Coefficient	Maximum Coefficient	S. E. at Maximum	R-squared at Maximum	Rank with Maximum Coefficient	Maximum Coefficient	S. E. at Maximum	R-squared at Maximum
Merchandise exports (logged)	M49 Minor	0.527	0.110	0.778	2,600	0.625	0.0904	0.778	8	0.403	0.0968	0.778
Services exports (logged)	**GCI Region**	**0.496**	**0.147**	**0.882**	12,000	0.272	0.0973	0.882	14	0.404	0.0985	0.882
FDI outward stocks (logged)	–	–	–	–	12,100	0.512	0.169	0.753	**65**	**0.520**	**0.150**	**0.753**
Portfolio equity assets stocks (logged)	**GCI Region**	**0.653**	**0.200**	**0.767**	12,000	0.595	0.145	0.768	29	0.535	0.144	0.767
Portfolio long-term debt stocks (logged)	GCI Region	0.541	0.158	0.763	12,100	0.500	0.123	0.763	**25**	**0.565**	**0.131**	**0.763**
Outgoing phone calls (logged)	Continent	0.318	0.0819	0.894	**3,400**	**0.448**	**0.112**	**0.894**	8	0.162	0.0819	0.893

Printed publications exports (logged)	**GCI Region**	1.032	**0.111**	**0.704**	11,300	0.528	0.0790	0.702	62	0.316	0.0760	0.701
Patent applications (logged)	**M49 Minor**	0.428	**0.0998**	**0.822**	15,800	0.375	0.0796	0.821	90	0.319	0.0919	0.821
Emigrant stocks (logged)	**Continent**	0.557	**0.0871**	**0.804**	3,200	0.464	0.107	0.803	8	0.410	0.0948	0.803
Tourist arrivals (logged)	Continent	0.773	0.114	0.884	**15,700**	**0.906**	**0.135**	**0.882**	17	0.565	0.127	0.880
Tertiary students inbound (logged)	GCI Region	0.363	0.114	0.716	**12,400**	**0.489**	**0.0839**	**0.720**	23	0.383	0.0910	0.719
FDI Outward Flows (PPML)	GCI Region	1.049	0.319	0.478	**6,800**	**1.305**	**0.219**	**0.482**	47	1.031	0.240	0.477
Announced Greenfield FDI (PPML)	GCI Region	0.371	0.159	0.558	12,200	0.390	0.131	0.531	**88**	**0.526**	**0.134**	**0.533**
Fortune Global 500 Subsidiaries (PPML)	GCI Region	0.554	0.113	0.524	**5,800**	**0.625**	**0.0933**	**0.525**	37	0.532	0.0618	0.527

physical distance-based proximity, and rank-based proximity – we have selected the region classification scheme or proximity variable that was associated with the largest effect, based on the magnitudes of positive and significant coefficients. Note that the magnitudes of the coefficients are all comparable (within rows) because they all pertain to binary variables in otherwise equivalent regressions. Across the three best-in-class models for each type of international interaction, the one with the largest significant and positive coefficient is highlighted in bold.[21]

From the standpoint of selecting between regions and proximity variables, the results are mixed. Focusing first on the usual set of interactions covered in Chapter 5 and Table 10.3, six of the largest coefficients pertained to proximity (4 based on physical distance and 2 based on ranks) while five pertained to regions (3 with GCI regions, 1 with M49 minor, and 1 with continents). It is also interesting to note the large differences across flows within each of the three categories of models. The best performing regions range from the small M49 minor (for merchandise exports and international patenting) to continents (telephone calls, emigration, and tourist arrivals). Using physical distance-based proximity, the largest coefficients fall into two clusters: one between 2,500 and 3,500 km (merchandise exports, telephone calls, and emigration) and another between 11,000 and 13,500 km (all others except patents and tourism). The best performing rank boundaries range from the closest eight countries (for merchandise exports, telephone calls, and emigration) up to the closest ninety (for patents).

The physical distance- and rank-based proximity variables outperform regions for the three additional types of activity covered at the bottom of Table 10.5: FDI outward flows, announced greenfield FDI and counts of Fortune Global 500 subsidiaries. Across two of these (FDI outward flows and Fortune Global 500 subsidiaries), the largest significant coefficients were obtained using physical distance-based proximity, whereas for announced greenfield FDI, the largest significant coefficient was obtained using ranks.

Apart from underscoring the need for further research on this topic, we view these results as more consistent with the view that continuous distance effects have complex contours than the view that large discontinuities arise at region boundaries. Distance effects are captured remarkably well by the continuous logged physical distance specification in the baseline model, but that specification represents only a broad generalization: one can think of many causes of irregularities that crop up at varying distances, not only at the region boundary. Focusing only on physical flows, think, for example, of shifts at distances where there would be a change in the dominant mode of transport.[22]

Box 10.1. Defining Regions

The abundance of differing region definitions reflects the fact that regional schemes are neither fully intellectual nor political (Agnew 1999, 95). Even the continents are only partially defined by geography, with the large landmass of Europe and Asia being divided arbitrarily by the Urals and the Black Sea, but not by the more formidable Himalayas. Plate tectonics would split off India and Arabia – but not Europe – from the rest of Asia (Frisch, Meschede, and Blakey 2011, 5). In terms of politics, the boundaries of regions are even messier. The European Union includes Cyprus, though it is much closer to Turkey and Syria than to Greece. The United Nations' Economic and Social Commission for Western Asia and the Economic Commission for Africa (two of the five regional commissions with broadly comparable mandates) have an overlap of six members, all in northern Africa (United Nations "ECA Members" 2016; "ESCWA Members" 2016). The Asia-Pacific Economic Cooperation members span 18½ time zones from Kaliningrad to Newfoundland, and yet it is considered a regional organization.

As background research for this chapter, we made several attempts at generating new region classifications based on international flows as well as countries' CAGE (cultural, administrative/institutional, geographic, and economic) characteristics. We used the k-means algorithm (a cluster analysis method that seeks to create groupings that minimize the within-group Euclidean distance) to generate regions endogenously: maximizing intraregional flow intensity, minimizing CAGE distance within regions, as well as minimizing distance between centroids of countries' international flows. We also used a hill-climbing algorithm as a simple method to revise existing region classifications, experimenting both with boosting the intraregional percent of interactions as well as the significance of the intraregional binary variable in our gravity model regressions.

Selected results from this analysis are available in the online appendix. To summarize them here, rather than a clear pattern of convergence across these various attempts, we obtained regions of greatly varying shapes and sizes, which often did not conform to typical standards of regional classifications, such as geographic compactness. Therefore, we restricted our focus in the main body of this chapter to traditional region classifications and to purely geographic alternatives (proximity based on simple distance radii and based on ranks of closest countries).

Regions and the Rest of the CAGE Framework

Why does geography – whether conceived of in terms of distance effects or regionalization – seem to matter so much, even for "weightless" interactions that require no physical transportation of any kind? Recall that Head and Mayer (2013) estimate that only 4–28 percent of distance-driven trade costs are attributable to transportation costs. Instead, they argue that geography has such a strong inhibiting effect on trade because of the historical legacy of geographic separation in which "cultural difference and inadequate information manifest themselves most strongly at national borders and over distance." More generally, geography seems to have such a large dampening effect on international interactions – both tangible and intangible ones – in substantial part because of its correlations with the other dimensions of the CAGE Framework.

Table 10.6 compares similarities and differences across the CAGE Framework between countries that are located in the same versus different GCI regions, based on both simple and GDP-weighted averages.[23] Across almost all of the factors shown on the table, countries that are located in the same region are, on average, more similar than countries located in different regions. Based on simple averages, for example, countries in the same region are 2.6 times as likely as countries in different regions to share a common official language (30 percent of countries in the same region do as compared to only 12 percent in different regions). Note that the common language coefficient from the baseline merchandise trade gravity model indicates that a common language more than doubles trade, illustrating how greater similarity within regions can boost intraregional interactions.

The same basic pattern – greater similarity within as compared to between regions driving more intraregional than interregional interactions – tends to apply across the other factors shown in Table 10.6. With the exception of colony/colonizer ties, there is significantly greater similarity within regions than between them with respect to all of the distance variables covered in the baseline gravity models in Chapter 5.[24]

The pattern that proximate countries are more similar than distant ones can also be analyzed with respect to physical distance rather than region boundaries. Figure 10.4 provides an illustration by plotting the proportion of countries that share a trade agreement, regional trade bloc, official language, and colonial linkage as well as average per capita income ratios[25] against the percentile ranks of the physical distances between the country pairs (with calculations performed at intervals of five percentile points). The figure shows that there is a steep drop in all five commonalities over even the shortest distances. The proportions of countries within the same GCI and broad triad regions are also shown to highlight how most of this drop-off takes place before reaching the

Table 10.6 *Average CAGE Commonalities/Differences among Countries in Same versus Different GCI Regions*

		Simple Average				GDP-weighted Average			
		Same Region	Different Region	Ratio	Sig.	Same Region	Different Region	Ratio	Sig.
Cultural	Common official language	30%	12%	2.62	***	14%	15%	0.97	
	Common religion	85%	48%	1.77	***	73%	45%	1.62	***
	Power distance[†]	24.93	24.91	1.00		23.43	24.08	0.97	
	Uncertainty avoidance[†]	25.38	27.52	0.92	***	26.03	28.71	0.91	***
	Individualism (vs. collectivism)[†]	20.37	30.45	0.67	***	21.41	35.79	0.60	***
	Masculinity (vs. femininity)[†]	25.35	20.66	1.23	***	24.25	21.03	1.15	***
	Long- (vs. short-) term orientation[†]	19.88	29.09	0.68	***	21.75	31.03	0.70	***
Administrative	Colonial linkage	1%	1%	1.02		3%	4%	0.88	
	Common legal origin	44%	29%	1.52	***	25%	27%	0.91	***
	Common currency	7%	0%	183.35	***	9%	0%	21.69	***
	Regional bloc	17%	0%	–	***	31%	0%	–	***
	Trade agreement	35%	7%	5.14	***	54%	10%	5.41	***
	Rule of law[^†]	0.22	0.28	0.76	***	0.26	0.36	0.72	***
	Political stability and absence of violence[^†]	0.20	0.26	0.76	***	0.19	0.24	0.77	***
	Control of corruption[^†]	0.23	0.28	0.82	***	0.27	0.33	0.81	***
Geographic	Physical distance (km)	3,145	9,518	0.33	***	2968	9213	0.32	***
	Common border	8%	0%	30.86	***	15%	1%	15.28	***
	Population density (people per sq. km of land area)[‡]	15.64	16.82	0.93		16.82	13.66	1.23	**
	Urban population (% of total)[†]	20.76	28.29	0.73	***	20.50	27.87	0.74	***
	Hours of time zone difference	1.34	5.33	0.25	***	1.43	6.25	0.23	***

(continued)

Table 10.6 (cont.)

	Simple Average				GDP-weighted Average			
	Same Region	Different Region	Ratio	Sig.	Same Region	Different Region	Ratio	Sig.
Economic								
GDP per capita (current US$)‡	5.17	13.61	0.38	***	4.89	16.99	0.29	***
GDP per capita, PPP (current international $)‡	3.93	7.85	0.50	***	3.27	8.28	0.40	***
Real GDP growth rate 2004-2014†	0.02	0.03	0.79	***	0.03	0.03	0.77	***
Volatility of GDP growth 2004-2014†	2.65	2.70	0.98	***	1.61	2.05	0.78	***
Agriculture, value added (% of GDP)†	10.22	13.52	0.76	***	6.37	11.68	0.55	***
Industry, value added (% of GDP)†	11.52	13.65	0.84	***	10.59	12.20	0.87	***
Services, etc., value added (% of GDP)†	12.41	16.07	0.77	***	11.34	16.89	0.67	***
Research and development expenditure (% of GDP)†	0.89	1.04	0.85	***	1.16	1.57	0.74	***
Human Development Index 2014 (HDI)†	0.10	0.19	0.52	***	0.10	0.20	0.48	***

*** p<0.01, ** p<0.05, * p<0.1.

Note: ^ Max-min normalization; † Difference in absolute value; ‡ Max-min ratio; Cells shaded in gray indicate greater similarity either within or across regions.

Sources: Centre d'Etudes Prospectives et d'Informations Internationales (CEPII), Trade Agreement augmented using data from the World Trade Organization; Dow and Karunaratna (2006); World Bank World Governance Indicators (2014); World Bank World Development Indicators (2016) reporting 2014 or most recent year available, IMF World Economic Outlook (October 2015), United Nations Development Program (2015); Geert Hofstede Dimension Data Matrix (2015).

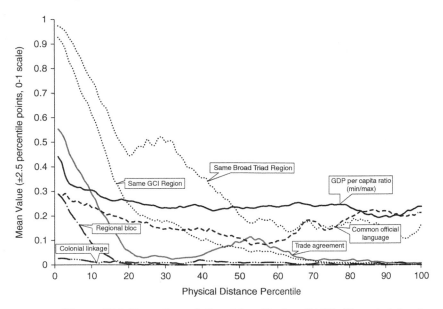

Figure 10.4 Proportion of Countries Sharing CAGE Characteristics by Physical Distance Percentile.
Source: Authors' analysis.

GCI region boundary and thus well within the broad triad region boundary.[26] Interestingly, the common official language measure first goes down and then back up, reflecting the historical legacy of far-flung colonial empires.

The same correlations also imply that physical distance can serve as a useful shorthand heuristic for composite distance across all four of the CAGE dimensions. Figure 10.5 presents the results of an analysis that tested this intuition. The composite CAGE distance values discussed in Chapter 5 pertaining to each of the flows analyzed in that chapter's gravity models were correlated here with physical distance. The correlation coefficients all exceed 60 percent, except in the case of the portfolio long-term debt. For the majority of flows, they exceed 80 percent.

Another illustration of this pattern is provided by ranking, from a focal country's perspective, its largest partner countries across multiple types of interactions. For the United States, Canada ranks among the top five partners across all of the interactions covered in Figure 10.5. The United States is Canada's top partner across all of the interactions except one (inbound students). Similar patterns tend to apply for other focal countries, with most international interactions involving countries that are geographically proximate and also share similarities on other CAGE dimensions. Given the correlations between physical and other types of distance, physical distance often provides a reasonable proxy for overall (relative) distance.

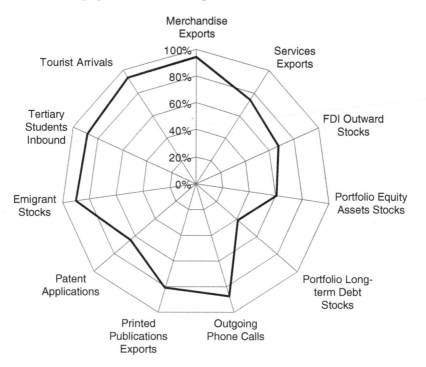

Figure 10.5 Correlations of Composite CAGE Distance with Physical Distance.
Source: Ghemawat, Pankaj, and Tamara de la Mata. "Globalization and Gravity." unpublished working paper, IESE Business School, 2015, Figure 1B.

Regional Business Strategies

The correlations between geographic and composite CAGE distance described in the previous section also underpin some of the value of regional strategies at the firm level. Regardless of whether or not there are true distance discontinuities at the region boundary, the greater similarity within as compared to between regions makes them a convenient base upon which firms may construct aggregation strategies. Ghemawat (2005) and Chapter 5 of Ghemawat (2007) are both devoted entirely to the topic of regional aggregation strategies, so we will summarize that content only briefly here.

Figure 10.6 illustrates six regional strategy archetypes. Note that the focus of boxes 1 through 3 is intraregional, in a sense, while that of boxes 4 through 6 is interregional. The boxes represent progressively more complex – and less common – approaches to dealing with regional boundaries. However,

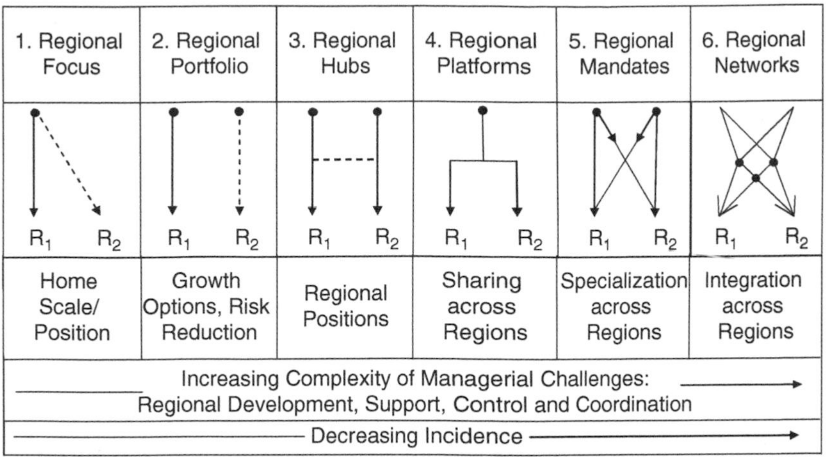

1. Regional Focus	2. Regional Portfolio	3. Regional Hubs	4. Regional Platforms	5. Regional Mandates	6. Regional Networks
R_1 R_2	R_1 R_2	R_1 R_2	R_1 R_2	R_1 R_2	R_1 R_2
Home Scale/ Position	Growth Options, Risk Reduction	Regional Positions	Sharing across Regions	Specialization across Regions	Integration across Regions

Increasing Complexity of Managerial Challenges: ⟶
Regional Development, Support, Control and Coordination

⟵——————————— Decreasing Incidence ⟶

Note: The solid circle (•) can be interpreted as distinct product types; R_1 and R_2 represent two regions.

Figure 10.6 Regional Strategy Archetypes.
Ghemawat, Pankaj. 2007. *Redefining Global Strategy: Crossing Borders in a World Where Differences Still Matter.* Boston, MA: Harvard Business School Press. Figure 5.3, p. 145.

it is worth noting that there is no natural order of progression through these regional strategy archetypes. Different regional strategies make sense for different businesses.

Regional or Home Focus

Focusing on the home region is worth emphasizing as a strategy because virtually all companies start off in this box, except for the very few that are "born global," often in high-technology areas. This is also the box in which most of the Fortune Global 500 still reside based on the geography of their sales. Focusing on selling to regional markets is favorable in a number of circumstances, including:

- A particularly profitable regional or home market (although this is likely to attract entrants from other regions)
- A need for deep local knowledge that reduces efficient breadth
- A high sensitivity to regional free-trade arrangements and regional preferences
- Other factors that effectively collapse the distance *within* regions relative to the distance *between* them (e.g., regional energy grids)

Other companies should be placed in this box based on their production footprints. Thus, in the highly globalized memory chip (DRAM) business, Samsung sells worldwide but considers the co-location of most R&D and production around one main site in South Korea as a key competitive advantage. Given how low transport costs are relative to product value, global concentration – which permits rapid iteration across R&D and production – dominates geographic dispersion. More generally, a regional or home focus for production activities is attractive when global scale economies are strong enough to permit centralization of at least some activities in one region or location, or when key economies of scale operate at the regional, rather than local or global, level.

Many of the risks associated with regional or home focus relate to the erosion of the conditions underpinning its viability relative to more globally standardized strategies. Also, regional focusers can run out of room to grow or fail to hedge risk adequately, motivating broader expansion efforts.

Regional Portfolio

Box 2 – the regional portfolio – comprises strategies that involve more extensive operation outside a single region. When companies look to move from box 1 to box 2, they often cite growth options and risk reduction. Particular stimulants to move in this direction include faster growth in nonhome regions, significant home positions that generate substantial free cash flow, local investment requirements to access foreign markets, and the opportunity to "average out" shocks, cycles, and so forth, across regions. Regional portfolio strategies tend to migrate some resource allocation and monitoring roles from corporate headquarters to regional entities. Apart from that migration, however, they offer little opportunity for regional considerations to influence what happens on the ground at a local level.

Regional Hubs

A more active alternative for adding value at the regional level was originally articulated by Kenichi Ohmae in the context of his notion of the "triad." This involves building regional bases or hubs that provide a variety of shared resources or services to the local (country) operations. The logic is that these hubs may – because of lumpiness, or increasing returns to scale, or externalities – be hard for any one country to justify, but may still be worth investing in from a cross-border perspective. Although a single or few locations often provide such shared resources and services, in some cases, the hub may be a virtual one.

Regional hub strategies in their purest form – that is, those focused solely on regional position – represent a structured, multiregional version of the regionally focused strategies discussed in box 1. Therefore, some of the same conditions that favor a regional focus also favor regional hubs: (1) economies of scale at the regional level; (2) factors that effectively collapse the distance within regions relative to the distance between them; and (3) other conditions that lead to battles to build position at the regional level. The difference is that with more than one region, considerations of interregional heterogeneity also come into play. The more that regions differ in their requirements, the weaker the rationale for the multiple, regionally focused entities within such a company to share resources and services.

A regional headquarters (RHQ) can be seen as a minimalist version of a regional hub. The impact of an RHQ is typically limited, however, by a focus on support functions, with limited links to operating activities. Phillipe Lasserre (1996) has developed a list of key RHQ functions that can help broaden the possibilities companies may wish to consider: scouting (business development), strategic stimulation (helping organizational subunits understand and deal with the regional environment), signaling commitment to a region (to internal and external audiences), coordination (ensuring the exploitation of synergies and the pursuit of consistent policies across the region), and pooling resources (to take advantage of regional scale economies).

Regional Platforms

Regional hubs, as we have seen, spread fixed costs across the countries within a region. Regional platforms, by contrast, spread fixed costs across regions – and could, therefore, also be described as "interregional platforms." Platforming, as noted in Chapter 4, is typically emphasized for back-end activities that deliver scale and scope benefits if coordinated across regions. Thus, major automakers attempt to reduce the number of basic platforms they offer worldwide to achieve greater economies of scale in terms of design costs, engineering, administration, procurement, and operations. The goal is not to reduce the *amount of product variety* on offer, but instead to *deliver variety more cost effectively* by building local customization atop common platforms explicitly engineered for adaptability along these lines.

The principal risk inherent in platforming strategies is that companies may take standardization too far, at the expense of the variation required for the local marketplace. A tendency toward centralization of key decisions at the corporate headquarters reinforces the risk of excessive standardization of platforms across regions.

Regional Mandates

Regional mandates could also be described as interregional mandates, because they involve awarding broader mandates to certain regions to supply particular products or to perform particular organizational roles in order to tap economies of *specialization* as well as scale. Whirlpool, for example, sources most of its small kitchen appliances from India. And a host of global companies have broadened the mandates of their production operations in China.

(Inter)regional mandates also show up in areas that go beyond product development and production. Thus, global consulting, engineering, financial services, and other service businesses often feature centers of excellence – repositories of particular knowledge and skills that are charged with making them available to the rest of the firm.

Again, there are several risks associated with assigning broad geographic mandates to particular locations. First, they can supply cover for local, national, or regional interests to unduly influence, or even hijack, a firm's global strategy. Second, broad mandates are not well suited to picking up on variations in local, national, or regional conditions, although overlaying other approaches such as platforming can be of some help here. And finally, carrying the degree of specialization to extremes can create inflexibility and lack of redundancy. In a volatile world, these are non-trivial concerns.

Regional Networks

To achieve complementarities across different regions, while avoiding excessive specialization and inflexibility, regional networks involve *integration* as well as division of labor among resources located in different regions. Although academics have discussed networking extensively, most companies merely *aspire* to such integration.

Having introduced this array of strategies, it is worth adding that analogues can be applied at geographic levels of aggregation other than international regions. Thus, Ghemawat (2015) discusses applications to intranational regions, and Prahalad and Bhattacharyya discuss global strategies built around global cities (2008).

Regionalization in Retreat?

The penultimate section of Chapter 5 highlighted how the average physical distance traversed by the interactions measured in the *DHL Global Connectedness Index* has increased since 2005. Over the same period, unsurprisingly in light of the distance trends, the proportion of each of those interactions taking place

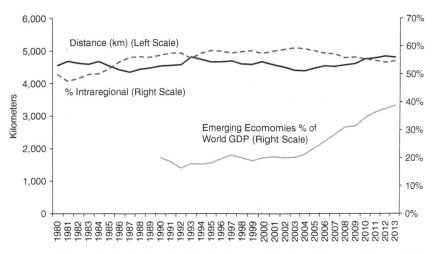

Figure 10.7 Merchandise Trade Average Physical Distance Traversed (in Kilometers) and Percent Intraregional, Emerging Economies Percent of World GDP, 1980–2013.
Source: Ghemawat, Pankaj, and Steven A. Altman. 2014. *"DHL Global Connectedness Index* 2014: Analyzing Global Flows and Their Power to Increase Prosperity." Deutsche Post DHL. www.dhl.com/gci. Figure 4.11, p. 68.

within (GCI) regions decreased (refer back to Figure 10.1). Here, we focus in on one of those country-level interactions – merchandise trade – extending the analysis back to 1980, and then turn to firm-level trends, focusing again on the Fortune Global 500. The discussion in Chapter 5 pointed to the rising proportion of international interactions involving emerging economies as the most likely driver of international interactions taking place over greater distances, a theme we will develop in greater detail here.

Country-Level Trends

The rich historical data available on geographic patterns of merchandise trade enables longer-term trend analysis. Figure 10.7 reveals that the current trend toward increasing distance and declining regionalization of merchandise trade began in 2003 and coincided with a sharp increase in the emerging economies' share of world GDP. Declining regionalization since 2003 has rolled back a large part of the increase on this measure that had taken place since 1980. By 2013, the regionalization of merchandise trade had fallen all the way back to a level last observed in 1986!

A region-by-region examination of changes that took place since 2005, shown in Figure 10.8, illustrates how the rising share of exports coming from

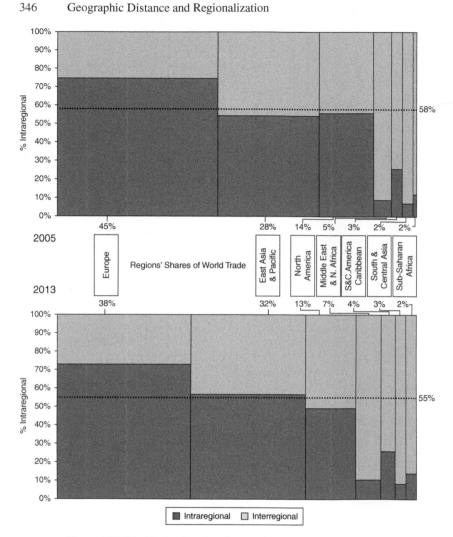

Figure 10.8 World Merchandise Exports Split by Region and by Intraregional versus Interregional, 2005 and 2013.
Ghemawat, Pankaj, and Steven A. Altman. 2014. "DHL *Global Connectedness Index* 2014: Analyzing Global Flows and Their Power to Increase Prosperity." Deutsche Post DHL. www.dhl.com/gci. Figure 4.12, p. 69.

emerging economies drove down the intraregional share of exports. Had all of the individual regions' levels of regionalization changed as they did from 2005 to 2013 (shown on the vertical axes of the figure) without any share shifts among regions (shown on the horizontal axis), the intraregional share would have gone down only one-quarter as much as it actually did over the period. More specifically, since Europe's trade is substantially more regionalized than that of any other region, Europe's falling share of global exports (from 45 percent to 38 percent) alone significantly reduced the intraregional share of world trade. East Asia & Pacific, the region with the largest gain in share of world exports, did continue its three decade long trend toward a higher proportion of intraregional trade (up from only 35 percent in the mid-1980s to over 55 percent in 2013), but its trade still remained significantly less regionalized than Europe's (which has tended to hover between 70 percent and 75 percent since the 1970s).

The rising intraregional share of trade in East Asia & Pacific also presents an interesting contrast to regionalization in Europe. While East Asian trade integration has been driven more by the creation of multi-country regional production chains, a higher share of intra-European trade involves final goods. Parts and components comprise 38 percent of intraregional manufacturing exports in Asia, nearly double their 21 percent share in Europe (and also far exceeding their 28 percent and 17 percent shares respectively in North America and in South and Central America) (World Trade Organization (WTO) 2013, 79).

What does this analysis imply about efforts undertaken in advanced economies to boost exports to faraway emerging economies? The average distance traversed by advanced economies' exports (holding their shares constant) has not increased appreciably since 2005. However, finer-grained analysis by region does indicate some success at targeting export growth from distant emerging economies. Exports from North America and Europe (even with constant shares) traversed 7 percent and 5 percent greater physical distances respectively in 2013 than in 2005, while exports from advanced economies in Asia traversed shorter distances (Taiwan 11 percent shorter, Singapore 7 percent, South Korea 6 percent, and Japan 5 percent). This distinction provides a valuable reminder that particularly when undertaking geographic analysis, a shift toward emerging economies in general is often better understood as a shift specifically toward Asia. The earth's economic center of gravity has shifted from somewhere in the mid-Atlantic in 1980 to somewhere in Turkey today and it is projected to be more than halfway across Asia by 2050 (Quah 2011; Dobbs et al. June 2012). We examine this big shift further in Chapter 11.

Firm-Level Trends

Shifting from country- to firm-level analysis, our research with Niccolò Pisani of the University of Amsterdam also reveals evidence of declining levels of regionalization based on the sales distributions of the Fortune Global 500. For comparability, we followed Rugman and Verbeke's definition of intraregional sales as those taking place inside the three broad triad regions of North America, Europe, and Asia Pacific and included domestic as well as international sales. Among the firms listed on the 2014 Fortune Global 500 that released 2013 sales data by region, the average firm earned 35 percent of its revenue outside of its home region, up from 31 percent in 2008 (Oh and Rugman 2014) and 28 percent in 2001, as reported in Rugman and Verbeke's original study of the regionalization of this sample of firms (Rugman and Verbeke 2004).[27]

The rise from 2008 to 2013 in the proportion of sales these firms generated in distant regions contrasts with how the Fortune Global 500's sales footprints evolved between 2001 and 2008. Over that period, Oh and Rugman (2014) report that their sales became more international – but via growth *within* their home regions rather than beyond them. Between 2008 and 2013, the opposite pattern appears to hold, although that conclusion is qualified by differences in the samples. Over the latter period, we observe a higher proportion of interregional sales *and* a higher proportion of domestic sales, implying on average a shift from foreign sales close to home to foreign sales in more distant markets.

Further evidence that the Fortune Global 500 have become less regionalized comes from classifying each firm (among the 301 with sufficient data reported to do so) as either *"global," "bi-regional," "host-region oriented," or "home-region oriented."* Here, again, we follow the classification scheme introduced by Rugman and Verbeke (2004). A "global" firm has 20 percent or more of its sales in each of the three broad triad regions and less than 50 percent in any one region. A "bi-regional" firm earns at least 20 percent of its sales in two regions and less than 50 percent in one. To be classified as "host-region oriented," a firm must generate more than 50 percent of its sales in a region other than its home region. "Home-region oriented" firms earn more than 50 percent of their sales in their home regions. Table 10.7 compares our classification of the 2013 sales of the Fortune Global 500 with Rugman and Verbeke's analysis of the 2001 data.

From 2001 to 2013, the proportions of "global," "bi-regional," and "host-region oriented" firms all rose, while the proportion of "home-region oriented" firms declined. Most strikingly, 10.6 percent of the firms met Rugman and Verbeke's criteria for classification as "global" in 2013, versus only 2.4 percent in their original study. The increases in the "bi-regional" and "host-region oriented" categories were smaller. The proportion of firms classified as "home-region oriented" fell from 84 percent to 68 percent.[28]

Table 10.7 *Regionalization of the Fortune Global 500, 2001 vs. 2013*

Type of MNE	Definition	Rugman and Verbeke (2004) Data from fiscal year 2001			2014 FG500 Dataset Data from fiscal year 2013		
		No. of MNEs	Percentage of 380 MNEs reporting pertinent data	Percentage of intraregional sales	No. of MNEs	Percentage of 301 MNEs reporting pertinent data	Percentage of intraregional sales
Global	At least 20% of sales in each of the three regions of the triad.	9	2.4%	38.3%	32	10.6%	33.7%
Bi-regional	At least 20% of sales in each of two regions, but less than 50% in any one region	25	6.6%	42.0%	38	12.6%	39.2%
Host region oriented	More than 50% of sales in a triad market other than the home region	11	2.9%	30.9%	19	6.3%	25.5%
Home region oriented	At least 50% of sales in the home region of the triad	320	84.2%	80.3%	204	67.8%	78.8%
Insufficient data		15	3.9%	40.9%	8	2.7%	21.8%
No data		120			199		
	Total	500	100%	71.9%	500	100%	65.3%

Source: **Rugman and Verbeke (2004)** and authors' analysis.

There are important differences between the 2001 and 2013 datasets, most notably the arrival of a critical mass of firms based in emerging economies. In 2001, less than 5 percent of the firms were based in emerging economies; by 2013, a full 25 percent were from such countries (19 percent from China alone). Many of these newcomers – especially domestically focused Chinese state-owned enterprises – do not report international sales data. However, splitting the sample of firms with data available into those from advanced versus emerging economies reveals a stark contrast, and further illuminates the results already reported (see Table 10.8).

None of the Fortune Global 500 firms based in emerging markets could be classified as "global" firms, so removing them from the sample pushed the proportion of the advanced economy based firms that are "global" to 11.7 percent. Since the 2001 sample consisted almost exclusively of firms from advanced economies, we can conclude that a like-for-like comparison shows that the largest firms from advanced economies have indeed become less regionalized – and that firms based in emerging economies continue to lag behind on interregional expansion.

Another contrast between the Fortune Global 500 firms from advanced versus emerging economies is the higher proportion of the latter in the "host-region oriented" category. This presumably reflects the subset of emerging market multinationals that focus on selling to customers in advanced economies. One should be careful, however, not to read too much into this pattern since the majority of the Fortune Global 500 firms from emerging economies do not release their sales by geographic region.

While the preceding discussion followed Rugman and Verbeke by including both domestic and international sales in the analysis, for comparability with our country-level results, it is also worthwhile to look at the international sales of the Fortune Global 500 alone (excluding domestic sales). Across the 320 firms in the 2014 Fortune Global 500 that reported a split of domestic and international sales, the average firm generated 46 percent of its sales outside of its home country. Focusing in on the 237 firms that report both foreign/domestic and regional splits, the average intraregional share of international revenue was 37 percent (down slightly from about 38 percent in 2008 based on data deplotted from Figure 1 of Oh and Rugman [2014]). To provide some basis for comparison, this roughly matches the level of regionalization of international students, one of the least regionalized of the country-level interactions included in our analysis. The Fortune Global 500 are, of course, the world's largest firms and one would expect substantially higher levels of regionalization among smaller firms.

Conclusion

In this chapter, we have examined the idea, influential in the international business literature, that there is a substantial regional boundary effect that dampens

Table 10.8 Regionalization Comparison between Fortune Global 500 Firms Based in Advanced and Emerging Economies, 2013

Type of MNE	2014 FG500 dataset Data from fiscal year 2013			Advanced economies Data from fiscal year 2013			Emerging economies Data from fiscal year 2013		
	No. of MNEs	Percentage of 301 MNEs reporting pertinent data	Percentage of intraregional sales	No. of MNEs	Percentage of 273	Percentage of intraregional sales	No. of MNEs	Percentage of 28	Percentage of intraregional sales
Global	32	10.6%	33.7%	32	11.7%	33.7%	0	0.0%	–
Bi-regional	38	12.6%	39.2%	35	12.8%	39.1%	3	10.7%	40.5%
Host region oriented	19	6.3%	25.5%	15	5.5%	26.1%	4	14.3%	23.5%
Home region oriented	204	67.8%	78.8%	184	67.4%	77.9%	20	71.4%	87.3%
Insufficient data	8	2.7%	21.8%	7	2.6%	19.1%	1	3.6%	40.6%
No data	199			93			106		
Total	500	100%	65.3%	366	100%	64.5%	134	100%	73.1%

interregional interactions relative to intraregional ones. While our analysis does uncover some evidence of a region effect, it also suggests that this is probably better understood in terms of effects of physical (and other dimensions of) distance that are not fully captured in our baseline gravity model specifications rather than by spikes at region boundaries. It also suggests a need for further research to better pin down the relationship between distance effects and regionalization.

Our analysis of potential region effects also has implications for the selection of region classifications in international business research. While prior literature has focused on the broad triad (often grouping most of the world into only three regions), we generally obtained stronger results using classification schemes that allow for six or seven regions. This provides support for continued use of our GCI regions as well as standard continents. While the broad triad regions often seem too broad for this type of analysis, the M49 Minor classification (with its 22 regions) seems too narrow.

While it can be difficult to separate physical distance effects from region effects, some of the value of regions lies in their correlations with the nongeographic dimensions of the CAGE Framework. Countries located in the same region tend to be more similar culturally, administratively, and economically, than countries located in different regions. This makes regions particularly helpful building blocks for firms to use in thinking about how to achieve economies of scale and scope that extend beyond national borders.

We concluded this chapter by presenting evidence of declining levels of regionalization in recent years. This serves as a reminder that the geographic structure of international interactions is not fixed. These recent changes seem to reflect how the rising share of economic activity taking place in emerging economies is bringing about a dramatic restructuring of the geography of trade and to a lesser extent the geography of capital, information, and people flows. We will dig deeper into the rise of emerging economies – and how they differ from advanced economies – in the next chapter, which focuses on the economic dimension of the CAGE Framework.

Notes

1 Time zone differences are sourced from the CEPII Gravity dataset (www.cepii.fr/ CEPII/en/bdd_modele/presentation.asp?id=8). Unlike most continuous variables included in these models, this is not logged, as doing so would result in country pairs in the same time zone being excluded. This variable is significant with a negative sign for merchandise exports, tertiary students, emigration, tourist arrivals, outgoing phone calls, printed publications exports, and international patenting activity.

2 Average yearly precipitation data (in millimeters) are as reported in the World Bank Climate Change Knowledge Portal (http://data.worldbank.org/data-catalog/cckp_ historical_data). The historical data cover the years 1961–1999 and are incorporated into the model as a logged max/min ratio. This variable is significant with a negative

sign for merchandise exports, services exports, portfolio equity stocks, printed publications exports, and international patenting activity, and with a positive sign for tourist arrivals.

3 Average yearly temperature data (in centigrade) are as reported in the World Bank Climate Change Knowledge Portal (http://data.worldbank.org/data-catalog/cckp_historical_data). The historical data cover the years 1961–1999 and are incorporated into the models as a logged absolute difference. We do this instead of the max/min ratio because the logged specification would have excluded countries with an average annual temperature below 0 centigrade. Furthermore, the arbitrary level of 0 centigrade means that the typical interpretation of ratios does not apply (that is, a country that averages 20 degrees centigrade cannot be logically said to be twice as hot as one that averages 10 degrees centigrade – indeed it is only 36 percent warmer when measured in Fahrenheit). This variable was significant with a positive coefficient for merchandise exports, services exports, and tourist arrivals, and with a negative coefficient for tertiary students.

4 Population densities are taken from the World Bank's World Development Indicators and are incorporated in the models as a logged max/min ratio. The coefficients were significant with a positive sign for merchandise exports, international student arrivals, emigrant stocks and outgoing phone calls, and with a negative sign for international patenting activity.

5 The authors would like to thank Phillip Bastian for his assistance with the modeling for this section.

6 The region classification scheme employed here is based on the World Bank's region classification scheme, with modifications made to incorporate advanced economies into appropriate regions and to include all of the current members of the European Union in the Europe category. The North America category here refers only to the member countries of the North American Free Trade Agreement (Canada, Mexico, and United States). The regions that result are as follows: East Asia and Pacific (Australia, Brunei Darussalam, Cambodia, China, Fiji, Hong Kong SAR (China), Indonesia, Japan, Republic of Korea, Lao PDR, Malaysia, Mongolia, Myanmar, New Zealand, Papua New Guinea, Philippines, Singapore, Taiwan (China), Thailand, and Vietnam), Europe (Albania, Austria, Belarus, Belgium, Bosnia and Herzegovina, Bulgaria, Croatia, Cyprus, Czech Republic, Denmark, Estonia, Finland, France, Germany, Greece, Hungary, Iceland, Ireland, Italy, Latvia, Lithuania, Luxembourg, FYR Macedonia, Malta, Moldova, Netherlands, Norway, Poland, Portugal, Romania, Russian Federation, Serbia, Slovakia, Slovenia, Spain, Sweden, Switzerland, Ukraine, and United Kingdom), Middle East and North Africa (Bahrain, Egypt, Iran, Israel, Jordan, Kuwait, Lebanon, Morocco, Oman, Qatar, Saudi Arabia, Syria, Tunisia, United Arab Emirates, and Yemen), North America (Canada, Mexico, and United States), South and Central America and the Caribbean (Argentina, Bahamas, Barbados, Bolivia, Brazil, Chile, Colombia, Costa Rica, Dominican Republic, Ecuador, El Salvador, Guatemala, Guyana, Honduras, Jamaica, Nicaragua, Panama, Paraguay, Peru, Suriname, Trinidad and Tobago, Uruguay, and Venezuela), South and Central Asia (Armenia, Azerbaijan, Bangladesh, Georgia, India, Kazakhstan, Kyrgyz Republic, Nepal, Pakistan, Sri Lanka, Tajikistan, Turkey, and Uzbekistan), and Sub-Saharan Africa (Angola, Benin, Botswana, Burkina Faso, Burundi, Cameroon, Central African Republic, Republic of Congo, Côte d'Ivoire, Ethiopia, Gabon, Gambia, Ghana, Kenya, Madagascar, Mali, Mauritius, Mozambique, Namibia, Niger, Nigeria, Rwanda, Senegal, South Africa, Uganda, Zambia, and Zimbabwe).

7 The frictionless benchmarks discussed here are analogous to those used in Chapter 5, themselves based on benchmarks discussed in Head and Mayer (2013).

8 For students, we retain the same 14 percent population weighted benchmark as used for tourism. For portfolio equity investment, an analogous benchmark based on stock market capitalization is 19 percent.

9 The top five countries in 2013 (Japan, the United States, Germany, the Republic of Korea, and France) were responsible for 66 percent of international patent applications; the top five patent offices (the United States, the European Patent Office, China, Japan, and the Republic of Korea) received 71 percent of international patent applications.

10 Due to concerns about multicollinearity, we ran these analyses both including and excluding the trade agreement/regional trade bloc variables. Since the results were usually similar across these variants, we report here the results from models that retain these variables, for consistency with Chapter 5 and other related content elsewhere in this book.

11 Several countries span two continents, but for this analysis, are not divided across regions. Island countries also present some issues. For this analysis, all countries of the Caribbean are part of North America; Egypt is part of Africa; Panama is part of North America; Russia is part of Europe; Turkey is part of Asia; Indonesia, the Philippines, and Timor-Leste are part of Asia; and Papua New Guinea is part of Oceania.

12 Only 149 countries (out of 218) are part of any broad triad region. In the gravity models that follow, only 56 of the 97 countries in the limited sample are in any broad triad region. Interactions involving any countries not in a broad triad region are coded as interregional in the broad triad gravity models.

13 We are again using the ninety-seven country sample used in Chapter 5.

14 As in Chapter 5, these models use ordinary least squares (OLS).

15 FDI flows are based primarily on OECD data, supplemented with data from national sources for selected non-OECD countries. For details, refer to Appendix B, Table B.2 of Ghemawat and Altman (2014).

16 The data on announced greenfield FDI are drawn from the fDi Markets database.

17 The Fortune Global 500 data are based on the dataset we compiled with Niccolò Pisani that was described in Chapter 6. As in that chapter, we again control here for firm fixed effects.

18 This approach builds on the methodology employed in Gallego and Llano (2014).

19 For the distance based analysis, we tested distances between 200 and 19,600 km. These limits were set so that at least one country always falls into the range and at least one falls outside the range. The closest two countries in the sample were Belgium and the Netherlands, separated by 161 km. The most distant country pairs in the sample, Ecuador and Singapore, were 19,650 km apart; the theoretical maximum, given the planetary circumference is 20,038 km.

20 Each binary physical distance-based proximity variable was tested in a separate regression. Thus, Figure 10.3 summarizes the results of 195 regressions.

21 For proximity based models, we restricted our search for largest coefficients to those obtained with distance stretches and ranks between the fifth and ninety-fifth percentiles, to avoid focusing on anomalous results sometimes obtained when boundaries are set either very close or very far.

22 Additionally, it is worth noting the relative magnitudes of the distance effects in our standard models as compared to those we have considered in this section. The average distance between two countries in the same GCI region is 3,145 km, roughly one third of the average distance between countries in different regions (9,518 km). The baseline model, holding all else equal, predicts more than five times as much trade between countries at the interregional average distance, as compared to the intraregional average. In Table 10.5, the largest coefficient for merchandise exports was only 0.63 (using a maximum distance of 2,600 km), implying less than a doubling of trade within that radius. This fits with our view that it is best to make continuous distance effects a primary focus, while still devoting secondary attention to improving our understanding of regions and other areas within which there may be additional proximity effects of interest.

23 While the comparisons here focus on similarities/differences between regions, it is also important to remember that regions themselves vary in terms of their internal distances and differences. Given its size and diversity, internal distances within Asia can be especially formidable.

24 This holds for both simple and GDP-weighted averages in all cases except common language, for which there is only greater similarity within regions when using simple averages.

25 This time calculated as lower divided by higher to produce a measure of similarity rather than difference, for consistency with the other measures on the chart.

26 This provides further support for the view that there do not seem to be substantial discontinuities at region boundaries.

27 Our 2013 calculation was based on 316 firms with sufficient data available. The sample of firms covered in this analysis varied across the years. Therefore, the trends described pertain to the Fortune Global 500 as an evolving collection of firms rather than to changes over time in a fixed sample of firms. The 2008 value reported by Oh and Rugman (2014) included all the firms listed in the Fortune Global 500 between 2000 and 2009 (based on data from 1999 to 2008). Our calculation included only firms in the 2014 Fortune Global 500 (which was selected based on 2013 data). Oh and Rugman (2014) report 30 percent of sales being interregional in both 1999 and 2001.

28 While Oh and Rugman (2014) emphasized the persistence of regionalization over time, looking back on their results in the context of ours reinforces the sense of firms reaching farther over time. They report that the proportion of global firms rose from 2.4 percent to 4.0 percent from 1999 to 2008, biregional firms from 4.7 percent to 10.7 percent, and host-region oriented firms from 1.6 percent to 2.8 percent (while the proportion of home-region oriented firms fell from 89.9 percent to 79.1 percent).

References

Agnew, John. 1999. "Regions on the Mind Does Not Equal Regions of the Mind." *Progress in Human Geography* 23 (1):91–96. doi: 10.1191/030913299677849788.

Aguilera, Ruth V., Ricardo Flores, and Jin Uk Kim. 2015. "Re-Examining Regional Borders and the Multinational Enterprise." *Multinational Business Review* 23 (4):374–394. doi: 10.1002/smj.2356.

Asmussen, Christian Geisler. 2009. "Local, Regional, or Global? Quantifying MNE Geographic Scope." *Journal of International Business Studies* 40 (7):1192–1205. doi: 10.1057/jibs.2008.85.

Asmussen, Christian Geisler, Bo Bernhard Nielsen, Tom Osegowitsch, and Andre Sammartino. 2015. "The Dynamics of Regional and Global Expansion." *Multinational Business Review* 23 (4):306–327.

Dobbs, Richard, Jaana Remes, James Manyika, Charles Roxburgh, Sven Smit, and Fabian Schaer. June 2012. "Urban World: Cities and the Rise of the Consuming Class." McKinsey Global Institute. www.mckinsey.com/insights/urbanization/urban_world_cities_and_the_rise_of_the_consuming_class.

Frisch, Wolfgang, Martin Meschede, and Ronald Blakey. 2011. *Plate Tectonics: Continental Drift and Mountain Building*. Berlin, Heidelberg: Springer Berlin Heidelberg.

Gallego, Nuria, and Carlos Llano. "On the Non-Linear Relation between Trade and Distance: New Results for the Border Effect Using Region-to-Region National and Inter-National Flows." Economic Analysis Working Paper Series 6/2014, Universidad Autónoma de Madrid, Madrid.

Ghemawat, Pankaj. 2005. "Regional Strategies for Global Leadership." *Harvard Business Review* December: 98–108.

2007. *Redefining Global Strategy: Crossing Borders in a World Where Differences Still Matter*. Boston, MA: Harvard Business School Press.

2015. "From International Business to Intranational Business." In *Emerging Economies and Multinational Enterprises*, edited by Laszlo Tihanyi, Elitsa R. Banalieva, Timothy M. Devinney, and Torben Pedersen, 5–28. Emerald Group Publishing Limited.

Ghemawat, Pankaj, and Steven A. Altman. 2014. "DHL Global Connectedness Index 2014: Analyzing Global Flows and Their Power to Increase Prosperity." Deutsche Post DHL. www.dhl.com/gci.

Head, Keith, and Thierry Mayer. 2013. "What Separates Us? Sources of Resistance to Globalization." *Canadian Journal of Economics/Revue canadienne d'économique* 46 (4):1196–1231. doi: 10.1111/caje.12055.

Hejazi, Walid. 2005. "Are Regional Concentrations of OECD Exports and Outward FDI Consistent with Gravity?" *Atlantic Economic Journal* 33 (4):423–436. doi: 10.1007/s11293-005-2870-2.

2007. "The Regional Nature of MNE Activities and the Gravity Model." In *Regional Aspects of Multinationality and Performance*, edited by Alan M. Rugman. Oxford: Elsevier JAI.

Hutzschenreuter, Thomas, Ingo Kleindienst, and Sandra Lange. 2015. "The Concept of Distance in International Business Research: A Review and Research Agenda." *International Journal of Management Reviews*. http://dx.doi.org/10.1111/ijmr.12065.

Lasserre, Philippe. 1996. "Regional Headquarters: The Spearhead for Asia Pacific Markets." *Long Range Planning* 29 (1):30–37. doi: 10.1016/0024-6301(95)00063-1.

Oh, Chang Hoon, and Alan M. Rugman. 2014. "The Dynamics of Regional and Global Multinationals, 1999–2008." *Multinational Business Review* 22 (2):108–117. doi: 10.1108/MBR-04-2014-0015.

Ohmae, Kenichi. 1985. *Triad Power: The Coming Shape of Global Competition*. New York, NY; London: Free Press; Collier Macmillan.

Prahalad, C. K., and Hrishi Bhattacharyya. 2008. "Twenty Hubs and No HQ." *strategy+business* (Spring). PwC. www.strategy-business.com/article/08102.

Quah, Danny. 2011. "The Global Economy's Shifting Centre of Gravity." *Global Policy* 2 (1):3–9. doi: 10.1111/j.1758-5899.2010.00066.x.

Rugman, Alan M., and Alain Verbeke. 2004. "A Perspective on Regional and Global Strategies of Multinational Enterprises." *Journal of International Business Studies* 35 (1):3–18.

Sammartino, Andre, and Thomas Osegowitsch. 2013. "Dissecting Home Regionalization: How Large Does the Region Loom?" *Multinational Business Review* 21 (1):45–64. doi: 10.1108/15253831311309483.

United Nations (UN). 2013. "Composition of Macro Geographical (Continental) Regions, Geographical Sub-Regions, and Selected Economic and Other Groupings." United Nations Statistics Division, Last Modified October 31, 2013. http://unstats.un.org/unsd/methods/m49/m49regin.htm.

2016. "Member States (ECA)." Economic Commission for Africa (ECA). Accessed 2016. www.uneca.org/pages/member-states.

2016. "Member States (ESCWA)." Economic and Social Commission for Western Asia (ESCWA). Accessed 2016. www.unescwa.org/about-escwa/overview/member-states.

Verbeke, Alain, and Christian Geisler Asmussen. 2016. "Global, Local, or Regional? The Locus of MNE Strategies." *Journal of Management Studies*. doi: 10.1111/joms.12190.

World Health Organization (WHO), UNICEF, UNFPA, World Bank Group, and United Nations Population Division. "Trends in Maternal Mortality: 1990 to 2015: Estimates by Who, UNICEF, UNFPA, World Bank Group and the United Nations Population Division." WHO /RHR/15.23, Geneva, November 2015. www.who.int/entity/reproductivehealth/publications/monitoring/maternal-mortality-2015/en/.

World Trade Organization (WTO). 2013. "World Trade Report 2013: Factors Shaping the Future of World Trade." www.wto.org/english/res_e/booksp_e/world_trade_report13_e.pdf.

11 Economic Distance and the Big Shift to Emerging Economies

Pankaj Ghemawat and Steven A. Altman

In the early decades after World War II, the advanced economies of the "First World" dominated the world economy. Countries in the top quintile on GDP per capita generated 69 percent of global economic output (adjusted for purchasing power parity) in 1950, and this ratio averaged 60 percent throughout the second half of the twentieth century.[1] For multinational corporations – then almost all based in advanced economies – the most important foreign markets were in other advanced economies, limiting the economic distance to be traversed.

The rapid growth of emerging economies in the early twenty-first century has dramatically altered that pattern. By 2008,[2] countries in the top quintile on GDP per capita accounted for only 48 percent of world output, and emerging economies became the world's largest markets for many industries. The shift of economic activity to emerging economies requires multinationals from advanced economies to bridge greater economic distance: selling to customers across income levels, competing with firms from both advanced and emerging economies, and assembling value chains that tap into distinct resources and cost levels across advanced and emerging economies.

Meanwhile, the rise of multinationals based in emerging economies has created the possibility of new competitors taking over global industry leadership from advanced economy incumbents. Firms from emerging economies, however, also face challenges bridging economic distance – and generally have less experience addressing other dimensions of distance as well. Whether or not the big shift will lead to a big shakeup in global leadership across many industries remains an open question.

This chapter will focus primarily on the most prominent type of economic distance that separates advanced and emerging economies: income distance, that is, differences in per capita income levels. Other types of economic distance, which we will not emphasize here, include differences in capital costs, factor endowments, and economic size. Although these other variables are certainly also of interest, they do not – as of this writing – present firms with the sort of novel challenges that the emergence of middle income countries as major players in international business does, suggesting that a focus on income distance is particularly timely from the perspective of management practice.

The first section of this chapter presents an analysis of how differences in levels of economic development relate to international interactions. We show that per capita income differences inhibit most types of international interactions but do boost those that are motivated by arbitrage (e.g., exports of labor-intensive manufactures from low wage countries). The second section tracks the "big shift" of a rising proportion of economic activity to emerging economies, comparing the extent and speed of that shift across a variety of macroeconomic, corporate, and other indicators. The third section systematically examines differences between advanced and emerging economies that firms must account for when doing business between them. The fourth section discusses the question of whether the big shift will lead to a big shakeup of the corporate pecking order, with firms from emerging economies displacing incumbents from advanced economies as global industry leaders. The final substantive section considers early evidence on how such competition is playing out by examining patterns of industry leadership within China.

Before proceeding, however, we must briefly address how emerging economies are defined. Antoine W. van Agtmael coined the term "emerging markets" in 1981, while trying to sell the idea of a Third World investment fund on behalf of the International Finance Corporation. He recalled, "people looked down upon the 'Third World.' It sounded so distasteful. I thought people with that feeling would never invest … we had to use a more uplifting term" (quoted in Knowledge@Wharton 2008). As van Agtmael's motivation suggests, the classification of economies based on levels of development is a politically sensitive and divisive issue. And the fact that van Agtmael recently declared the United States the next great emerging market (Zweig 2013) and McKinsey managing director Dominic Barton also referred to the United States in this context (Raghavan 2015) underscores the need for more definitional clarity.

In line with the discussion in the rest of this book, this chapter employs the IMF's classification system, which divides countries into "advanced" and "emerging and developing" economies.[3] While the IMF's current *World Economic Outlook* states that "this classification is not based on strict criteria, economic or otherwise, and it has evolved over time" (2015, 145), its country lists still seem to be shaped by criteria for countries that are advanced economies enumerated in earlier editions. The 1997 *World Economic Outlook* mentions: "per capita income levels well within the range indicated by the group of industrial countries, well-developed financial markets and high degrees of financial intermediation, and diversified economic structures with relatively large and rapidly growing service sectors" (IMF 1997, Box 1).[4]

Figure 11.1 compares lists of emerging economies or analogous categorizations (low and middle income, etc.) across commonly used classification systems. There are 149 countries that appear on at least one of these lists. Of those, 23 are also considered advanced (or its analogue)

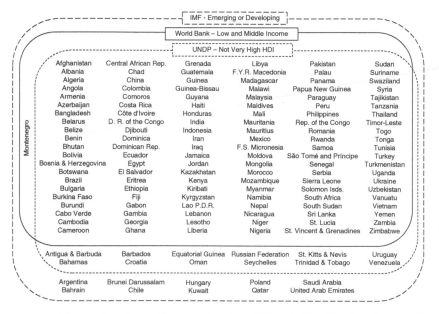

Figure 11.1 Venn Diagram Showing Different Classification Systems for Emerging and Developing Countries.
Sources: IMF, World Bank, UNDP.

on at least one list. Together, these 23 make up roughly 7.5 percent of world GDP. These discrepancies are easier to understand in light of how the different lists are compiled. The IMF criteria have already been discussed. The World Bank defines low- and middle-income countries as those with purchasing power parity-adjusted GNI of less than $12,736,[5] thus excluding many oil-rich countries as well as several others, primarily in Latin America and the Caribbean. The UN Development Program uses their Human Development Index (HDI), comprised of per capita income, educational attainment, and life expectancy, and classifies countries without "very high" HDI as those below 0.8[6] (on a 0 to 1 scale), again excluding several oil-rich countries as well as Argentina, Chile, Hungary, and Poland.

Another approach that is particularly popular in international business is to focus on enabling institutions rather than outcomes. Thus, Khanna and Palepu (1997) focus on the absence of well-functioning market institutions ("institutional voids") as the criterion for identifying emerging markets. On this basis, they see possibilities for emerging markets to exist within otherwise advanced economies. Khanna (2012) argues that the dot-com meltdown and subprime crisis resulted from emerging market conditions within the United States. While we prefer to rely instead on standard economic definitions of emerging economies,

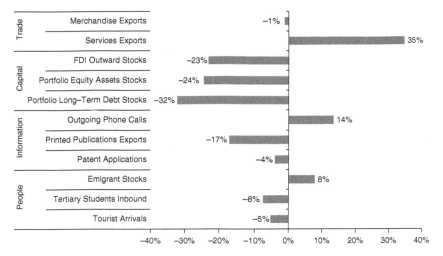

Figure 11.2 The General Effects of Doubling Per Capita Income Ratios (Higher/Lower).
Note: All effects statistically significant except merchandise exports.
Source: Based on gravity model analysis elaborated in Ghemawat and de la Mata (2015).

we revisit later on how they differ from advanced ones along all the dimensions of the CAGE Distance Framework, not just the administrative/institutional one.

Economic Distance and International Interactions

Economic distance inhibits most – but not all – types of international interactions. Figure 11.2 compares the impacts of doubling per capita income disparities across eleven types of international interactions, as estimated based on the gravity models described in Chapter 5. For this analysis, we measure per capita income disparities based on the ratios of country pairs' per capita incomes (higher divided by lower).[7] If countries have the same per capita income, the ratio is one, and it rises as their per capita incomes become more different. Doubling per capita income disparities implies, for example, shifting from a country pair such as France (GDP per capita ~$40,000) and Portugal (~$20,000) (ratio = 2) to a pair such as France and Mexico (~$10,000) (ratio = 4).

The only interaction, among the eleven covered on Figure 11.2, where per capita income disparities were not statistically significant was merchandise exports.[8] This does not mean that merchandise exports are unrelated to per capita income disparities. Rather, it reflects how trade can be both motivated and inhibited by income distance. Recall from Chapter 6 that estimating gravity models by product category showed positive and significant coefficients for ratio of GDP per capita in many industries, but also negative and significant coefficients for that variable in many others. Trade that is motivated by per capita income disparities often seeks to arbitrage across wage levels by exporting labor-intensive products and services from poorer countries to richer countries. Of course, other aspects of economic distance such as differences in countries' natural resource endowments can also motivate trade. Traditional Ricardian and Heckscher-Ohlin trade theories focus on trade that is motivated by such differences.

Trade can also be motivated by economic similarities (i.e., inhibited by differences). The Linder hypothesis suggests that countries with similar per capita income levels will trade more intensively with one another (Linder 1961). In countries with similar per capita incomes, buyers are more likely to be able to afford and to be interested in purchasing similar products. Thus, firms can often sell products they develop for their home markets in other countries with similar levels of economic development without investing as much in adapting to foreign markets as would be necessary to sell in economies with greater differences in development levels. Large observed intraindustry trade flows between countries with similar levels of economic development motivated the development of "New Trade Theory" by Paul Krugman and others (see, e.g., Krugman 1979).

Looking beyond merchandise trade, income distance has statistically significant effects on all the other types of international interactions shown in Figure 11.2. In seven of the ten cases, the effects are negative, indicating that increasing per capita income ratios dampens interactions. These cases are consistent with the general pattern implied by the law of distance with respect to other types of distance: interactions are more intense among countries that are more similar and decline as countries become more different.

The interactions for which per capita income differences have the largest inhibiting effect are the capital market interactions: doubling per capita income ratios reduces portfolio long-term debt by 32 percent, portfolio equity assets by 24 percent, and foreign direct investment by 23 percent. Portfolio investment, in particular, still takes place primarily between advanced economies, with upwards of three-quarters of these interactions (by value) involving one advanced economy investing in another advanced economy (and an even higher proportion if tax havens are excluded from the calculations).[9] The other interactions on which per capita income differences have smaller but still significant negative effects are trade in printed publications, international patenting, and international movements of students and tourists.

Among the interactions that are positively associated with differences in per capita income, the largest effect pertains to services trade. Doubling per capita income ratios is associated with a 35 percent increase in services exports. One possible explanation is that arbitrage motivates many services exports. India's IT services exports, which are almost all destined for advanced economies, present an obvious example.[10] And advanced economies export services to emerging economies by arbitraging across differences in the availability of specialized skills. For example, as of early 2014, the five tallest buildings in China were all designed by architects based in the United States and the UK.

Migration and telephone calling patterns were also positively associated with per capita income disparities. The result for migration is unsurprising, since migrants often seek opportunities in countries with higher wage levels. According to a World Bank estimate, workers who move from developing to developed countries triple their real incomes, on average (World Bank 2006). More emigrants from emerging economies, however, move to other emerging economies rather than to advanced economies, in part due to restrictions on people flows associated with visa and work permit requirements (UNDP 2009, 29). The telephone call results seem to reflect their association with migration patterns (people keeping in touch after moving),[11] as well as the fact that phone calls between advanced and emerging economies tend more often to be placed by the party in the advanced economy. A rough analysis indicates more than three times as many minutes of calls were placed from advanced economies to emerging economies than vice versa in 2012.[12]

In summary, economic distance can both motivate and inhibit international interactions, but the inhibiting effect tends to be stronger across the majority of the types of interactions studied here. These effects are becoming increasingly important to firms as the share of economic activity taking place in emerging economies rises, as discussed next.

The Big Shift to Emerging Economies

In 2014, emerging economies generated 39 percent of the world's economic output in US dollar terms, nearly double their 20 percent share in 2000. (In purchasing power parity or PPP terms, emerging economies' share of world GDP rose from 42 percent in 2000 to 57 percent in 2014.) Between 2008 and 2012, as the economic crisis battered most advanced economies, 79 percent of the world's economic growth took place in emerging economies.[13] Between 2014 and 2020, the IMF projects that 59 percent of global growth will take place in emerging economies (71 percent at PPP) (IMF October 2015). These projections assume that on average, emerging markets grow their per capita incomes more quickly than developed ones, but even demographic trends alone suggest faster growth in emerging economies. Over the 2014–2020 period, only 4 percent of population growth is expected to come from developed countries.[14] Thus, even if per capita incomes were stagnant, emerging markets would still grow more quickly.

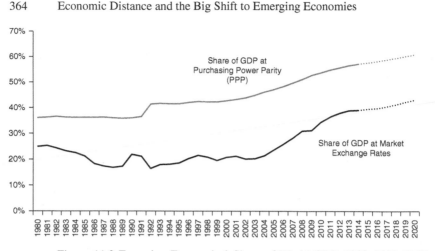

Figure 11.3 Emerging Economies' Share of World GDP, 1980–2020 (IMF Projections).
Source: Based on data from IMF World Economic Outlook, October 2015.

As shown in Figure 11.3, the big shift of economic activity to emerging economies predates the financial crisis of 2008, with the emerging economies' share of world GDP having started a strong upward trend in the early 2000s (with a pronounced uptick after 2003). The rising share of output generated in emerging economies is causing the planet's economic center of gravity to shift eastward. It had already moved from the mid-Atlantic in 1980 to the rough longitude of Turkey by the late 2000s, and forecasts suggest that it could be on the Chinese-Indian border by 2050 (Quah 2011; Dobbs et al. June 2012). One of the advantages of visualizing the big shift in terms of a moving center of gravity is that it helps to avoid mistaking the declining relative share of activity in advanced economies with absolute decline. Note that output per person (in constant terms) in the advanced economies, in spite of the crisis centered in those economies, was 14 percent greater in 2014 than in 2000 (versus 75 percent greater in the emerging economies).[15]

A finer-grained analysis of this big shift is important because its extent and velocity vary widely across different types of activity. Figure 11.4 compares emerging economies' shares of world totals across seventy-five metrics. Without purporting to be exhaustive, this list encompasses a wide range of indicators that we have categorized into seven major groups. The bars on the left show their levels in 2000, whereas the bars on the right show the most recent year for which data are available.

Starting at the top of the figure, in light of emerging economies' lower per capita incomes, it is unsurprising that population is the variable with the highest emerging country share – 86 percent in 2014, up from 84 percent in 2000 – and that six of the ten variables on which they score highest are demographic or other

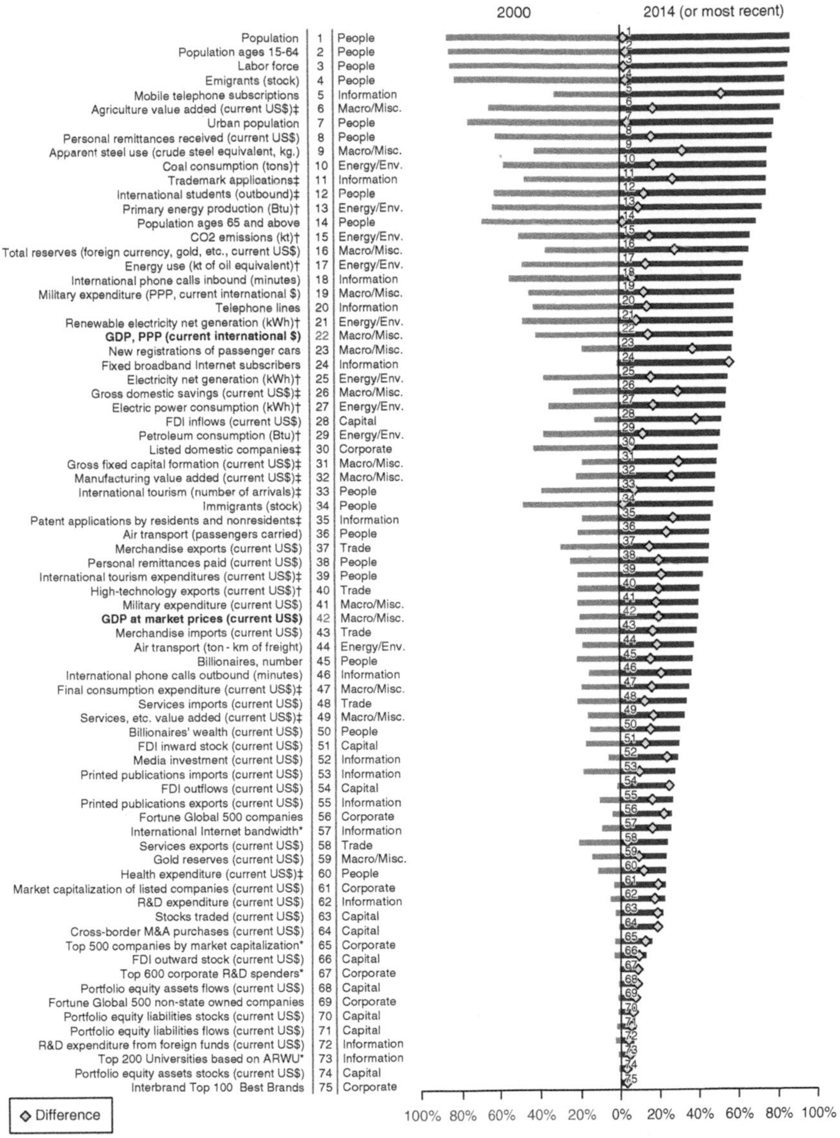

Figure 11.4 Emerging Economies' Share of World Totals, 2000 versus 2014 (or most recent available).

Note: Unless otherwise noted, 2014 values are based on 2014 or 2015 data. Items marked with † are based on 2011 or 2012 data. Items marked with ‡ are based on 2013 data. For items marked with * 2000 data were unavailable: top 500 companies by market capitalization substitute 2002 data; top 600 corporate R&D spenders and top 200 universities based on ARWU substitute 2003 data; international internet bandwidth substitute 2005 data.

Figure 11.4 (*cont.*)

Sources: Based on data from European Commision, Euromonitor Passport, Forbes magazine, Fortune magazine, Financial Times, GroupM This Year Next Year report (various editions), International Copper Study Group, International Monetary Fund, Interbrand, ITU, Shanghai Academic Ranking of World Universities, Telegeography International Traffic Database, United Nations Comtrade, UNCTAD World Investment Report, United Nations Population Division, US Energy Information Administration, World Bank World Development Indicators, World Steel Association, World Trade Organization.

people-related variables. Note that this 86 percent of world population accounted for only 35 percent of the world's final consumption expenditure in 2013 – although this did reflect a significant improvement versus 19 percent in 2000.[16]

The five metrics with the largest shifts from advanced to emerging economies since 2000 were fixed broadband Internet subscribers (emerging share up from 1 percent in 2000 to 56 percent in 2014), mobile telephone subscriptions (up from 32 percent to 83 percent), FDI inflows (up from 13 percent to 51 percent), new registrations of passenger cars (up from 20 percent to 56 percent), and apparent steel use (up from 42 percent to 74 percent).[17] These metrics exemplify the fast shifts taking place across a broad range of economic activities.

Merchandise exports ranks thirty-seventh out of the seventy-five categories, with 42 percent of merchandise exports coming from emerging economies (up from 30 percent in 2000). Figure 11.5 provides additional perspective by tracking the changing composition of global merchandise exports since 2005. It reveals that the growth of merchandise trade since 2005 has been driven by trade flows involving emerging economies (as exporters, importers, or both). From 2005 to 2014, "South-South" trade between emerging economies was the fastest growing component of merchandise trade flows, expanding five times as fast (in US dollar terms) as trade between advanced economies and almost twice as fast as trade between advanced and emerging economies. The rise of emerging economies has also contributed to deepening trade integration by spreading the world's economic activity more broadly across countries. According to one estimate, roughly one-third of the increase in trade intensity since the early 1990s was caused by economic output becoming less concentrated among a small number of large economies (Subramanian and Kessler 2013).

Turning to the bottom of the list, five of the bottom ten metrics involve capital flows and stocks, particularly portfolio equity. In 2014, emerging economies accounted for only 4 percent and 7 percent, respectively, of portfolio equity stock assets and liabilities, and only 9 percent and 7 percent, respectively, of portfolio equity flow assets and liabilities (well below their share of market capitalization). This reflects the limited development of stock markets across many emerging economies as well as the use of capital controls in some. The emerging economies' share of outward FDI stocks, 13 percent, also places this metric among the bottom ten (IMF BOP 2016).

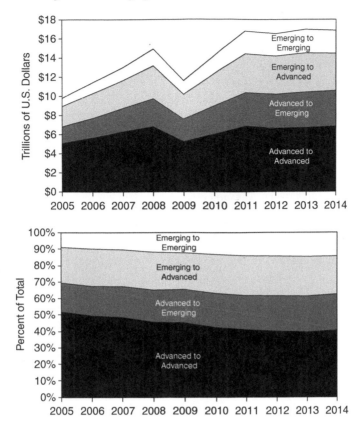

Figure 11.5 Merchandise Trade, Advanced versus Emerging: Value (Top), Share (Bottom), 2005–2014.
Source: Based on data from UN Comtrade Database.

Corporate metrics are also concentrated near the bottom of Figure 11.4, with three finishing in the bottom ten. While emerging economies' share of the world's 500 largest firms by revenue (the Fortune Global 500) rose from 4 percent to 26 percent from 2000 to 2014 (with acceleration since 2010, when the emerging share stood at 15 percent),[18] that rise was driven by Chinese state-owned firms, many of which focus primarily on the Chinese domestic market. Excluding state-owned firms, the emerging economies' share of the Fortune Global 500 rose only from 1 percent in 2000 to 9 percent in 2014 (ranking sixty-ninth on the chart) (Fortune 2015). And on corporate measures that proxy more for capabilities than for size, emerging economies are also very thinly represented. Only 9 percent of the world's top 600 firms ranked by their R&D

expenditures and only 3 percent of the top 100 based on their brand values were from emerging economies in 2014 (European Union 2015; Interbrand 2015). The penultimate section of this chapter – on the possibility of a "big shakeup" in the corporate pecking order – will return to the topic of the growth of firms based in emerging economies.

In between the macroeconomic and firm levels, Figure 11.6 traces the shift of production and consumption to emerging economies across a dozen industries. The automotive industry exhibited the largest shift, moving from having roughly 70 percent of its production and consumption in advanced economies in 2005 to roughly 45 percent in 2014. In contrast, the share of meat production and consumption in emerging economies only increased by about five percentage points each between 2000 and 2011. Consistent with what one would expect given the laws of globalization, most of the industries shown in the figure cluster along the diagonal line, implying limited net flows between advanced and emerging economies. An exception with large flows from emerging economies to advanced economies is microwave ovens – well above the diagonal line – of which 98 percent were produced in emerging economies but only 54 percent were sold in those economies in 2014.[19] The opposite pattern holds for large commercial jet aircraft – well below the diagonal line – with only 4 percent of production but 52 percent of sales in emerging economies in 2014.[20]

What Is Different about Emerging Economies?

The rise of emerging economies has prompted many to probe more deeply how they differ from advanced economies, beyond having lower per capita incomes ($17,198 based on a PPP-adjusted GDP-weighted average in 2014 versus $46,670 across advanced economies) and faster real growth rates (6.5 percent as compared to 1.4 percent between 2004 and 2014) (IMF October 2015). This section provides a data-driven approach to answering that question, covering cultural, administrative, and geographic metrics as well as economic ones. We focus here on GDP-weighted averages in order to place more emphasis on the differences that business practitioners will encounter in the large markets on which they are likely to focus.[21]

Due to space limitations, these comparisons do not segment economies more finely than the broad categories of advanced versus emerging. So they should be prefaced by noting that there is substantial diversity within both groups of countries, and especially among emerging economies. In 2014, for example, the fastest growing emerging economy was Ethiopia with 10 percent GDP growth, but Libya was also classified as an emerging or developing economy although its GDP shrank 24 percent in that year. And per capita GDP among emerging or developing economies ranged from $336 (Burundi) to $93,900 (Qatar), with the latter ranked as the third highest in the world (IMF April 2015). Furthermore, as mentioned in Chapter 2, despite their

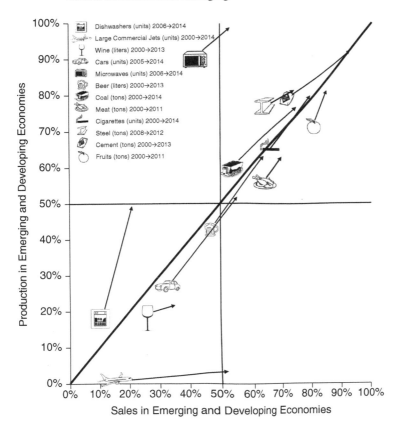

Figure 11.6 Industry Level Shift of Production and Consumption to Emerging Economies.
Sources: Based on data from Euromonitor Passport except for: Large Commercial Jets (Boeing, SpeedNews, Bloomberg and Planespotters), Steel (World Steel Association and UN Commodity Production Statistics), and Cement (Portland Cement Association, Deutsche Bank Global Cement Review and UN Commodity Production Statistics).

faster growth rates, there is little evidence of general convergence of income levels between advanced and emerging economies: the four Asian "tigers," which are now widely considered to be advanced, are the only group that has achieved high income relatively recently without resource-based wealth.[22]

To start with economic differences that have not already been discussed, Figure 11.7 indicates that emerging economies derive more of their GDP from agriculture and less from services, and exhibit higher levels of inequality. From an international business perspective, the lower R&D intensity in emerging economies is particularly salient, given the association between R&D (and advertising) intensity with resources that enable firms to become multinational.

Also, the higher proportion of GDP coming from the industrial sector in emerging economies implies that it is no longer appropriate to treat "industrialized countries" and "advanced economies" as synonymous.

Emerging economies also differ from advanced economies on the other dimensions of the CAGE Framework. Culturally, there are statistically significant differences on three of Hofstede's dimensions of national culture (Hofstede 1980; Hofstede and Bond 1988). Greater power distance, collectivism, and long-term orientation in emerging economies all imply requirements for varying leadership practices. Based on data from the World Values Survey, people in emerging economies accord work a higher priority in their lives – presumably an advantage for employers – but have lower levels of trust in foreigners – which can complicate international business activities in particular.[23] Furthermore, the higher cultural fractionalization within emerging economies provides a reminder of the importance of not treating large emerging economies as monolithic entities (Fearon 2003). And the lower representation of women on boards in emerging economies highlights how the issues surrounding gender and other aspects of diversity also vary with countries' levels of economic development.

Administratively, emerging economies rank significantly worse than advanced economies on the indicators of administrative/institutional quality that were discussed in Chapter 9's analysis of vertical institutional distance, for example, rule of law, political stability, and corruption. The latter is of particular importance with respect to international interactions. According to an estimate by Shang-Jin Wei (2000, 1), "an increase in the corruption level from that of Singapore to that of Mexico would have the same negative effect on inward FDI as raising the tax rate by fifty percentage points." Emerging economies also require more documents to conduct international trade and rank lower on the World Economic Forum's Enabling Trade Index. Surprisingly, despite their administrative weaknesses, publics in emerging economies seem to express greater confidence in their governments.

Emerging economies also present distinct geographic conditions. They average lower levels of urbanization which impact both demand patterns and supply chains. Temperature levels are also higher, on average, in emerging economies. And while emerging economies' higher likelihood of being landlocked is not statistically significant, infrastructure deficiencies make landlocked emerging economies far less accessible than landlocked advanced economies.

Some types of cross-country differences, such as the presence or absence of a common language, can only be measured relationally (i.e., with respect to bilateral country pairs), and so could not be included in Figure 11.7. Figure 11.8 provides a set of bilateral comparisons along the cultural, administrative, and geographic dimensions of the CAGE Framework, incorporating variables for which gravity models have shown that greater distance significantly dampens trade and/or FDI.[24] It compares commonalities and distances across pairs of two advanced economies, of one advanced economy and one emerging

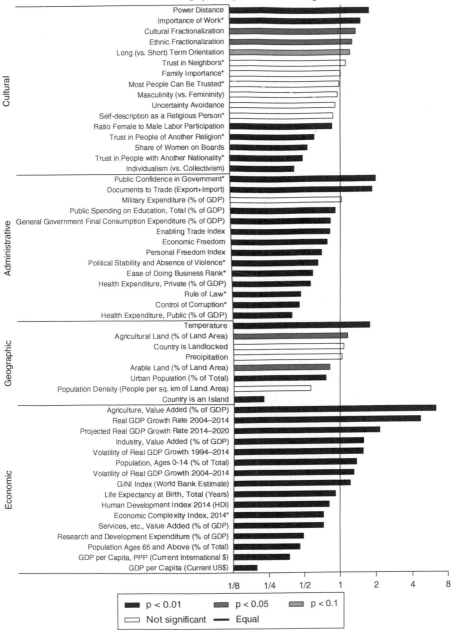

Figure 11.7 Unilateral Comparisons between Advanced and Emerging Economies (Weighted by GDP).

economy, and of two emerging economies. Here, we utilize country pairs' GDPs as weights to compute weighted averages for each of the categories.

It is useful to consider the analyses summarized in Figure 11.8 separately from the perspectives of firms based in advanced and emerging economies. From the perspective of a firm based in an advanced economy, emerging economies are more different or distant – to a statistically significant extent – than other advanced economies on every variable except language and legal origins. Physically, emerging economies are more than one-quarter more distant, and administratively, advanced economies are about two-and-a-half times as likely to have trade agreements with other advanced economies as with emerging economies. Based on a gravity model with the measures shown in the figure as explanatory variables (along with origin and destination country GDPs and fixed effects), shifting from the weighted average distance between two advanced economies to the weighted average distance between one advanced and one emerging economy is expected to reduce merchandise trade by 36 percent and FDI stocks by 29 percent! Incremental distance, thus, clearly imposes substantial challenges on firms from advanced economies pursuing growth in emerging markets.

For firms expanding abroad from emerging economies, while similar levels of development create economic proximity with other emerging economies, many of the other commonalities that bind advanced economies together are absent. Emerging economies share common languages, common religions,

Figure 11.7 (*cont.*)

Notes: Variables marked with asterisk (*) were transformed using min-max normalization prior to calculating comparisons.[25]
Sources: World Values Survey (waves 2005–2009 and 2010–2014); Fearon, "Ethnic and cultural diversity by country," (2003); Geert Hofstede Dimension Data Matrix (2015); World Bank World Development Indicators (2016); World Bank Climate Change Knowledge Portal; Catalyst Knowledge Center (2014); GMI Ratings Women on Boards Survey (2013); World Bank Worldwide Governance Indicators (2014); Heritage Foundation Index of Economic Freedom (2015); World Economic Forum Global Enabling Trade Report (2014); World Bank Ease of Doing Business (2016); Centre d'Etudes Prospectives et d'Informations Internationales (CEPII) Geography Database; Google Maps; International Monetary Fund World Economic Outlook Database (October 2015), United Nations Development Program HDI (2015); Cato Institute, Fraser Institute and Friedrich Naumann Foundation for Freedom Human Freedom Index (2015); Ricardo Hausmann, César A. Hidalgo, et al. *The Atlas of Economic Complexity: Mapping Paths to Prosperity.* (Cambridge, MA.: Harvard's Center for International Development (CID)); Harvard Kennedy School; MIT Media Lab, 2011), www.atlas.cid.harvard.edu/book/.

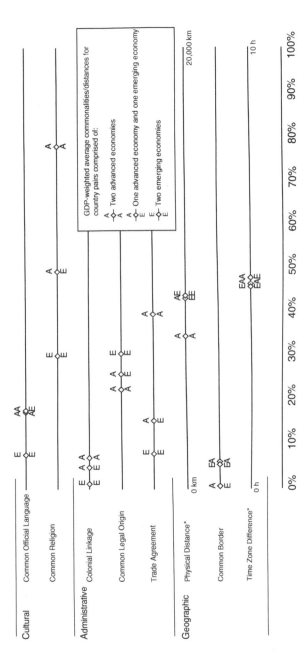

Figure 11.8 Bilateral Comparisons between Advanced and Emerging Economies.

Notes: For variables marked with asterisk (*), distance rises from left-to-right across the chart; for all other variables, commonality/proximity rises from left-to-right. All differences (AA vs. AE, AE vs. EE, and AA vs. EE) are significant at the 0.01 level, except for Physical Distance (AE vs. EE) and Common Border (AA vs. EE) that are significant at the 0.05 level and Time Zone Differences (AA vs. AE and AA vs. EE) that are significant at the 0.1 level. The only difference that is not significant at any standard level is Common Official Language (AA vs. AE).

Sources: Based on data from Centre d'Etudes Prospectives et d'Informations Internationales (CEPII), Dow and Karunaratna (2006) (using series R1 and treating scores of 1-3 as reflecting a common religion), and World Trade Organization (WTO).

colonial linkages, and trade agreements more often with advanced economies than they do with each other. The paucity of trade agreements between emerging economies is particularly striking: two emerging economies are half as likely as a pair comprised of one advanced and one emerging and one-fifth as likely as two advanced economies to have a trade agreement. The only variable where two emerging economies benefit from the greatest commonalities is legal origins.[26]

Considering all of the variables in Figure 11.8 together, gravity models indicate that firms from emerging economies face *greater* resistance due to noneconomic distance when trading and investing in other emerging economies than they do in advanced economies: shifting from two emerging economies to one emerging and one advanced is expected to boost both trade and FDI by 15 percent as a result of greater noneconomic distances, on average, between emerging economies. And, of course, firms from emerging economies face far greater distance-related challenges in advanced economies than do competitors from advanced economies. Many factors that make emerging economies harder for advanced economy based firms also apply in the reverse direction, and may even get amplified. Thus, in the context of the kind of vertical segmentation revealed by the case study of China in the final section of this chapter, it may be easier for advanced country companies to move down from high-end positions than for emerging economy companies to move up from low-end positons. All of which suggests that distance imposes even greater challenges on multinationals from emerging economies than on those from advanced economies. Furthermore, in light of the results of the analysis in Chapter 6 of firm characteristics associated with operating across greater distances, the lower R&D intensity, advertising intensity, and top management team non-nativity of large firms from emerging markets suggests that they may also have weaker capabilities for traversing distance.

The greater distances faced by emerging economies as well as some of their country-level characteristics contribute to another barrier to business into and out of emerging economies: their lower depth of globalization as measured by our *DHL Global Connectedness Index* (Ghemawat and Altman, 2014) and shown in Figure 11.9. Advanced and emerging economies are roughly at parity with respect to trade intensity – exports and imports of goods and services as a share of GDP. However, with respect to capital and people flows, advanced economies are three to six times as deeply globalized as emerging economies, and they are nine times as deeply globalized with respect to international information flows.

Consider examples for each of these categories: While emerging economies attracted 51 percent of FDI inflows in 2014, advanced economies still provided 74 percent of FDI outflows. On the basis of 2013 data, emerging economies still have only 15 percent as much international internet bandwidth per internet

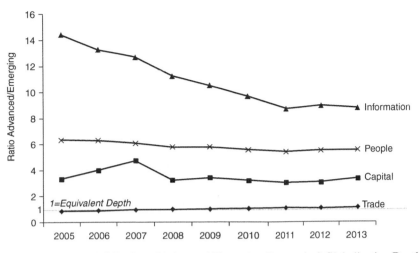

Figure 11.9 Ratios of Advanced/Emerging Economies' Globalization Depth
Scores by Pillar (Trade, Capital, Information, People) on the *DHL Global
Connectedness Index.*
Source: Figure 3.11 of *DHL Global Connectedness Index 2014*, p. 55.

user as advanced economies, and people in emerging economies only travel
outside of their countries' borders on average once every thirteen years (as
compared to every 1.7 years in advanced economies). If one expects emerging
economies to grow to look more like (today's) advanced economies, this
implies that people and information flows and, to a lesser extent, outward FDI,
may be subject to particularly rapid increases going forward.

The multifaceted differences between emerging and advanced economies
that we have highlighted in this section hint at the limitations of previous
efforts to characterize the salient differences among them in terms of one
CAGE dimension – whether it be power distance (cultural), institutional
voids (administrative), higher temperatures (geographic), or lower per capita
incomes (economic) – rather than more broadly. Previous characterizations are
also limited by a focus on (an unduly narrow subset of) unilateral differences
at the expense of bilateral (or multilateral) differences, even though the latter
have been shown to have profound influences on international interactions.

Will the Big Shift Lead to a Big Shakeup?

The firms that prove themselves most adept at bridging the differences
between advanced and emerging economies covered in the previous section

will gain a large edge over their rivals as they compete for global leadership of their respective industries. This section considers whether firms from emerging economies will shake up the global pecking order and displace many incumbents from advanced economies as industry leaders. We begin by drawing attention to the distinction between size and leadership. Then, we review considerations that favor such a shakeup, followed by perspectives that point toward incumbents sustaining their leadership positions. The following section zooms in on the case of China to look at how this competition is playing out in the largest emerging economy.

Guillén and García-Canal (2012) predict that half of the world's 500 largest firms will be based in emerging economies by 2030. A McKinsey report released in October 2013 concurs, projecting that 45 percent of the Fortune Global 500 will be based in emerging economies by 2025 (Dobbs et al. October 2013). These predictions imply a considerable leap from the 26 percent in 2014, but they seem consistent with recent historical trends, both in terms of emerging economy growth rates and growth of the emerging market share of the Fortune Global 500. Note, however, that there is nothing necessarily "global" about the Fortune Global 500. Firm size should not be conflated with global leadership, since even very large emerging economy companies tend to be more domestically focused than their advanced economy counterparts.

As we reported in Chapter 10, none of the emerging economy based firms on the 2014 Fortune Global 500 could be classified as "global" according to the criteria proposed by Rugman and Verbeke (2004). Among the more internationally oriented minority of these firms that report sales data by world region, interregional sales (based on "broad triad" regions) average 27 percent, compared to 36 percent for firms based in advanced economies.[27] And, if the world's largest corporations are ranked based on their total foreign assets (instead of their revenues), only 7 of the top 100 are from emerging economies (UNCTAD 2013). This pattern underscores how having more companies in the ranks of the world's largest is not the same as assuming global leadership.

It is also important to recognize that multinationals from advanced economies *do not* currently hold dominant positions broadly across sectors in emerging economies. Santos and Williamson report that the top two multinationals in each of the BRIC countries have smaller market shares than the top two local companies across several industries (Santos and Williamson 2015). More generally, one hundred of the world's largest companies headquartered in advanced economies derived just 17 percent of their total revenue in 2010 from emerging economies – even though those markets accounted for 36 percent of global GDP and were projected to contribute more than 70 percent of global GDP growth through 2025 (Atsmon et al. August 2012). This alone suggests that without any changes in their market shares in emerging economies, the rising proportion of economic activity taking place in emerging economies will shrink the global market shares of firms from advanced economies.

Recent growth trends also point toward further market share erosion for multinationals from advanced economies. Analysis over time frames from 1999 to 2008 indicates that emerging economy companies not only grew 10 percentage points faster annually at home than companies from advanced economies (18 percent vs. 8 percent) but also enjoyed a similar edge (22 percent vs. 12 percent) in advanced economies and an even bigger one in other (foreign) emerging economies (31 percent vs. 13 percent) (Atsmon et al. August 2012)!

Surveys also indicate a growing recognition among executives in multinational firms from advanced economies of the problems their firms face dealing with the big shift. A recent survey by the Boston Consulting Group (BCG) indicated that while 78 percent of multinationals expect to gain market share in emerging economies, only 13 percent say they have an advantage over local competitors. BCG also reported that more respondents cited local competitors as a major threat in emerging economies than multinationals from either advanced or emerging economies (Mall et al. 2013).

Limited representation of executives from emerging markets within their leadership teams is probably among the reasons why executives at multinationals from advanced economies report they do not understand local business practices well enough in emerging economies. Among companies from advanced economies in the Fortune Global 500, only 4 percent have CEOs from emerging economies. And below the CEO level, a recent McKinsey survey of leading Western companies found that just 2 percent of their top 200 employees hailed from key Asian emerging economies (Atsmon et al. August 2012). Nonetheless, from a competitive standpoint, one should recall that – as discussed in Chapter 4 – Fortune Global 500 firms from emerging economies have even less top management national diversity than firms from advanced economies: only 2 percent have nonnative CEOs and 3 percent of their top management teams are nonnative (Ghemawat and Vantrappen 2015).

Although moving executives to emerging economies could help address this talent gap, according to the same BCG survey of large multinationals, only 9 percent of the companies' top twenty leaders were located in these markets, versus an average of 28 percent of their revenues. BCG also found that companies with some of their top executives located in emerging economies were more likely to outperform in those markets (Mall et al. 2013). Hiring local talent is also getting harder for Western multinationals in emerging economies. According to a Corporate Executive Board survey, highly skilled Chinese professionals' preference for working in multinational over domestic companies in 2010 was only half as strong as it was in 2007 (Schmidt 2011).

Turning to companies from emerging economies, Chinese and Indian companies, in particular, have developed low-cost capabilities that are the envy of competitors from advanced countries. And while governments have a poor track record at picking winners to become "national champions," the high priority the Chinese government places on fostering the growth of Chinese multinationals – including via channeling cheap credit to them – is also a factor that must be recognized. Guillén and García-Canal (2013) also argue that multinationals from emerging economies tend to be less focused on short-term results (better able to pursue long-term strategies due to state or business group backing), are less encumbered by tradition, and are more willing to pursue growth in difficult and potentially dangerous locations.[28] It should be noted, however, that such discretion can drive value destruction as well as value creation.

Of course, established multinationals also enjoy significant advantages that could help them defend against new rivals from emerging economies. As Figure 11.4 shows, firms from advanced economies still have a very large lead with respect to R&D expenditure and own almost all of the world's most valuable brands. The *Best Global Brands*, a report by the consulting firm Interbrand that ranks the top 100 brands in the world, lists only 3 developing country brands: Huawei (88), Corona (93), and Lenovo (100) (Interbrand 2015). As the incumbents with first mover advantages, established multinationals also have a disproportionate ability to dictate the terms of engagement.

Given that competitors from both advanced and emerging economies have their relative strengths and weaknesses, it is useful to consider models that permit one to think about how they may net out. One theoretical model that describes which firms have the capability to compete in a given industry was developed by John Sutton. He looks at equilibrium in the space of outcomes rather than equilibrium in the space of strategies and thereby manages to pin down the range of possible outcomes without making nearly as many assumptions about functional forms as game-theoretic models generally do (Sutton 1997). His key results concerning globalization and competition among firms of differing capabilities can be summarized in terms of the "window of viability." Thus, in Figure 11.10, firm A has the highest level of capability and therefore is the market leader. The area between the curve on which point A is located and the market threshold for entry (the bottom curve) forms the window of viability. Points B and C, which are within this window are also viable, whereas D and E are not. Note that firm D would be viable if it had a similar productivity level to the other firms, whereas firm E would need to improve its quality level.

As markets become more integrated, the window of capabilities that are viable shifts upward. More specifically, trade liberalization causes the bottom of the window to shift upward, that is, a higher level of wage-adjusted capability (quality divided by unit cost) is needed to be viable, putting pressure on firms from emerging economies that compete on low costs. And pressure from them

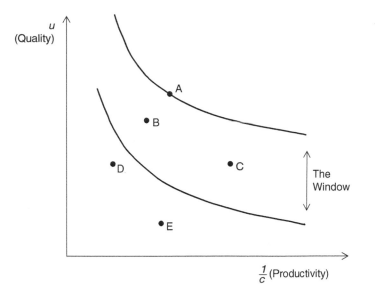

Figure 11.10 Capabilities and the Window of Viability.
Source: Sutton, John. 2012. *Competing in Capabilities: The Globalization Process*, Fig. 1.2, pg. 13.

on firms from advanced economies that compete on quality and innovation causes the top of the window to shift upward as well. The next section looks at how well this model explains competitive outcomes in one of the key arenas being contested by multinationals and domestic companies: China.

A Case Study of Competition within China

The big shift described earlier in this chapter reflects not just the ascendency of emerging economies in general, but also the rising economic power of one in particular: China. China accounted for about 20 percent of world GDP growth between 2000 and 2014. As discussed in Chapter 5, it has already become a larger trading partner than the United States for most countries. And the "made in China" sticker has moved from simple manufactured goods to computers and smartphones. But what underlies these aggregate outcomes? Ghemawat and Hout (2016) take an industry-level perspective on this question, focused on China, that is drawn upon here.

Table 11.1 summarizes the arguments about why China is an appealing test-bed for such analysis. It corresponds to the cell, shaded for emphasis, in the matrix that presents the most ambiguous – and interesting – set

Table 11.1 *Market Sizes, Vertical Capability Differences, and Likely Winners*

		Host market size	
		Small	Large
Vertical capability differences between MNCs and emerging/local challengers	Small	Uncontested?	Local heroes
	Large	Global champions	China/focus of research

of possibilities. Focusing on China sets up a test of whether vertically-advantaged multinationals from advanced countries – competitors that still typically hold an edge in terms of marketing and technological know-how – will win or lose ground in emerging host markets to less vertically differentiated (lower cost/lower quality) challengers from there that are likely growing faster.

China makes for a particularly interesting host market because it has become the largest or second-largest market in the world for a wide array of products. Across a sample of forty industries, China ranked first in market size for nineteen and second for another twelve. China ranked first in sales volume or value in 2012 across nearly all types of commodities and industrial products for which data were available (e.g., chemicals, steel, gold, soybeans, tobacco) and first or second for most consumer durables (e.g., first on consumer appliances and mobile phones, second on computers and peripherals and consumer electronics). China's ranks were more varied on services (e.g., second on car rentals and fourth on insurance) and soft goods (e.g., first on apparel but twenty-fifth on pet care products).[29] Large domestic markets make it more likely that local firms can hold their own against multinationals from advanced economies: with small home markets, local firms are likely to be subject to crushing scale-related disadvantages.

Relative to many other emerging economies, conditions seem to have been in place for (at least some) Chinese firms, particularly the private ones, to actually climb the vertical ladder of capabilities. In contrast, with a stunted domestic response (and there do seem to be examples of emerging economies caught in such a bind), there would be no point to the kind of analysis, domestic versus foreign, attempted here: the all-too-predictable outcome would be that locals would be wiped out in proportion to the degree of opening up. Thus, according to Sutton, companies from Sub-Saharan Africa have yet to follow leading companies from China and India in "moving into the window" of viability (2012, 181).

Of course, there are drawbacks to looking at China as well, most prominently the fact that many sectors in China are still officially or unofficially closed to foreign competition. Indeed, there is even a sense that such official home-bias may be getting worse as China turns to a more domestically driven, services-led growth model and continues to emphasize the development of technological self-sufficiency (European Chamber 2014). The analysis that follows focuses on sectors where the Chinese government does allow meaningful foreign competition.

Recall Sutton's baseline model from the previous section. In addition to its formal attractions, it helps one think about these patterns in the context of competition to develop capabilities. As low-wage competitors upgrade, the bottom of the window in Figure 11.10 shifts upward. To maintain their relative positions, vertically differentiated multinationals have to shift the top end of the window upward as well. Industries in which there are actually opportunities to do so – industries that advanced country multinationals can continue to lead – tend to be the ones in which it is possible to sink costs into improving products and operating margins by enhancing intangible assets, the general intensity of which, as Chapter 3 pointed out, has increased greatly in the last few decades. Intangible assets associated with image/reputation and know-how can roughly be proxied for by advertising-intensity and R&D-intensity respectively. Figure 11.11 plots industry leadership in China by industry against advertising and R&D intensity on the horizontal and vertical axes respectively in 2012–2013.

As the figure shows, Chinese companies' strongest domestic positions are in relatively low R&D- and advertising-intensity industries, and not coincidentally, China's multinationals in manufacturing are mostly drawn from the same group (see Box 11.1). The more intensive in R&D and advertising an industry is, the more likely foreign multinationals are to do well. In the most R&D intensive industries – modern patented pharmaceuticals, packaged software, commercial jet aircraft, etc., foreign multinationals continue to lead. The only major exception to the rule about R&D-intensity is internet hardware, currently dominated by Huawei Technologies and ZTE – and one arguably shrouded in some mystery insofar as links with and support by the Chinese military are concerned. Foreign multinationals also lead in industries such as personal care and carbonated beverages that are very advertising-intensive and, apparently, in ones that combine relatively high levels of the two, most notably sports apparel and athletic shoes.

There are also a few industries in which foreign multinationals lead even though they would seem to fall below the R&D-plus-advertising thresh-old that generally separates multinational-led industries from ones led by Chinese companies: industries such as elevators and aseptic food packaging. Elevators are dominated by Otis and aseptic packaging by TetraPak. Both

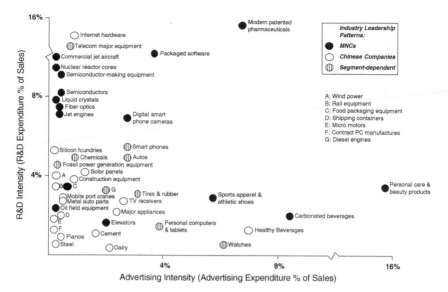

Figure 11.11 Industry Leadership: Chinese Companies versus Foreign MNCs (2012–2013).

Note: Estimates of market share leaders in sample of forty-four industries open to foreign competition. Industries are mainly product-defined and follow the conventions of the industry associations that provided the data. Source: Ghemawat and Hout (2016) based on R&D Intensity from DTI's R&D Scoreboard, UK; Advertising Intensity from Schonfeld & Associates Ad/Sales report and 10-K's; China literature search.

entered China early (in the mid-1980s) and established large installed bases and networks of local service operations, contributing to the sustainability of their positions.

The analysis around Figure 11.11 was a snapshot of a process that is supposed to be dynamic. Fortunately, we can develop some sense of the dynamics by juxtaposing it against a snapshot taken earlier by Ghemawat and Hout (2008): it is interesting to compare the data for 2012–2013 to the 2006 data used in that piece. The most striking aspect of the comparison is how little change there has been over the years. To focus on just the changes, there has been some strengthening of Chinese positions, especially in internet hardware and in popular-priced smartphones. Chinese firms have also taken leadership in solar panels, another relatively high R&D-intensity industry. Three of the four leading silicon-based solar panel producers globally – Trina, Ying Li, and Jinko – are Chinese. Construction equipment leadership was formerly

Box 11.1. China's Multinationals

Most of China's multinationals are entrepreneurial companies, started in the 1980s (or 1990s), often privately held but typically with good connections to the Communist Party apparatus and state organizations. Thus Haier began as a township enterprise, one of the two listed Haier entities is still considered state-owned, and its founder, Zhang Ruimin, occupies a high rank in the Party. Lenovo was started by state-employed scientists. Huawei was started by former members of the military. Others were launched with offshore support, often from Hong Kong or Singapore, including CIMC and Pearl River Piano.

The development of China's first generation of multinationals closely followed the patterns that are predicted by Sutton's model. Many started as contractors, providing services to foreign companies. As their capabilities grew, they were able to take on more of the manufacturing, and eventually, the design and marketing. Many of China's top multinationals, such as Wanxiang (auto parts), Galanz (microwave ovens), and Haier (home appliances) started this way.

Other companies took advantage of markets where advanced economy multinationals were not particularly strong to become major suppliers of products under their own brands. Companies such as Pearl River Pianos (upright pianos), Goodbaby (baby strollers), and China International Container Corporation (shipping containers) are good examples. Big-ticket capital goods companies took much longer to gain acceptance in global markets. Examples include Huawei (IP and telecom equipment) and Shanghai Zhenhua (port cranes) and Lenovo (computers). Most of these companies compete in low to medium R&D- and advertising-intensity industries with the possible exception of Lenovo, which gained market acceptance after buying IBM's personal computer business. Other Chinese companies are now making large acquisitions in advanced economies with similar motives (e.g., Geely's acquisition of Volvo and Haier's of GE Appliances).

Many of the multinationals mentioned here now have more foreign sales than domestic. An estimated two-thirds of Huawei, Shanghai Zhenhua and CIMC's revenues are foreign, and the shares are roughly evenly divided between advanced and emerging markets. Early successes in capital goods were more often in other emerging markets with lower barriers to entry, but Goodbaby's and Lenovo's international revenues are distributed across advanced and emerging markets.

Source: Adapted from Ghemawat and Hout (2016).

segment dependent but Sany now rivals Komatsu for overall leadership. And Chinese producers still lag on quality at the high-end, but do now lead, overall, in the local consumer electronics market. But in the meantime, multinationals have retaken the lead in sports apparel and shoes as well as in food packaging. Overall, R&D intensity and advertising intensity remain robust predictors for both periods of where advanced country multinationals will do well relative to Chinese firms within China.

While the Chinese data presented by Ghemawat and Hout (2016) are novel, their basic finding is not: the success of multinationals from advanced economies in R&D- and advertising-intensive sectors reminds us of the basic theory of the (horizontal) multinational enterprise developed more than forty years ago by Richard Caves, in which such intangible assets, and the increasing returns to scale that underlie them, are what typically propel companies to expand across national borders (Caves 1971). Sutton provides a formalization, with an explicit model of product market interactions over time embedded in a general equilibrium context, of a mechanism that generates the basic patterns described above for competition within China.

But that said, the type of vertical economic differences on which Sutton focuses captures only a subset of the CAGE distance effects that influence outcomes in a given market. Horizontal cultural, administrative, and geographic distances also matter. Again, consider the case of China:

> **Cultural Distance:** The most advertising-intensive industry in which Chinese companies lead is healthy beverages, where local cultural insight is presumably more important than in colas. More broadly, local consumer goods companies often have stronger knowledge of local customs and are better able to monitor their customers' preferences. For example, Joyoung took advantage of consumers' disaffection with food contamination, creating a home soymilk maker that presses fresh soybeans, giving homemakers an alternative to pesticide-contaminated products.

> **Administrative Distance:** Beyond the fact that many industries are not fully open to multinationals, local favoritism can take place in others. Local companies may be better able to affect local Party or state gatekeepers, and are in a better position to make deals than multinationals, which may be constrained by their home countries' legal requirements. In addition, locals' advantages are often cemented by the difficulty of working within the Chinese legal system, which is an essential part of operating for a Chinese firm, but can be too cumbersome for some multinationals.

> **Geographic Distance:** China's geographic proximity to the advanced manufacturing centers of Japan and Korea makes it a natural host to

low-cost assembly of products made from components developed
in these countries. Furthermore, local clustering makes local capability pools more than the sum of their parts because of spillovers.
Many of China's early exporters were able to achieve success due
to a large scale of production within small geographic regions, a
pattern that still persists today.

So cultural, administrative and geographic distances, many of them horizontal, do seem to play a role in affecting competitive outcomes, as one might
expect theoretically since they soften the viability constraints facing local
firms relative to the ones they would face if horizontal distance offered them
no protection from the vertical economic differences whose evolution Sutton
models.

Shifting attention from industry environments to how firms compete in
those contexts, it is natural, especially in a practical context, to turn to the
AAA strategies – adaptation, aggregation, and arbitrage – for dealing with
differences, as discussed in Chapter 6. The AAA strategies (Ghemawat 2007)
embody a set of possible responses to a broader range of differences across
countries than just vertical positioning – ones that encompasses horizontal
distance as well. More specifically, *adaptation* to achieve local responsiveness is neither necessary nor feasible – except in terms of vertical positioning
– in Sutton's model. Also missing are regional and other *aggregation* strategies aimed at achieving cross-border economies of scale and scope – even
though regional groupings often account for the bulk of international interactions and most of the Fortune Global 500 derive the majority of their sales
from their home regions, as discussed in Chapter 10. And finally, *arbitrage*
to exploit differences does appear in Sutton's model, but it is of a specific
economic sort. There is no provision, for instance, for international expansion based on cultural arbitrage (e.g., the advantages of French origins in
perfumes or Italian in luxury handbags) or for that matter, of administrative
arbitrage (across differences in tax or regulatory systems, for example). Yet
when one actually looks at competition in and out of China, one observes the
broad range of AAA strategies. And underlying conceptions of horizontal
distance are essential to making sense of some of the patterns of overseas
activity by Chinese firms, for example, China's dominance of exports to the
rest of Asia and Africa.

As foreign multinationals try to adapt better to China or to arbitrage more
effectively out of China if their activities there are focused on globalizing production rather than globalizing markets, and as local firms try to upgrade, there
is the potential for a "race to the middle." But, to speculate about the eventual
outcome, it seems unlikely that the two types of firms would entirely give up
their initial advantages relative to each other. For multinationals to succeed in

China requires, in addition to official sanction, organizational patience, attitudinal changes, and considerable investments in the development of locally relevant capabilities. Some multinationals succeed, but many continue to struggle with this AAA balancing act, since in striving to adapt and arbitrage, they cannot give up on aggregation, which remains their key strength relative to local competitors.

Meanwhile, local challengers continue to cultivate the adaptation and/or arbitrage advantages that got them started but also typically have to make a start at aggregation en route to becoming truly multinational, that is, to competing on an equal strategic footing with existing multinationals (although many do, of course, opt to remain local). There are exceptions when global challengers have some other attribute that renders the additional A of aggregation unnecessary (e.g., an arbitrage strategy sustained by proprietary access to cheap resources, as in the case of Gazprom and Russian natural gas). Otherwise, however, building up intangible assets related to marketing, technology and, in many cases, management capabilities that can be applied across borders is indicated.

Conclusion

The rising share of economic activity taking place in emerging economies implies that it is along the economic dimension of the CAGE Framework that firms are likely to face the most dramatic changes over the medium term. The economic dimension differs from the others, in the greater importance of arbitrage strategies along this dimension. Firms can and do arbitrage across cultural differences (e.g., French wines are especially prized in the market due to their long history and tradition), geographic differences (e.g., fruit is imported from other regions when out of season or cannot be cultivated locally), and administrative differences (e.g., differing tax policies create loopholes). However, it is only on the economic dimension of the CAGE Framework where arbitrage strategies – particularly those focused on labor costs – are so central to the operations of many firms. Strategies for bridging economic distance will therefore remain a key focus, and must pay careful attention to both its attractions and its challenges.

The economic dimension is also perhaps the only dimension of the CAGE Framework where a broad range of actors is making a concerted effort to move toward convergence. While globalization has sparked fears of cultural and administrative convergence and suggestions that geographic distance no longer matters, these concerns mostly seem to be overstated, as we discussed in Chapter 1. By contrast, inclusive economic development is one of the key espoused goals of the international community (which is not to say that there is universal belief in that objective).

But convergence – even with deliberate efforts in that direction – is a slow process. The era we live in will not see a world in which the GDP per capita ratios in our gravity models are all one, or even near one. Partial convergence is perhaps the most likely outcome as some (but probably not all) emerging economies narrow the economic gap with advanced economies. Emerging and developing country firms are moving up in the ranks of the world's largest (although as noted earlier, that measure does have its limitations), and emerging countries increasingly rank among the top markets for many products.

This dramatic shift implies both new opportunities and new competition for multinational firms. As advanced country multinationals enter emerging and developing country markets that previously held little interest, both as buyers and sellers, they will encounter challenges that are very different from those they faced entering other advanced markets. Companies will be best placed to take advantage of new opportunities by using the strategies discussed earlier. And as emerging and developing country firms grow in size and capabilities, they will increasingly find themselves in competition with advanced country firms, both domestically and in foreign markets, and likewise, they will have to make the most of their natural advantages, especially in terms of economic arbitrage on costs.

To conclude this book as well as this chapter: this book has considered a wide range of models, frameworks, tools, empirical regularities, and case examples that can be useful in understanding and adapting to changes in the structure of the world economy. The big shift may not change culture, but it may lead to new opportunities for intercultural interaction. Globalization may not lead to a unified government, but it has already affected how companies interact with legal systems, both domestic and foreign. Geography is perhaps the most immutable of all, but understanding its role in shaping international interactions remains essential. The precise outcomes remain to be determined: they will reflect, along with chance and circumstance, many individual decisions – by politicians, managers, individuals – that influence the way globalization and the big shift proceed. But given the evidence presented in this book, it would be surprising if the outcomes reflected neither home bias nor any effects of distance, the two kinds of regularities highlighted by the laws of globalization.

Notes

1 These calculations are based on (Maddison "Historical Statistics").

2 Angus Maddison passed away in 2010, and thus the last update of the full dataset only includes years up to 2008. Thus, for consistency with the earlier data presented, we end the series with 2008 here.

3 We selected the IMF's classification scheme both because of the apparently broader set of criteria employed by the IMF (as discussed later in this paragraph) and for convenience and consistency in our analyses which often use IMF macroeconomic data as inputs. The advanced economies are Australia, Austria, Belgium, Canada, Cyprus, the Czech Republic, Denmark, Estonia, Finland, France, Germany, Greece, Hong Kong (China), Iceland, Ireland, Israel, Italy, Japan, the Republic of Korea, Latvia, Lithuania, Luxembourg, Malta, the Netherlands, New Zealand, Norway,

Portugal, San Marino, Singapore, Slovakia, Slovenia, Spain, Sweden, Switzerland, Taiwan, the United Kingdom, and the United States, including all territories, protectorates and autonomous regions.

4 For more elaboration of the IMF's as well as other classification systems, refer to Nielsen (2011).

5 More specifically, for the 2016 fiscal year, high-income economies are those that had a gross national income per capita of $12,736 or more in 2014, as reported at http://data.worldbank.org/about/country-and-lending-groups.

6 As reported in the technical notes section of the UNDP's 2015 Human Development Report.

7 These ratios are logged in the gravity models, and the coefficients are interpreted here as elasticities. The data pertain to GDP per capita in US dollars at market exchanges rates (i.e., without adjusting for purchasing power parity).

8 As noted in Chapter 5, when expanding the number of countries and territories included in the gravity model from from 97 to 224, this variable does becomes significant with a negative sign but its effect remains smaller for merchandise exports than for all of the other flows analyzed.

9 On the basis of data from the IMF Coordinated Portfolio Investment Survey (CPIS). Available at: http://cpis.imf.org/.

10 Geographic distribution of India's IT Services exports based on data reported by Nasscom.

11 The United States, as a country of immigrants, figures in eight of the top ten bilateral flows of phone calls. The top two destinations of international calls placed from the United States are Mexico (the largest source of first-generation immigrants) and India (the third largest). All of the United States' country partners in the top ten figure in the top fifteen sources of immigrants to the United States (out of more than two hundred countries and territories) with the exception of Brazil, which ranks twenty-sixth. The inference of an immigrant effect is backstopped by the observation that the two flows of the largest ten that do not involve the United States are from Hong Kong to China and from the United Kingdom to India (the largest source of first-generation immigrants to the United Kingdom based on immigrants' birth countries).

12 Based on data from Telegeography Traffic Database.

13 This calculation does not take differing inflation levels or exchange rates into account.

14 This calculation uses the UN classification for developed and developing regions, as well as UN population projections.

15 Authors' calculations based on data from World Development Indicators.

16 Based on data from World Bank World Development Indicators.

17 See the sources listed for Figure 11.4.

18 Note that the 2014 Fortune Global 500 reflects data on firms' revenues during 2013.

19 Recall that among the products covered in Figure 5.2 in Chapter 5, microwaves were traded over the second longest average distance.

20 Calculations cited in this paragraph were based on data from Euromonitor Passport, Boeing, Bloomberg, Deutsche Bank Global Cement Review, Planespotters, Portland

Cement Association, SpeedNews, UN Commodity Production Statistics, and World Steel Association. Production data are based on final production/assembly locations, without any consideration of imported content.

21 For weights, we used GDP in US dollars at market exchange rates. Analysis based on simple averages is more strongly affected by small economies that receive less attention from multinational firms. Nevertheless, there is a 0.9 correlation between ratios calcualted in weighted and unweighted versions of this analysis, and in most cases, ratios that were greater than one in the weighted version were also greater than one in the unweighted version (and vice versa).

22 An analysis of real GDP per capita in PPP terms since the 1960s highlights only Hong Kong, Singapore, South Korea, and Taiwan as having converged to the levels of the industrialized economies.

23 Calculated using data from Wave 5 (2005–2009) and Wave 6 (2010–2014) of the World Values Survey.

24 In these gravity models (which follow the methodology used in Chapter 5 except for adjustments to the set of explanatory variables covered), all of the variables shown in the figure were significant for merchandise exports at the 0.01 level with expected signs except common legal origin which was significant at the 0.05 level. For FDI outward stocks, they were all significant at the 0.01 level except common religion, time zone difference, trade agreement, and common border which retained their expected signs but were not significant at any standard level.

25 Min-max normalization rescaled values to lie between 0 and 1 without changing the shapes of the relevant distributions. Variables from World Governance Indicators and Economic Complexity Index were normalized to avoid incorporating negative values into the ratio calculations; variables from World Values Survey were coded based on answers to individual survey questions and made comparable via normalization; World Bank's Ease of Doing Business ranks were normalized in order to reverse order and improve comparability with other data components.

26 To test the effect of common colonial histories on international interactions, we added a variable reflecting a common colonial heritage to the baseline gravity models in Chapter 5 (in addition to the colony-colonizer variable). This variable achieves significance for all flows except patents, though generally with a smaller effect than the colony/colonizer relationship. The "Empire" variable in CEPII's gravity dataset was used in this analysis to proxy common colonizer relationships. The dataset is available at www.cepii.fr/CEPII/en/bdd_modele/presentation. asp?id=8.

27 Dobbs et al. (October 2013) report, based on data for a larger sample of firms with available data from the 2012 Fortune Global 500 (but with unspecified region definitions), that the emerging economy based firms in their sample generated only 14 percent of their sales outside of their home regions as compared to 24 percent for firms from advanced economies.

28 This is consistent with Hofstede's research on short- vs. long-term orientation discussed in Chapter 8.

29 Based primarily on data from Euromonitor Passport database, supplemented with industry-specific sources to fill gaps.

References

Atsmon, Yuval, Peter Child, Richard Dobbs, and Laxman Narasimhan. August 2012. "Winning the $30 Trillion Decathlon: Going for Gold in Emerging Markets." *McKinsey Quarterly*. www.mckinsey.com/insights/strategy/winning_the_30_trillion_decathlon_going_for_gold_in_emerging_markets.

Caves, Richard E. 1971. "International Corporations: The Industrial Economics of Foreign Investment." *Economica* 38 (149):1–27. doi: 10.2307/2551748.

Dobbs, Richard, Jaana Remes, James Manyika, Charles Roxburgh, Sven Smit, and Fabian Schaer. June 2012. "Urban World: Cities and the Rise of the Consuming Class." McKinsey Global Institute. www.mckinsey.com/insights/urbanization/urban_world_cities_and_the_rise_of_the_consuming_class.

Dobbs, Richard, Jaana Remes, Sven Smit, James Manyika, Jonathan Woetzel, and Yaw Agyenim-Boateng. October 2013. "Urban World: The Shifting Global Business Landscape." www.mckinsey.com/global-themes/urbanization/urban-world-the-shifting-global-business-landscape.

Dow, D., and A. Karunaratna. 2006. "Developing a Multidimensional Instrument to Measure Psychic Distance Stimuli." *Journal of International Business Studies* 37 (5): 578–602.

European Chamber. 2014. "Business Confidence Survey 2014." *European Chamber Publications*. www.europeanchamber.com.cn/en/publications-business-confidence-survey.

European Union. 2015. "2015 EU Industrial R&D Investment Scoreboard." http://iri.jrc.ec.europa.eu/scoreboard15.html.

Fearon, James D. 2003. "Ethnic and Cultural Diversity by Country." *Journal of Economic Growth* 8 (2):195–222. doi: 10.2307/40215943.

Fortune. 2015. "Fortune Global 500 Database." Time, Inc. Available for purchase at: www.fortunedatastore.com/index.html.

Ghemawat, Pankaj. 2007. *Redefining Global Strategy: Crossing Borders in a World Where Differences Still Matter*. Boston, MA: Harvard Business School Press.

Ghemawat, Pankaj, and Steven A. Altman. 2014. "DHL Global Connectedness Index 2014: Analyzing Global Flows and Their Power to Increase Prosperity." Deutsche Post DHL. www.dhl.com/gci.

Ghemawat, Pankaj, and Tamara de la Mata. "Globalization and Gravity." Unpublished working paper, IESE Business School, 2015.

Ghemawat, Pankaj, and Thomas Hout. 2008. "Tomorrow's Global Giants? Not the Usual Suspects." *Harvard Business Review* 86 (11):80–88.

2016. "Globalization, Capabilities, and Distance: Theory and a Case Study (of China)." In *Oxford Handbook of Dynamic Capabilities*, edited by David J. Teece. Oxford; New York: Oxford University Press.

Ghemawat, Pankaj, and Herman Vantrappen. 2015. "How Global Is Your C-Suite?" *MIT Sloan Management Review* 56 (4):73–82.

Guillén, Mauro F., and Esteban García-Canal. 2012. "The Rise of the Emerging-Market Multinationals." In *Global Turning Points: Understanding the Challenges for Business in the 21st Century*, edited by Mauro F. Guillén, and Emilio Ontiveros Baeza, 26–43. Cambridge: Cambridge University Press.

2013. *Emerging Markets Rule: Growth Strategies of the New Global Giants*. New York: McGraw-Hill.

Hofstede, Geert. 1980. *Culture's Consequences*. Beverly Hills. Ca: Sage.

Hofstede, G., and Michael H. Bond. 1988. "The Confucius Connection: From Cultural Roots to Economic Growth." *Organizational Dynamics* 16 (4): 5–21. doi:10.1016/0090-2616(88)90009-5

Interbrand. 2015. "The Best 100 Brands." London. http://interbrand.com/best-brands/best-global-brands/2015/.

International Monetary Fund (IMF). "Coordinated Portfolio Investment Survey (CPIS)." http://cpis.imf.org/.

———. 1997. "World Economic Outlook: A Survey by the Staff of the International Monetary Fund." May 1997 ed. Washington: IMF. www.imf.org/external/pubs/weomay/weocon.htm.

———. April 2015. "World Economic Outlook: Adjusting to Lower Commodity Prices." Washington, DC: IMF. www.imf.org/external/pubs/ft/weo/2015/02/pdf/text.pdf.

———. October 2015. "World Economic Outlook (WEO) Database." https://www.imf.org/external/pubs/ft/weo/2015/02/weodata/index.aspx.

———. 2016. "Balance of Payments and International Investment Position Statistics." Last Modified January 26, 2016. http://data.imf.org/?sk=7A51304B-6426-40C0-83DD-CA473CA1FD52.

Khanna, Tarun. 2012. "What the U.S. Has in Common with Emerging Markets." *Harvard Business Review*. Harvard Business Publishing. https://hbr.org/2012/03/what-the-us-has-in-common-with.

Khanna, Tarun, and Krishna Palepu. 1997. "Why Focused Strategies May Be Wrong for Emerging Markets." *Harvard Business Review* 75 (4):41–51.

Knowledge@Wharton. 2008. "When Are Emerging Markets No Longer 'Emerging'?" *Global Focus*. http://knowledge.wharton.upenn.edu/article/when-are-emerging-markets-no-longer-emerging/.

Krugman, Paul R. 1979. "Increasing Returns, Monopolistic Competition, and International Trade." *Journal of International Economics* 9 (4):469–479. doi: 10.1016/0022-1996(79)90017-5.

Linder, Staffan Burenstam. 1961. *An Essay on Trade and Transformation.* Uppsalla: Almqvist A. Wicksell.

Maddison, Angus. "Historical Statistics of the World Economy: 1–2008 AD." www.ggdc.net/maddison/Historical_Statistics/vertical-file_02-2010.xls.

Mall, Amitabh, David C. Michael, Lori Spivey, Andrew Tratz, Bernd Waltermann, and Jeff Walters. 2013. "Playing to Win in Emerging Markets." *BCG Perspectives*. https://www.bcgperspectives.com/content/articles/globalization_growth_playing_win_emerging_markets/.

Nielsen, Lynge. 2011. "Classifications of Countries Based on Their Level of Development: How It Is Done and How It Could Be Done." *IMF Working Papers*:1–45.

Quah, Danny. 2011. "The Global Economy's Shifting Centre of Gravity." *Global Policy* 2 (1):3–9. doi: 10.1111/j.1758-5899.2010.00066.x.

Raghavan, Anita. 2015. "Head of McKinsey is Elected to a Third Term." The New York Times, February 2.

Rugman, Alan M., and Alain Verbeke. 2004. "A Perspective on Regional and Global Strategies of Multinational Enterprises." *Journal of International Business Studies* 35 (1):3–18.

Santos, José F. P., and Peter J. Williamson. 2015. "The New Mission for Multinationals." *MIT Sloan Management Review* 56 (4):45–54. Massachusetts Institute of Technology. http://sloanreview.mit.edu/article/the-new-mission-for-multinationals/.

Schmidt, Conrad "The Battle for China's Talent," Harvard Business Review 89 (3): 25–27. Available at https://hbr.org/2011/03/the-battle-for-chinas-talent.

Subramanian, Arvind, and Martin Kessler. "The Hyperglobalization of Trade and Its Future." Peterson Institute for International Economics Working Paper 13–6, July 24, 2013. Available at SSRN: http://ssrn.com/abstract=2297994 or http://dx.doi.org/10.2139/ssrn.2297994.

Sutton, John. 1997. "One Smart Agent." *The Rand Journal of Economics* 28 (4):605–628.
    2012. *Competing in Capabilities: The Globalization Process*, Clarendon Lectures in Economics. Oxford: Oxford University Press.

TeleGeography. 2015. "Telegeography Report & Database." www.telegeography.com/research-services/telegeography-report-database/.

UNCTAD. 2013. "World Investment Report 2013: Global Value Chains: Investment and Trade for Development." United Nations. http://unctad.org/en/PublicationsLibrary/wir2013_en.pdf.
    2015. "World Investment Report 2015: Reforming International Investment Governance." United Nations. http://unctad.org/en/PublicationsLibrary/wir2015_en.pdf.

United Nations Development Programme (UNDP). 2009. "Human Development Report 2009: Overcoming Barriers: Human Mobility and Development." http://hdr.undp.org/sites/default/files/reports/269/hdr_2009_en_complete.pdf.

UNU-IHDP, and UNEP. 2014. "Inclusive Wealth Report 2014: Measuring Progress toward Sustainability." Cambridge: Cambridge University Press. http://inclusivewealthindex.org/#the-world-wants-to-know-how-its-doing

Wei, Shang-Jin. 2000. "How Taxing Is Corruption on International Investors?" *Review of Economics and Statistics* 82 (1):1–11.

World Bank. 2006. "Global Economic Prospects 2006: Economic Implications of Remittances and Migration."

Zweig, Jason. 2013. "Here Comes the Next Hot Emerging Market: the U.S." *The Wall Street Journal*, April 24.

Index